# For Robert Cooper

Robert Cooper, who died in 2013, was the leading theorist of organization working in England over the past few decades. Describing himself as a 'social philosopher,' he was one of the first writers to introduce post-structuralist and postmodern thought into theories of organization but was always reluctant to reduce what he did to being part of 'Management.' Instead, he concentrated on thinking about organizations and organizing, working with ideas about entity and process views of organizations, and also the dualisms of organization/environment, organization/disorganization, and concentrating particularly on ideas of the boundary or seam which divides and conjoins. He wrote about, and was influenced by, systems theory and post-structuralist philosophy, particularly Whitehead, Bateson, Deleuze, Derrida, Foucault and Simmel.

Cooper has already been the subject of much commentary, but much of his work is not well known, and it deserves a wider readership. The purpose of this collection is to gather together a body of essays which are widely dispersed in journals and edited collections. This is a repository of pieces and extracts which stand the test of time, and scholars will benefit from a collection which pulls together some of his most influential work. The collection also contains two essays, one biographical and one intellectual, about Cooper and his work.

**Gibson Burrell** is Professor of Organization Theory at the University of Leicester, UK.

**Martin Parker** is Professor of Organization and Culture at the University of Leicester School of Management, UK.

# Routledge Studies in Management, Organizations and Society

This series presents innovative work grounded in new realities, addressing issues crucial to an understanding of the contemporary world. This is the world of organised societies, where boundaries between formal and informal, public and private, local and global organizations have been displaced or have vanished, along with other nineteenth-century dichotomies and oppositions. Management, apart from becoming a specialized profession for a growing number of people, is an everyday activity for most members of modern societies.

Similarly, at the level of enquiry, culture and technology, and literature and economics, can no longer be conceived as isolated intellectual fields; conventional canons and established mainstreams are contested. **Management, Organizations and Society** addresses these contemporary dynamics of transformation in a manner that transcends disciplinary boundaries, with books that will appeal to researchers, students and practitioners alike.

# For Robert Cooper
Collected Work

**Edited by Gibson Burrell and
Martin Parker**

Routledge
Taylor & Francis Group

LONDON AND NEW YORK

First published 2016 by Routledge

2 Park Square, Milton Park, Abingdon, Oxfordshire OX14 4RN
711 Third Avenue, New York, NY 10017

*Routledge is an imprint of the Taylor & Francis Group, an informa business*

First issued in paperback 2018

*Library of Congress Cataloging-in-Publication Data*
CIP data has been applied for.

ISBN: 978-1-138-94079-6 (hbk)
ISBN: 978-1-138-61710-0 (pbk)

Typeset in Sabon
by Apex CoVantage, LLC

# Contents

    MARTIN PARKER AND ROBERT COOPER

12  Primary and Secondary Thinking in Social Theory:
    The Case of Mass Society                                     253
    ROBERT COOPER

13  Making Present: Autopoiesis as Human Production              280
    ROBERT COOPER

14  The Generalized Social Body: Distance and Technology         303
    ROBERT COOPER

15  Main Features of My Approach                                 318
    ROBERT COOPER

16  Complete List of Robert Cooper's Work                        325

    *Contributors*                                               329
    *Index*                                                      331

# 1  Organizing a Life

*Gibson Burrell and Martin Parker*

"The two of us wrote *Anti-Oedipus* together. Since each of us was several, there was already quite a crowd."

—Deleuze and Guattari

How do we stitch together a story from a life?[1] The two authors knew Robert Cooper well, in different places and at different times, and he had a huge influence on their thinking and writing. But they didn't know him any more than did the various colleagues and friends whose words and memories we will borrow for this introduction. Bob expressed an intellectual distrust of boundaries and stressed the need to both problematize them and subject any and all divisions (which he called di-visions) to intense scrutiny. Yet his life and the compartments into which he placed it remain incredibly bounded one from the other. It is as if he had several different lives, not just one, and we don't have the evidence to tell you anything about some of them. His colleagues, his friends and perhaps even his family knew only a part of the whole man, if indeed there was ever a whole man to know. Perhaps we are all severed, several, di-vided.

From what we know, and his friend Harry Jamieson has been crucial here, Robert Christopher Cooper was born on the nineteenth of August 1931 to parents who lived in the port city of Liverpool in the north-west of the United Kingdom. His father was the owner of a hardware shop and died when Bob was a child. Bob was successful in gaining entry to the Bluecoats school as a boarder, and when the Second World War began, the whole school was moved out of Liverpool to Beaumaris on Anglesey. As an 'evacuee', Bob lived in this part of North Wales as a Bluecoats school boarder until the war was almost over and it was deemed safe for the school to return to the city. Bob completed his education back in Liverpool. Harry recalls that he and Bob would drive into North Wales when both were retired and sit with take-away beer on a hill side enjoying the scenery that Bob had come to admire whilst an evacuee.

After leaving school, Bob's curriculum vitae from about 1994 states, "Before I did a degree, I worked variously as a junior reporter on a local newspaper, National Service (RAF) and administrative assistant in the hospital service".

We know that the local newspaper was the *Birkenhead News* and that his national service in the RAF around 1950 did not take him to the far-flung points of the 'Commonwealth' but to Liverpool itself and the docks from which RAF personnel were despatched to their posts by sea. Whereas for some, National Service had broadened their horizons via foreign travel, for Bob, these two years meant a growing familiarity with and abiding affection for his home city. Whilst working in the hospital service, he undertook evening classes in Latin and set up a poetry group which attracted local, national and US interest throughout the 1950s. He edited a magazine called *Artisan* which ran to seven issues between 1951 and 1955, particularly publishing North American poets such as Charles Olson, Denise Levertov, Robert Duncan and Robert Creeley. An account of his ill-fated visit to see the lattermost in 1953 can be found in a biography of Creeley (Faas 2001: 119). Sverre Spoelstra's essay on Bob's work that follows this one in the book suggests that this period shaped Bob's writing in many ways. He was to continue to write poetry all his life but would only entrust very few close friends, of whom a Lancaster colleague Alan Whitaker was one, to a reading of his work, late in the evening.

Bob had gained a Higher School Leavers Certificate which was necessary for entry into university, so in 1957, he went to Reading University, about 200 miles south of Liverpool, to read for a degree in psychology. He learnt statistics there as part of his studies, and after graduating in 1960 he moved back to Liverpool to the Department of Sociology in the University of Liverpool to undertake a PhD. The Department at the time was a leading centre for industrial sociology and saw pass through its doors luminaries like W. H. Scott, Joe and Olive Banks, Tom Lupton, A. H. Halsey and Andrew Pettigrew. Bob was awarded his PhD after three years and decided to stay in the university. From 1963, he was (according to his CV) 'Research Officer, Medical Research Council Unit for Research on Occupational Aspects of Ageing, Department of Psychology, Liverpool University', where his statistical skills had won him the post and were put to good use. It was here that he met Harry Jamieson (who in the 1970s helped to found the Department of Communication at Liverpool), who remembers that "Although the origins of our interests were divergent, Bob's towards the verbal, and mine towards the visual, we found common ground in, for example, the work of Gregory Bateson, and [*George*] Spencer-Brown".

Around this time he published two sole authored pieces in the social science magazine *New Society* (see the bibliography at the end of this book for full details of his publications) and with his friend Roy Payne wrote an article that appeared in *Occupational Psychology*. In dealing with the Tavistock Institute, who controlled the journal *Human Relations*, Bob came across Michael Foster around 1966, and this friendship was also to prove important.

When this research funding ran out in 1966, Bob moved to become a 'Lecturer in Social Psychology, Aston University, 1966–69'. His friends of this period reported that he did not enjoy this time working in Birmingham nor did he identify in any way with the approach being developed to the study of organizations by the later-famous 'Aston School' of Industrial Administration. Bob left there in 1969 having published three pieces on boredom and alienation (sic) to return to his beloved Liverpool as 'Research Fellow, School of Business Studies, Liverpool University, 1969–76'. At this time, Bob knew Philip Baxendale, who was part of a family based to the south of Preston who owned a firm of manufacturers of central heating boilers. The company used the trade name 'Baxi', and the firm was experimental with regard to HR practices. Bob held a 'Baxi Fellowship' for a number of years at this time in which he did not pursue anything like the approach developed at Aston. Several more pieces appeared in this period of his life, one with Roy Payne and one with Michael Foster, but most being sole authored. These show a move into an interest in technology, or sociotechnical systems, and might in some small way reflect the interests of the Baxi board. His 1974 book *Job Motivation and Job Design* for the Institute of Personnel Management provides more evidence of this trend. Its approach and language were not warmly humanist as might be expected given the topic, but cool and abstract, treating the human element as part of a system.

In 1976, Baxi was unable to carry on with the funding of their fellowship and Bob moved to Lancaster University in the north-west of England, in part through his friendship with Frank Blackler, who had moved to Lancaster from Liverpool a few years earlier. Frank remembers Bob's advocacy at the time of Robert Pirsig's *Zen and the Art of Motorcycle Maintenance*. "Pirsig's intellectual interests were, as his book reveals, closely interrelated to his personal experiences and state of mind. Similarly, for Bob there was a passion and urgency in his academic work. This could be inspirational, but it was not always easy for those around him. Bob was deeply scornful of approaches to organisational studies he considered misguided (the so-called Aston Studies were a regular target of his)". Bob was to spend the next eighteen years in Lancaster and to influence a significant number of staff and students but never lived anywhere near that city, preferring to commute by car and then later by train from Liverpool, which lies almost fifty miles away.

It's at this point that Gibson Burrell got to know something of Bob and he can tell a story of Bob's intellectual contribution to academic life in Lancaster and beyond at that time. In 1976 Bob came to a department of predominantly young men. Sylvia Shimmin was Professor and there were two lecturers of more mature vintage, but the rest of the staff—all 'junior' lecturers—were in their late twenties or early thirties. Bob was forty-five years old and was coming for a lectureship in a competitive environment fuelled in part by youthful testosterone. He was not everyone's chosen candidate, partly because of staff prejudices regarding age (what is now known as 'chrononormativity'), but also because he stated clearly and without subterfuge that he would not be moving to Lancaster if successful. But Bob succeeded in the interview and entered the Department of Behaviour in Organisations (decidedly not a 'z' but an 's') in October 1976. What persuaded some of the staff that this was a good appointment was a sight of Bob's piece, "The Open Field", which appeared that year in *Human Relations* and which we reprint here as the first example of his mature thought. It seemed poetic in its writing style, philosophically informed, and partial to European thinkers. It was antithetical to much that was being written in the 'organizational behaviour' textbooks of the time, many of which came from North America. For some readers, it was a breath of fresh air, showing that it was possible to broaden the range of writing that one engaged in. But there was little pressure to publish in those days and people read much more than they wrote. And often the standard by which they judged their own work prior to publication was mountainously high. Bob empathised with this approach. He polished and polished and polished—perhaps reflecting the work of the poet who is reluctant to let their work be seen by wider audiences until it is word-perfect.

Frank Blackler recalls that Bob "always pushed himself to the limit in whatever he was writing but could be highly critical of work that he found short of the standards he was creating. But one memory I have was how supportive he could be of colleagues or students whose work he did approve of. In his lectures too he would sometimes go to extraordinary lengths to introduce students to the detail of approaches he believed important".

Bob had very good relationships with a number of PhD students whose work came to be published from their theses. Brian Baxter, Phil Leather and Eric Lefevbre were three at least whose book-length publications arose from Bob's influence. He liked the intensity of intellectual dialogue, and doctoral supervision and very small group meetings around ideas allowed this to flourish. He was more nervous in front of large packed lecture theatres, but in later years he could walk into such a room with a copy of that day's *Sun* newspaper and then extemporize about the state of the world, how one might understand it and what methods you might need to employ, from the front page alone. This, on many occasions, worked beautifully, an improvised illumination that showed Bob's thought at its most pyrotechnical. John Bergin, a student of Bob's, remembers, "Bob had a great gift of revealing insight, almost effortlessly, even in something as prosaic as a bar of Sunlight soap. Fostering understanding of meaning in human experience was core to Bob's life's work." John Hassard was taught by Bob when he was an undergraduate at Lancaster. "Bob would occasionally drop little conceptual bombs. In one lecture he made an elliptical remark to the effect that 'well if you take the people out of the organization, there's no organization'. I thought—'what the hell is he on about'? However catching a train later that day I passed an office block and thought: 'Got it—no people, no meaning.' I guess I wasn't the sharpest of Bob's students!"

Bob's politics were liberal humanist—or perhaps as Spoelstra suggests in the essay that follows, vitalist—but he was by no means a socialist, so it came as a surprise to us when, at a time of crisis in the life of the Department, he was labelled by someone as a 'Marxist'. This description bore no weight whatsoever (yet to some of us would have been seen as a badge of honour), but it was meant to be a denigratory smear upon Bob and his work aimed at the ears of those in higher reaches of the University. A report on the Department's future which fell into Gibson Burrell's hands after the untimely death of one of its authors maintained that no evidence had been found of Marxism in Bob's work. This was indeed correct, for Bob had little if any interest in the politics of his own institutions—nor even more widely. At his leaving event in 1994 before Bob moved on to Keele, he was presented by a colleague with a set of videotapes entitled, "The Thatcher Years". He was told in front of well-wishers, "This is what Thatcherism was like Bob, because we all protected you from it".

Freed from any concerns to be active in university or departmental politics, Bob threw himself into the issue that was appearing to have some relevance at the time—postmodernism. The putative decline and thus neglect of big-party politics within postmodernity may have fitted in with Bob's lower level of political commitment, but this was not the major reason for his delight in this material. Rather, it seemed to genuinely resonate with his predilections for philosophically informed approaches that saw the science envy of some social science as deeply problematic. His reading on this topic was vast, and he devoured the literature coming out of France in particular. There is a period in his CV between 1978 and 1983 in which nothing was published but during which he was assembling notes on the emerging question of postmodernism. Bob produced a piece for Gareth Morgan's *Beyond Method* edited collection in 1983 which marked the end of his period of theoretical reassessment, and which we include here. Gareth was nominally supervised by Bob for his doctorate, and although Gareth's thesis did not reflect much of Bob's interests, there was a mutual respect between them engendered by that burst of creativity in Behaviour in Organisations. "I had the highest regard for Bob. He was a great intellectual who had a phenomenal impact on Lancaster's intellectual and social culture and his influence on those who converted to his cause was immense."

Bob Cooper soon had a comprehensive 'line' on modernism and postmodernism and sought to build up an interest within the Department and its PhDs on the topic. He and Brian Baxter introduced Gibson Burrell to the work of Foucault, which was (not to overegg the pudding) to represent an overnight gestalt switch after reading *Discipline and Punish*. Bob's recommendations for reading, in a department where reading was seen as essential, were taken very seriously indeed. For his friend Harry Jamieson, the metaphor most apt for Bob was that "he was a signpost, directing attention to ways of understanding that are original, meaningful, and interesting, leading to a destination that can be fulfilling." For John Bergin the same metaphor holds. "What a library I now have of books I would never have read were it not for meeting Bob in 1980 and knowing him for another three decades".

Bob also recommended certain lifestyle choices to do with food and drink where the latter was to be imbibed for preference on a Friday. This matched the departmental culture where the feast of Saint Friday was respected by many academic and administrative colleagues. For some of his closest students it appeared that his intellectual arena was more the pub than the university.

Bob's recommendations about Liverpool and its pub life were taken up by members of the Department and several trips were made—on a Friday—to the birthplace of the Beatles where Bob was keen to show us the city-centre drinking places that John and Paul had frequented. A favourite of Bob Cooper's at this time was the 'Philharmonic', which was an enormous and beautifully decorated public house that had Victorian green tiles every-where, especially in the gents lavatory, and reflected a city that had seen better days when the docks were thriving. But in those days, UK licensing laws meant that pubs shut at two in the afternoon and did not reopen till 6 pm. There were thus collective requirements for carrying on drinking when thrown out of the Philharmonic. One could buy alcohol and sit by the River Mersey in the sun listening to Bob discoursing on the nature of contemporary French thought, but on several inclement days we attempted to gain access to 'The Hole in the Wall'.

This was an amazing place—an oasis—that Bob knew well. At about 2.30 in the afternoon, one appeared, as well dressed and as apparently sober as possible, in front of a door in a wall in Liverpool city centre and knocked three times. A shutter would open in the door and an eye would peruse those that stood outside. Bob would proffer some incantation and access to this demi-world was allowed. It was a very large place teeming with males who turned out to be well-dressed solicitors, bank managers and estate agents. They had worked until lunchtime and then abandoned their offices for 'doing business' in the Hole in the Wall. Some of us assumed that a Masonic handshake would be required to enter any conversation going on around us and the espoused politics on show were not to all our tastes, but the freedom to carry on buying alcohol all afternoon was magical for a generation that had known for all their lives that disappointing postprandial ejection from any decent pubs. Once licensing laws changed, the satisfaction of illegal drinking was lost, but civilisation was to be welcomed in its stead.

It was Bob's signal that you were accepted into his world to be invited to Liverpool for a day's refreshment, and many of us remember his pride in showing the novitiate around. He was particularly proud when Liverpool gained some cultural cachet with the opening of the Tate Modern Art Gal-lery in the renovated Albert Dock in 1988. Given the relaxation over licens-ing hours in later years, the day would be reshaped to embrace culture first and then drinking. He would insist that visitors toured the galleries of the

Tate before getting down to socialising over a beer. Bob did 'insist' a lot. Norman Jackson and Pippa Carter recall this aspect of his persona:

> He was a man who had no qualms about magisterially deciding, while others, more democratically, and probably more long-windedly, debated. At a conference in Brussels, that cornucopia of fine food, where a group of colleagues were positively salivating about the prospects for a gourmet evening off the *Grand Place*, we ended up, somehow, at Bob's behest and to his satisfaction, at an unbelievably dire pizza place on the ring-road. Even as we ate, there were puzzled murmurings as to how this had happened. Such was Bob's ability to influence—he certainly knew a thing or two about organising.

Back in Lancaster, Bob was concentrating on certain developments which he had identified and selected through extensive reading and which questioned much of what had been taken for granted in western social theory. He was putting together a clear understanding of these developments and persuaded several people of the excitement that this could and would generate. His energy levels went up as he was carried along by the traction of the material. And this gave him the confidence to see a programme of work. Thus the series of pieces on modernism and postmodernism that appeared in *Organization Studies* was mooted to the editors and publishers and was very quickly accepted as a proposal about 1986. On publication of the first in the series (reprinted here), Bob came into heavy demand for his time and was being encouraged to attend many conferences in the UK and in Europe. This was most fitting because that first piece is almost entirely Bob's contribution. The second name on that article was offered by Bob as a courtesy that he need not have done. One more attuned to the singularity of career would have insisted on sole authorship, but Bob was not like that in his generosity of spirit.

Various conferences and workshops took place where Bob was invited to speak, and Gibson remembers one of these vividly. In a sense it is a moment, and as the reader will see, a phrase that captures Bob's essential attitude to life and his work. This was a workshop in Amsterdam organised by a Dutch quasi-academic who charged for attendance at various seminars in a private non-university location as an academic impresario. Not that Bob or Gibson, having had both their trip funded and an audience delivered, were interested in the money, but it must have raised a profit for our Dutch colleague. Bob performed very well and refused to explain to a business audience how their world and his might interact. He did not wish their modern grappling irons to hook into his postmodern ship and successfully evaded answering direct questions on the direct organizational relevance of his position. It was a master class in that skill. As the workshop ended, we were asked to stand outside on the canal side to have our photograph taken. As we posed, the organiser surprised us by handing us bowler hats and umbrellas so we might be captured on picture as stereotypical southern British males.

Bob looked at these props in total disbelief and raised himself to his full height. His sense of outrage was palpable. He pushed the hat and umbrella straight back into Dutch arms, and said very loudly and aggressively up-close in the face of our host, stressing each carefully considered word as a refutation of the gross liberties being taken, "WE. . . ARE. . . PROPER. . . FUCKING. . . ACADEMICS". In his case at least, he was correct.

Later, we were sent the newspaper cutting of an article written about the presentations we had undertaken accompanied by the photograph that was eventually allowed—after Bob had cooled down—and without the clichéd London accoutrements. A friend was a Dutch speaker and I asked her if she would translate the newspaper piece for us. She did so and told us a day or two later with a disarming frankness that we wouldn't want to know what it said!

Whilst at Lancaster and now aged in his mid-fifties, Bob wrote and published his most well-known pieces, if citations are anything to go by. The "Introduction to Modernism and Postmodernism" reprinted here is currently Bob's most influential piece, followed by his 1989 piece in the same series on Derrida, and then a piece from 1986 called "Organization/Disorganization" (also reprinted here), which appeared in *Social Science Information*. A planned article on Niklas Luhmann for *Organization Studies* was sketched out but did not appear. However, Bob wrote with Stephen Fox, who was also at Lancaster at this time in the Department of Management Learning, and also collaborated with Mick Dillon in Lancaster's Department of Politics. The latter still jokes that working with Bob held back his publications for years because he had to rethink everything he'd ever believed.

Bob Cooper could have this effect upon people with whom he collaborated, and they usually saw it in a positive light. But like many academics, Bob had views about his colleagues that he was willing to share with others late into the evening when these colleagues were not there. Bob once said of a close co-worker that this person "had knocked at the door of knowledge but had not bothered to go in". Of another (somewhat over-eagerly reported back to Gibson by others), that "once he had shown promise, but he had never delivered on it". These one-liners reflect someone who was wholeheartedly committed to the task of being a proper (fucking) academic and who had extraordinarily high standards as to what being an 'intellectual' entailed. But living up to these ideals is impossible for most.

Bob left Lancaster for Keele University in the North Midlands and a Chair there in 1994. His leaving event was a disastrous occasion because rather than saying generously what Behaviour in Organisations had done for him, it became an event for delivering home truths about what Bob thought of the intellectual atmosphere and what had driven him away. Rather than speak of the pull factors of his new institution, he spoke of the elements pushing him away from Lancaster. Whilst it was heartfelt, it was by no means a diplomatic triumph and turned acrimoniously into a really uncomfortable event for all concerned. It was the end of something that had been mutually beneficial, but the evening functioned as the severing of once-close ties with a few at Lancaster. And thus Bob moved on to Keele where Martin Parker takes up the story.

Though I had met him before, my first memory of Bob comes before I joined Keele, at a workshop where he was presenting a version of the proximal and distal paper that he wrote with John Law, and that we reprint here. I, young smart arse that I was, tried to take the old man down with some question about how this was all very similar to Tony Giddens's structuration theory. He snorted back at me, letting me know that I simply hadn't understood the depth of his argument. I later heard that he sometimes described that paper as merely 'A level sociology', thinking perhaps that the dull dualisms of agents and structures were simply pale reflections of the seething mess of movement and boundary-making that he could see beyond the world.

Bob's appointment at Keele coincided with a real burst of creativity there. Together with John Law from Sociology and John Hassard and Rolland Munro from Management, he created the Centre for Social Theory and Technology (CSTT), a multi-disciplinary assemblage that brought together those departments with people from Geography, Literature and Politics. It allowed a lot of the staff in Management to pretend they weren't from Management, including Bob and me. Indeed, the earlier Cooper who wrote about job design and leadership was erased, and I remember Bob's embarrassment when he caught me reading a copy of his job design book from twenty years previous. Conversations with him would often begin with some sort of distancing from the dull universe of dull utilitarians, perhaps with reference to some resented character from his Lancaster past. "You and me, we're not part of Management, are we?" Positions emplaced, he a 'social philosopher', me a 'sociologist', we could move on (and since I had the office next door to him, we often did) to conversations about ontology, the inadequacies of people we knew in common, or our latest plans to go drinking.

By then, Bob was becoming well known, with two edited books concerning his work (Chia 1998a, 1998b), a special issue of a journal (Böhm and Jones 2001) and later a chapter about his work (Spoelstra 2005). There was a regular procession of people coming to see him, the 'mini-coopers' as we called them. He clearly enjoyed the attention, but never gloried in it, always being careful and attentive with visitors. He was also part of a flurry of seminars, conferences and workshops with various people from CSTT which led to edited books on Bob neologisms such as 'The Labour of Division' (Hetherington and Munro 1997) and 'The Consumption of Mass' (Lee and Munro 2001), as well as popular culture (Hassard and Holliday 1998), Actor Network Theory (Law and Hassard 1999), the body (Hassard, Holliday and Wilmott 2000), complexity theory, science fiction and so on. One I remember particularly well concerned art and social theory and took place in Liverpool's Institute for Performing Arts, with a reception in his beloved

Liverpool Tate art gallery. I had an odd sense that Bob felt that this was something really important, to be talking about art, and the ways in which it could reveal something significant about the world, with an audience of people from the humanities. Amongst the canapés and chattering academics, he looked at home and alive. Still funny and rude, but with less need to position himself, either in terms of class or discipline. He was talking about art and social theory, laughing, and seemed as happy as I remember him.

Because most of the time, in the seminar room as some august speaker or earnest PhD rolled their theoretical piano into the room, Bob just squirmed. He would throw me theatrically desperate winks, as if we were the only two people in the room who could see just how intellectually hollow the presenter was, and then leave early, or deliver a question (prefaced with much odd throat clearing and which was more assertion than query). He was always impatient with people who he felt lacked 'rigour' in their thought, but was encouraging to those who he thought showed promise, particularly if they were younger, and seemed to be trying rather than posing. Sverre Spoelstra remembers Bob visiting Copenhagen in 2006 for a PhD course that was organized around his work. "About twenty PhD students discussed their research projects with Bob for three days. All made explicit connections to Bob's writings. I think he enjoyed the interest in his work, but his input always followed what the students were trying to achieve. It was never concerned with interpretations or misinterpretations of his own work."

We wrote together once, though we never actually did it together. Deciding to write a chapter on cyborgs, and cyborganization (a concept in the Cooper and Law essay), I wrote a few pages. He wrote something too, and then I made the mistake of editing it, deleting what I thought were some repetitions. This resulted in a tense conversation, in which I was clearly told that I should not edit his words again, and we agreed on a compromise. I would write some text, and he would provide footnotes, with neither editing the other. It was probably for the best, but resulted in a chapter with two parts which barely engaged with each other. One of those parts is reprinted here. I thought he was writing glacier-cool unadorned social science, when perhaps he always imagined it as a terse poetry with its own economies and repetitions. As Geoff Lightfoot, a colleague at Keele, told me, Bob once complained that he would take hours trying to find the right word.

I met his wife Maxine once, for five minutes in a bookshop, but never visited his house, or met his children. I never read his poetry. I think he liked cats, because he stayed in my house once and met a cat or two, but I never really knew him. Others might have known him better. Despite this, he is someone whose thinking has shaped mine (see Parker forthcoming) and that of many other people I know, too. His insistence on academic work being carried out slowly, with creativity and integrity, is increasingly alien to a university system which values narrow senses of performativity and rewards people who do what they are told. Bob was a terrible colleague in the sense that he refused to fill in the right forms, and was sometimes grumpy and rude, but he made people think, if they were open to thought. Steve Brown, another Keele colleague, said, "I think Bob liked me, for a while at least. He encouraged me to read his copy of Michel Serres' *The Parasite* at a time when it was long out of print. He could be so unnecessarily and delight-fully rude about Actor-Network Theory. Cups of coffee became impromptu seminars on whatever he was passionate about at the time ('hand-made space' has stuck with me). 'Canetti's Sting' was once named as the work he was most proud of, despite, or perhaps because of its obscurity."

As the essays in this collection show, as well as the beautiful assessment by Sverre Spoelstra, he refused to let concepts settle, always trying to torture and stretch each word, each join and separation. Often, he spins the reader around an etymological merry-go-round, ending up where they began, but much wiser. I'm not sure that he would have survived in the university now-adays. He would have been repelled by journal rankings, impact factors and impact cases, and been incapable of ensuring that students gave him high satisfaction scores on their end-of-term questionnaires. Marshall McLuhan expressed it well:

> The poet, the artist, the sleuth—whoever sharpens our perception tends to be antisocial; rarely "well-adjusted", he cannot go along with cur-rents and trends. A strange bond often exists among anti-social types in their power to see environments as they really are. (1967: no page numbers)

I think Bob must have been a poet, because he was a terrible employee.

He formally retired from Keele in the late 1990s, but then became an honorary research professor there for several more years, and eventually a visiting professor who never visited, with an honorary appointment at Leicester University, too. By then, most of his friends had left Keele anyway. He stayed in Liverpool, holding court with the people who came to see him for a tour of grand old pubs full of carved wood and lunchtime drinkers, and perhaps followed by a Chinese meal. Sverre Spoelstra, then a PhD stu-dent at Leicester University, stayed at his house twice, and remembers that Bob "complained about not finding enough time to write because his son played games on his computer and he didn't have access to online journal articles. The solution to his 'problem' seemed so obvious: get another com-puter and use someone's university login. It was too obvious so I didn't dare to suggest it—there was clearly something else, beyond 'the practical-useful' as he would put it, at work in his complaints." He kept on writing though, perhaps a little more slowly, and sometimes complaining of his dislike of public places (particularly supermarkets) because of tinnitus.

I only saw him a few times in the last few years, in pubs in Liverpool, and when he died in 2013, I remembered a backwards glance, something I now remember as a thoughtful and lengthy assessment, as he left the pub that we were in the year before. He looked back at tableful of braying academics in front of a table full of empty glasses, and then he was off to catch his bus back home. To wherever he lived.

After his funeral, a few of Bob's friends that had known him through university life, found a pub in Liverpool close to the crematorium. The beer was incredibly cheap, and it was remarked upon that Bob would have liked its ambience. As Norman and Pippa noted at the time, Bob had an aversion to food—he was always a man who ate to live, often dwelling amongst those who live to eat. We were dressed in black and were talking animatedly about him and his life, remembering stories, like the ones we have told here, to unify us as mourners. Dispersed around us throughout the pub sat a team of six silent painters and decorators, all dressed in white overalls and reading their newspapers. In their leisured lunchtime they were differentiated by the large spaces by which they had chosen to separate one from another. These labours of di-vision in the black and white colours of our dress, the presence/absence of talking, the spatial and temporal contiguity or separation of when and where we sat would have been perfect for Bob to analyse. But he was not there, and it dawned that we had lost Professor Robert Cooper. This book is simply an attempt to make sure that his work—and some memory of him—lives on.[2]

## NOTES

1  Grateful thanks to Abbie Sleath, for her wonderfully efficient retyping of the Cooper pieces we reprint here. Thanks to Priya Dey for her help with the diagrams. Also to Sverre Spoelstra for his help with our introduction and list of publications. Finally, thanks to the College of Social Sciences at the University of Leicester for a 2014–15 grant to fund the permissions and the typing and hence which made this book possible.

2  We have selected what we think are twelve of the most useful or revealing of Cooper's essays, and bookended the earlier ones with sections from an extended interview with him that was published in 1998. The book concludes with another section from that interview, followed by a bibliography of his work. Note that the references for the interview sections are all collected at the end of the final interview fragment, and edits to the interview sections are marked with [. . .].

## REFERENCES

Böhm, S. and Jones, C. (2001) 'Responding: To Cooper' *ephemera* 4/1: 314–422.
Chia, R. (ed) (1998a) *In the Realm of Organization: Essays for Robert Cooper.* London: Routledge.
Chia, R. (ed) (1998b) *Organized Worlds: Explorations in Technology and Organization with Robert Cooper.* London: Routledge.
Faas, E. (with Maria Trombacco) (2001) *Robert Creeley: A Biography.* Hanover, NE: University Press of New England.

Hassard, J. and Holliday, R. (eds) (1998) *Organization—Representation: Work and Organization in Popular Culture*. London: Sage.

Hassard, J., Holliday, R. and Willmott, H. (eds) (2000) *Body and Organization*. London: Sage.

Hetherington, K. and Munro, R. (eds) (1997) *Ideas of Difference: Social Ordering and the Labour of Division*. Oxford: Blackwell.

Law, J. and Hassard, J. (eds) (1999) *Actor Network Theory and After*. Oxford: Blackwell.

Lee, N. and Munro, R. (2001) *The Consumption of Mass*. London: Wiley-Blackwell.

McLuhan, M., Fiore, Q. and Agel, J. (1967) *The Medium Is the Massage*. London: Penguin.

Parker, M. (2016) 'Organization and Philosophy: Vision and Division.' In R. Mir, H. Willmott and M. Greenwood (eds) *Companion to Philosophy in Organization Studies*. London: Routledge.

Spoelstra, S. (2005) 'Robert Cooper: Beyond Organization'. In C. Jones and R. Munro (eds) *Contemporary Organization Theory*. Oxford: Blackwell, 106–119.

# 2 Robert Cooper
## Beyond Organization

*Sverre Spoelstra*

(A revised, updated and expanded version of a chapter that was originally published in C. Jones and R. Munro (eds.) *Contemporary Organization Theory*. Oxford: Blackwell, 2005.)

## INTRODUCTION

Apart from one short book on work design, Robert Cooper exclusively wrote articles and book chapters. This early book (Cooper, 1974) and other works from the 1960s and early 1970s (e.g., Cooper, 1966; Cooper and Foster, 1971; Cooper, 1973) were part of a programme at the Tavistock Institute of Human Relations, whose object was to translate some of the theoretical ideas from sociotechnical systems thinking into practical language. Although interesting in its own right, it is Cooper's later work, roughly starting with his 1976 essay 'The Open Field', which is of greater interest for the study of organization, primarily because it raises profound theoretical questions concerning the ontological underpinnings of organization. In this chapter I am concerned with these later works, in which Cooper turns away from the core concerns of the Tavistock programme to address more general philosophical and sociological questions concerning the nature of organization.

From 1976 until 1994, when he went to Keele University, Cooper worked in the Department of Behaviour in Organisations at Lancaster University. The 'Lancaster group', which in the late 1970s and early 1980s included Gibson Burrell and Gareth Morgan among others, questioned the status quo of organization theory by inquiring into its roots in sociology and philosophy. One of the key publications of these years is Burrell and Morgan's *Sociological Paradigms and Organizational Analysis*, first published in 1979. Cooper and Burrell's introduction of postmodernism and poststructuralism to the study of organizations in the late 1980s (Cooper, 1987; 1989b; Cooper and Burrell, 1988; Burrell, 1988; 1994) was also strongly connected to the research performed by the Lancaster group. At Keele University, Cooper became the director of the interdisciplinary Centre for Social Theory and

Technology, which was one of the largest groups of poststructuralists in the United Kingdom at that time. In his years at Keele Cooper further developed poststructuralist-inspired ideas (e.g., 1998a; 2001a), in collaboration with the sociologist John Law among others. After his retirement, Cooper was a visiting professor at Keele University.

It would be a mistake to limit a discussion of Cooper's work to his 'contributions' to the study of organizations, since his elaborations on organization resonate with much wider theoretical and practical concerns. In spite of Cooper's well-documented importance for organization theory (e.g., Chia 1998a; 1998b, Böhm and Jones, 2001), Cooper never studied 'real' organizations as such. In fact, much of his work, as I will explain in the next section, is directed against the idea of a 'real' or 'completed' organization and, consequently, questions the tradition in the social sciences that has made the individual organization its object of study. In this context, Cooper distinguishes 'theory of organizations' from 'organization theory' (Cooper and Law, 1995): the first studies organizations as bounded entities, which is what Cooper cautions against, whereas the latter is interested in the organizing processes out of which these organizations emerge and disappear.

Related to discussion of the nature of organization, conceived as a social practice rather than a bounded thing in the world (Cooper, 1986; 1987; Cooper and Law, 1995), important themes in Cooper's writings are culture (Cooper, 2001a), cyborganization (Cooper and Law, 1995; Parker and Cooper, 1998), distance (Cooper, 2009; 2010), information (Cooper 1976; 1986; 1987), mass (Cooper, 2001b; 2003), Otherness (Cooper, 1983; 1998a), process (Cooper, 1976; 2007; 2014), representation (Cooper, 1992; 1993) and visibility/division (Cooper, 1989a, 2006; 2014). His theoretical inspirations are equally diverse: from contemporary French and Italian philosophy to anthropology, sociology, psychoanalysis, pragmatism, systems theory, chaos theory, cybernetics and art theory—to name only a few primary sources. What is remarkable is the lightness with which Cooper crosses these boundaries, or perhaps we should say in which he *un-forms* boundaries. Cooper moves almost effortlessly from one discipline to another as if there were no boundaries between them.

This style of thinking and writing, in which authors from different backgrounds are connected to one another, can be confusing. What is confusing is precisely the 'everybody knows' which Cooper often seems to disregard. This, however, is a conscious strategy, for it is precisely the 'everybody knows' (or simply 'knowledge') which Cooper seeks to unmask. Cooper is not interested in the knowledge embedded in the separate disciplines. What interests him is what moves through disciplines (or systems, organizations), what keeps them together and what allows them to fall apart. What is especially important for Cooper, as I see it, is the question of the *beyond*: What is *beyond* discipline? What is *beyond* knowledge? What is *beyond* subjectivity? What is *beyond* organization? The question of the beyond is primarily an ontological question, an investigation into the formation and—simultaneously—displacement of order, as well as its relation to the human condition. From these questions of the beyond other questions follow: technical questions (How is the unknown made knowable?), sociological questions (What does it mean to have agency? How do humans participate in organizing processes?) and epistemological questions (How to know the beyond? Is there a method to reach out to the beyond?).

Cooper's style of writing is unique and stands as a powerful reminder that articles do not need to be formulaic exercises in making 'a contribution' to the field. Characteristic for Cooper's style is his frequent use of the word 'again'. In many of his writings he reworks the problem he is addressing, again and again. This is not a repetition of the same, even though some concepts (e.g., vision as division) can be found in many of his writings. Whenever Cooper takes up one of his concepts again, it is put in relation to another term, another author or another theme, whereby the new inevitably slips in. This way of working invites the new to appear beyond the control of the author. Cooper (1998a: 112) quotes Deleuze: 'Movement always happens behind the thinker's back, or in the moment when he blinks'. Cooper's writing is a tireless re-working or re-reading that results in a series of small displacements of what has come before. His texts move along, but defy a linear narrative. The idea is always to unfold the immediate possibility of the beyond.

As Burrell and Parker mention in their introduction to this volume, Cooper was very fond of poetry (and he wrote poems himself). As editor of the little magazine *Artisan* in the early 1950s, he introduced a number of North-American poets to an English audience, including the poets Charles Olson and Robert Creeley, who were to become the most influential of the Black Mountain poets. Cooper's essay 'The Open Field' is partly inspired by what Olson called 'open field composition' or 'projective verse', which went radically against the closed-form poetry of the mainstream at the time. One of the guiding ideas of open field poetry is that every line has a singular force which should neither be pre-structured by images of what a poem ought to be like (e.g., in terms of rhythm, meter and stanza) nor held in check by the intentions of the poet (see Kwasny, 2004). Olson (1997: 240, capitals in original) writes, 'From the moment he [the poet] ventures into FIELD COMPOSITION—puts himself in the open—he can go by no track other than the poem under hand declares, for itself'. For Cooper, this is much more than a poetic device; it is a way of being a scholar and academic and, ultimately, a human being. In 'The Open Field' Cooper (1976: 1002) writes, 'The man who enters the Open Field uses action as a means of revealing the latent in himself and his world'. This is how Cooper approached writing; his essay 'The Open Field', and all papers that followed, are not to be read as reflections on the open field, but foremost as a step into it.

My reading of Cooper in this chapter, despite my attempts to find running threads in his work, is a partial reading. It is an attempt to step into the space that Cooper's work has opened up. Realizing that Cooper's writings, by definition, do not form one closed system, also means that any representation of his writings will be equally partial. I have chosen to focus on Cooper's ontology of organization—in my view his most important displacement of organization theory. This is where Cooper takes organization theory beyond organization theory.


## AGAINST SIMPLE LOCATION

If there is one common theme in all of Cooper's later writings, then it is a negative theme. This is, at times passionate, a not *that* kind of thinking, a not *that* type of knowledge. Cooper has used various labels to designate this adversary to his thought, the adversary of the open. The clearest expression, perhaps, is one he borrowed from Whitehead: the logic of simple location (Cooper, 1997; 1998a; 1998b; see also Chia, 1998c). Whitehead defines simple location as the idea which says that 'material can be said to be *here* in space and *here* in time, or *here* in space-time, in a perfectly definite sense which does not require for its explanation any reference to other regions of space-time' (Whitehead, 1967: 62). For Whitehead, the logic of simple location is intimately related to the concept of Euclidean space: the idea that clearly distinguishable things, defined by their locations, move from one place to another by the force of universal laws (such as gravity). Once we 'know' these 'laws' the world becomes entirely predictable. According to Whitehead this idea is based on simplification, missing primary forces not *in* time and space, but from which time and space effectuate. For Whitehead, true movement is a distortion of nature as a whole, simultaneously redefining time-space relations as well as the identity of 'things'. Whitehead was thus concerned with what we miss out when we present things as complete in universal time and space. To Bertrand Russell, who defended the idea that the world is formed of independent and complete entities, Whitehead once said, 'You think the world is what it looks like in fine weather at noon day; I think it is what it seems like in the early morning when one first wakes from deep sleep' (Russell, 1956: 41). Whitehead was interested in the point where the clear evaporates into the unclear. This is exactly what interests Cooper as well.

The logic of simple location, as Cooper understands it, attempts to translate raw matter into 'things' (Cooper, 1998b: 137). It is based on the idea that the conditions which define what a thing is capable of are located in the thing itself. Every idea of the fixed is based on the flawed idea of simple location, the idea that there is no beyond: 'What you see is all there is', 'What you know is all there is'. According to Cooper, however, entities (and identities) do not have natural locations, and 'things' do not have an essence that keeps them together: 'Social terms are not bounded by "walls"—there are no containers and no contained in the social world' (Cooper and Law, 1995: 243). Identities, subjects, and organizations are generated, and continuously require regeneration, from a groundless mass or abstract field (Cooper, 1976). This groundless mass, which I will discuss in more detail shortly, is a field of absolute potentiality, i.e., potentiality not tied to actuality. Forms derive their existence from this mass. In the idea of simple location this mass is denied: the potential that surrounds any being, which is present in its absence, is excluded from analysis and excluded from knowing. There clearly is a violence to this: Drawing on Derrida and Serres, Cooper warns that the purity of an inside 'can only be attained . . . if the outside is branded as a supplement, something inessential, even parasitical' (Cooper, 1989b: 487). By ascertaining the purity of the inside, the outside is by implication denunciated.

As with Whitehead, Cooper's dismissal of simple location is equally directed against the idea of the universal in general: the idea that nature consists of a fixed set of laws which determine the 'simple movement' of 'clear-cut, definite things' (Cooper, 1998a: 108). The social and technical world we inhabit, says Cooper, cannot be understood on the basis of universal laws. The idea of the universal is another example of simple location, or the representation of partiality as wholeness. A universal law, even if infinite in its power, is finite in being forever closed: its formula remains forever the same. We find the same idea in Deleuze and Guattari. They say, 'We think the universal explains, whereas it is what must be explained' (Deleuze and Guattari, 1994: 49). So, for Cooper, as well as for Deleuze and Guattari, the moment we have established a bounded entity or a universal (Whitehead's noon), that is the moment when we need to start asking questions—that is when there is an opportunity and a need for thinking. Thinking for Cooper thus involves a displacement of established forms. It reaches beyond the immediately visible and knowable, which is to say that it dwells in the open or the 'abstract field' (Cooper, 1976).

## THE POTENTIAL OF THE ABSTRACT FIELD

Let us try to translate Cooper's dismissal of simple location in terms of potentiality. What does potentiality mean? What does it mean to be capable of something? In Book Theta of *Metaphysics*, where Aristotle developed his ontology of potentiality, one finds a critique of thinkers of the Megarian school, who argued that a being has potency only when this potency is active, when it is exercised. According to Aristotle, this is an absurd idea, leading to beliefs such as:

> that which is standing will always stand and that which is sitting will always sit; for that which sits will not get up, since it will be impossible for it to get up if it does not have the power to get up.
>
> (Aristotle, 1966: 149)

For Aristotle, a human being has the potentiality to stand when sitting, or to sit when standing. That is, human beings can be the moving cause of their own movement. This idea is safeguarded by the idea that being human is grounded in a substance in which the potentiality to sit and to get up find their natural location: as a human being I can talk; as a chair I can bear a human being. It is uncontested, says Aristotle, that to be able to do something is not the same as exercising this potentiality: the potential is different from its actual expression. To get up when one sits, one needs to possess the potentiality or the power to get up, and in getting up one's potentiality to get up is actualized.

According to Agamben (1999), however, there is more to Aristotle's concept of potentiality than the idea that something is potential when there is a possibility of actualization. The true potential, says Agamben, does not exhaust itself in actualization, which is to say that something does not give over to actuality when one does what one is capable of. Agamben (1993: 36) gives the example of the piano player. Having the potential (to be capable) of playing the piano is not simply actualized when playing the piano. What is carried over from potentiality to actuality in the act of playing the piano is the potential not to play: when the piano player plays the piano, the potential not to play is 'set aside'—but not lost—in playing. Paradoxically, then, to be capable of something means that one is capable of one's own impotentiality. For Agamben, the potential to act and the potential not to act go together and are ultimately identical: 'all potentiality is impotentiality' (Agamben, 1999: 181). The important point that Agamben makes is that potentiality is not a derivative of actuality, which is how the potential is normally understood.

What Cooper calls 'the abstract field' (1976) can be understood as pure potential in the sense of Agamben. Agamben's impotentiality (or 'pure negativity') is Cooper's 'constitutive absence' (2014: 586), 'constitutive negativity' (2014: 596) or, following the poet Keats, 'negative capability' (Cooper, 1976: 1009; Cooper, 1987: 400). These are all concepts that stress that the actual, far from being the actualization of the potential, remains grounded in the potential. The abstract field is Cooper's name for the 'potential of existence which the immediate utility of everyday life conceals from us' (Cooper, 2007: 1565). Potentiality for Cooper is never *located* within substance, genus or species (frames or boundaries which keep a set of potentialities together), or *defined* by function or law (the idea of the universal). The power is not a power from within, nor a power located in universal laws, but a power from the abstract field. Actualization is grounded in the abstract field (or rather 'ungrounded') from which what is known as reality folds and unfolds. Heidegger's influence on Cooper can clearly be felt here: Heidegger's Nothing as the background out of which everything emerges resembles Cooper's concept of the abstract field.

For Cooper, the popular idea that employees have a potential, and that good managers can help employees to realize their full potential, is a fiction that is again based on the logic of simple location. Yes, people do have potential, in a sense, but this potential is not an inherent property waiting to be actualized; it is rather a necessarily 'dormant' and 'invisible' force that keeps us on the move and that at no point dissolves in actuality. It is something that 'seems to resist conceptual and practical appropriation' (Cooper, 2005: 1693). Staying in touch with this potentiality is what Cooper's politics amounts to, which couldn't be further away from party politics—it is therefore entirely consistent with his thinking that Cooper rarely had something to say about the political tides of his time, as the editors note in the introduction to this volume. What is often understood as 'politics', namely the formulation of desirable ends and the struggle to get there, is at odds with Cooper's idea of staying in touch with the abstract field. Politics, for Cooper, is about reaching out to pure potential, rather than the reduction of life to particular ends.

For Cooper, the abstract field can never be touched directly. It can only be approached through the divisions we recognize as our world: 'The primary whole is always a lost whole, one which we can only see through the work of division' (Cooper, 1987: 402). We see a resemblance with Spinoza's thinking. In Spinoza's *Ethics* (2002) the finite and the infinite form one substance, Nature or God, where the finite beings (modes) express infinity through infinite attributes (thinking, extension). Cooper argues that the only key to the infinite (the abstract field) is through the finite: 'Unity or wholeness can emerge only through division or difference' (1983: 213). For this reason, one can only sense the infinite whole, or abstract field, in its absent presence. The abstract field is present in the incompleteness and mutability of actualities. Actualities are always unfinished, or partial, continuously moving through clouds of potentialities:

> Each object—chair, cup, spoon—can never be separate and self-contained; by definition, it is always partial, a *con-verse* in a dynamic network of *convertibilities*. The body, too, is necessarily partial, momentarily defining itself through assemblage with another partial object. The understanding and definition of the human agent as essentially purposeful and self-directive now takes second place to agency as the general collection and dispersion of parts and fragments which co-define each other in a mutable and transient assemblage of possibilities and relations.
>
> (Cooper, 2001b: 25, emphasis in original)

Partiality, for Cooper, means that anything we conceive of as a bounded thing (the possessor of boundaries), is in fact generated from these boundaries, continually transforming itself through interaction with other partialities. The potentiality of a human body, for example, can only be understood through the interactions with other partialities. To sit on a chair means entering a relation with this chair: the human body and the chair temporarily co-define each other.

These interactions between partialities, which continuously reinvent our world, cannot be captured in knowledge because they resist abstraction. It is therefore important to realize that Cooper's abstract field is not abstract in itself. We think of it as abstract because we cannot define its essence or draw its borders. That is to say, we *abstract* from the abstract field. One may even argue that Cooper's abstract field is concrete just like abstract art may be said to be concrete (there is a tradition of 'concrete art' and 'concrete poetry' that most people would qualify as 'abstract'). An abstract painting of, say, a human body reminds us of the complex *concreteness* of what it means to be human. As Sørensen put it, 'all abstractions are simple; everything that is concrete is complex' (2004: 12). The concrete, in this sense, does not stand for 'the actual' or 'the solid', as the term is often understood, but as the actual in its relation to the absent presence of potentiality. Cooper's abstract field, as abstract art, thus reminds us of our forgetfulness of the concreteness of potentiality. We tend to make the concrete abstract through the logic of simple location.

## SIMPLE LOCATION AND ORGANIZATION THEORY

Cooper's dismissal of simple location is primarily directed at dominant discourse in the social sciences. Social science has attributed social origins to complete structures, such as systems and organizations, which are in fact abstractions from far more complex processes of composition and decomposition. Establishing things or 'forevers in thought' stops thinking. It consists of building walls around the present, i.e., locating that which is unlocatable, with the double purpose of creating certainty and advancing 'knowledge'. Simple presence, in its most extreme forms, becomes a collection of moments where one declares the infinite to be finite. This is how some versions of 'progress' in research should be understood. Disciplines such as sociology or organization theory are thought to progress through abstraction upon abstraction. Sociology and organization theory, Cooper argues, all too often blind themselves from what goes beyond simple location. They tend to accept simple location as a given, as a natural fact of life, while the true task for thinking is to ask fundamental questions such as: Where does the logic of simple location lead us? Where would a distal (Cooper, 1998b) or proximal (Cooper and Law, 1995) way of thinking, sensitive to the abstract field, take us? This, of course, is not to say that sociologists have only been preoccupied with simple location. The question of the beyond is clearly present in Max Weber's thinking and can also be felt in systems thinking of the 1960s and 1970s, both important sources of inspiration for Cooper. Nor would it be fair to say that organization theorists have only been preoccupied with simple location. There are strands within organization theory directed against the idea of simple location (and some of it has been inspired by Cooper). But the logic of simple location continues to dominate thinking about organization and management.

An illuminating example of simple location in the social sciences, according to Cooper, is Herbert Simon's (1957) idea of bounded rationality. Simon critiques the idea of Economic Man, he who possesses all relevant information and who makes rational decisions based on this information. Simon corrected models of rational decision-making by arguing that (1) agents face uncertainty about the future, and (2) that there are costs and difficulties in acquiring the required information. In making decisions, Simon argues, decision-makers therefore have to rely on bounded rationality. Decision-making thus becomes a matter of satisficing rather than optimizing. Cooper, in his critique of Simon, says that rationality and prediction are not locatable potentialities in the first place: 'we recognize that it's not the rationality that is bounded but rather that the *boundedness* is *rationalized*' (Cooper, 1998b: 148; emphasis in original; see also Cooper, 1992). In the idea of bounded rationality the ideas of subjectivity and rationality remain unquestioned. That is, in bounded rationality, rationality is located within the minds of individual decision-makers: rationality is bounded because boundedness is attributed to the form of the human mind. Mind, however, is something much more fundamental for Cooper since it directly links us with the undivided mass: the unconsciousness of mind touches the absent presence of potentiality. Forcing the mind to exclusively think in terms of bounded things loses sight of the formation and deformation processes of boundaries.

Another example is the idea of the division of labour. The division of labour, dividing labour into specific tasks or functions, is one of the key concepts in sociology and economics (classic studies are Braverman, 1974; Durkheim, 1984; Marx, 1992; Smith, 1979). While these studies certainly highlight important developments in the industrialization processes that characterize the past three centuries, what is usually forgotten, says Cooper, is what lies beyond the division of labour. This is what Cooper calls the *labour of division* (Cooper, 1989a; 1998a; Cooper, 2006; see also Hetherington and Munro, 1997): the production of the visible in the stabilized forms of social knowledge, social objects or social objectives. Through labour of division human beings are able to give meaning and purpose to their lives. Vision, as we have seen, is always division. That is, through acts of division are we able to see, are we able to create meaning and are we able to find purpose. Work or labour serves precisely this function. Hence what you see is not the unorganized or uninformed mass itself: you see products of the labour of division. Nor are what you hear and what you say rough data (as statisticians would have it): words are formed through division and are therefore meaningful to us.

For Cooper, for the socially and technically informed world at least, these variations on the idea of simple location are based upon an ontological error: the idea that difference is secondary to being: 'differentiation is not a process that occurs (naturally) in the world; rather, it is the world that occurs within the differentiation of dedifferentiation, displacement and uncertainty' (Cooper, 1997: 12). Cooper's point is not that organization theory, or the social sciences in general, focus too much on organization, and that, as 'poststructuralists', we should celebrate process and disorganization. The point is that the establishment of 'an organization' closes the door for thinking about organization as a generic process. That is, precisely by being satisfied with 'an organization' as a completed structure we forget the beyond. Being occupied with organizations is thus a way to stop thinking about organization, i.e., life's immanent organization.

## ORGANIZATION AS THE TRANSFORMATION OF BOUNDARY RELATIONSHIPS

In saying that boundaries do not belong to the entities that they shape, Cooper is not saying that boundaries do not exist. His point is that boundaries do not *belong*. As dividers, boundaries make up the world, i.e., the world belongs to boundaries. To think of walls not as an effect (of building, as in simple location) but as origin, is to move from atoms and laws as object for research to boundary-activity (Cooper, 1986), division (Cooper, 1989a), or framing (1986; 1991b) as the unfolding of life and thought:

> Any 'I' is the transient and uncertain result of boundaries dynamically shared with 'you', 'he', 'she', 'it', and 'them'. This shared 'I' is therefore *common* and *communal* in the most radical sense of a boundary as that which *separates and joins at the same time*.
> (Cooper, 2003: 166, emphases in original)

Boundary-activity, division, or framing, is to separate and to connect at the same time; a condensing of time and space (unthinkable in Euclidean space where time and space are universal dimensions) where what comes after simultaneously comes before: the copy creates the original as much as the original creates the copy.

The reorganization of form is what Cooper calls information. Information must be taken literally here: to in-form, that which goes into form (Cooper, 1976). As we noted earlier, the formed is only partial, looking for further connections that will change its identity. Thus, 'information is not a property of the individual message but of the set of possibilities which surround the message' (Cooper, 1991b: 3). Here we see a direct link to what Whitehead said to Russell: the moment when one wakes up from a deep sleep is the moment of information: 'in that imperceptible moment between the known and the unknown. [Information] lasts but an instant and is quickly gone' (Cooper, 2001a: 169). Similarly, the poet Charles Olson, whose presence—as mentioned—is clearly felt in Cooper's 'The Open Field', described himself as 'an archeologist of morning' (Olson, 1997: 207), where the morning stands for the moment of information.

To think about boundaries, frames and divisions is to think of action (Cooper, 1976; Cooper and Law, 1995). Action does not take place inside or outside boundaries: action takes place in the midst of things, continuously redefining the actual whilst maintaining a cloud of potentialities. Cooper seeks to disentangle the act from actuality or the actor (the agent), similar to the way in which Agamben's potential survives actualization. Much like Agamben stresses the 'nonaction-as-action', as Hamacher (1999: 333) puts it, Cooper conceptualizes the act as that which relieves actuality from itself. The act in Cooper is what the 'event' is in much poststructuralist theorizing (e.g., Badiou, Lyotard): 'action (at least initially) occurs in a meaning vacuum, having become detached from clear purpose and outcome' (Cooper, 1976: 1002). Actions (or events) make present what was absent, they make visible what was invisible, possible what was impossible, and they can do this because of their refusal to be steered by functions or intended outcomes.

This is also how Cooper understands organization: 'Organizing activity is the transformation of boundary relationships' (Cooper, 1992: 257). Organization or information is always a reorganization of presence and absence. 'Organizations' (what we in language refer to as organizations) do not organize. The earth organizes. What we commonly conceive as 'an organization' is the result of symbolic reproduction. The ontological moment of information or organization is not to be understood as a simplification of things (in translating matter into form); it is the moment when potentialities come into being, without exhausting themselves in actuality. It is the moment when space, or 'world' (as Heidegger would put it) is revealed (Cooper, 2001b).

One might object that if 'organizations' were in fact continually changing, or continually informing, it would be impossible to actually work in an organization, or to recognize an organization as such. Cooper has two answers. The first we have already seen: what we see is not sheer matter, or sheer potentiality. What we see is the symbolic order, the already divided, the already signified. This answer, however, is not enough in itself, for the question is: How do we act upon this symbolic order? This is Cooper's second answer: What we call an organization, in this regard, is no different from what we call an 'I', a 'we' or an 'it'. Just as 'we' continuously regenerate ourselves by speaking the already-formed concepts (conforming) and by inventing new concepts (informing), 'organizations' also continuously regenerate themselves. Newspapers, for example, recreate themselves on a daily basis through their reports (Cooper, 2005: 1690). On an ontological level there is no categorical distinction between human being and organization: 'We' are equally part of 'organizations' as 'organizations' are part of 'us'. 'We', as well as 'organizations', produce what it means to be a 'we' or 'an organization' in taking part of the primary processes of formation and deformation—in short: in organizing.

## HUMAN PRODUCTION SYSTEMS

Production, as Cooper understands it, is not simply the making of useful and desired objects. It is also the structuring of a world so that it endures into the future as a knowable creation in space and time (Cooper, 2001a). If we were only to experience the unformed or abstract field, consciousness would not be possible. As Schelling (1980) argues, we need objects in order to be reflexive because a thought can only turn back to itself (which, for Cooper, is no longer itself *because* of this return) after it has hit an object. Humans, by giving meaning and purpose to their lives, constitute themselves as objects: 'The subject has to posit itself as an object in order to know [or form] itself' (Cooper, 1987: 413). The formation of matter into graspable and controllable forms is what Cooper also calls institutionalization. Institutionalization is not separate from human acts; we partly define ourselves by institutionalization, or by constituting ourselves as objects. Subjectivity is the product of institutionalization, not the origin.

To say that institutionalization is necessary for thinking is not the same as saying that institutionalization is something that stimulates thinking. Even though one needs to encounter objects in order to think, these very same objects make thinking difficult: 'The object is that which objects' (Cooper, 1987: 408). By definition, objects refuse thought since the thinking, of which objects are the result, has already been done. This is, as we have already seen, Cooper's problem with the idea of the organization as object: thinking in terms of organizations will refuse thinking of organization. Thus institutions

> make it difficult for us to think of the 'nowness' or sublimity of the event, since they are continually structuring our thoughts and thinking processes for us. Universities, schools, political programmes, religious credos, academic theories are all 'infected' with the 'practical-useful'.
> (Cooper, 1991a: 11)

The danger inherent to any form of institutionalization is that we stop to think and question. To be concerned with the 'practical-useful' means to be guided by what has already been actualized: one caters to problems, demands or goals that are already formed, instead of opening up for that what actuality represses in order to assume its current form. Through institutions we can undergo the structures of daily existence without acting upon these institutions. We affirm, hence regenerate, without thought. By affirming institutions the human becomes dominated by 'human production systems' (Cooper, 2001c)—a process that, according to Cooper, is characteristic for our age. Indeed, some 'systems have lives of their own which make them fundamentally independent of human control' (Cooper and Burrell, 1988: 94).

This development, says Cooper, has to a large extent to do with the nature of post-industrial systems of production. Not only do modern corporations incorporate bodies into their production, the products (or objects) that these processes produce enter these very same bodies:

> The institutional product is also a social product in that we eat it, we wear it, we speak it; it enters our minds and bodies in such a way as to constitute us as a corporate body.
>
> (Cooper, 2001c: 326)

Human beings, or the 'innocent' human body, sheer matter and potentiality, is thus inscribed by institutionalization, which resists 'human' intervention: 'Without our realising it, we are in danger of becoming technical products of the technology we have produced' (Cooper, 2001a: 334). We have withdrawn ourselves from where the action is.

## TO THINK OPENLY

How do we overcome the passivity that characterizes our (consumer) society? How do we re-engage in the human production systems that seek to reduce life to the interaction between discrete entities defined by functions and goals?

We have already seen versions of Cooper's answers: to think in terms of organization instead of organizations, to think with boundaries instead of within boundaries, to think the beyond (or the abstract field), to think openness itself. Cooper's 'objects' of thinking are not objects but that which goes beyond objects. It is not the objects that resist meaning (as we have seen they are full of meaning), but what goes beyond such objects. In order to see what lies beyond objects, however, one paradoxically needs objects: only through the divided the undivided can be felt. One might therefore ask if scholars of organization theory continue to think if they no longer accept 'real' organizations (i.e., identities, functions) as the objects of thinking. We are again reminded of Schelling's observation that without objects there is nothing to think, or better: our thoughts will never return to us, forever lost in the abstract field. Thus the further we reach into and become ungrounded mass, the less we experience, and the more consciousness disappears. As such, the resulting 'thoughts' would be unable to emancipate or re-enlighten the bodies that are captured by un-human human production systems.

Cooper is well aware of this limit. We can never become one with the abstract field—we can only temporally approach it. The life of the mind, as well as of the body, is a continuous process of learning and unlearning (Cooper, 2003). In order to make room for the new, one must first negate that which is taken as positive. In other words, one must find the partiality in anything that is taken as a bounded whole in order to inform. While we are generally good at learning, i.e., finding a simple location for 'real' things, what Cooper 'teaches' us is that renewal, and hence the possibility of ethics and politics, is grounded in unlearning. Unlearning, however, is not possible to zero degree. In approaching the abstract field one needs to be careful not to reach the point of no return.

So the question becomes: how do you escape from a life that is dictated by the finished or the practical-useful without losing your mind or your body in the abstract field? Building on Anton Ehrenzweig's *The Hidden Order of Art* (2000), Cooper has used the concepts of 'scattered attention' and 'undifferentiation' in attempts to suggest theoretical answers to these questions (Cooper, 1998b; 2001c; 2003). Methods, for Cooper, do not provide solutions that can be used to arrive at a desired end; they become part of the forms that we ourselves assume: *'we become the methods* that we use to understand what is "out there"' (Cooper, 1983: 218, emphasis in original). The real 'escape' must be understood as action itself, rather than in speculations about methods that allow one to enter an action mode. There is a long tradition in philosophy that separates thought from action (e.g., Arendt, 1958), but for Cooper thought and action are indivisible. Thought that is worthy of the name is not an abstraction from the world (of action), but rather an active approach to the concrete that opens things up. It is in this sense that thought is affiliated to politics, which is a link that Agamben also stresses: 'thought—that is, politics' (Agamben, 1995: 98).

One mode of action, for academics generally the most important mode, is writing. Writing can be a dislocation of seeing, testing the limit of what is possible, or seeking contact with the absent presence of potentialities. One can certainly find demonstrations of this power of writing in Cooper. As mentioned in the introduction, Cooper is a master in displacing words and concepts, at times starting from their etymological roots in Heideggerian fashion. In this manner you control words and concepts as much as they control you. As a result, boundaries, including the boundaries that define your own being, become fluid and open up to the beyond.

It is hard to think without objects or live without objectives. It is therefore unavoidable that, in acting, one *selects* objects for displacement. Cooper does not go into the question on what basis we make this selection. We have nevertheless identified one important ethical or political moment in Cooper's writings: the idea that human production systems in which humans do not actively take part need to be resisted. This is another way of saying that there is a necessity for action in post-industrial times. How, exactly? Cooper does not answer this question in terms of a programme or in terms of techniques, which would, in his view, close things down rather than open up. What he suggests instead is that there is a need to think as concretely as we possibly can: 'As soon as you get towards the concrete, you cannot exclude action' (Whitehead, cited in Cooper, 1976: 1006). We must approach writing and thinking as a mode of action. We have a tendency to try to 'understand' the finished rather than to engage with the partial. This is particularly true for organization theory, which, at least in some manifestations, seems to have *founded* itself on this tendency. In doing so, we lose sight of the potentialities through which we continually move and which continually move us. More importantly perhaps: we lose the potentiality to see new sights.

## A GREAT CONSISTENCY

Bergson once said that true philosophers have one original idea, which they express in many different ways (de la Durantaye, 2009). This strikes me as an accurate description of Cooper's work: I don't think it is an exaggeration to say that his work since 'The Open Field' is an endless re-working of one problem, which is addressed through many different concepts, many different authors and many different themes. There is a great consistency in Cooper's later work that never reaches closure.

Cooper's early papers on job motivation, task relevance and leadership in the 1960s and early 1970s lack the style and novelty that characterizes his later work. It seems to me that Cooper found his idea when he allowed his early interest in radical poetry and philosophy to inform his work on organizations. In the early 1970s references to Whitehead start to enter his work, even though it is still concerned with the 'theory of organizations' rather than 'organization theory' (Cooper and Law, 1995).

There is one particular quotation from Whitehead that is cited in three of Cooper's papers from the 1970s that offers a trace of this development in his thinking:

> A factory, with its machinery, its community of operatives, its social service to the general population, its dependence upon organizing and designing genius, its potentialities as a source of wealth to the holders of its stock is an organism exhibiting a variety of vivid values. What we want to train is the habit of apprehending such an organism in its completeness.
>
> (Whitehead, cited in Cooper, 1970: 290; Cooper and Foster, 1971: 467; Gadalla and Cooper, 1978: 360).

Cooper's initial reading of this quotation is typical of the open systems approach. In a direct comment on the cited passage, Cooper applauds the fact that social scientists have started to view organizations as 'dynamic complex structures in symbiotic relationship with their environment' (Cooper and Foster, 1971: 467), which is typical of sociotechnical systems thinking. In 'The Open Field', however, the emphasis is no longer on the idea of thinking organizations as organisms but on Whitehead's notion of completeness. Completeness for Whitehead means 'to include apprehension of what lies beyond oneself' (Whitehead, 1967: 200), which, translated into Cooper's terms, is an apprehension of the abstract field. Paradoxically, to understand something in its completeness means understanding how 'nothing is allowed to complete itself' (Cooper, 2006: 64). In the paper that

Cooper cites, Whitehead further warns against the specialization in the sciences and calls for the importance of 'immediate' or 'aesthetic' apprehension in scientific research (Whitehead, 1967: 199), similar to what Cooper later calls 'scattered attention' (Cooper, 2003).

Still in the same Whitehead paper, we come across a passage that, I have been told, was a favourite of Cooper: 'When you understand all about the sun and all about the atmosphere and all about the rotation of the earth, you may still miss the radiance of the sunset' (Whitehead, 1967: 199). It is easy to see why this appealed to Cooper: it calls for a move away from the 'noons of thought', that Whitehead saw as characteristic for Russell, and shows how thinking and writing is not to be located on the outside but in the midst of action.

I have never felt that humour played much of a role in Cooper's work. But the title of Cooper's final publication, 'Process and reality', after Whitehead's seminal work, is rather humorous. It reminds me of a philosophical joke by Foucault, who wrote an entry in a French encyclopaedia under the pseudonym of 'Maurice Florence'. Foucault (1994: 315) writes: 'if Foucault is indeed perfectly at home in the philosophical tradition, it is within the critical tradition of Kant'. With his final publication, written shortly before his death, it is as if Cooper is saying: 'If Cooper is indeed perfectly at home in organization theory, it is in the process tradition of Whitehead'. Both Foucault and Cooper clearly did not belong to a school in the sense of 'Whitehead studies' or 'Kant studies'. Cooper made connections to Whitehead and to many others, but as part of a method to step into the open or, better still, to step into the open as method.

## ACKNOWLEDGEMENT

Many thanks to Gibson Burrell, Nick Butler, Robert Cooper, Campbell Jones, Ruud Kaulingfreks, Martin Parker, Stefan Tramer and two anonymous reviewers for their helpful comments on earlier versions of this chapter.

## REFERENCES

Agamben, G. (1993) *The Coming Community*, tr. M. Sullivan and S. Whitsitt. Minneapolis, MN: University of Minnesota Press.
Agamben, G. (1995) *Idea of Prose*, tr. M. Hardt. Albany, NY: State University of New York.
Agamben, G. (1999) 'On potentiality' in *Potentialities: Collected Essays in Philosophy*, tr. D. Heller-Roazen. Stanford, CA: Stanford University Press, 177–184.
Arendt, H. (1958) *The Human Condition*. Chicago: University of Chicago Press.
Aristotle (1966) *Metaphysics*, tr. H. G. Apostle. Bloomington: Indiana University Press.
Böhm, S. and C. Jones (eds.) (2001) 'Responding: To Cooper' *ephemera*, 1(4): 314–320.

Braverman, H. (1974) *Labor and Monopoly Capital: The Degradation of Work in the Twentieth Century*. New York: Monthly Review.

Burrell, G. (1988) 'Modernism, postmodernism and organizational analysis 2: The contribution of Michel Foucault' *Organization Studies*, 9(2): 221–235.

Burrell, G. (1994) 'Modernism, postmodernism and organizational analysis 4: The contribution of Jürgen Habermas' *Organization Studies*, 15(1): 1–19.

Burrell, G. and G. Morgan (1979) *Sociological Paradigms and Organizational Analysis*. London: Heinemann.

Chia, R. (ed.) (1998a) *Organized Worlds: Explorations in Technology and Organization with Robert Cooper*. London: Routledge.

Chia, R. (ed.) (1998b) *In the Realm of Organization: Essays for Robert Cooper*. London: Routledge.

Chia, R. (1998c) 'From complexity science to complex thinking: Organization as simple location' *Organization*, 5(3): 341–369.

Cooper, R. (1966) 'Leader's task relevance and subordinate behaviour in industrial work groups' *Human Relations*, 19(1): 57–84.

Cooper, R. (1970) 'A summing up', in B. M. Bass, R. Cooper and J. A. Haas (eds.) *Managing for Accomplishment*. Lexington, MA: DC Heath and Co, 286–294.

Cooper, R. (1973) 'Task characteristics and intrinsic motivation' *Human Relations*, 26(3): 387–413.

Cooper, R. (1974) *Job Motivation and Job Design*. London: Institute of Personnel Management.

Cooper, R. (1976) 'The open field' *Human Relations*, 29(11): 999–1017.

Cooper, R. (1983) 'The other: A model of human structuring' in G. Morgan (ed.) *Beyond Method: Strategies for Social Research*. Newbury Park, CA: Sage, 208–218.

Cooper, R. (1986) 'Organization/disorganization' *Social Science Information*, 25(2): 299–335.

Cooper, R. (1987) 'Information, communication and organization: A post-structural revision' *The Journal of Mind and Behavior*, 8(3): 395–416.

Cooper, R. (1989a) 'The visibility of social systems' in M. C. Jackson, P. Keys and S. A. Cropper (eds.) *Operational Research and the Social Sciences*. New York: Plenum.

Cooper, R. (1989b) 'Modernism, postmodernism and organizational analysis 3: The contribution of Jacques Derrida' *Organization Studies*, 10(4): 479–502.

Cooper, R. (1991a) 'Institutional aesthetics: The case of "contestation"'. Paper presented at Utrecht University, The Netherlands, January.

Cooper, R. (1991b) 'Information theory and organizational analysis'. Paper presented to the Institute of Advanced Studies in Administration, Caracas, Venezuela, 12 March.

Cooper, R. (1992) 'Formal organization as representation: Remote control, displacement and abbreviation' in M. Reed and M. Hughes (eds.) *Rethinking Organization*. London: Sage, 254–272.

Cooper, R. (1993) 'Technologies of representation' in P. Ahonen (ed.) *Tracing the Semiotic Boundaries of Politics*. Berlin: Mouton de Gruyter, 279–312.

Cooper, R. (1997) 'Symmetry: Uncertainty as displacement'. Paper presented at Uncertainty, Knowledge and Skill conference, University of Limburg, Belgium, 6–9 November.

Cooper, R. (1998a) 'Assemblage notes' in R. C. H. Chia (ed.) *Organized Worlds: Explorations in Technology and Organization with Robert Cooper*. London: Routledge, 108–129.

Cooper, R. (1998b) 'Interview with Robert Cooper' in R. C. H. Chia (ed.) *Organized Worlds: Explorations in Technology and Organization with Robert Cooper*. London: Routledge, 121–165.

Cooper, R. (2001a) 'A Matter of Culture' *Cultural Values*, 5(2): 163–197.

Cooper, R. (2001b) 'Interpreting mass: Collection/dispersion' in N. Lee and R. Munro (eds.) *The Consumption of Mass*. Oxford: Blackwell, 16–43.

Cooper, R. (2001c) 'Un-timely mediations: Questing thought' *ephemera*, 1(4): 321–347.

Cooper, R. (2003) 'Primary and secondary thinking in social theory: The case of mass society' *Journal of Classical Sociology*, 3(2): 145–172.

Cooper, R. (2005) 'Relationality' *Organization Studies*, 26(11): 1689–1710.

Cooper, R. (2006) 'Making present: Autopoeisis as human production' *Organization*, 13(1): 59–81.

Cooper, R. (2007) 'Organs of process: Rethinking human organization' *Organization Studies*, 28(10): 1547–1573.

Cooper, R. (2009) 'The generalized social body: Distance and technology' *Organization*, 17(2): 242–256.

Cooper, R. (2010) 'Georg Simmel and the transmission of distance', *Journal of Classical Sociology*, 10(1): 69–86.

Cooper, R. (2014) 'Process and reality' in J. Helin, T. Hernes, D. Hjort and R. Holt (eds.) *The Oxford Handbook of Process Philosophy and Organization Studies*. Oxford: Oxford University Press, 585–604.

Cooper, R. and G. Burrell (1988) 'Modernism, postmodernism and organizational analysis 1: An introduction' *Organization Studies*, 10(4): 479–502.

Cooper, R. and M. Foster (1971) 'Sociotechnical systems' *American Psychologist*, 26(5): 467–474.

Cooper, R. and J. Law (1995) 'Organization: Distal and proximal views' in S. B. Bacharach, P. Gagliardi and B. Mundell (eds.) *Research in the Sociology of Organization*. Greenwich, CT: JAI Press, 275–301.

De la Durantaye, L. (2009) *Giorgio Agamben: A Critical Introduction*. Stanford, CA: Stanford University Press.

Deleuze, G. and F. Guattari (1994) *What Is Philosophy?*, tr. G. Burchell and H. Tomlinson. London: Verso.

Durkheim, E. (1984) *The Division of Labour in Society*, tr. W. D. Halls. New York: Free Press.

Ehrenzweig, A. (2000) *The Hidden Order of Art*. London: Phoenix.

Foucault, M. (1987) *Death and the Labyrinth: The World of Raymond Roussel*, tr. C. Ruas. London: Athlone.

Foucault, M. ["Maurice Florence"] (1994) 'Foucault, Michel, 1926–', in G. Gutting (ed.) *The Cambridge Companion to Foucault*. Cambridge: Cambridge University Press, 314–19.

Gadalla, I. and R. Cooper (1978) 'Towards an epistemology of management' *Social Science Information*, 17(3): 349–383.

Hamacher, W. (1999) *Premises: Essays on Philosophy and Literature from Kant to Celan*, tr. P. Fenves. Stanford, CA: Stanford University Press.

Hetherington, K. and R. Munro (eds.) (1997) *Ideas of Difference: Stability, Social Spaces and Labour of Division*. Oxford: Blackwell.

Kwasny, M. (ed.) (2004) *Toward the Open Field: Poets on the Art of Poetry 1800–1950*. Middletown, CT: Wesleyan University Press.

Marx, K. (1992) *Capital: A Critique of Political Economy Vol. 1*, tr. B. Fowkes. London: Penguin.

Olson, C. (1997) *Collected Prose*, ed. D. Allen and B. Friedlander. Berkeley: University of California Press.

Parker, M. and R. Cooper (1998) 'Cyborganization: Cinema as nervous system' in J. Hassard and R. Holliday (eds.) *Organization/Representation: Work and Organizations in Popular Culture*. London: Sage, 201–28.

Russell, B. (1956) 'Beliefs: Discarded and retained' in *Portraits from Memory and Other Essays*. London: Allen & Unwin.

Schelling, F. W. J. (1980) 'Philosophical letters on dogmatism and criticism' in *The Unconditional in Human Knowledge: Four Early Essays: 1794–1796*, tr. F. Marti. Lewisburg: Bucknell University Press, 156–218.

Simon, H. A. (1957) *Administrative Behavior: A Study of Decision-Making Processes in Administrative Organization* (second edition). New York: Macmillan.

Smith, A. (1979) *The Wealth of Nations: Books I-III*. Harmondsworth: Penguin.

Sørensen, B. (2004) *Making Events Work, or, How to Multiply Your Crisis*. Copenhagen: Samfundslitteratur.

Spinoza, B. (2002) *Complete Works*, tr. Samuel Shirley. Indianapolis: Hackett.

Whitehead, A. N. (1967) *Science and the Modern World*. New York: Free Press.

# 3 The Open Field

*Robert Cooper*

(*Human Relations*, 1976, 29(11):999–1017. Reproduced by permission of SAGE Publications Ltd., London, Los Angeles, New Delhi, Singapore and Washington DC, Copyright © SAGE publications.)

*The paper attempts to define an epistemology of process as a basis for the development of expressive and creative action. Five conditions of process are identified—unstructured action, projectability, the situation, the abstract field—and their behavioural implications are discussed. Finally, a methodology for the personal use of process is presented.*

As social scientists, we are probably less attentive than we should be to the wavering balance between structure and process in understanding human action. Structure is the invariant pattern of relationships among functional points in a system, while process is the continuous emergence of new elements from those already existing. Structure concerns itself with stability or quasi-stability; process, with change. Though seemingly in contrast, structure and process complement each other both as concepts and in the real world: to paraphrase Whitehead (1929) structure can be snatched only out of process; and the novelty that emerges from process can realize itself only by submitting to structure.

As men, we need to recognize the implications of the structure-process dichotomy for the ordering of our lives. There is a choice at both individual and societal levels in the forms that we and our environment can assume. Three basic forms can be identified:

1 *The Structural Form.* Its main features are preservation of itself at the expense of environment and subordination of its parts to the whole. Men's energies, therefore, are directed to the maintenance of the system more or less as it is, and also of themselves as they occupy the functional roles of the system. It is the world of Classical Rationalism.

2   *The Process Form.* Through flux and chance, events coincide to make novel forms. In the extreme, there is no guiding purpose; things merely happen. The precondition for process is the abnegation of control; men have to deny their existing structures in order to lay themselves open to the creative possibilities of chance. It is questionable whether men can assume the process form for long periods without dissipating themselves into chronic nonstructure, e.g., madness and chaos. The paradigm for process is Surrealism.

3   *The Structure-Process Balance.* Structure and process complement each other in a state of "regenerative equilibrium" (Koestler, 1964). The relationship is cyclic: the disintegration of structure → a temporary immersion in process → the attainment of a new, more creative structure. In this form, men continually have to disapprove the adequacy of their own structures without having detailed preconceptions of what should take their place. The relevant paradigm is Creative Evolution (Bergson, 1944).

The key to understanding the structure-process relationship in human systems lies in the concept of *purpose*. Purpose binds together and gives direction to the system; it preserves structure at the expense of process. Put more exactly, fixed, specific purposes make fixed, specific structures, and process therefore is inversely related to the degree of fixity and specificity of purpose. Given a fixed, specific purpose, everything adjusts itself to that purpose.

Classifying by purpose suggests two different types of system: (1) *instrumental*, and (2) *expressive*. It is in the nature of instrumental systems to use themselves as means for attaining goals external to themselves (e.g., production units). Their organizational form is one that stresses structure over process; their purposes are relatively specific. In contrast, expressive systems use environmental resources as means to cultivate their own varied possibilities (e.g., creative artists). Their organizational form is of "structure-process balance"; their purposes, diffuse,

The two types of system follow different principles of development: (1) *linear*, and (2) *contingent*. Linear development proceeds by preset purpose and structure *from the known to the known*; the system grows by imposing its own image on the environment. The characteristic strategy of linear development is *regulation*, i.e., the control of variance likely to hinder goal attainment. Instrumental systems develop linearly by sharpening their instrumentality and/or increasing their size. Contingent development explicitly rejects the restrictions of prior purpose and structure; every contingency is valued as a potential source of growth. The system is viewed as a mosaic of possibilities whose actualization depends upon chance factors; its growth is multiform, dependent on adventure and discovery. Development occurs through a strategy of *revelation* whereby the system, abandoning conscious purpose, experiences its environment as an ingression of unfolding forms.

The existential choice for man lies in understanding himself and his institutions in terms of instrumental/expressive systems and in deciding which of these should characterize his social forms.

Despite the increasing humanization of the social sciences, we are still short of concepts which would enable us to see experience in process terms. As a discipline, social science seems almost naturally disposed to expressing itself in structural terms, where structure becomes an end in itself and not a means. There is some promise of a fuller conceptualization of process in Systems Theory, especially in concepts such as "variety" and "morphogenesis" (Buckley, 1967), but these processes constructs are yoked to purposeful systems whose aims are to subjugate process to their own particular structural designs. Systems Theory, as presently conceived, has, therefore, an inbuilt structural bias.

We have to move out of social science proper in order to find a conceptualization appropriate to the process view of man. There are two requirements for such a view: (1) a Whiteheadian conception of man and environment as mutually immanent in a unitary field: "In an act of perception, the person involved is neither a merely passive reflector nor a dominating actor who imposes his preconceived scheme of things on to his surroundings, but is instead a knot or focus in a network of to-and-fro influences" (Waddington, 1969): (2) a definition of man as "ever open" and "unfinished" in the sense of Heidegger's *Dasein*. Man thus experiences himself and his world as an Open Field.

The Open Field defines the conditions necessary for process and the emergence of expressive systems. But definition itself is never enough; though its purpose is to put sense on experience, it unwittingly serves to arrest the course of process, to freeze it in a concept. The validity of the Open Field lies in its *enactment*. Yet we have come so far from the possibility of unselected experience that it now seems necessary to spell out exactly the conditions which will enable us to repossess it.

## THE PRIMACY OF "ACTION"

Theories of human action typically assume that the content of most action is determined by the images people have of their environments. Images precede actions and give them meaning. The image is an active organization of past experience through which history writes the future. As such, the image inhibits the possibility of creative transformation which may be required for personal renewal or to meet novel demands. In order to subvert the tyranny of the image, pure action, uncontaminated by a directing image, must be generated. The point of such "action" is to create a cognitive vacuum which man must fill—since he so abhors a void—with images that break new ground. Thus, action becomes the dynamo for change and the basis of growth. The man who enters the Open Field uses action as a means of revealing the latent in himself and his world; his action makes visible what is invisible. The habits of action are to be seen at their most lucid in the work of the "action painters" described by Rosenberg (1962):

> The painter no longer approached his easel with an image in his mind; he went up to it with material in his hand to do something to that other piece of material in front of him. The image would be the result of this encounter . . . in this mood there is no point to an act if you already know what it contains . . . what matters always is the revelation contained in the act . . . art as action rests on the enormous assumption that the artist accepts as real only that which he is in the process of creating . . . the artist works in a condition of open possibility, risking, to follow Kierkegaard, the anguish of the aesthetic, which accompanies possibility lacking in reality. To maintain the force to refrain from settling anything, he must exercise in himself a constant No.

Action penetrates the social world via three mechanisms of change: (1) the "open model" form of planned change, (2) crisis, and (3) rupture.

The open model form of planned change begins with a rudimentary program of desired change which avoids specifying a priori strategies and solutions, thus permitting the program to unfold and define itself over time. In such circumstances, the change agent is immediately involved in the change process and so helps to shape action and in turn is shaped by it. The situation transforms the program as much as the program transforms the situation. Specific examples of open model approaches to change are "broad-aim" programs in community development (Weiss & Rein, 1970) and action research (Chein, Cook & Harding, 1948).

Crisis is an experience, externally generated, which destroys or radically questions one or more of man's central values and which he has no ready means of coping with. Learned behaviour breaks down because (1) the agent is "robbed of essential purpose, as in severe personal bereavement," (2) events cannot be understood in terms of existing categories, and/or (3) the "same event falls into more than one category" so that "there may then no longer be one best action but two or more which mutually exclude each other . . ." (Marris, 1974). The essential feature of crisis is loss of control by the agent: action (at least initially) occurs in a meaning vacuum, having become detached from clear purpose and outcome. The course of action must follow its uncertain context, like the behaviour of the mariner in Poe's story *A Descent into the Maelstrom*, who learned that the only way to survive the vortex was to be incorporated into the form of the vortex itself.

The role of action in crisis is vividly seen in the early stages of the T Group. Group members are thrust without warning into a social void created by the absence of collective expectations and purpose. "If there are no meanings, no values, no source of sustenance or help, then man, as creator, must invent, conjure up meanings and values, sustenance and succour out of nothing" (Laing, 1967). In the group, every action is a gesture which seeks to define the conditions of meaningful community but, paradoxically, that community can only be achieved through the members' active participation in the chaos—chaos, being the source of infinite possibilities, is the royal road to creation—conceived by their diverse unstructured actions.

Rupture is a self-generated break with established structures; it seeks to free the agent from the thrall of the inhabited context and to create the conditions necessary for imageless action and the emergence of new forms and meanings. Rupture was the basic working method of Surrealism which was specifically intended to realize "that unlimited capacity for rejection that is the whole secret of human advance . . ." (Breton, 1935). In the French revolution of 1968, rupture as the operational means of bringing about the "shock of freedom" required for the development of personal and social creative change. "The transition from . . . the liberating shock (induced by rupture) . . . to the self-management of life and work . . . takes place so quickly that during such a period of improvisation repressed desires rise to the surface and produce, as it were automatically, by simultaneous emergence, a natural reinvention—or rather, the *discovery* of what was only latent—of schemes of community life, such as self-management" (Willener, 1970).

## CHANCE

Chance is when the unexpected coincide. Through chance, man communes with possibilities. Chance, therefore, becomes the device by which man amplifies his capacity for spontaneous growth.

There is a preparatory problem in that the mind has to assume a form that will enable it to experience chance. It is Suzuki's (1974) problem of how to relate man to nature ". . . unknown and mind must be somehow of the same nature and cherish a mutual communication." This connection can be realized through the strategies of (1) suspended purpose, and (2) induced disorder.

The strategy of suspended purpose expresses Cage's (1968) instruction that the mind must surrender its right to control in order to enhance its awareness of the world: "The highest purpose is to have no purpose at all. This puts one in accord with nature in her manner of operation." The world of meaning expands so that (to quote the painter Arp) a broken twig becomes equal to the stars. The experience of this "objective chance" is described by Breton (1960) in his imaginative *Nadja*:

> I am concerned . . . with facts which may belong to the order of pure observation, but which can on each occasion present all the appearance of a signal, without our being able to say precisely which signal, and of what; facts which when I am alone permit me to enjoy unlikely complicities, which convince me of my error in occasionally presuming I stand

at the helm alone. Such facts, from the simplest to the most complex, should be assigned a hierarchy, from the special, indefinable reaction at the sight of extremely rare objects or upon our arrival in a strange place (both accompanied by the distinct sensation that something momentous, something essential depends upon them), to the complete lack of peace with ourselves provoked by certain juxtapositions, certain combinations of circumstances which greatly surpass our understanding and permit us to resume rational activity only if, in most cases, we call upon our very instinct of self-preservation to enable us to do so.[1]

The facts of "objective chance" reveal a contingent rather than an instrumental truth or a truth which you see *laterally*, out of the corner of your eye: lateral truth is a

> Knowledge that doesn't move forward like an arrow in flight, but expands sideways, like an arrow enlarging in flight, or like the archer, discovering that although he has hit the bull's-eye and won the prize, his head is on a pillow and the sun is coming through the window. Lateral knowledge is knowledge that's from a wholly unexpected direction, from a direction that's not even understood as a direction until the knowledge forces itself upon one. (Pirsig, 1974).

This is also the metaphor of the "kaleidoscope equipped with consciousness" which Baudelaire used to describe the *flâneur* who drifted through the Paris crowds sensitive only to the creative flow of chance and which, a century later, was incorporated into the theory of urban design known as "psychogeography"(Ivain, 1974).

Through induced disorder, man challenges himself with the exigencies of self-imposed chaos whose possibilities he permutes into another beginning. The recognition that creative renewal depends upon disorder is as old as civilized life (Wind, 1969) but it has been left to our own time to apotheosize the relationship into a genera cultural—political praxis (Marcuse, 1969). The direction of induced disorder may be inward on the self or outward on the world. Rimbaud disordered himself in order to create the ultimate magic world ("Le poéte se fait *voyant* par un long, immense et raisonné dérèglement de tous les sens") while the painter Pollock disordered the world in order to discover himself (". . . it was as if he crashed an immensely heavy object on to a table and sent flying in all directions some sticks that had been lying in carefully arranged groups. This was his attempt to disrupt the time flux and to invoke a new contingency. To throw his own presence into the smoothly modulated pattern of existence. Or violently shake an all too predictable kaleidoscope") (Robinson, 1960). In these private acts, men can remake themselves but not their fellow men. For men to remake each other requires the translation of the strategy of induced disorder into a principle of social design such as we see in Sennett's (1971) vision of urban life where the "brute chance" of spontaneous social instructions becomes a major means of personal and interpersonal growth.

## PROJECTABILITY

The essence of projectability lies in (1) the power of men to project their unconscious forces into the external world, and (2) the power of external forms to draw out and give substance to the unconscious content. Projectability is, therefore, a quality which pervades the total field.

How men project their unconscious forces depends on their ability to manage them. If the appropriate skills are there, projection is expressed in the form of a creative art which enriches the projector and his world.

> The forces of the imagination, from which (the artist) draws his strength, have a disruptive and capricious power which he must manage with economy. If he indulges his imagination too freely, it may run wild and destroy him and his work by excess . . . yet if he plagues his genius with the wrong kind of drill, and uses too many contrivances and refinements, the imagination may shrivel; it can atrophy. (Wind, 1969).

If the skills are absent, the unconscious forces insinuate themselves into the fabric of the world and work for its dissolution or else explode in a rush of contemptuous violence that seeks to destroy everything in its path. In such ways, the unconscious forces contribute to the psychopathology of groups (Bion, 1961) and help explain the latent brittleness of human organization.

The forms of the world are ambiguous (though we may fight to deny this fact) and so demand our participation: "it is the way of the earth to make no display of completed work but rather to bring everything to completion vicariously" (the *I Ching*). We are led to fill in the gaps, find the keys to the cryptic, elaborate the allusory, create out of chaos—whether it be as the mimesis which fills out the latency of an institutional role or as that more elemental process described by Gaston Bachelard (e.g., 1969) in his psychoanalyses of the material world.

The *project* is the vehicle for projectability. The project is that which is "thrown forward" to modify the future. The project is a process which moves between *projection* and *construction*. The projection is a *coming into being* of the inner content; the construction is the *form* taken by the projection in the external world. In one usage, the project moves naturally *from* projection *to* construction, in which the inner forces direct the development of the construction according to a principle of "organic incrementalism." Pollock's paintings are projects of this kind. Here, the problem is of managing the individual products that break into light in the course of projection *as a field*—that is, the products in their relations with each other—which gets continually redefined as new products emerge. The construction, therefore, is a moving field which exists not for itself but to give form to an interior content. In a different usage, the project—perhaps impatient to be realized—seeks first a form in the external world as its construction. (Consider Lukács' description of form as "the shortest way to the top") (Goldmann, 1969). In this case, the borrowed construction directs the projection in proportion to the specificity of its own structure. The project develops "epigenetically," that is, by elaborating and expanding on the "program"of structures contained in its construction. The paradigms portrayed by Kuhn (1962) as shaping the form and content of scientific knowledge are such epigenetic constructions—"paradigms provide scientists not only with a map but also with some of the directions for map-making."

Finally, there are constructions which, by communal consent, we deny projectability to. These I call "self-defining reifications." The positivist's world is made up of constructions of this kind—pure facts, autonomous, inviolable. They have their own meanings, their own definitional limbo, as things "out there," separated from their spectators in the human world. It is a world "experienced by man as a strange facticity, an *opus alienum* over which he has no control rather than as the *opus proprium* of his own productive activity" (Berger and Luckmann, 1967).


## THE SITUATION

The situation is the immediately perceived field of actualities (objects, events) the concrete context in which we carry on our lives. It is the pith of existential meaning, where the perceptions do their work and find a unity. The situation is the rudimentary morphology of everyday experience—discrete, vivid, multiple. Man-in-the-world is an endless, all-over apposition of man-in-situations.

The first thing about the situation is its concreteness. It is full of definite objects and events which strike the senses and shape their perceptions in definite ways; the situation embodies "that *definiteness* to which our experience has to conform" (Whitehead, 1929). The interacting actualities that make up the situation are both source of and target for a man's attentions, those disciplined perceptions which must go and before all our acts of personal and social growth. We live among and through *things*, from them we get our natural power, our impetus to act and create beyond ourselves. "As soon as you get towards the concrete, you cannot exclude action" (Whitehead, 1925). The other extreme is the way of the "abstract" generalization whose appeal is to the intellect only and not to the vivacity of the senses themselves, and which, lacking the focus of the object or thing, forces man, if he is not careful, into a state of clouded subjectivity in which he has, unnaturally, to propel himself. Any excessive subjectivity or concern for self precludes him from participating fully in the situation.

The philosophy of the situation demands a theory of discontinuous and heterogeneous experience whose parts are multiple and individually active.

Only in conditions of difference and autonomy can man find his own internal power, be his own measure. Otherwise, inertia reigns. The logic is given by Reimann's principle that "the inertia and the metrical structures of the world are so intimately connected . . . and the metrical field will of necessity become flexible as soon as the inertial field is deprived of its geometric rigidity" (Weyl, 1949). The metric is the key to the inertia problem. When the metric is based on static, homogeneous forms, as in Euclidean space, the inertial field is absolute and immutable. For evidence, see Whorf's (1956a) treatment of our time metric and how it adduces our thoughts and energies. The power of the inertial field is cut down to the extent that the metric rests upon the concepts of the *local* and the *variable* which together characterize the uniqueness of the situation. Such situational metrics are found in post-Newtonian physics and information theory. When the metric becomes situational it becomes flexible and this more amenable to the intimate requirements of the human grain. A corollary is this: that the management of self must always begin with a situational metric; otherwise control must, by definition, reside somewhere else.

Psychological definitions of the person overwork the past and the power of habit. In psychoanalysis, he is fixated in early childhood. In behaviourism, he is shaped through the tedious accretion of habits. For situationism, the here-and-now and the response to it is what matters. It is the old truism that men become what they experience, but this time in different guise, that of the unique present. If the potentialities of men are manifold, they are so only as they materialize in a manifold of situations. There lies the situational thrust to man's use and growth: he makes himself to the degree he makes use of the situation.

The converse is "spectatorism" or the blandishment, by others, of spectacle in which one as no true part. Is the experience of the image of the thing rather than the thing itself. And when images are set up, men are put down, dispersed from the very events which alone can give them back their desired sharpness.

The opening of the field must go by way of the situation, of the things themselves in their interactions. For this is the situational key to process: that is viewed as a nexus of things and happenings between them. (We destroy the living root of the situation when we do, as we often do, that most pernicious form of abstraction which is to take thing and activity and treat them separately). Two appreciations follow from this view. One is, the form of the situation follows the logic of discursive action and not the logic of linear structure, for things can and do happen according to their own impulse and direction. The happenings are their own ends, not a progress to some other state. ("We torture ourselves getting somewhere, and when we get there it is nowhere, for there is nowhere to get to" [Lawrence, 1974]). The second is, things act *and* are acted on, that is, they are both cause *and* effect of their happenings as the other objects about him, and what he creates turns back and creates him.

## THE ABSTRACT FIELD

But the field goes beyond the situation to find its larger meaning. For what is discrete and singular is, by that very token, alone. The field of larger meaning resides in a concept of the world as a penetralium of relationships in which the many become one. Spelled out, it is three things:

1 The basis of meaning is *relationship*, which gives the principle: *only connect.*
2 Relationship is the stem of unity and through it the many become one.
3 The combinatorics of relationship make possible the evaluation of the field above the literal and obvious. The many can combine variously ad infinitum to give a field of endless depth and extent, a unity of difference.

The Abstract Field is what Whitehead (1929) would call an "extensive continuum," whose immanent structure is the very axis of process:

> This extensive continuum is one relational complex in which all potential objectifications find their niche. It underlies the whole world, past, present, and future . . . An extensive continuum is a complex of entities united by the various allied relationships of whole to part, and of overlapping so as to possess common parts, and of contact, and of other relationships derived from these primary relationships. The notion of a "continuum" involves both the property of indefinite divisibility and the property of unbounded extension. There are always entities beyond entities, because nonentity is no boundary. This extensive continuum expresses the solidarity of all possible standpoints throughout the whole process of the world. It is not a fact prior to the world: it is the first determination of order—that is, of real potentiality—arising out of the general character of the world.[2]

The use of the Abstract Field is as a cosmology which joins the order of unity with the unction of transcendent creation. This is the cosmology of process through which my personal causality connects with the world's ontogeny.

Equal to the Abstract Field is the tendency of man's thought to reach for a noumenal world of pure pattern beyond his own physicality. As the Abstract Field is the pristine continuity of form-not-yet-realized, so in the realm of the human mind is the unconscious through which the Abstract Field comes to form, naturally, as an act of nature, without strain. But man lives within two field, the Abstract and the Literal, and may find the noumenal properties of the first only through the firm ground of the second. The Literal Field is the discrete, denotable world in space and time, around which we weave and hang our lights. Whorf (1956b) brings out the specific workings of distinction in his discussion of language and *Manas*:

> It is said that in the plane of *Manas* there are two great levels, called *Rupa* and *Arupa* levels. The lower is the realm of "name and form", *Nana* and *Rupa*. Here "form" means organisation in space ("our" three-dimensional space). This is far from being coextensive with pattern in a universal sense. And *Nana*, "name," is not language or the linguistic order, but only one level in it, the level of the process of "lexation" or of giving words (names) to parts of the whole manifold of experience, parts which are thereby made to stand out in a semi-fictitious isolation. Thus a word like "sky" which in English can be treated like "board" (the sky, a sky, skies, some skies, piece of sky, etc.) leads us to think of a mere optical apparition in some ways appropriate only to relatively isolated solid bodies. "Hill" and "swamp" persuade us to regard local variations in altitude or soil composition of the ground as distinct THINGS like tables and chairs. Each language performs this artificial chopping up of the continuous spread and flow of existence in a different way. Word and speech are not the same thing . . . Thus the level of *Rupa* and *Nama*—shape-segmentation and vocabulary—is part of the linguistic order, but a somewhat rudimentary and not self-sufficient part. It depends upon a higher level of organisation, the level at which its COMBINATORY SCHEME appears. This is the *Arupa* level—the pattern world par excellence. *Arupa*, "formless," does not mean without linguistic form or organisation, but without reference to spatial, visual shape, marking out in space, which as we saw with "hill" and "swamp" is an important feature of reference on the lexical level. *Arupa* is a realm of patterns that can be "actualized" in space and time in the materials of lower planes, but are themselves indifferent to space and time. Such patterns are not like the meanings of words, but they are somewhat like the way meaning appears in sentences. They are not like individual sentences but like SCHEMES of sentences and designs of sentence structure. Our personal conscious "minds" can understand such patterns in a limited way by using mathematical or grammatical FORMULAS into which words, values, quantities, etc., can be substituted.[3]

In other words, the *materials* of expression are in the Literal Field but the *method* of expression is elsewhere. The method is tied to the autonomous processes of decision and creation within the unconscious which serve the latter's special will to reveal the larger mystery of the "primitive abstract"—". . . the riddle is that the true self is not the asserting function but an obeying one, that the actionable is *larger* than the individual and can be obeyed to" (Olson, 1970). The method is the putting of oneself among uncertainties and staying there, or what Keats called "Negative

Capability"—the capability "of being in uncertainties, mysteries, doubts, without any irritable reaching after fact and reason." Out of this swirl of indeterminacy, a creation delivers itself in its own wisdom and needs no pulling. It is the work of the Intelligence that *breathes*. The opposite is the "irritable reaching after fact and reason," preoccupation with Literal Field.

Our curse is that we are slaves to an epistemology that separates the knower from the known, the knavish subject-object split systematized and promulgated by Plato in his flawed program to make man "autonomous." Its ostensive purpose was to give man *control* over nature (including himself) by developing the twin functions of intellection and reflection so that he could stand apart (a "thinking reed") from the vivid flow of experience, distance being a necessary condition of mastery (Havelock, 1964). Its covert effects were *reductive* because its method was based on "the absolute necessity of the isolation of the per se" through the permanence of timeless categories.

> Their syntax excludes tenses of the verb *to be*. Principles and properties and topics just *are*. When placed in relationship with each other they provide the terms of analytical statements or of equations, which cannot share in the syntax of process and time, for they are not statements of specific situations and instances, not statements of action.
>
> (Havelock, 1964)

Thus ripped out of a context and set in the aspic of man's controlling subjectivity, they can never go beyond themselves into that variable, wider world of the Abstract Field. Two delusions mark this epistemology: one, that through it man became autonomous; two, that it gave a unitary framework to diverse experience. The first requires the insight that man gets autonomy when he *uses tools*, not when he is *wedded to ends*, and the force of the Platonic system was that it was a specific end just as much as it was a specific tool. That end was the *law* or *principle*, the essence beyond change. Therein lay the power, not in man who was mere messenger. The second is that the unity of the system is built on division, for the whole is an integration of individual categories that theoretically exhaust the knowledge of the world. The root and norm is "divide and rule" to produce a hierarchy of categories, but this logic cannot deal with unity based on interaction of multiplicity of function. Its unity is essentially reductive:

> "To *reduce*" means not only to simplify, schematize, dogmatize, and classify. It means also to arrest and to fix, to change the total into the partial while yet laying claim to totality through extrapolation; it means to transform totality into a closed circle.
>
> (Lefebvre, 1969)

The motive of Platonic systems and their life is for order as priority and their consequent strategy is regulative. Or put this another way: to regulate, as a priority of life, is to forbid or dampen down difference so that regulative systems can know nothing other than themselves, they cannot enter the larger area of the actionable which is the Abstract Field. The true, and only, way in the latter's possibilities is the three-fold cycle: (1) suspension of conscious, specific purpose, (2) embracing of, and staying among, uncertainties, (3) creation through the passive voice, i.e., the Casual Unconscious. The heart has its epistemology . . .

## ENVOI: THE USES OF THE FIELD[4]

The Open Field is the condition of process. Process is the creative advance of events, according to a law of parsimonious action, in a field of intensive relationships, whose main terms, exposited, are:

> *Creative advance*: process of becoming, the action between beginning and end; in human affairs, realized through unstructured action, chance connections, projection.

> *Parsimonious action*: that which goes by the straightest possible path, without fault, effort or encumbrance; "like snow that falls from a bamboo leaf." Via the mastery of parsimonious action, man is enabled to pass through the literal to the abstract, to go behind appearance.

> *Intensive relationships*: literally, relationships in tension, for Whitehead a defining characteristic of "life." Intensity is got by realizing and maintaining (i.e., not resolving) a variety of contraries while eliminating incompatibilities or those opposites that would cancel each other.

The whole is a field of process in tensive order, not just change or novelty, rather the *dance* of things.

The point of the Field is its use, not analysis. Use is what makes ideas move. There is a mode of use that short-circuits the human core by directing man's values to ends outside himself as in the diagnosis that in getting and spending we lay waste our powers. Instead, a contrasting use is now needed to show the Field as a means of illuminating man as the source of his own life-nourishing process. The use is *homotopic*. The homotopic processes are: *to find out* and *to make*. Through these, the individual dimensions of the Field are convened and gain direction: The Field becomes homotopic, open to man's proper use. To "find out" is to explore and discover the possibilities of a situation through un- (or semi-) structured action, chance connections, projection, etc., while to "make" is to construct a form which will show these discoveries as happenings in a field of process. To find out is to get knowledge of process as is, rough and not through the neat telling of another's logic or self-interest. There are just two ways of finding out: to place oneself directly in the experience of process and/or, though with care, use the evidence of men who have recorded the essential forms of process via the right methodologies. What you find out (and this is the key) is *information*. Information is two things: it is *difference* (in the cybernetic sense) and it is *what goes into form*, i.e., in-forms. Ergo: difference is the key to form. So to find out is to be in form i.e., literally inside it, be part of. To be open to process is to be open to a field of dynamic difference (a bit is static difference, not true process) which means to be engaged with the Field at all possible points and not lose any of its active content through laziness or an act of prior selection. It is to know oneself more fully "in the world," not as separate from it.

To "make" is to present what is found out in a form that will validly express the variety in process. The problem is to contain ("hold together") diversity "like it is." Only right form makes man content. To make it is to put the content of process into right form. What you make has both *express* and *impress*. Express is the style in which you manage the bringing of content into form; the express of process in right form is "grace." Impress is the moral effect of what you make either upon the world of nature of the community of men; grace and right form make good impress. To find out and to make are correlative: the more you find out, the more you can make.

If such are the uses of the Field, what are the mechanics of those uses, how does a man come to a methodology of its practice? It is a question, finally and when all the theory is done, of how we manage ourselves in our daily reality. A needed recognition is that we are systemic, that we are not simply parts of our ecology but flow with it: ". . . the mental characteristics of the system are immanent, not in some part, but in the system as a whole" (Bateson, 1972). The mind is the flow of information in balance throughout the man-field system. To derive a practice from this is another and more difficult matter but it requires that man learn to become a less wilful creature than he is abjuring his cataleptic dependence for the management of his affairs on the inflated faculty of "conscious purpose" and permit himself to be guided more by the systemic wisdom of his unconscious processes. The specifics of such a substitute system, must lie in the functions of (1) perception, and (2) "parcratic" wholeness. Perception is primary to an engagement with process not just because here is the locus of man's meeting with the world but because of perception's ability to register the small grain of process through the diverse sensations at nerve ending and in complex feeling system and orchestrate them in a synergic analogue of multiphasic experience. We miss this vital thing if we think "behaviour" is what life is all about. The system must recognize its wholeness through the character of its individual parts—hence "paracratic," the power of the whole residing in the parts. The whole must be ever present in the parts. Not one dominates, for then the whole loses its systemic wisdom. The intellect is there of course, one among equals, not suborned to control in the interests of "conscious purpose." Expressed like this, the two functions lead us to the principle that process can only be got through *particulars*, not through systems per se. It is in the particular of ourselves and what is about us that true process moves. Particulars are primary, systems secondary. If we reverse this, we cut ourselves off from the use of reality as process. This must be a discoverable condition, else we are lost. I am not sure, but I want to suggest that a methodology to do this would revolve around the issues of:

Force        Medium        Form        Meaning

I submit these are the launching points for a practice of process.

*Force.* All process is in essence transference of force from agent to object. The process is the force; agent and object, the reference points. But force is something more: it is the energy of process, of the action between terms. And there is a choice in how we may use this force. We can reduce its immediacy for us by translating the reference points into limiting terms as we do in the structure of logical thought when subject and object are the framework for a complete thought and the action, the doing, is just something that joins the two terms together. Or we can imitate nature is its continuity of action and not seek the terminal satisfaction of completeness. This is to go straight for the tensions operating as indeterminate relationships between objects—which we do when we "find out" and "make"—and by doing so become engrossed in the uncertainties for their own sake and not for their resolution. The last point is crucial. It is to treat uncertainty instrumentally as a temporary source of interest with a soluble state at the end, which is one of man's ways of backing off from reality. But to complete is a step back from process and lose force. The practice is to get in there and stay there. Is this learnable? Not as dialectic, or even a trialectic, but as a *field* of such tension. As truth is natural force between things, to take up force is to participate in truth, as in the "purposeless tension" of Zen.

*Medium.* Man, more exactly his psychophysiology, is his own medium for process. His work is done literally through the senses and neutral pathways and it is precisely these informational sinews of the body that have to be cultivated—not the imperious egohood of the self—in order for man to take up the process, the life, within himself and the Field. We have the choice of perceiving through the senses or through the ego. Though we do not see it, they are incompatible opposites. The ego structures experience to complement itself. Its habit is to do this at the expense of the external world, maximizing its own ease and welfare in technicity. There is no way it can meet reality as a humble process. That what lies in the meticulous use of the senses among the particulars of situations so that perception becomes both a seeing and a feeling through the organs, enabling perception and action to run together in the "flash of lightning" that needs no reflecting intelligence. The synchrony moves at 100mph. In other words, perception, control and action are always one, though the words alone give no idea of the enormous discipline needed for such skilful use. It is the skill of containing, without

conscious thought, a complex perceptual process which develops only gradually, as the power of holding together the parts develops, from the simple
registration of raw sensation to the complex appreciation of systemic relationships, *in order to free* the "workings of the heart"—the skill which uses
the concrete to reveal the abstract. This is an accomplishment which goes
beyond the simple punctuation of experience into instrumental contexts (in
which the "total context is made to fit the expected punctuation") to a facil-
ity to stay among and weave together the dissimilar and conflicting contexts
of wider field. The attentions must be poised at all times and all angles
to take in the world of particulars to make this possible. Life begins with
alertness to difference and falls away when the attentions sag. Such practice
must be sustained by reverence and care, for only through the cathection of
his affections on the objects and events of his immediate attention can man
bind himself authentically to the wider world. How can one love a system
per se? We must always be in the grain of it. The lesson, at least as old as
Pythagoras is: right management of our world begins with right management of ourselves. Is this learnable?

*Form.* The problem of form is the containment of difference. Good form
is the unity of difference. There are two basic and opposed methods for
containing difference. One is to categorize differences into similarities on
the basis of shared criteria—this is formation through classification. It has
order but no real unity since the whole is a sum of homogenized separates
and difference of particulars is lost, pre-empted by difference at the level
of gross categories. It reduces the world to a convenience. The other is to
capture the field as an imbrication of differences, in which events move out
in all directions, penetrating and being penetrating by each other and so
revealing their uniqueness through contrast with all other events in the field.
What matters is that the individual parts gain from the wider field, and not
the field per se. This is good form or form that respects its content. There
is a model for this: form emerges from events through context, the steps
being: event ↔ context of event ↔ context of context of event ↔ and so on.
This form is always leading on beyond itself, hinting—through contrasts,
ambiguities, resistances—at contexts yet to come. It is form as unfinished
business. Form operates from within towards the outside world, Kandinsky
said. In other words, content in, form out. The rule is always to focus on
the field of content—objects and events—for the form will, by a process of
unconscious syncretism, always look after itself. Beware the seduction by
form per se; there lies our ruin.

*Meaning.* The ontological meaning of process resides in the principle of
*individuated wholeness*, which is the process of the psyche towards self-real-
ization. The origin is Jung's (1953) picture of the self as *center and circumference*, unconscious to conscious. The center is (1) a gravity point for creation:
". . . the center—itself virtually unknowable—acts like a magnet on the
disparate materials and processes of the unconscious and gradually captures
them as in a crystal lattice," and (2) a force that moves out to express itself

through an ever-widening integration of events in the conscious world, the circumference representing this movement out. Center is at once continuous, whole yet undifferentiated in nature, and its task is to express itself as a unity while at the same time differentiating itself as a unique process; hence the circumference seeks a form of individuated wholeness. But there is a paradox in that individuation means separation while wholeness means integration. Individuation rests on the creation of identifiable boundaries which separate the system from its setting. Methodology, space and time are the bases of all system boundaries. Wholeness depends upon coincidence among these three root parameters of life. Meaning resides in events as individuated wholes. The center is motive for metaphor, from the small tropes we trip over daily to the cosmos that contains it all—"through metaphor to reconcile the people and the stones" (William Carlos Williams). Here is the rhythm, the natural flow, of center and circumference in its course of growth. He who has wholeness has rhythm and he who has rhythm has the universe. Meaning is also rhythm.

So these are the issues we have to take up, I believe, in order to get to a practice of the Open Field. It comes down in the end to how we use ourselves. If there is nothing "in here," there is nothing (of ours) "out there." Process begins with oneself and moves out from here. One is ever open. The alternative is the rule of structure outside you—in fact, that which measures you—and to which, having no meaning to call your own, you refer everything. You are thus always closed, you do not own the key.

We have not yet properly understood the human cost tolled by the systems we have built to assuage our fears of uncertainty and the void. Nor the thick grip they have on us in consequence. Somewhere McLuhan says the old world was a world of roles and the modern world is a world of jobs. It is so because our systems demand our efforts and our beliefs for their continued maintenance and growth. We are conduits for them. Yet, as Blake divined at the birth pangs of the organizational society (it is only 200 years ago now?), we endure a profound psychic hurt in serving systems and not being allowed to find our own deep centers. The result is an inner rage which often disrupts. There is no parting from your own shadow, Whitehead said. Here is the real why of the Open Field. Can anything, then, be more imperative than to find the lost land of the soul and make it pragmatic? At bottom, it is a question of locating that point of balance which enables the satisfaction of outside *and* the expression of inside and thereafter managing the weights to keep it right. There is evidence we had it once and after that some few have it still (Bateson, 1972; Lévi-Strauss, 1966). Our task, though an archaeology of man, is to get back and redeem that past wisdom for present use. For the repossession of ourselves inside (as primary process or primitive abstract) is the repossession of process outside, and vice versa.

Meanwhile, we are overfaced with what Lefebvre (1971) would call the systems of compulsion. How can we do the two necessary things: (1) make them equal to us, and (2) scramble them into a workable process? For myself, the means exist and are there, in social science, to be picked up for this use. The one is self-management generalized to all our activities—working, learning, etc.—not just as a way of socializing a la Marx the institutions through which society keeps moving, but as a way of making space for the definition of our real selves. The challenge is to manage ourselves all ways, in and out and right across, not be steered, however benignly, by that which is external and above. Democracy is not enough. The second is to make process out of institutional stasis by working on the syntax of life precisely where the rules of stasis are felt, the threshing floor—what Lefebvre (1971) calls the recreation of everyday life—literally the only place where we can recognize the system as ourselves. The one rule for the inversion of stasis to process if, hew close to the experience that quickens. Despite entropy, to be fought for in every act.

## NOTES

1 Quoted by permission of John Calder.
2 Quoted by permission of The Macmillan Company.
3 Quoted by permission of The Massachusetts Institute of Technology Press.
4 Throughout this section I have freely borrowed and adapted idea from Bateson (1972), Olson, (1970), and Whitehead (1929).

## REFERENCES

Bachelard, G. (1969) *The Poetics of Space*. Boston: Beacon Press.
Bateson, G. (1972). *Steps to an Ecology of Mind*. London: Intertext.
Berger, P. L. and Luckmann, T. (1967) *The Social Construction of Reality*. London: Allen Lane.
Bergson, H. (1944) *Creative Evolution*. New York: Modern Library.
Bion, R. (1961) *Experiences in Groups*. London: Tavistock Publications.
Breton, A. (1935) *Position Politique du Surréalisme*. Paris: Editions du Sagittaire.
Breton, A. (1960) *Nadja*. New York: Grove Press.
Buckley, W. (1967) *Sociology and Modern Systems Theory*. Englewood Cliffs, New Jersey: Prentice-Hall.
Cage, J. (1968) *Silence*. London: Calder and Boyars.
Chein, I., Cook, S., and Harding, J. (1948) 'The Field of Action Research', *American Psychologist* 3: 43–50.
Goldman, L. (1969) *The Human Sciences and Philosophy*. London: Jonathan Cape.
Havelock, E. (1964) *Preface to Plato*. Oxford: Blackwell.
Ivain, G. (1974) 'Formula for a New City' in C. Gray (ed.) *Leaving the 20th Century*. London: Free Fall Publications.
Jung, C. G. (1953) *Psychology and Alchemy*. London: Routledge and Kegan Paul.
Koestler, A. (1964) *The Act of Creation*. London: Hutchinson.
Kuhn, T. S. (1962) *The Structure of Scientific Revolutions*. Chicago: University of Chicago Press.
Laing, R. D. (1967) *The Politics of Experience and the Bird of Paradise*. Harmondsworth: Penguin Books.
Lawrence, D. H. (1974) *Apocalypse*. Harmondsworth: Penguin Books.
Lefebvre, H. (1969) *The Explosion: Marxism and the French Upheaval*. London: Monthly Review.

Lefebvre, H. (1971) *Everyday Life in the Modern World*. London: Allen Lane.
Lévi-Strauss, C. (1966) *The Savage Mind*. London: Weidenfeld and Nicholson.
Marcuse, H. (1969) *An Essay on Liberation*. London: Allen Lane.
Marris, P. (1974) *Loss and Change*. London: Routledge and Kegan Paul.
Olson, C. (1970) *The Special View of History*. Berkeley, California: Oyez.
Pirsig, R. M. (1974) *Zen and the Art of Motorcycle Maintenance*. London: Bodley Head.
Robertson, B. (1960) *Jackson Pollock*. London: Thames and Hudson.
Rosenberg, H. (1962) *The Tradition of the New*. London: Thames and Hudson.
Sennett, R. (1971) *The Uses of Disorder*. London: Allen Lane.
Suzuki, D. T. (1974) 'Lectures on Zen Buddhism', in D. T. Suzuki, E. Fromm and R. D. Martino *Zen Buddhism and Psychoanalysis*. London: Souvenir Press.
Waddington, C. H. (1969) *Behind Appearance*. Edinburgh: Edinburgh University Press.
Weiss, R. S. and Rein, M. (1970) 'The Evaluation of Broad-Aim Programmes: Experimental Design, it's Difficulties, and an Alternative, *Administrative Science Quarterly* 15: 97–109.
Weyl, H. (1949) *Philosophy of Mathematics and Natural Science*. Princeton: Princeton University Press.
Whitehead, A. N. (1925) *Science and the Modern World*. London: Macmillan.
Whitehead, A. N. (1929) *Process and Reality*. London: Cambridge University Press.
Whorf, B. L. (1956a) 'The Relation of Habitual Thought and Behaviour to Language', in J.B. Carroll (ed.) *Language, Thought and Reality*. Cambridge, Mass.: The Massachusetts Institute of Technology Press.
Whorf, B. L. (1956b) 'Language, Mind and Reality', in J.B. Carroll (ed.) *Language, Thought and Reality*. Cambridge, Mass.: The Massachusetts Institute of Technology Press.
Willener, A. (1970) *The Action-Image of Society*. London: Tavistock Publications.
Wind, E. (1969) *Art and Anarchy*. New York: Vintage Books.

(Excerpt from 'Interview with Robert Cooper' Robert C. H. Chia and Jannis Kallinikos, in Chia, R. (ed) (1998) *Organized Worlds: Explorations in Technology and Organization with Robert Cooper*. London: Routledge, 139–45.)

*In 'The Open Field' (Cooper, 1976), an essay published in the journal* Human Relations *over twenty years ago, you attempted to articulate what you called an 'epistemology of process' in which you drew substantially from the work of the philosophers Alfred North Whitehead and Henri Bergson. It seems to me that this essay in particular was intended as a polemical statement drawing attention to the possibility of an alternative set of theoretical concerns for the social sciences. To what extent do you think this essay and its concerns relate to the work you are currently doing, and what particular virtues do you see in this approach?*

The 'Open Field' essay was a very personal expression of my general reflections on the social sciences and their theoretical and practical relevance. The essay grew out of a set of political concerns I had been engaged with since the mid-1960s—the practical use of theoretical ideas at both personal and social levels. I worked on several practical projects that were related to the realization of these interests. For some years I collaborated with the Tavistock Institute of Human Relations in London on its Industrial Democracy programme. The Tavistock researchers had been developing action-orientated theory and consultancy in industry and the community for some years. My work with them was theory-based and specifically dealt with refining existing ideas on socio-technical systems and autonomous work groups. I published several technical papers on these and related topics. I was also involved in the early 1970s with the successful transformation of a family-owned factory in Northern England into a workers' co-operative. During the same period, I worked as a consultant on a community development programme in Liverpool, which was part of the then Labour government's national programme of Inner City Renewal. The work examined the administrative relationship between a local community and the city council with the aim of transferring control over local matters to the community itself. (The general theory and philosophy behind these various projects in self-management are described in Herbst's 1976, *Alternative to Hierarchies*.) But I was personally dissatisfied with both the social science theory and the change programmes. Local autonomy was a beginning but not an end in itself. So I began to review my involvement in this work and this led to a fundamental questioning of the nature of science writing lacked imagination or spirit, that it was too limited in its conception of the human world, that it was overly normative and too irreflective to do more than represent a conventionally restricted view of that world. Instead of describing the world 'as it is' with the implicit assumption that this is the way to do respectable social science and that alternatives are necessarily limited by the intrinsic intractability of things, I began to think of what was excluded from social science thinking.

My reading in philosophy and literature contrasted significantly with my reading in social science. Ostensibly, all these disciplines were *human* sciences since they all dealt with human experience. But the differences I saw suggested that an institutional division of labour had occurred at some point so that philosophy and literature had been accorded the 'rights' to certain areas of human experience and to certain methodologies or analytical strategies which were deemed to be less 'authoritative' than those of the academic social sciences. This was especially marked in the case of literature which reflected fictive life while social science was somehow seem to be 'realistic' and hence more veridical. But the real difference, as I saw it, was that philosophy and literature addressed the imagination and the domain of the spirit—*vital* features of human community—while social science seemed not to admit these as defining criteria of social and cultural life. I wanted to open up social science to neglected and excluded possibilities, to draw attention to its dereliction of intellectual duty, to its lack of vision, to its limiting positivism and its squeamish obeisance to the mundane. This, then, was my general state of mind when I wrote 'The Open Field'.

It may help if I comment on the actual title of that essay. The title has several sources. I took it directly from a poem of the same title by Robert Duncan, which explored the notion of the poetic imagination as an ingredient of everyday life. Another important source was field theory, which the social sciences began to adopt from the physical sciences in the 1930s. Field theory thought in terms of fields of relationships rather than self-contained things or structures. It emphasized the dynamic nature of the world, its constant movement, its conflicts and tensions. (See Mey, 1972, for a detailed overview of field theory in the social sciences.) It also revealed the world as an open, unfinished process. Gaston Bachelard's *The New Scientific Spirit* (1937) is a splendid exposition of the philosophy of the new physics—quantum physics and the Uncertainty Principle—which shows the relationship between the human observer and its world to be basically 'open', that is, heterogeneous, unlocalizable, differential, ambiguous, and apparitional. So the philosophy and methodology of my essay came from a range of vastly different intellectual fields which I saw as different expressions of the same underlying ideas.

Modern science expressed the same intellectual methodology as modern literature. Interchangeability and exchangeability, transformation and deformation, became key terms in understanding both the human and the physical worlds. (Strictly speaking, the distinction between the human and the physical is a fictional convenience which the philosophy of 'The Open Field' does not recognize in its problematizing of reality.) All this was echoed in my essay and its attempt to articulate a view of the process as chaos, chance, enactment, situatedness and generic abstraction, and its interlacing of the work of philosophers (Bachelard, Heidegger, Whitehead), writers and artists (Breton, Cage, Olson, Pollock, Rimbaud) and social thinkers (Bateson, Berger and Luckman, Lefebvre, Whorf). The concerns addressed by 'The Open Field' were also related, I felt, to Max Weber's critique of the modern world's preoccupation with rationality and the 'purging of magic from the world'. Institutional and organizational rationality has changed our ways of thinking, both about the world and ourselves in relation to it. We have become manipulative and predatory, subverting the naturalness of the earth to our 'will to power'. And in this process we have lost the sense of the 'open' possibilities of the world, of the infinite mystery of nature. Heidegger's later philosophy is essentially an exploration of Weber's 'purging of magic from the world'. Heidegger's concept of 'the Open' is both a critique of modern instrumentality and an exposition of the meaning of 'magic'. For Heidegger, the earth had become simply a pool of resources to be manipulated at will. The forest is now perceived as a resource for the timber-newsprint industry, the river provides power for electricity. Human beings turn themselves into human resources. Everything subserves what Heidegger calls 'the will to will'. Yet beyond all this is the Open, that which can't be contained in the manipulative categories of techno-scientific organization, that which denies the humanistic perspective that the world exists simply for us. In the Open we experience something other than ourselves, something 'grander' (or 'grounder') than our obsession with specific, anthropomorphic objects and goals. This larger 'ground' Heidegger calls Being, which is another way of saying 'openness'.

All my work since 'The Open Field' has followed up the general theme of openness. In various papers dealing with the nature of *organization* (e.g., Cooper, 1986; Cooper and Law, 1995), I have examined the interdependence between organization and disorganization, between systemness and unsystemness. Always my purpose has been to remind ourselves that the understanding of *organizing* as an ontological process is more important than the study of *organizations*. For this reason, I see my work as a reflection on Weber's general concern with the opposition between instrumental rationality and 'magic'. If we insist on thinking in terms of *organizations*, we miss the bigger question of how organization as a generic process both structures and destructures our world, how our minds and bodies are caught up in its complex, reflexive dynamics. To think of *organizations* is to think of specific objects external to us. To think of *organization* is to recognise a more general force which includes us in its perpetual movement between order and disorder, certainty and uncertainty. (Weber himself exemplified this conflict, for his life oscillated dramatically between a commitment to rationalism and a subjection to personal and professional ambiguities.) Again, to think in terms of *organization* is to think of specific objects that we *use*—tools, plans, rules etc. In this sense, *organizations* are a form of instrumental rationality. But *organization* as a general force, an ontological process, is *not about use* but about active *participation* in the living world. This is the message we get from modern science where the scientist is not merely an observer of the external world but an active participator in it, so that the world is no longer external to us. We are it and it is us. This insight is basic to the ideas of openness. It's what Heidegger means by the Open, that sense of a 'ground' that is 'grander' than our instrumentality agency.

All this means that we have to think *openly*, to develop a general methodology of openness. This if course is the significance of much poststructuralist philosophy, which—perhaps curiously—echoes the 'participative' message of modern science. To say that we are the world and the world is us is to underline the central role of *mediation* in 'The Open Field'. Mark Taylor's (1995) concept of the *mediatrix* is one interesting attempt to represent the participative, interactive character of mediation and media. Drawing on poststructuralist theory, Taylor shows that the emergence of the electronic media and (what he calls) compu-telecommunications technology is forcing us to recognize the participative, open nature of modern life: 'New spaces and new times are timings of the past or present. Openings that open a midst that is not precisely "our" midst' (p. 24). It's not 'our' world—it's rather than we're 'possessed' by the mediations and media of the world. The mediatrix explores mediation as a complex, dynamic processes of *interstanding*, which is another way of saying participation and openness. It's no longer a question of *understanding* a world that's external to us but of *interstanding* the Open as a 'between' in which 'things neither come together nor fall apart' and which is contingent, heterogeneous, both mergent and emergent.

I've tried in some recent work to apply this approach to the analysis of the human-technology relationship, using ideas from cybernetics (see Part 2 of Parker and Cooper, 1998). To reflect the *interstanding* of human-technology interactions, I devised the term 'cyberorganization', a neologism of 'cybernetics' and 'organization'. Cybernetics deals in patterns of information rather than things—patterns that continually reconstitute themselves out of unstable contexts, patterns in constant movement. Cybernetics denies the fixed term and the specific location. For cybernetics, organization is the action or practice of constructing and maintaining pattern or order in a continually dissolving world—organization is stability in motion. It's important to recognize here that organization is not a self-contained entity and that it's always unfinished. This really means that organization and disorganization, order and disorder, are *mutually constituting forces*. Amongst other things, this means that human agents are necessarily 'open', they *need* disorder and unpredictability. In fact, they actively seek it. But there's more to openness than this. There's also what I call 'techno-imitation'—the 'imitation' (taken in the widest sense) of human agents by machines and vice versa. In techno-imitation, we see the merging together of agents and machines in a process of mutual mimesis that exemplifies Taylor's (1995) *interstanding*. Human agent and machine *become each other* in a process of unfinished openness. It's this mutual becoming that I call cyberorganization—the patterning or ordering *between* the mutually constituting forces of human and machine. But this becoming, by definition, is *always* unfinished—it never arrives at a completed state. Becoming is repeated beginning. It's that state of dynamic suspension that Taylor (1995) sees in the mediatrix, in which 'things neither come together nor fall apart' (p.34). Now, this state of dynamic suspension that I call 'becoming' is equivalent to the definition of cyberorganization as the mutual constitution of organization—disorganization. This is one way of approaching openness. There's another way of thinking openness that's perhaps more radical. This is through Gaston Bachelard's (1937) brilliant characterization of modern science in what he calls the 'New Scientific Spirit'. Where older forms of scientific thinking assumed a natural separation of thought from the so-called objective world with the implication that the latter is both independent of and prior to the world of thought, modern science shows the observer and the observed, the subject and the object, to be co-implicated process that defines both terms in the relationship. There is no objective external world which has its own independent properties and which exists in its own limbo of permanent forms. Instead, observer and observed continually *interact* to produce a world of ever-changing forms in which *deformation* and *transformation* dominate. It's a provisional, heterogeneous and probabilistic. All this, of course, is another way of talking about cyberorganization and the mutual constitution of organization-disorganization. It's also another way of talking about *becoming* and the *infinite* or 'unfinished', another way of saying 'openness'. Now, this equivalence between different ways of thinking openness suggests an important feature of openness itself—that it lies beyond the divisions and boundaries of *specific* disciplines and languages, that it exceeds these and thus always offers 'more'. It's a kind of negative space—a space of 'negative capability'—which seems to deny the world of fact and reason, of specific subjects and objects with their specific questions and their specific answers, and which even resists representation (Scott, 1969). It's a space that is *negative* in a special sense—a space of uncertainty, mystery, doubt, where human *being* is that process of *unfinished becoming* highlighted by Deleuze (Deleuze and Parnet, 1987). It's that space that Foucault termed the 'outside' of thought, or the 'unthought', which lies hauntingly beyond and between the representations that modern knowledge has constructed to reassure us that we exist in a secure and dependable world—those representations constructed by the modern human sciences (sociology, psychology, psychiatry, etc.) that persuade us that there *are* the *facts* of 'society', 'individuals', 'organizations', 'human minds', 'mental health', etc. It's that space that Foucault borrowed from Maurice Blanchot's (1982) 'space of literature'—a space that is always *lateral* to the divided, disciplined spaces of conventional representation, a negative space of pure deferral, a bottomless, infinite void that human work continually attempts to fill in. For Blanchot, it was a space where, strangely, science and literature came together, or, perhaps more accurately, where there was no difference between them. A sacred space Blanchot distinguished his negative space from the positive spaces of everyday life, employing fundamentally different interpretations of the concept of 'work'. The work of the conventional world, the work of modern organizations, he called *le travail*, by which he meant labour, purposeful action, productive organization, all with their senses of getting somewhere, of accomplishing goals. The work of negative space he called *l'oeuvre*, a form of work which leads nowhere, in which the human agent gives itself up the void of the 'unthought', to a space that resists purpose and production.

In science, Bachelard (1968) reinterpreted the concept of *mass* in similarly negative terms. In conventional interpretations, mass is a positive thing and an object of *le travail*. In Bachelard's interpretation, mass is a 'space' that is infinitely pliable, open to endless transformation and deformation, to inexhaustible possibilities—the 'negative capability' of *l'oeuvre*. Bachelard saw this interpretation of mass not only in modern science but in literature, in poetry, as well as in the hidden corners of the everyday world. In Bachelard's eyes, modern science and literature assume the nature of Blanchot's 'lateral space', and in that space are equivalent. In recognizing the significance of negative space, Bachelard (like Blanchot) showed it to be *the* source of the imagination, and his later work especially was wholly devoted to exploring the distinction in the human condition between the positive space of *le travail* with its concern for productive organization and the negative space of *l'oeuvre* with its requirement of passive obeisance to the transformations and deformations of the imagination.

My commitment to the questions raised in 'The Open Field', as you can see, are still very much alive but they're now expressed as a struggle, or rather an agonistics, between these two forms of space—that of conventional representation in an increasingly organized and institutionalized world, and that which lies 'outside' the world of seemingly purposeful and productive structures, in the secret and even sacred spectres of the imagination. My current work on information, cybernetics and technology, in particular represents this continuing concern with the problematics of openness. The special virtue of this approach lies in its potential for radically reinterpreting the overly limited use of the term 'open' in the social sciences (e.g., the concept of open system in systems theory) which is still conceived in terms of objects in positive (i.e., closed) spaces. The negative space of the Open Field knows no positive terms—it denies the existence of objects and entities in *single* locations. Instead, it requires us to think of a field of transformations in continuous movement of solution and dissolution. As yet, the social sciences have not event begun to consider the implications of such an approach for the study of social life. When they do so, they will have to take their cues from literature, art theory and philosophy.

## Editors' Note

All the references for these interview sections can be found after the final interview extract, 'Main features of my approach . . .', in section 15.

# 4    The Other
## A Model of Human Structuring

*Robert Cooper*

(From G. Morgan (ed.), 1983, *Beyond Method: Strategies for Social Research* Newbury Park, CA: Sage, 202–218. Copyright © 1983 by SAGE publications. Reprinted by permission of SAGE publications, Inc.)

The self is a function of the other.

*G. H. Mead*

Everyone is the other, and no one is himself.

*M. Heidegger*

Man's desire is the desire of the Other.

*J. Lacan*

The logic of Otherness is immanent in social structure. Structure is always relationship between "others."

The Greek myth of Echo and Narcissus allegorizes the significance of the Other as a human ontology. Narcissus was the solipsist who rejected the affections of the nymph Echo, who eventually wasted away until only her voice remained. As punishment for his inability to love others, the gods made Narcissus fall in love with his own reflection, which paradoxically he both possessed and yet could not possess. Finally, he thrust a dagger into his heart. The myth's meaning lies in the necessarily ill-fated attempt by Narcissus to live through himself alone and to reject the live-giving structure of the outside society, mediated by other people. We know ourselves only through the echo of the Other.

In everyday thought, the Other is that which is separate in the sense of not being *this* but *that;* it is disjunctive, alternating between the either . . . or. Its deeper ontological meaning reaches down to the ancient Greek sense of a condition that uniquely characterizes human experience and which the Greek's enshrined in their term for man, *anthropos*, whose root *anthr* later gave the German *andere(r)*, meaning "other" or "different". As ontology, the Other is that which includes disjunction *and* conjunction. It is like the rim of a glass, which while separating inside from outside at the same time brings them together, or the edge of a coin, which separates as well as joins the obverse and the reverse.

In our time, it has been Heidegger's special task to recover this original but lost meaning of the Other as the "original unifying unity of what tends apart." In *Being and Time*, Heidegger thought of the Other as an "in-one-anotherness." In later works, the *concept* is analysed in terms of *difference*—from the Greek *diaphora*, which means a double crossing or reversing. Difference us that which mediates between two and, in doing, holds apart while holding together. We talk of the turning of the year or the turning of a page, by which we actually mean a crossing. It is impossible to think of the action of crossing without the action of reversing, for one crosses from A to B and only knows that one has reached B by returning, in the mind at least, to A. In the progress of the year, Otherness emerges through the reversal (the point of difference) of spring and summer into autumn and winter. It would be appropriate to say that the seasons are in-one-another through a process of mutual reflection or reversal much as you can see yourself *in* a mirror, which is equivalent to saying that the mirror returns you to yourself. In the turning of a page we reverse one side into the other and the point of difference or in-one-anotherness is the edge of the page that both divides *and* joins.

The humble screw and nut are further everyday reminders of the Other inasmuch as a screw is a nut without a hole just as a nut is a screw with a hole. We may say that screw and complete each other through the mediation of lacks and fills, for a screw is the fill of a nut that lacks and, conversely, a nut is the fill of a screw that lacks. In this way, screw and nut are in-one-another, reflectively returning.

Such a conception of Otherness informs Merleau-Ponty's ontology, in which reflexiveness and reversibility become the essential means by which the human being knows his or her world. In various works, Merleau-Ponty (1964a, 1969) pursued and elaborated this definitive feature of his proprioceptive phenomenology, namely, that the body knows itself only through taking the position of another through which it comes back to itself. "Vision is not a certain mode of thought or presence to self: it is the means given me for being absent from myself, for being present at the fission of Being from the inside—the fission at whose termination, and not before, I come back to myself" (Merleau-Ponty, 1964a: 186). Here, the fission is the point of difference, of disjunction/conjunction. Kant's gloves can be understood in this way. The left and right gloves, as mirror images of each other, represent reversal in one dimension and, in that *dimension*, are not interchangeable and so must remain different. But one glove, say the left, can be turned inside out (i.e., reversed) to become the same as the other (right) glove. In this second step, the "termination of the fission" is represented by the fingertips of the glove, the points at which inside becomes outside, left becomes right. For Merleau-Ponty, the ontological significance of the point of difference lies in its pivotal or axial function: it is the point at which things turn round each other. The Other is no longer simple reflection but a structure in which actions take place in one another.

## THE SOCIAL OTHER

We know that Freud recognized the pervasiveness of Otherness in the structure of human activity, especially the work of reversibility as a characteristic of unconscious and primitive formations. To indicate the primary role of reversibility in human experience, Freud (1957) draws our attention to the philologist Karl Abel's analysis of the "antithetical meanings " behind "primal words". In the most ancient languages, contraries such as "strong/ weak", "light/dark", "big/small" were expressed by the same verbal roots. In Ancient Egyptian, *ken* represented "strong" *and* "weak". In Latin, *altus* means "high" *and* "deep"; *sacer*, "sacred" *and* "accursed". An additional mark in the form of intonation, gesture, or other device was normally associated with the concept in order to give it an unambiguous meaning; for instance, by a picture of a man, limply squatting or sitting erect, according to whether the ambiguous hierograph *ken* was to mean "weak" or "strong". The determining mark essentially transformed a reversible process into an irreversible state. Such reversible structures are seen in Freud's dream work, especially in the more elaborate form of "over determination", and also characterize social relationships from the process of primary socialization to the joke.

Complex reversible or circular structures, called "overdetermined" in psychoanalysis, emerge as "total social facts" in the ethnology of social structure. A social fact "totalizes" in the sense that it condenses within itself, like a symbol, a multitude of social dimensions and meanings. Despite its complexity it is reducible to the concept of reversibility, and for Lévi-Strauss is epitomized by the gift. Now the essence of the gift is that it must be *returned* in some form; it sets up an obligation or claim. Despite their structuralist provenance, both Mauss (1967) and Lévi-Strauss (1969), and perhaps especially the latter, limit their interpretation of gift exchange to its essentially bonding nature. Yet in the date they both present, there are at least hints that the structure of gift giving is somewhat more than they indicate. At the level of the obvious, we can easily see that gifts are accompanied by a sort of rule of return. A bit of thought is required to realize the gift, to quite Merleau-Ponty (1964a) in a related context, implies for the giver a "double reference to himself and the other person", and since every receiver is also a giver, the double reference is also mirrored in the other.

It is precisely this point that Mead (1934) assumes to be basic to the social process and indeed to the development of mind: "Reflexiveness . . . is the essential condition, within the social process, for the development of mind." (Mead, 1934: 134.) Mead tells us that reflexiveness means the *turning back* of the individual's experience on him-or herself, which suggests that his ontology is similar to that of Heidegger and Merleau-Ponty.

For Mead, the "double reference" occurs in the "conversation of gestures," the building block of communication, in which A's stimulus calls out B's response, and B's response returns as the stimulus for A's response, and so on. B is the other for A, and A is the other for B. Here, as elsewhere, Otherness does not reside in any one term but lies between terms, as it were.

In Mead's conception of the process of human communication, the "I" is spoken by the "generalized other," which is a pooling of the attitudes of others. Specifically, other's attitudes are pooled into the "me," which is a mean or average of the positions of "I" and "Others." The "me," therefore, functions as a medium or central axis that enables social structure to be. In this context, we can speak of any single term's meaning as being "authored" by the "other," and it is no accident that these two latter terms are lexically so alike.

The special character of the medium or mean may be better understood through Merleau-Ponty's (1964a) suggestion that reversibility is analogous to the linguist's "zero phoneme," a kind of imaginary place that has no value in itself but serves to bring out values in others such as we see in Helson's (1964) conception of the "mean" as a functional zero in psychophysical judgements. Given a range of stimulus values to identify, the human subject can only respond by first locating their mean or average value, from which he or she is then able to estimate the remaining values as "deviations" of "differences." In effect, the mean is that which divides the total range of values into two subranges that are understood as mirror images or "returns" of each other.

In analysing the social structure of a South American people, the Bororo, Lévi-Strauss (1963a) reveals the workings of a similar process in suggesting that the mute role of a certain institutional axis was to "give meaning" to the social structure as a whole. Ostensibly, the Bororo village is optimized on an exogamous East-West axis that is crossed perpendicularly by a North-South axis whose function is not empirically clear but which appears to serve as the sole unifying devise in the Bororo social structure, joining together otherwise disparate elements. In itself, the second axis has no value and exists simply for the benefit of other terms in the structure. For this reason, Lévi-Strauss ascribes it to a *Zero-Value* (whose structural resemblance to Helson's *functional zero* may be noted in passing). Yet this second axis, like the determinative added to the ambiguity of primal expressions, serves to signify inasmuch as it creates conditions for two otherwise separate moieties to exist in one another. In other words, this axis creates the "double reference."

Both Parsons (Parsons and Bales 1955) and Lacan (1977) have dealt, in their different ways, with the double reference. In his analysis of family structure and socialization, Parsons relies on logic and psychoanalysis to argue the fundamental role that the double reference plays in structure, especially social structure. His conception of the double reference is presented in terms of disjunction and conjunction which he equates with the individual and social dimensions of social structure, respectively. Parson's originality lies in refusing to see the individual-disjunctive and social-conjunctive as separate features of structure. For him, they are complementary facets of the same structure.

It is necessary to remind ourselves exactly what Parsons means by the logic of disjunction and conjunction. Both processes are regarded as fundamental to human thinking and occur simultaneously in any act of thought. In adding together four different things—say, apple, orange, pear, banana—we reason by conjunction: $1+1+1+1=4$. At the same time, we reason by disjunction because each one of these different things is made by the *same* in the sense that it becomes simply one more thing to be added up.

In this sense, being "individual" means that you and me are "undivided" symbols of the concept "human being." Any one of us taken separately makes up a whole human being. Following Parsons, we can say that you *or* me is a human being, but we are not allowed to say that you *and* me is a human being for this involves at least two human beings. So we are "disjointed." But in conjunction we are "divided" and we become "undivided" by joining together in the same group. Mother, father, daughter, and son added together make up the family group. We cannot say that mother *or* father is the family, for the family is a conjunction of these individuals.

Basing his analysis of the socialization process on Freud and (to a lesser extent) Mead, Parsons views the first stage of this process, the mother/child identity, as conjunctive since it is structured in terms of absolute identification of mother and child who are joined as one; at this stage, disjunction has not appeared. Disjunction or individual identity is realized through the Oedipus phase, where the father intervenes to break up the absolute relationship between mother and child and places himself between them as a third term. In so doing he creates a double reference that integrates the conjunctive and the disjunctive.

A similar analysis constitutes the theory of human development in Lacan's psychoanalysis, especially in the so-called Imaginary and Symbolic orders. In the Imaginary, there is no distinction, only a perpetual merging of terms into each other: no "I," no "you," no "me," to speak of. The Imaginary is the order of the conjunctive. In the Symbolic, a sense of the individual who is part of a structure is introduced through the process of naming, which ascribes a fixed position in the social structure. The Symbolic is the order of the conjunctive/disjunctive.

In Lacan's *mirror stage* the child identifies itself with and through the image of the "other"—the mother, other children; there is no understanding of itself as a separate "I": it imagines itself as the "other." In the particular case of the mother/male child relationship, the child fuses with the mother in a process of imaginary mutual appropriation in which each lives through the other. This moment of continuity is suppressed by *the Name-of-the-Father*, when the father imposes constraint by naming the specific roles in the family structure. The function of the name is to constrain, and constraint is the source of pattern. (The Etymology of "father" as *pater* reflects that of "pattern"). At this magical point the social becomes individual and the individual becomes social.

In small group studies of social structure, especially studies based on factor analysis, two dimensions—individuality and sociability—are consistently reported. But a defect of much of this work is that these factors are interpreted as being separate. Yet they are clearly equivalent to the individual (disjunctive) and social (conjunctive) facets of social structure noted by Parsons, whose special merit in the present context was to view them as mutually defining. It is this fact of interdependence or coupling between individual and social that is of high significance in understanding Otherness as the basis of social structure, for, among other things, it implies recursiveness or circularity which is merely another way of saying in-one-anotherness.

## A METHODOLOGY OF THE OTHER

The mathematical logic of circular order has been worked out by Guttman (1954) in his concept of the *circumplex*. Guttman has shown that when you intercorrelate measurements of polarized variables (i.e., which have both negative and positive values), the latent structure that emerges is of a circular order. Circular structure has been demonstrated in regard to human intelligence, attitudes, and so on.

Perhaps the most systematic empirical studies of circular structure have been carried out by social psychologists in the field of interpersonal behaviour. Foa (1961), in a neglected but important paper, has discussed much of the background literature and has presented a mathematically based case for circular structure, much of it coming from Guttman's model.

To demonstrate the methodology of the circular model, let us take one study, reported by the psychologist Timothy Leary (1957), of the personality structures of psychiatric patients. Leary describes the circular organization of sixteen behavioural variables around two orthogonal axes: dominance/submission and hostility/affection, the former representing the individual facet of structure, the latter, the social facet.

It is worth noting that Leary justifies his circular rationale by discussing similar methodologies put forward by various scholars including Parsons and Freud, who, in particular, considered Lichtenberg's "compass of motives" as a model especially appropriate to the circular structures latent in human action.

Leary's main types of behaviour were:

(1)   Managerial-Autocratic
(2)   Competitive-Narcissistic
(3)   Aggressive-Sadistic

(4)   Rebellious-Distrustful
(5)   Self-Effacing-Masochistic
(6)   Docile-Dependent
(7)   Cooperative-Overconventional
(8)   Responsible-Hypernormal

He reports that the quantitative relationships (expressed in terms of correlation coefficients) between these behavioural characteristics are arranged in a circular order and that the "average size of the correlation coefficients decreases systematically as the intervariable distance on the circular arrangement increases."

Foa's fuller demonstration of the circular logic behind Leary's findings depends on a reanalysis of the latter's concepts in terms of three facets: the *context* of the action (rejection or acceptance), the *object* of the action (self or other), and the *psychological mode* of the action (emotional or social) which yields eight profiles:

(A)   Rejection of self, emotional
(B)   Rejection of self, social
(C)   Rejection of other, social
(D)   Rejection of other, emotional
(E)   Acceptance of self, emotional
(F)   Acceptance of self, social
(G)   Acceptance of other, social
(H)   Acceptance of other, emotional

The circular structure of the profiles, when viewed as a system, is more easily seen in Figure 4.1.

We can now apply Foa's scheme to understand more precisely the nature of the circularity in Leary's original data. In Figure 4.2, A through H represent Foa's eight profiles (see above), while plus and minus signs represent the presence or absence, respectively of a particular profile.

From the table, we see that Leary's Managerial-Autocratic type is interpreted in Foa's scheme as a mix of social and emotional rejection of other and social and emotional acceptance of self. The rest of the types can be interpreted in the same way. But the real point of the exercise is to indicate that these various types of psychiatric behaviour may only be understood in terms of their interrelationships. In other words, meaning derives from the types *turning round each other*, and Figure 4.2 suggests how this may occur.

First, let us make explicit the circular structure of Figure 4.2 by looping type 8 (Responsible-Hypernormal) back to connect with type 1 (Managerial-Autocratic). When this is done, we find that those types that are farthest from each other on the circular structure are also diametrically opposed in terms of their constituent variables. Type 1 (Managerial-Autocratic) is the exact opposite of type 5 (Self-Effacing-Masochistic), that is types 1 and 5

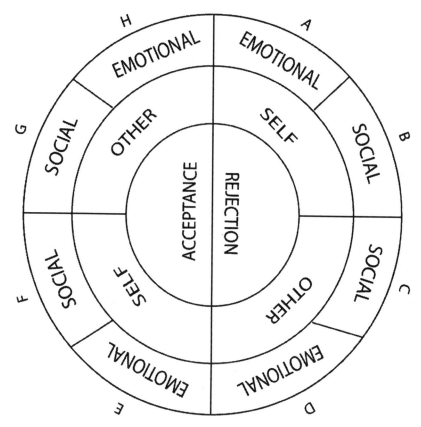

*Figure 4.1*   The Circular Logic of Leary's Analysis Behaviour Types

|                                   | A | B | C | D | E | F | G | H |
|-----------------------------------|---|---|---|---|---|---|---|---|
| (1) Managerial-Autocratic         | − | − | + | + | + | + | − | − |
| (2) Competitive-Narcissistic      | − | + | + | + | + | − | − | − |
| (3) Aggressive-Sadistic           | + | + | + | + | − | − | − | − |
| (4) Rebellious-Distrustful        | + | + | + | − | − | − | − | + |
| (5) Self-Effacing-Masochistic     | + | + | − | − | − | − | + | + |
| (6) Docile-Dependent              | + | − | − | − | − | + | + | + |
| (7) Cooperative-Overconventional  | − | − | − | − | + | + | + | + |
| (8) Responsible-Hypernormal       | − | − | − | + | + | + | + | − |

*Figure 4.2*   Foa's Eight Profiles/Leary's Behaviour Types

are *inverted reflections of each other*. Likewise, types 4 and 8 invert each other. By the same logic we find that the nearer to each other the types are *on the circular order*, the more similar they are in character. The movements of this structure bear a remarkable similarity to the movement of time throughout a 24-hour period. We might characterize this movement as a cycle of progression-regression, in which the crepuscular light of dawn gradually turns into the brighter light of midday, thereafter falling away to dusk and finally reaching its darkest period at midnight, at which point the cycle begins again. The points of extreme inversion return to each other, as it were, through a logical and stepwise process at can be observed in the Foa-Leary space by taking A and looping it around to meet H. This enables one to see the continuous, step-by-step movement of the elements around the circle so constituted.

However, the circularity of this space moves in two directions at the same time. As well as the A-H loop, there is also, as we noted earlier, the loop made by connecting Leary's types 1 and 8. It is of interest to note that we cannot create this double circularity by shaping the actual page on which the data are presented. We can do this in one dimension only if we reply on the page—if we turn the page round so that A meets H, it becomes impossible to do the same with types 1 and 8 *at the same time*. In order to think of such double circularity, a torus structure is required.

The two-directional nature of the structure involves a continuous turning round each other of types and profiles in the sense that the rows (types) of the table connect horizontally and the columns (profiles) connect vertically. There is also a horizontal/vertical interaction that reveals itself by analysing neighbouring rows and columns—each row and column moves, as it were, into its neighbour by means of a single discrete change of position of sign (+, −), thus giving to the whole structure a spiral movement in two planes at the same time.

Combinations of signs (types, profiles) represent the logic of conjunction; the differences between them, the disjunctive. But the above analysis suggests that this structure corresponds to an in-one-anotherness in which conjunction and disjunction combine and define each other. It seems that conjunctive and disjunctive processes each occur within a frame defined by the other.

In this connection, the Foa-Leary space as the character of a Möbius strip, a ring-shaped band having two separate surfaces, one inside and one outside, but twisted at one point so that the two surfaces become one to symbolize a divided whole. Now the point of twist is equivalent to the point of reversal, which in its turn is a point of lack since it is neither one thing nor the other, neither this side of the Möbius strip nor the other side. Lack, as neither one thing nor the other, lies *between* terms; in other words, it is Heidegger's concept of "difference" (i.e., "that which mediates between two and in so doing holds apart while holding together"). A lack is therefore a medium. In the Foa-Leary space, lack as mediation has a clearly defined character. If, as before, we take types 1 and 5 as examples of binary oppositions or inversions of each other (i.e., their constituent variables are diametrically opposed), type 3 occupies the role of medium in that it shares exactly and in a lawful way the variables that make up types 1 and 5. Also types 1 and 5 are media for other types. We thus see that the medium is that which *lacks* the clear and unmistakable characteristics of the terms it mediates. In other words, a special feature of the medium is that it is ambiguous in relation to the terms it mediates, for the property of combining within itself the differences of its mediated terms means that the medium negates such differences and makes them, in some sense, the same.

It is possible to see this feature of medium as equivalent to measurement, which itself is necessary step in the institution of human structuring. The essence of measurement is that it enables comparison by making differences the same through the use of symmetrical or equal units; and what is the same is also timeless (i.e., permanent and indestructible). These characteristics of medium explain its function of "returning" or "reversing" inasmuch as one returns to that necessary and fundamental operation of symmetrizing, which gives meaning to all differences, whether temporal or spatial. Differences have no separate, individual meanings and may be understood only in terms of each other, which is simply another way of saying mediation. We echo here a basic principle of information theory where information emerges only from a *set of equally likely possibilities*—randomness, if you like—without which no form or structure is possible. In other words, information or structure is not properly of individuals but of, let us say, otherness. In terms of the Foa-Leary space, each personality type possesses a "double reference": As a disjunction, it is paired with another type in a binary opposition, and, as a conjunction, it is a third term, a medium, which gives both measure and meaning to the other oppositions in its space. It is essentially a matter of parts being shared among a whole. The parts or disjunctions share the "whole" of the medium, while, the medium, in a reverse action, unifies the parts. This double role entails a continuous oscillation, a kind of alternating current, between medium and mediated, which Derrida (1978) recognizes in his concept of *difference* as a process that continuously defers the return to the same. As we have noted, the medium symmetrizes or homogenizes the field of experience. Carried to the extreme, this would mean the loss of the medium itself since it can be known only through the terms it mediates. Hence the necessity to postpone the lack or loss of distinction bought about by mediation; yet distinctions, in their turn, must refer or return to a center or medium by means of which they can be compared and thus evaluated.

## SOCIAL ORGANIZATION AND THE OTHER

The Other is a structure—not simply another person or thing—that characterizes social organization. The essence of structure or organization is that of two terms mediated by a third, the relationship between the three terms being characterized by a process that alternates between division and combination. In the social sciences it is usual to think of social organization in terms of the "individual" and the "social." In the present context, the social is simply the process of otherness or mediation that occurs (minimally) between two individuals, the nature of this process being expressed as the *combination* of the two parts into the one of a larger whole and the *division* of the larger one into two smaller parts. This draws attention to a paradoxical feature of otherness, namely, that unit or wholeness can emerge only through division or difference.

> For nothing can be sole or whole
> That has not been rent [Yeats, 1933: 294]

This principle lies at the heart of social organization, which, because of it, is fated to perpetual division and to mourn the loss of a supposed anterior unity.

We can picture the medium as a center or nucleus with properties that make it, as we have already suggested, analogous to measurement, the essence of which is reference to a standard. But the standard has to be understood as being more than a point of reference and more like a dynamic constraint on variation and difference. A tension, of the order of a compulsion, operates in which the medium exerts a centripetal effect on its differences. This is, again, the point at which things turn round each other—the rim of a glass, the edge of a coin, the fingertips of Kant's gloves. It is at this point of meeting that the differences become symmetrical, equal, where they share the same measure (more precisely, they are the same) and thus, of course, do not differ. At this primal point, this origin, everything condenses into a unity, which we can only know indirectly, in inference and deferment i.e. through difference, as a *lost* whole. (In the language of information theory, the "lost whole" can be recognized in the concepts of variety and constraint (Ashby, 1956). "Wholeness" occurs when all elements in a given set can vary independently of each other, thus giving absolute freedom. The idea of a medium's "symmetry" means that all its elements are "equally possible" as parts of a larger set from which the differences are taken. But wholeness in this sense is a form of randomness and so has to be constrained. Constraint therefore reduces the freedom intrinsic to the whole, and "loss" is the loss of possibilities or freedom that constraint brings about, which, paradoxically, can only be understood as loss through the imposition of constraint.) However, to know something by inference and deferment is to know something that is not irrevocably lost but merely held in suspension, placed in limbo. This is exactly the timeless quality of the medium as measure, which, since it is permanent and indestructible, is resistant to all change. The whole or unitary character of the medium is therefore essentially *indivisible* and resists differentiation. This means that a principle of symmetry operates in human structures so that differences are understood fundamentally as inversions of each other and thus are seen as necessarily equivalent. It suggests that symmetry acts as a loadstone to draw all the differences back to a common source where, and only where, they can be understood—compared, evaluated—in terms of each other. The implications for social organization are especially significant, for the essential invisibility of symmetry means that it refuses to accept the absolute dominion of asymmetry or differentiation that characterizes the "division of labour" in social existence, and in fact *it seeks to reverse such division*.

In his analysis of social power, Canetti (1962) has caught the essence of this reversal of social division in his concept of the "sting." Power, it seems, is the expression of order via command. A command consists of *momentum* and *sting*. The momentum is the force on the person to act, while the sting, invisible and mute, remains behind after every command is obeyed. The sting is indestructible and waits, often for years, for the chance to avenge itself by reversing the original command. "What spurs men on to achievement is the deep urge to be rid of the commands once laid on them" (Canetti, 1962: 306). The sting is therefore a devise whose goal is to free the command's recipient of a "deference order" and thereby make the relationship "whole." (Elsewhere Canetti [1974] has demonstrated the significant role of the sting in Kafka's social relationships). The sting is yet another way of expressing the idea of return or otherness as an a priori structure governing social organization. Hughes's (1951) account of the relationship between the Chicago apartment house janitor and his tenants, focusing on the garbage that serves as a medium between the two, vividly illustrates the workings of the sting. It is apparently not the garbage per se that is troublesome to the janitor, but the perception that it reflects the tenants' low valuation of him. But as a true medium, the garbage can be turned against the tenant: bits of torn-up letter paper in the waste inform the janitor about hidden love affairs, unopened letters tell him of impending financial disaster or of financial tall talk. "The garbage gives the janitor the makings of a kind of magical power over that pretentious villain, the tenant" (Hughes, 1951: 320).

When Mauss (1967) examined the functions of gifts in ancient societies, he emphasized the obligatoriness of giving *and* receiving them. That is, gifts, far from being voluntarily exchanged, symbolize an instinctive and impulsive form of action over which we have no control. It is important to understand that the gift is not the result of an act of kindness. In fact, Mauss's evidence is that an act that is intended to place the other *in debt* so that the return of the gift serves to free the recipient from the state of "deference" created by the "kindness" of another. The form instituted by the gift is that of the medium, which here very clearly functions as a measure that evaluates the "division of labor" according to a pre-existing and sacred symmetry. To accept a gift without returning it is to disequilibrate a relationship and do violence to the concept of measure itself.

Both in the sting and in the gift we observe what appears to be a basic social force in which symmetry or wholeness continually tries to reconstitute itself against an equally continuous fore of differentiation. More simply, we might say that symmetry resists being shared, and this resistance constitutes an ineffable core that is beyond rational, conscious management.

Information theory, it is worth noting, is based on the idea of binary division but this is invariably limited to choice between objects or events viewed from the position of an *individual* decision maker. It seems not to occur to the information theorist to reverse his or her customary usage of the binary idea by asking what happens when a single object or event is chosen by two people. If he or she were to do this, he or she would reveal the operation of two desires competing for the same object. The essence of desire in social organization is that it is *shared* (i.e., divided) among people *and* objects. Its etymology also reflects this—"desire" is to cognate with the French *déchirer*, to tear or rend, and with the Latin *desiderium*, a longing for that which is lost. What is rent and lost is the idea of the whole.

It is precisely this sense of loss that defines the human condition. To be human is to enter the social structure as a duality and not as a unity. Mead's (1934) model of human interaction is a formalization of this insight, and the whole of psychoanalysis rests on it. Social organization is a system of information exchange whose function, as we have said, is to defer the loss of itself. The actors in the social structure thus represent themselves to each other as lacks of a larger whole. Desire is the presence of a lack of loss that is represented to us by another, whose desire is the reflection of our own lack. It underlines the ontological, as opposed to the instrumental, basis of knowledge, that it, lack is information that is missing to being.

For Hegel (1931), desire is the desire for *recognition* (i.e., to be valued by the other). In other words, desire is the desire to be desired, to be wanted; since a want is a lack, when you want me, you fill my lack.

A's lack is expressed, through language, as a call to B to fill the former's lack. B, as the other, is the sign of A's lack as A is the sign of B's lack. The call is of one desire to another desire. It is not the call to fill in a biological need such as hunger but *an appeal for valuation*, which is why Hegel says that desire is the desire for recognition. Value, as the complement of desire, seeks to fill the list whole of the lack.

All this comes down to saying that B's response to A's call is essentially a token or sign of the latter's lack, and this is equivalent to saying that it valorises or fills the lack. This is why the lack has the character of mediation, for, as we have already noted, a medium (such as the spoken or written word) provides information that is missing to being: i.e., it fills a hole and thereby makes a whole. (In this connection, we may note that "word" is etymologically related to "worth" [i.e., value] and that the latter derives from Old English *weorthan*, to become [to which the modern German *warden*, to become, is related]).

We can now perhaps see that sting, gift, and desire are different ways of expressing the mediating function of the Other in social organization, for they are all premised on the paradoxical principle of sharing an essentially indivisible and permanent whole. Sharing or division is the potential destruction of the whole, but nothing must be allowed to destroy that which is the very source of division itself; hence the force that lies behind sting, gift, and desire is the force that seeks to preserve the whole. The central role of this force in social processes is recognized by Mauss (1967) in his discussion of modern formal organizations. Despite their much flaunted rationality, formal organizations are ruled by an essentially intractable structure— the Other—which is the nucleus of all social organization. In *Finnegans Wake*, James Joyce encapsulated the intractability of social relationship in the covert notion of symmetrical human bondage, thus: "His producers are they are his consumers?" This symmetry of reversed opposition represents the obduracy of the Other, and the desire to actualize it is a fundamental compulsion in social life, which Mauss (1967: 75) expressed in the following words: "The producer-exchanger feels not as he has always felt—but this time he feels it more acutely—that he is giving something of himself, his time and his life. Thus he wants recompense . . . for his gift." The giving of time, of effort, of a significant portion of a life, is seen as a call that demands as adequate and just response from the other since only this form of reciprocation can give individual actions both measure and meaning. It seems that this is what Goffman had in mind when he depicted formal organization as a superstructure on a more primitive social core:

> In our society . . . a formal instrumental organization does not merely use the activity of its members. The organization also delineates what are considered to be officially appropriate standards of welfare, joint values, incentives, and penalties. These conceptions expand a mere participation contract onto a definition of the participant's nature of social being. These implicit images form an important element of the values which every organization sustains, regardless of the degree of its efficiency or impersonality. Built right into the social arrangements of an organization, then is a thoroughly embracing conception of the member— and not merely a conception of him *qua* member, but, behind this a conception of him *qua* human being [1968: 164].

The significance of Goffman's quotation is contained in the idea that formal organization is at bottom social organization that defines "social being" and not "organizational membership." It is the social measure, the symmetrically bonded relationship with the Other, that above everything else constitutes the nub of formal organization. In a footnote, Goffman alludes to Gouldner's (1955) analysis of the "indulgency pattern" of management that informally underpinned the bureaucratic organization of the General Gypsum Company to support the priority of "social being" over the "organizational member." In this still-classic study, pervaded by a sensitive sociology of the human condition, Gouldner reveals the central issue of all formal organization when he questions Weber's treatment of the concept of rational-legal authority. "For Weber, authority was given consent *because* it was legitimate, rather than being legitimate *because* it evoked consent" (1955: 223)—so that consent, for Weber, was taken for granted and therefore unproblematical. However, if one takes the concept of otherness as the central problematic of social organization, consent as the expression of "social being" and the satisfaction of social demand becomes the source of rational-legal authority. We may understand this connection through the original meaning of "rational," which, rather than the idea of "instrumental efficiency", refers to an equitable sharing or "rationing" of the goods and bads that characterise all other-centered activity. Consent is given to another on the understanding that what is given is returned in some way. The idea of equivalence, one thing for another, is implied. Hence the concept of consent is bound up with the idea of symmetry or return, which Gouldner (1973) elsewhere calls the "norm of reciprocity."

Formal organization, like all conscious and rational social arrangements, entails the differentiation of people and objects in time and space. In contrast, the Other, especially in its function of mediation, draws differences back to a supposed state of wholeness unconstrained by time and space in which there are no gaps, no discrepancies, where everything is full and equal. Despite the Other being a "perfect" form that can exist only in certain privileged states of suspension (such as the mathematically pure world of measurement and the condition of the "sacred" in religion), the fact that it is ever present as a desired yet impossible absence in social relationships suggests that what ultimately organizes the social world is not the tangible and immediate reality of people and things but the structural presence of a metalogical absence.

## REFERENCES

Ashby, W. R. (1956) *An Introduction to Cybernetics*. London: Chapman & Hall.

Canetti, E. (1962) *Crowds and Power*. London: Gollancz.

Canetti, E. (1974) *Kafka's Other Trial*. London: Calder & Boyers.

Derrida, J. (1978) *Writing and Difference*. London: Routledge & Kegan Paul.

Foa, U. (1961) "Convergencies in the analysis of the structure of interpersonal Behaviour." *Psychological Review* 68: 341–353.

Freud, Sigmund. (1957) *Standard Edition of the Complete Psychological Works, Vol II*. London: Hogarth.

Goffman, Erving. (1968) *Asylums*. Garden City, NY: Double Day.

Gouldner, A. W. (1955) *Patterns of Industrial Bureaucracy*. London: Routledge & Kegan Paul.

Gouldner, A. W. (1973) "Reciprocity and autonomy in functional theory," pp. 190–225 in *For Sociology*. London: Harmondsworth.

Guttman, L. (1954) "A new approach to factor analysis: The radix," P. Lazarsfeld (ed.) *Mathematical Thinking in the Social Sciences*. New York: Free Press.

Hegel, G. W. F. (1931) *The Phenomenology of Mind*. London: Macmillan.

Helson, H. (1964) *Adaption-Level Theory*. New York: Harper & Row.

Hughes, E. C. (1951) "Work and the self," in J. H. Rohrer and M. Sherif (eds.) *Social Psychology at the Crossroads*. New York: Harper.

Lacan, J. (1977) *Ecrits*. London: Tavistock.

Leary, T. (1957) *Interpersonal Diagnosis of Personality*. New York: Ronald Press.

Lévi-Strauss, Claude. (1963a) *Structural Anthropology*. New York: Basic Books.

Lévi-Strauss, Claude. (1969) *The Elementary Structures of Kinship*. London: Eyre Spottiswode.

Mauss, Marcel. (1967) *The Gift*. New York: W.W. Norton.

Mead, G. H. (1934) *Mind, Self and Society*. Chicago: University of Chicago Press.

Merleau-Ponty, Maurice. (1964a) *Primacy of Perception*. Evanston, IL: Northwestern University Press.

Merleau-Ponty, Maurice. (1969) *The Visible and the Invisible*. Evanston, IL: Northwestern University Press.

Parsons, Talcott and R. F. Bales (1955) *Family, Socialization and Interaction Process*. Glencoe, IL: Free Press.

Yeats, W. B. (1933) "Crazy Jane Talks with the Bishop" pp. 294–295 in *Collected Poems*. London: Macmillan.

(Excerpt from 'Interview with Robert Cooper' Robert C. H. Chia and Jannis Kallinikos, in Chia, R. (ed) (1998) *Organized Worlds: Explorations in Technology and Organization with Robert Cooper*. London: Routledge, 152–56.)

*You have written about the concept of the 'Other'. Who or what is the Other and how do we find it in organizational analysis?*

The Other—or Otherness, Othering—draws attention to the deeply *relational* nature of the social world. I don't mean the obvious fact that we live in networks of relationships. Like the concept of division, the Other actually constitutes social life. In fact, the Other can be said to *supplement* the labour of division. It's what the labour of division marginalizes yet cannot do without.

There are various ways of talking about the Other. There are 'thin' and 'thick' ways of approaching it. Perhaps the most common way of thinking the Other is in terms of the conventional subject—object, dichotomy, or, rather, the assumption that the human subject is at the centre of the world. In this case, the Other is simply other people and objects which the subject sees in terms of its own needs and interpretations. Here, the Other is that which is *other than* the self, that which is *not-me*. Otherness is simply a network of relations between self-identical subjects and objects. This is the Other of 'thin' connections. A more complex (or 'thick) approach starts not from a world from self-identical subjects and objects but from an analysis of Otherness itself. Otherness is not a property of things but a field of continuously active relations *between* things. It's like language where the individual words get their meaning from other words. When we seek the definition of a word in a dictionary, we're referred to *other* words. When we read a word in a sentence, we have to wait for the end of the sentence to get its meaning, and that sentence in turn depends for its meaning on the paragraph it's in. It's not just a matter of context but of continuous, unfinished movement. The word is never just itself but always Other. It's *distributed throughout* a field of relations. Another way of expressing this is through the idea of *in-one-anotherness*—Otherness resides not in positive, self-enclosed spaces but in its *mediation between* terms. (It's this sense of mediation that Taylor, 1995, applies to the medium/media of the *mediatrix* [. . .])

The Other is not *here* and it's not *there*, it's not in you nor is it in *me*. It can't be said to *occupy* a *single* location but *mediates* in a field of constant transformation. This is exemplified in two ideas—repetition and iteration—often associated with Otherness. Repetition is when a 'second' repeats a 'first'. But, as we've already seen in the example of the original and the copy . . . it's the 'second' that gives primacy to the 'first', thus confusing conventional linear order and identity. Iteration (from *iter*, Latin for *again, other)* is a form of repetition that transforms that it repeats. Here we have repetition not simply as *again* but as *a gain*, a renewal. Otherness as mediation is thus everywhere and nowhere. When Heidegger said, 'Everyone is the other, and no one is himself', it was this spectre-like aspect of Otherness which he had in mind.

In another version of the Other, the anthropologist Michael Taussig (1993: 19) he used Walter Benjamin's idea of *mimesis* as the basis of what he calls 'the capacity to Other'. Mimesis is a primitive human compulsion to imitate an aspect of the world, to become like something or someone else. This is, again, a matter of original and copy since the imitator can only become something or someone by copying that Other, so that it's the something or someone else as Other that originates the imitator or copier as 'origin'. It's yet again a matter of *mediation* in space and time. An example of in-one-anotherness. Benjamin is careful to underline that mimesis is a process of *becoming*. In this respect, Benjamin's interpretation of mimetic Othering is very similar to Deleuze's (Deleuze and Parnet, 1987) conception of life as a network of *becomings* that occur *between* objects . . . Mimesis is the act, the action, of '*becoming* something else'. It's not the 'something else', the other term, that's important here but the action of Othering itself.

Taussig draws on some ideas from the French sociologist Roger Caillois to illustrate the workings of mimetic Othering. Caillois argues that living organisms are motivated to simulate aspects of their environments, for example, leaf insects simulate leaves. But it's not the case of the organism consciously deciding to simulate something other than itself. It's more like the two terms being appropriated by the space between them. In human terms, there is a loss of self: 'Then the body separates itself from thought, the individual breaks the boundary of his skin and occupies the other side of his senses . . . He feels himself becoming space . . . He is similar, not similar to something, but just *similar*' (Caillois, quoted by Taussig, 1993: 34). The Other is thus the dissolution of identity, of difference, by similarity. Taussig goes on to say that mimetic Othering is a primitive, unconscious process that consists of *contact* and *copy*: the material contact between material things (e.g., the physical contact between the rays of the rising sun and the retinal rods and cones of the human eye) and the copy (the image of the sun) that emerges out of this contact. Taussig then extends the contact-copy interpretation of mimetic Otherness to the technologies of what he calls 'mimetic machines' such as the camera. The significance of the camera (and its extensions, e.g., film, television) lies not so much in its ability to represent objects in the world but rather in its ability to *de-objectify* by the world. By this, I mean that it forces attention away from a world of self-identical objects and towards a recognition of reality based in the dynamic Otherness that flows *between* contact and copy. At the same time, it destabilizes and problematizes the objectified world through *repetition* and *iteration* which reveal the Other as an unlocalizable process that is everywhere and nowhere at the same time.

How do we understand the Other in the context of organization? For a start, we have to give up thinking in terms of organizations. Organizations are specific structures, self-identical objects. As we've noted, Otherness requires that we dissolve the object and try instead to understand *organization* as an active field of terms mediated by in-one-anotherness. The trick here is to recognize that Otherness is really continuous movement that you can't pin down. This means translating objects, structure, systems into fields of movement. In fact, this is what modern organizations already do. Looked at closely, organizations are not the monolithic systems that conventional economics or sociology likes to suppose. They're always on the move, always regenerating themselves through repetition and iteration. We have to transform the organization as object, as structure, into organization as regenerative action. This is when *organization* becomes *ergonization*, or the work of *becoming* . . . In the modern world, organization as Otherness, as negation of the world of objects, as mediation, can be seen as its simplest in mass production. From the perspective of Otherness, mass production is not the production of finished objects for the mass market. When we think of mass production we automatically think of the assembly line and its mass production of identical items. Fordism is the image that comes to mind. But we forget that Fordism is simply one step in a much larger scheme which starts with the general deconstruction of the natural world into pools of resources: coal, copper, uranium, oil, etc. The mining industry represents the first systematic attempt to translate the earth into lumps of pure matter which are then refined and eventually shaped into functional objects. In the modern economy, this generalized process of mass production occurs in four stages (Fisher, 1991: 223): (1) the stage of materials or stocks; (2) the stage of parts in which materials have been shaped into repeatable part elements; (3) the stage of assembly in which a functional object is made out of a pool of parts drawn from different stocks; (4) the stage of debris or junk where we see the remains of former objects. These stages help us to reinterpret Fordism, which is now no longer to be understood in terms of the *assembly line* but in terms of the principle of *assemblage*. Fordism represents the characteristic features of the modern production process—the focus on *parts and their assembly*. The finished object—the automobile—is a secondary aspect of the part-assembly process and of the mass production process more generally. To underlines this last point we may note that the automobile leaves the factory as an *incomplete* object (i.e., as a part) which seeks a further connection with its human driver—yet another step in the assemblage.

In all this, it's the *part* rather than the whole object that dominates. And it's the parts with their suggestion of transience and incompleteness that give us the idea of the relentless movement of Otherness: 'parts, in the long run, are the carriers of "being", not wholes, which are no more than provisional arrays of parts' (Fisher, 1991: 213). Otherness is always *de-parting*.

Giles Deleuze's various writings on assemblage help bring out the partial, fleeting, unlocalizable character of the Other (e.g., Deleuze and Guattari, 1983; Deleuze and Parnet, 1987). Deleuze used the French term *agencement*, which is usually translated as *assemblage* but can also mean *arrangement* or *organization*. But these terms—as well as assemblage itself—are liable to give the impression of a static structure that (however temporary) is complete in itself. So it's always the active nature *of assembling* that Deleuze wishes to foreground. First, an assemblage is 'neither a unity nor a totality' but a *multiplicity*. Multiplicity actively resists unification: 'In a multiplicity what counts are not the terms or the elements, but what there is "between", the between, a set of relations which are not separable from each other' (Deleuze and Parnet, 1987: viii). And it's *movement* that comes *between the parts* of the multiplicity which provides the inexorable, unlocalizable locomotions of Othering. But movement is a tricky 'thing' to handle, it's not easily thinkable. 'Movement always happens behind the thinker's back, or in the moment when he blinks' (Deleuze and Parnet, 1987: 1). Movement is 'almost imperceptible'. It occurs 'in' the 'between'. Deleuze calls it *becoming*. It's not a condition, nor a thing or state, but always an *ongoing* that never arrives anywhere, never completes itself. Deleuze illustrates becoming as Othering with the example of the wasp and the orchid:

> The orchid seems to form a wasp image, but in fact there is a wasp-becoming of the orchid, an orchid-becoming of the wasp, a double capture since 'what' each becomes changes no less than 'that which' becomes. The wasp becomes part of the orchid's reproductive apparatus at the same time as the orchid becomes the sexual organ of the wasp.
>
> (Deleuze and Parnet, 1987:2)

But, since we've been so conditioned by the logic of *simple location*, it's difficult for us to think becoming. We slide almost naturally into thinking in terms of bounded entities. The becomings of assemblages are not just intermittent acts of co-operation between essentially different terms or parts, for *part* really means *part of* in the most radical sense of mutual belongings and in-one-anotherness. To emphasize this point, Deleuze says that in this world of becomings there are no metaphors and the word 'like' does not exist because the logic of resemblance does not work here. Men are not *like* animals, nor animals *like* men. Instead, it is the becoming-animal of the man or the becoming-man of the animal. In this strong sense of Otherness, the part is always a double-part or *parasite (para*, equal, between; *site*, place, situation) that is doubled or 'devilled' by the tension it creates between being both *apart* and *a part of*, just like the queer tension we've already noted in the original-copy relationship . . .

It's this strong sense of Otherness as parasite that's exemplified in Donna Haraway's (1991) portrayal of the *cyborg*, 'a hybrid of machine and organism' in which the separate terms of machine and organism dissolve into a mixed space—an-in-anotherness—that is 'multiple, without clear boundary, frayed, insubstantial' (177). The cyborg is an assemblage of parts or components whose significance lies in its combinational possibilities for the disassembly and reassembly of new forms and patterns. The cyborg is less of a thing or object and more of a process of becoming. Biotechnology is the exemplary science of the cyborg because it transforms living organisms into biotic components that can be endlessly combined and recombined: 'In a sense, organisms have ceased to exist as objects of knowledge, giving way to biotic components' (Haraway, 1991: 164). The solid world dissolves and gives way to Otherness that's hybrid, parasitical and transient. In an essay on the significance of cybernetics in the modern world, Italo Calvino (1987) suggests that the mobile, liquefying logic of cybernetics creates a 'ghost-like' space that increasingly confutes the expectations of conventional thought for things and objects to stay in place. The Otherness of the cyberneticized organism—the cyborg—is Calvino's non-place where appearances (not things) move like apparitions and ghosts. And here we have *appearance* rather than substance—forms that *seem* and thus give the *semblance* to assemblage.

If assemblage *seems*, it's because it's non-localizable, transient and transitional—it always moves *between* parts in a non-completable *whole* that is destined always to remain a *hole* or absence. If assemblage *seems*, it also *seams*, i.e., connects and moves across divisions and parts. The worlds of industrial mass production and biotechnology, for example, share the common strategy of translating their raw material into parts that are then freely combined and recombined. As Calvino intimates, this is the also the strategy of language and mathematics which work through the combinability and permutability of letters, words and numbers. We are thus left with the suggestion that human systems, whatever their form and function, incline towards a common strategy of self-knowledge and self-renewal that revolves around the continuous assemblage of parts and the refusal of objecthood. It's this loss of object that prepares the way for Otherness as transient becoming and apparition, as the haunting of a *seeming* presence by an unnerving absence. It's exactly this Othering aspect of assemblage that Picasso dramatizes in his famous sculpture of a bull's head made out of the seat and handlebars of a bicycle. We *seem* to see an assemblage that strangely hovers *between* the world of mass-produced industrial parts and the image of a natural object that we know as a bull's head in an in-one-anotherness that, though divided refuses division.

## Editors' Note

All the references for these interview sections can be found after the final interview extract, 'Main features of my approach . . .', in section 15.

# 5 Organization/Disorganization

*Robert Cooper*

(*Social Science Information*, 1986, 25, 299–335. Reproduced by permission of SAGE Publications Ltd., London, Los Angeles, New Delhi, Singapore and Washington DC, Copyright © SAGE publications.)

## INTRODUCTION

> Two dangers continually threaten the world: order and disorder.
>
> Paul Valery

Contemporary usage of the concept of organization gives it a formal-functional emphasis and this is no more evident than in that branch of social science we call organization theory.[1] No doubt this is part of the long drift towards the economism of modern institutions so well described by Polanyi in his analysis of the difference between primitive and modern economies (Polanyi, 1969). However, the placing of organization theory within the wider field of social organization gives it a significantly different interpretive context in which rational-instrumental behaviour is subject to social or interactional forces. In an early paper on organizational analysis, Gouldner (1959) made a similar distinction in isolating the *rational* and *natural* systems of organization. The main purpose of that paper was to criticize the 'natural' mood for overemphasizing the tendency of organizational members to integrate their activities spontaneously and naturally. Against this view, Gouldner argued that system parts act in accordance with a principle of 'functional autonomy'; that is, far from willingly and spontaneously co-operating with others in the organization, sub-systems seeks to preserve a degree of distance from other sub-systems. In what is for us a most telling observation, Gouldner writes:

> Assuming that the organization's parts, no less than the organization as a whole, operate to maintain their boundaries and to remain in equilibrium, then the parts should be expected to defend their functional autonomy, or at least some measure of it, from encroachment.
>
> (Gouldner 1959: 420–1)

What is significant about this comment is the implication that organizational activity is focused on the boundaries between system parts (the 'equilibrium' tendency—a contentious notion, anyway, being derived from and therefore secondary to boundary activity). Organizational structure, writes Gouldner, 'is shaped by a tension between centrifugal and centripetal pressures, limiting as well as imposing control over parts, separating as well as joining them' (Gouldner, 1959: 423). Boundaries are thus seen as the loci of paradoxical interactions constituted by the mutuality of 'separation' and 'joining'.

A less explicit concern of Gouldner's paper was to tie the sociological analysis of organization into the still wider context of social and philosophical theory (an indication, incidentally, of Gouldner's own propensity to break down intellectual boundaries). In a footnote, Gouldner briefly casts his discussion of the 'rational' and 'natural' models (the latter now modified to take account of the autotropism of parts) in Apollonian and Dionysian terms respectively (Gouldner, 1959: 421). Thus he quite clearly saw the 'rational' model of organizations as an expression of classic control and the modified 'natural' model as a form of romantic freedom. In a later paper, Gouldner carried the discussion further in identifying classicism and romanticism as two 'deep structures in social science' (Gouldner, 1973: 323–66). Representing the perspective of order, classicism sees the world in terms of clear-cut boundaries and neat categories of thought which privilege the unities of time and space, the transparency of meaning and the fixity of form. In contrast, romanticism views reality as an 'intrinsic vagueness' in which objects and events blend into one another and thus lose their specific identities; against the universal and permanent, 'the contingent, the changing and local' are privileged; against the average, the special case is raised up; the disorderly is prized over the orderly. Here again Gouldner's subject matter revolves around the function of the boundary in social thought and action. Gouldner's main objective is to assess the pervasiveness of the two perspectives in Continental European and American social science. His characterization of 'Chicago School romanticism', for example, serves to underline the major differences between the Classic and Romantic modes in social science. What haunts the work of the Chicago School is the idea of active difference located within the boundaries between systems and their parts; the focus of interest moves away from the classic concern with the system *per se* in its ordered unity to the divisions and gaps that constitute the 'between' of systems. The deviant case is not only raised to question the 'logic' and structure of the boundaries between the cases so that, for instance, social roles are conceived as symmetric reversals of each other. Nothing is privileged, in this point of view, or at the very least the notion of a privileged system is raised as a 'construction' to be 'deconstructed'.

Gouldner's analysis draws our attention to the role of boundary as a complex, ambiguous structure around which are focused both the formal and information organizing processes of social life. The boundary emerges as an intrinsically indeterminate medium which requires structuring in a particular order. It is this ordering of an intrinsic disorder that constitutes organization and which prescribes the theoretical recuperation of the boundary concept from its present marginal position in social and organizational analysis.

To comprehend the full significance of this conceptual shift it would be necessary to retrace the history of 'system' as portrayed in the literature of sociology and systems theory where it would not be difficult to show that the concept of boundary has been displaced by the concept of system itself in all its unity.

## SYSTEM AND BOUNDARY

In the study of systems, social or otherwise, it is often forgotten that representation is a necessary part of the 'knowing' process. We do not experience the things of the world directly, but single out certain of their distinctive or differential features which we then perceive as mappings. In other words, we map out the world in terms of significant differences, selecting certain features and excluding others. In this operation our thinking often eludes the actual process of mediation itself and we think and act as though signs and symbols give us unmediated access to the world, reproducing it as it is without our selective intervention. In the discourse of the social and cultural sciences this art of elision, which supresses the fundamental operation of the medium in communication, leads us to assume that socio-cultural artefacts can be grasped in themselves and independently of the forms of human communication that actually constitute them.

The analysis of discourse examines this distinction in terms of 'metalanguage' and 'object-language'. A metalanguage contextualizes or 'talks about' an object-language, the relationship between the two being of form to content. The academic language of social science, for example, acts as a metalanguage to frame its object or content which of course is some aspect of social life. In this case the metalanguage implicitly says: 'This is not really social life—it is a way of talking about it, i.e. it is a substitute for it'. But to the extent that this substitute function remains implicit rather than explicit there exists a tendency to regard the metalanguage as the real thing. The metalanguage thus becomes a form of representation which ignores or hides its representing or framing role and which acts like a transparent window which surreptitiously—since the observer is usually aware of it—shapes what is perceived.

Systemness relies singularly on a conception of unity and unity itself is a product of framing. The frame both includes and excludes and what it includes is subjected by the metalanguage to a process of logical ordering and organization. Typically, what lies outside the system—or more accurately, what is said to life outside the frame that creates the system—is viewed as less ordered and less unitary than what is included. A privileging of unity and order is attributed to the inside of the system while the outside, presumed to be less organized, is by implication devalued.

Systematic approaches in social science distinguish between the system and its environment and often emphasize the importance of boundary maintenance between the two. It is of course recognized that boundaries may be more or less permeable to environmental influences. The term 'closed system' is used to describe a system that is relatively impermeable to influences from the environment, while 'open system' refers to one which has a high degree of commerce with its context. It is significant that the analysis is invariably couched in binary terms, revolving around the distinction between *system* and *environment*. It is also significant that it is the system that has the boundary and not the environment, i.e. the boundary belongs to the system and not to the environment, which further supports the idea that the boundary serves to frame the system, encapsulating it as a thinkable entity and thus preserving its metalinguistic identity.

Traditional conceptualizations of systems are therefore structured so as to give preference to the idea of systemness, of articulated unity and order. The system (with its boundary) becomes conceptually detached from background or environment and thus takes on a life of its own. This has the effect of diverting attention from the all-important function of the frame. Paradoxically, while the social system is defined as a pattern of relationships, the concept of relationship is its least systematically analyzed feature and this effectively means that we end up with a nepotistic conception of social system. It is, we would claim, the frame which constitutes the relationship between system and environment and consequently it is the frame which provides the key to understanding the relationship between the two. At its most fundamental, the frame is what differentiates between inside and outside and thus must be understood as a structure which produces two mutually-defining points of view. In this context, the system is just as much inside the environment as the environment is inside the system. Whatever point of view is ultimately preferred must be arbitrary be definition. The boundary or frame has now to be conceived not as a static concept, subservient to either term, but as an active process of differentiation which serves system and environment equally.

Within social science itself the study of systems has undoubtedly followed the model of viewing the boundary of the system as a kind of container which holds the system parts together and thus prevents their dispersal. For example, it is clear that Talcott Parsons brings to the study of social systems an acknowledged predisposition (which is itself a boundary or frame of reference) to view systems as *ordered* structures. In *The Social System*, for example, Parsons discussed key concepts such as 'boundary', 'interaction' and 'relation' always from the *point of view* of an ordered, unitary system and not in their own terms (Parsons, 1951). Social systems are 'boundary maintaining', differentiating themselves always from the 'environment'.

A 'persistent' order pervades the system which is based on the system's 'strains to consistency', 'consistency' itself being understood as 'the logical consistency of a cognitive system'. It is thus the 'system', with its correlates of 'logicality', 'consistency', and 'unity', that is privileged. The boundary, placed in a secondary and supplementary role, simply serves to frame (i.e. maintain) the 'system'. But supposing Parsons had decided to subvert this privileged position of 'system' by placing the emphasis on the differentiating or framing functions of the boundary. The whole nature of his theoretical enterprise would have been reversed and not only would he, like Gouldner, have revealed the significant social forces involved in the 'functional autonomy' of system parts but he would have been forced to recognize the primary (i.e. non-supplementary) role of boundary as the source of paradox and contradiction in social life and to relegate 'system' to the secondary and supplementary role. 'System' thus loses its position of centrality in the theoretical analysis and becomes an adjunct to 'boundary' and 'difference' which are then seen as the true problematics of social action.

Much the same sort of criticism could be addressed to the work of Peter Blau. In his work on formal organization, Blau shares the functional-system perspective of Parson and this emerges especially in his use of the concept of 'differentiation' in organizational structure (Blau, 1974). By 'differentiation' Blau means the divisions of labour (specialization) and authority. Like Parsons, Blau is predisposed to viewing organizations within the functional perspective of 'instrumental order':

> The defining criterion of formal organization—or an organization, for short, is the existence of procedures for mobilising and co-ordinating the efforts of various, usually specialised, subgroups in the pursuit of joint objectives . . . although the defining characteristic of an organization is that a collectivity is formally organized, what makes it of scientific interest is that the *developing* of social structure inevitably does not completely coincide with the *pre-established* forms.
>
> (Blau, 1974: 29, my italics)

Blau's functionalist orientation then leads him to place the emphasis on specialization and authority rather than on differentiation, i.e. the perceptual centering on 'instrumental order' seduces him into defining structure in terms of *static* differences in role and status and not in terms of the actual process of difference which then of course becomes hidden from awareness and therefore, unavailable to analysis.

Like most systems theorists, Parsons and Blau begin their analyses from a position which omits the foundationary step of division or differentiation in social life.[2] Social organization therefore appears already formed. In contrast, attention to the divisionary nature of the boundary reveals that the work of organization is focused upon transforming an intrinsically ambiguous condition into one that is ordered, so that organization as a process is constantly bound up with its contrary state of disorganization. Seen in this way, the mutuality of the organization-disorganization opposition becomes a central issue in the analysis of social organization and social action. It is to this question that we now turn.

## SYSTEM AND DIFFERENCE

### Organization and Information

Social organization may be defined as a structure which relates people to each other in the general process of managing nature and themselves: 'Nature, society and individual human beings are related to each other by the transformation of matter-energy and by the communication of information' (Wilden, 1982: 2). In the modern world, formal organization is the main device for transforming matter-energy but when the latter enters the social world it takes on informational character. Thus organizations, in the processing of raw materials, at the same time produce a communicational order which relates their members to each other.

The role of information is to mediate between form and matter, order and disorder; information is a process (and not a state) in which form is made out of non-form. Usually, information is defined in terms of its improbability; the less likely or more unexpected an event, the more information it carries. In a more fundamental sense, information derives its value from the inherent *undecidability* of matter. Mediating between form and matter, information contains a contradiction which is—curiously and significantly—reflected in its etymological affinities with, on the one hand, words of *order* (e.g. inform, enframe) and, one the other, words of *disorder* (e.g. unformed, infirm); while reproducing materially, information at the same time supresses it.

Within the social sciences and related disciplines, the concept of information as structure or organization is well-known though it may be construed in different ways (Buckley, 1967; Spencer Brown, 1969). However, there is a general agreement that information is a binary structure based on the idea of division or distinction. The human world is constituted by such divisions, e.g., man-woman, teacher-student, night-day, summer-winter, etc. There are two ways of interpreting such binarity: (a) by placing the emphasis on the two separate terms, or (b) by focusing on the division boundary *between* the terms. We have already suggested that (a) is the dominant mode of perception among systems theorists such as Parsons and Blau. To understand (b) requires that the division between terms be conceived no longer just as separation but also as a structure that joins terms together, i.e. division both separates and joins. In fact, it is the act of separation which, paradoxically, creates the perception of something that is also whole or unitary. This observation—of fundamental significance in understanding the nature of information or structure—can be more clearly seen in Figure 5.1, which

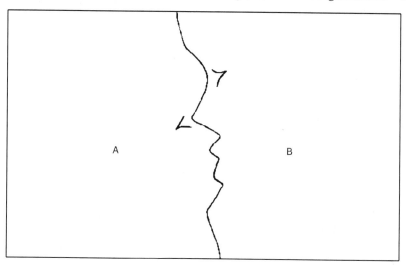

*Figure 5.1*  Information vs. alternating structure

illustrates the separation-wholeness paradox of information. The separate faces of Figure 5.1 share the same profile yet at the same time they repress each other in the sense that the perception of one face is always at the expense of the other. The profiles are thus mutually parasitic and it is this property which makes them inseparable and their overall structure radically undecidable.

Now no longer a simple binary structure, information appears as the sharing or alternation of a whole between two terms. It is specifically the idea of alternation or reversibility that distinguishes information. Though different, the profiles of Figure 5.1 are also the same in that they are the perfect reversals of each other. With this recognition we have gone beyond the common definition of information as merely 'useful knowledge' and have adumbrated its ontotheoretical status.

We have noted that social organization is structured around the communication of information or difference. It is perhaps more usual to express this in terms of the communication of signs, but a sign is merely another name for a difference. The sign enables the individual subject to mark itself off in a social space in relation to other signs—teacher/pupil, doctor/patient, producer/consumer, etc.—but this marking off is subject to the 'mutual parasitism' intrinsic to the boundary between signs. While belonging to neither one side nor the other and therefore being unapportionable by either, it is the boundary which structures the interaction and meaning *between* social actors. The boundary may be shared out: it is obdurate and intractable. This resistance to apportionment is a feature of the boundary's intrinsic undecidability. A more systematic characterization may be approached through

Saussure's ideas on the 'system of language' and the works of Bateson and Derrida on the concept of 'difference'.

## The Systems of Signs (Saussure) and Difference (Bateson)

Saussure's *Course in General Linguistics* (1974) provides a framework for understanding language as a structure or system; it may, therefore, serve as a model for all systems of communication, including social systems. For Saussure, language is a system of signs. A linguistic sign is a dual structure made up of concept (e.g. the *idea* of a tree) and sound-image (e.g. the spoken word 'tree'). The concept is called by Saussure the signified, meaning aspect of the sign, and the sound-image, the signifier. Saussure asserted that signifier and signified are inextricably intertwined. The signified receives the emphasis as the source of meaning, the signifier simply being the vehicle by which subjects exchange meaning. Saussure therefore describes a one-to-one correspondence between signifier and signified.

Later in his analysis, Saussure recasts his earlier interpretation of signification. Signification, he tells us, 'is only the counterpart of the sound-image' (Saussure, 1974: 114). But there is paradox, in that 'on the one hand the concept seems to be the counterpart of the sound image and on the other hand the sign itself is in turn the counterpart of the other signs of language'. The point then leads Saussure to argue that language is a system in which each term or sign is defined not by itself but by the presence of other terms from which it is seem to differ so that 'in language there are only differences'.

Clearly Saussure holds two different and apparently contradictory views of language: one that derives from a conception of the sign as the focus and carrier of meaning and the other, located at the level of the language system, which sees the sign as the effect of difference. In the first, division between signified and signifier is elided despite Saussure's insistence that the bond between the two is arbitrary (and that artbitrariness and difference are 'two correlative qualities') and one can suggest that this is because Saussure, understandably taking a 'common-sense' view of the sign which puts meaning before all else, gives priority to concept over phonetic substance. In this respect, Saussure's concept is the metalanguage to the object-language of the sound-image; the concept contextualizes the sound-image and gives it a place in a seemingly pre-formed world of meaning. Saussure thus provides theoretical support for what is really a semantic conception of language which orders everything according to meaning. But when he moves to the level of the system, Saussure does a complete reversal: the differential features of both signifier and signified are paramount, each linguistic term is a negative product of the other terms. Language is a structure of traces which, when followed, are seen to have no origin but are continually deferred and unfinished just as there is no absolute end to the process of looking up the meaning of a word in a dictionary where one definition can lead on to another, endlessly. Language as system reveals a structure that, far from the positivity and fixity of sign as meaning, is essentially incomplete and without solid foundation, with neither beginning nor end, based on the negative, on what is not. It is the continual deferral of presence that characterizes 'system' as a seriality of differences and which is further elaborated from a different intellectual standpoint by the social anthropologist Gregory Bateson (1972).

Bateson reminds us that we do not experience things in themselves in their full, unitary presence but as transforms or differences of them. The world of form and communication deals only in differences. In the mind there are no objects or events; the mind contains only differences. To talk about things in the mind is to commit the intellectual sin of reification. There is even a problem in talking about *the* mind since this gives the impression of a locatable place, a thing which contains other things. In fact, the mind, too, is difference. Difference, or information, cannot be localized or placed because it is dimensionless:

> It is flatly obvious that no variable of zero dimensions can be truly located. 'Information' and 'form' resemble contrast, frequency, symmetry, correspondence, congruence, conformity and the life in being of zero dimensions and, therefore, are not to be located. The contrast between this white paper and that black coffee is not somewhere between the paper and the coffee and, even if we bring the paper and the coffee into close juxtaposition, the contrast between them is not thereby located or pinched between them. Nor is that contrast located between the two objects and my eye. It is not even in my head; or, if it is, then it must also be in your head. But you, the reader, have not seen the paper and the coffee to which I was referring. I have in my head an image or transform or name of the contrast between them, and you have in your head a transform of what I have in mine. But the conformity between us it not localizable. In fact, information and form are not items which can be localized.
>
> (Bateson, 1972: 414–15)

A difference, then, is a transform of the world, and 'the mind' records the difference in much the same way as a map records the differences deemed significant by the map-maker. The territory itself does not of course appear on the map:

> What gets on to the map, in fact, is difference, be it a difference in altitude, a difference in vegetation, a difference in population structure, a difference in surface or whatever.
>
> (Bateson, 1972: 457)

With this insight, it is now more logical to view mind as a structure or circuit of differences; like difference, mind is not locatable but is a process that is immanent throughout a system of differences.

The relationship between information, or difference, and action is effected through exclusion:

> Information, in the technical sense, is that which *excludes* certain alternatives. The machine with a governor does not elect the steady state; it *prevents* itself from staying in any alternative stage; and in all such cybernetic systems, corrective action is bought about by *difference*. . . . The difference between some present state and some 'preferred' state activates the corrective response.
>
> (Bateson, 1972: 381)

In other words, difference leads to action prompted by a negation, by what is not. Information results from selecting one of two mutually exclusive choices which are *a priori* for the subject, i.e. difference corresponds to a dilemma which every message implies—yes or no, this or that, here or there, etc. The action of difference is the selection of one state over another and this is what Bateson means by the 'preferred' state—the lack or absence of the preferred state is what motivates action. Discussing the action of the nervous system, Bateson argues that is wrong to say that "impulses" travel in axons since the metaphor of "impulse" suggests a hard-science line of thought which will ramify only too easily into nonsense about "psychic energy"' (Bateson, 1972: 318). It is 'difference' that travels in the axon—in this case, difference between 'quiescence' and 'activity'. Quiescence and activity have equal informational value:

> It is even incorrect to speak of the 'message of activity' and the 'message of quiescence'. Always the fact that information is a transformation of difference should be remembered, and we might better call the one message 'activity—not quiescence' and the other 'quiescence—not activity'.
>
> (Bateson, 1972: 319)

Nevertheless, an act of exclusion does occur and Bateson analyses this as in the process of framing. To illustrate the concept of frame, he uses the analogies of the picture frame and the mathematical set. The functions of frames are:

1 To exclude: by including certain messages within a frame, certain others are *excluded*.
2 To include: by excluding certain messages certain others are included.

Now in set theory, as Bateson points out, these two functions are symmetrical and equivalent, being straightforward reversals of each other, but psychologically they are quite separate. The frame around the picture, for example, is really an instruction to the viewer telling him or her to attend to what is within the frame and to ignore what is outside it. Perception of the background has to be formally inhibited and that of the foreground enhanced. In addition, the frame informs the viewer that he or she may not utilize the same rules for interpreting the picture as for interpreting the wallpaper outside the frame. In terms of set theory, those elements outside the imaginary line are defined as members of the same class since they share common properties. Similarly, any message that gives instructions or provides an orientation or direction serves as a frame.

The frame's directing function helps elucidate Saussure's analysis of the signified (the meaning aspect of the sign). Significance rests on the idea of direction, moving in one way rather than another, that is, a selection process is at work which includes certain things while excluding others. Selection at this level is not voluntary but imperative; one is forced to choose one of the differences. It is in this sense that signification 'pre-vents' (i.e. 'comes before' a as 'pre-structure') the subject from occupying the *other* position, i.e. each signification is produced by its difference from or opposition to other significations.

## From Difference to Undecidability (Derrida)

Building on Saussure's conception of language as a system of differences, Derrida (1982) has introduced the concept of *différance*. In coining the term *différance* with an *a*, Derrida combines the two senses of the French *différer*—to differ (in space) and to defer (postpone in time)—into 'one designation for what both subverts and produces the illusion of presence, identity and consciousness' (Johnson 1980: 130). Explicating his conception of *différance*, Derrida begins with the traditional understanding of the sign as that which we put in place of the absent thing we wish to be present to us; in this way the sign represents the present in its absence. The sign is thus deferred presence. This classically conceived structure of the sign, in substituting the sign for the thing itself, treats the sign as a derivative of a lost presence towards which the sign carries the subject. The argument that Derrida advances can be said to be essentially against the idea of a fully present reality which we normally consider the world to be, directly and unitarily available to our understanding, and what is posited instead is a world that is continually deferred, postponed in space and time.

The principle of difference, Derrida continues, affects the sign in its entirety, that is, as both signified and signifier. The first implication of this is that the:

> signified concept is never present in and of itself, in a sufficient presence that would refer only to itself. Essentially and lawfully, every concept is inscribed in a chain or in a system within which it refers to the other, to other concepts, by means of the systematic play of differences.
>
> (Derrida, 198: 11)

The play of differences—*différance*, in effect—thus becomes not merely a concept or a word but instead 'the possibility of conceptuality, of a conceptual process and system in general' (Derrida, 1982: 11). Briefly, *différance* is that which occasions system and which at the same time lies beyond it. The essential point is that *différance*, just like Saussure's conception of difference, can never be fully grasped in the present since it is an active play that always runs before us. A taxonomic approach to the language system can reveal only an inert statistical and classificatory inventory of linguistic features and would not be able to bring out the essential play of differences, nor would it tell us that these differences are themselves 'effects' of something other than themselves, namely, *différance*.

> This does not mean that the *différance* that produces difference is somehow before them, in a simple and unmodified—in-different—present. *Différance* is the non-full, nonsimple, structured and differentiating origin of differences. Thus, the name 'origin' no longer suits it.
>
> (Derrida, 1982: 11)

Since *différance* is ever-active play, it cannot be located in any particular place, which is Derrida's way of characterizing Bateson's idea of information (differences) as a zero form which is not locatable. It may be thought that *différance* can at least be approached but it moves away before being fully caught. As Derrida says, the differences of language are effects which 'do not find their cause in a subject or a substance, in a thing in general, a being that is somewhere present' (Derrida, 1982: 11). The differences of *différance* have neither a locatable presence nor a specifiable cause. Like Borges' rediscovery of the ancient metaphor of God and Nature as a sphere whose centre is everywhere and circumferences nowhere, *différance* is a continuous centre that continually divides itself; *différance* is divided presence:

> An interval must be separate the presence what from it is not in order for the present to be itself, but this interval that constitutes it as present must, by the same token, divide the present in and of itself, thereby also dividing, along with the present, everything that is thought on the basis of the present. . . . In constituting itself, in dividing itself dynamically, this interval is what might be called spacing. . . .
>
> (Derrida, 1982: 13)

If we ask *what* or who produces differences, we couch the question in such a way that we expect an answer in terms of some thing or form or state—that is, some presence. But Saussure reminds us that language (which consists only of differences) is not an effect of the speaking subject but rather that the subject is a 'product' of language, that the subject speaks, is enabled to speak, through the system of differences that constitute language. It follows that a conception of 'social system' in these terms must dispense with the perception of an interactional structure that is fully given to us in the present; social structure can only become 'present' to us through *différance* which, though it constitutes presence, can never be present. This is a difficult point for us to understand since our habitual forms of thought privilege presence over absence, the positive over the negative. In general, we are given to thinking in binary or polar terms (i.e. not 'differentially') and in privileging one term over the other. Other examples of this bias offered by Derrida are: good-evil, truth-error, man-woman, nature-culture, mind-matter, life-death, where the second term in each pair is regarded as the perverted, corrupt and therefore undesirable version of the first.[3] A hierarchical order is thus set up which prerogates the classical desiderata of unity, identity, immediacy (i.e. spatio-temporal presence) over difference, interval and separation.[4] It should be clear by now that 'presence' (and its component features) is Derrida's way of talking about metalanguage.

Allied to the concept of presence as *différance* (i.e. as deferred presence) is the idea of undecidability, which is Derrida's way of expressing the non-form of information. A certain force or violence is required for the act of separating the decidable from the undecidable. The idea is reminiscent of Simmel's (1950) statement that: 'All system-building, whether of science, conduct or society, involves the assertion of power: it subjects material outside of thought to a form which thought has cast' (Simmel, 1950: 357). The concepts of the metalanguage or the frame (which are really the same) are devices for creating undecidability or meaning. An 'excess' always surrounds and surpasses systems which claim to be based on 'decidables' and which are therefore thought to be complete. A simple example is the series of graphic marks on a page—letters, words—which, from the point of view of a metalanguage, are ordered—assembled, categorized and unified—to produce a meaning that transcends the fragmentary, material characters of the text. Derrida argues that these material marks *and* the white spaces between them which lend them form are necessary for 'meaning' to be produced yet are themselves without meaning; they are undecidable in relation to the metalinguistic principles bought to bear on them. While being necessary to create the system of meaning, the material text contradicts the meaning system because it cannot be reduced to the decidability characteristic of the latter.

One of Derrida's best-known texts, 'Plato's Pharmacy', analyses the ancient Greek *pharmakon* as treated by Plato in the *Phaedrus* (Derrida, 1981: 61–171). Derrida's purpose in this exemplary dissection is to show how philosophy doctors its subject matter in the interests of a privileged point of view; in this respect philosophy simply exemplifies the bias that runs through all tests that assert or look for 'meanings' or 'formalisms'. The word *pharmakon* is intrinsically 'undecidable'; in ancient Greece it meant both remedy and poison, good *and* bad rolled into one. When Plato applies the term *pharmakon* to those he is criticizing (e.g. the Sophists, he intends it in its maleficent sense of 'poison'; applied to Socrates and the Socratic approach in general, which he favours, it means 'remedy'. However, it is less the truth position which Plato would like to establish that concerns Derrida but the intrinsic ambiguity of the term itself. The 'problem' of *pharmakon* is that it is the 'medium in which opposites are opposed' and in which one side (site) crosses over into the other (good/bad, inside/outside, etc.) in an ever-active play which brings to mind the 'mutual parasitic' structure of Figure 5.1 (page 85). It is this play or freedom of movement that Plato wishes to stop but which in itself is beyond control, i.e. undecidable.

Derrida elaborates his argument in terms of the inside/outside polarity: 'Apprehended as a blend and an impurity, the *pharmakon* also acts like an aggressor or a housebreaker, threatening some internal purity and security' (Derrida, 1981: 128). The 'inside' must fight to retain its 'purity' (this is another way of defining 'self-identity' and 'presence' against the 'impurity' of the 'outside') in much the same way that Plato cleansed 'truth' of contaminating 'error'. The purity of the inside can only be attained, says Derrida, if the outside is branded as a supplement, something extra (an 'excess') not necessary in itself. But the supplement is added in order to complete and compensate for a lack in what is thought to be complete. In order to cure the 'inside' of the 'undesired' aspect of the *pharmakon*, it is necessary to keep the outside out. In this very powerful and fundamental sense, the 'outside' as the undesired supplement plays a necessary constituting rule in the formation of the 'inside' and, far from being a mere accessory, is thus a central feature of the 'inside'. The supplement, therefore, acts as a frame or ground to the content of the inside to which it is marginal. In other words, the supplement supports the privileged 'inside'. But this metalinguistic view of the inside/outside relationship hides a paradox which we have already hinted at in drawing attention to the mutuality or interdependence of inside/ outside. Bateson, too, recognizes the existence of this same paradox when he discusses the contradiction inherent in framing where the outside can become the inside and vice versa. To illustrate this, Derrida uses examples from the human body, for its innermost spaces—mouth, stomach, etc.—are actually pockets of externality folded in. An 'outside' is thus seen to be the most intrinsic feature of a system, displacing the inside.

It is clear that the concept of difference provides a way of understanding social systems as contrived devices whose stability and identity rests to a large extent on the suppression of the movement of difference. Especially in the work of Derrida, concepts such as *différance*, undecidability, and supplement 'decompose' or 'deconstruct' the ordered and organized character of social systems to reveal their essentially precarious foundation which founders on the process of differentiation. There are here—and throughout the above accounts—two ways of approaching 'system' or 'organization'. The dominant mode of interpreting and understanding 'system' is by way of a fully present unity, hierarchical order and purpose. We have called this the metalinguistic model whose main epistemological prop id the asymmetrical frame or boundary. In contrast, the work of those writers—Saussure, Bateson, Derrida—who view structures differentially has bought to us an alternative conception of 'system' and 'organization' in which, perhaps at the level of what we might call the infrastructure, we discover an intrinsic undecidability which can only be 'organized' or 'systematized' through an external force that is wholly foreign to it. It is this level which is resistant to order and organization and which we call 'disorganization' or, as in the next session the zero degree of organization.

## THE ZERO DEGREE OF ORGANIZATION

Introduced in the social anthropology of Marcel Mauss through the concept of *mana*, zero degree or zero value has been used by Lévi-Strauss to facilitate the understanding of social structure in symbolic or linguistic terms. We may thing of zero degree essentially as a state—if this word can be properly applied to such a dynamic concept—of no specific order, organization or direction, a process of undecidability that pervades all social organization. Zero degree is always conceived as an excess to order or meaning, it is always 'more than', it is the overabundance of the signifier in contrast to the 'reduction' contained in the signified. In his 'Introduction to the work of Marcel Mauss', Lévi-Strauss captures his manifoldness of zero degree in the following words:

> In other words—and taking as a guide Mauss's precept that all social phenomena can be assimilated to language—we see in *mana*, *Wakan*, *oranda* and other notions of the same type, the conscious expression of a semantic function, whose role it is too permit symbolic thought to operate in spite of the contradiction which is proper to it. In this way are explained the apparently insoluble antinomies to this notion. . . . At one and the same time force and action, quality and state, noun and verb; abstract and concrete, omnipresent and localised—*mana* is in effect all these things. But it is not precisely because it is none of these things that *mana* is a simple form, or more exactly, a symbol in the pure state, and therefore capable of becoming charged with any sort of symbolic content whatever? In the system of symbols constituted by all cosmologies, *mana* would simply be a zero symbolic value, that is to say, a sign marking the *necessity of a symbolic content supplementary to that which the signified is already loaded* [our italics], but which can take on any value required, provided only that this value still remains part of the available reserve. . . .
>
> (Lévi-Strauss, 1950: XLIX-L)

The surplus or excess of zero degree, or what amounts to the same thing, the signifier, results from the finite, limited nature of the signified which is seen as a lack that must be filled in. It is this surplus or excess that occasions Derrida in his essay, 'Structure, sign and play in the discourse of the human sciences', to conceive of the 'zero symbolic value' of the signifier as play

(Derrida, 1978). Derrida's essay is worth summarizing in some detail since it reveals the essentially 'undecidable' character of the zero degree.

Derrida's starting point is 'structure'—let us also add 'organization'—and how we conceive it. Traditionally, structure has always been thought of in a limited way, limited by the idea of it necessarily having a fixed centre of point of origin:

> The function of this centre was not only to orient, balance and organize the structure. . . . but above all to make sure that the organizing principle of the structure would limit what we might call the *play* of the structure. By orientating and organizing the coherence of the system, the centre of a structure permits the play of its elements inside the total form.
> (Derrida, 1978: 278–9)

However, the centre 'closes off' the play it has made possible since it excludes itself from the very possibility of play; it creates 'a play constituted on the basis of a fundamental immobility and a reassuring certitude, which itself is beyond the reach of play' (Derrida, 1978: 279). In short, this playless centre whose lack of play assures our certainty is another name for *presence* or *meta-structure*:

> It could be shown that all the names related to fundamentals, to principles, or to the centre have always designated an invariable presence—*edios, arche*, telos, *energeia, ousia*, (essence, existence, substance, subject), *aletheia*, transcendentality, consciousness, God, man, and so forth.
> (Derrida, 1978: 279–80)

But modern thought has shaken this illusory edifice and is beginning to substitute for it a conception of centre based on non-presence *différance*:

> Henceforth, it was necessary to begin thinking that there was no centre, that the centre could not be thought in the form of a present-being, that the centre had no natural site, that it was not a fixed locus but a function, a sort of nonlocus in which an infinite number of sign-substitutions came into play. This was the moment when language invaded the universal problematic, the moment when, in the absence of a centre or origin, everything became discourse. . . . that is to say, system in which the central signified, the original or transcendental signified, is never absolutely present outside a system of differences.
> (Derrida, 1978: 280)

Exemplars of this radical shift in thought are Nietzsche for this critiques of metaphysics and absolute truth (for which he substituted the notions of play and sign); Freud for his critique of consciousness, of the 'individualized' subject in possession of itself; and Heidegger for his destruction of metaphysics and the idea of existence as 'presence'. Among the 'human sciences', one area stands out as especially reflecting this epistemological schism, and this is ethnology.

Ethnology, a European science, was born at the point when European culture (which would include political, economical, technical, as well as philosophical and scientific discourses) was forced to stop thinking of itself as the centre of the human universe, the standard by which all other cultures were to be judged. Derrida chooses the work of Lévi-Strauss who, perhaps more than any other social scientist, has concerned himself with self-reflection and self-criticism, with exposing ethnology to the contradictions inherent in its own methodology and discourse. This project is seen perhaps most explicitly in Lévi-Strauss' later work on myths and mythological activity in which he sees his own scientific endeavour as 'mythological' or 'mythopoetical'. The chief characteristics of 'this critical search for a new status of discourse is the stated abandonment of all reference to a *centre*, to a *subject*, to a *privileged reference*, to an origin, or to an absolute *archia*' (Derrida, 1978: 286). It is this that is revealed in the analysis of myth. In myth there is no one authoritative reference point or absolute source. For example, in *The Raw and the Cooked*, Lévi-Strauss (1970) realizes that the Bororo myth, which serves as the 'reference myth' for the analysis of all the other myths examined in the book, cannot properly be allotted this privileged referential position since it is simply a transformation of other myths either in the same community or in more remote societies. Because myths are cross-referential in this way, all are equal and hence they collectively refute the idea of one version being paramount for the understanding of all the others. There is also no unity or absolute centre of myth.

The 'differential' structure of myth necessarily preludes it being pinned down to any one position or point of view. Its understanding therefore requires a discourse which has the same 'form of that of which it speaks', i.e. which is itself *mythomorphic*. Traditional scientific and philosophical discourse is therefore inappropriate to the analysis of the zero-degree of myth because such a discourse organizes its interpretation according to the principles of an original, founding source or centre and therefore inflicts a violence on what is intrinsically without a clear organizing centre. Lévi-Strauss thus argues against the idea of a fixed origin that authors—gives authority or credence—to myth. There is no centre, just as there is no subject. The conception of a stable centre is equivalent to the signified whose *partial* nature, as we noted above, creates a lack which must be filled in. This is the nature of play in that it always runs beyond the constraint of the fixed position or meaning; play is another name for zero-degree as it is for myth, absence of centre, and authority (i.e. a determining author).[5]

It is curious that few writers on social systems have explicitly identified the concept of zero-degree or its like. Gouldner we have singled out as one of the rare exceptions, but while his characterization of the 'deep structure' of Romanticism institutes the notion of zero-degree it lacks the rigour that 'structuralist' (or 'post-structuralist') thought has added to it. It is also curious that of the thinkers cited by Gouldner as representative of this tendency in social science, none has really put his theoretical or conceptual finger on the definitive properties of zero-degree. Gouldner's exemplars of the counter-classical position are only hazily aware of the nature of the phenomena they are trying to express. It seems to us that Gouldner's case could have been significantly advanced by using the sociological insights of Georg Simmel, which, strangely, he completely neglects.

Simmel's theoretical position, especially his so-called 'theory of forms', is remarkably similar to the concept of zero-degree. Simmel's attack on the classical position echoes the critique of classical 'presence' that we find in Lévi-Strauss and Derrida. 'Classicism. . . . Is the ideology of form, which regards itself as the ultimate notion for life and creation' (Simmel, 1965: 21). The classical approach, based on the assumption of a privileged centre, is a 'closed system [which] aims to unite all truths, in their most general concepts, into a structure of higher and lower elements which extend from a basic theme, arranged symmetrically and balanced in all directions' (p. 21). Against this, Simmel argues that form, although necessary as a categorizing device, is partial, temporary and cannot exhaust (i.e. fully comprehend) the infinite nature of the raw material of life (Simmel, 1980).[6] This means that no one form can occupy a privileged position, hence differentiation becomes the definitive mark of form, as in Derrida's deconstruction of the classical 'centre' which becomes 'decentred'.

What is perhaps more relevant to our present purpose is Simmel's use of the concept of 'play'. Social structure is not a simple set of categorizations for Simmel, but a 'play' of relationships which is seen in much the same way as Derrida's conception of play. Let us remind ourselves that play as the movement *différance* is that which is always 'more than' a specific form or meaning; that which cannot be contained or limited. Play is that which is supplementary to form. In his analysis of the role of secrecy in social life, for example, it is clear that Simmel understands the secret as a process which supplements or compensates for the lack of play in formal structures (Simmel, 1950). The essence of the secret society, says Simmel, is autonomy or freedom. The autonomy indicated here is differential to the larger, more encompassing system from which a desired property is missing and which the autonomy seeks to supplement. As a sociological variable, autonomy is the movement of *différance*, of which secrecy, as Simmel suggests, is one of the major social expressions:

> The employment of secrecy as a sociological technique, as a form of action without which certain purposes—since we live in a social environment—can simply not be attained, is understandable immediately. Not quite so evident are the attractions and values of the secret beyond its significance as a mere means—the peculiar attraction of formally secretive behaviour irrespective of its momentary content. In the first place,

the strongly emphasised exclusion of all outsiders makes for a correspondingly strong feeling of possession. For many individuals, property does not fully gain its significance with mere ownership, but only with the consciousness that others must do without it. The basis for this, evidently, is the impressionability of our feelings through *differences*. Moreover, since the others are excluded from the possession—particularly when it is very valuable—the converse suggests itself psychologically, namely, that what is denied to many must have special value.

(Simmel, 1950: 332)

Here Simmel couches his analysis in terms of the inside/outside distinction; those excluded are placed outside and are thus *without*, i.e. they lack something in relation to those included. Simmel's equating of secrecy with autonomy, emphasizing as it does the ideas of inclusion and exclusion which mediate between the two, helps extend Gouldner's earlier mentioned analysis of organizational boundaries and the process of functional autonomy (i.e. the 'play' in the system which is beyond so-called 'rational' control). For Simmel, secrecy illustrates the infinite, unfinished character of social life, which not only refuses the fixity of a determined form, but which also transgresses it. As an expression of zero-degree, secrecy is a subversion of the known and formal term, a movement beyond that which can be publicly observed and hence organized; the secret—like the sacred with which it shares an ancient etymology—derives from an inviolable exigency to preserve what is expunged in every form, namely, the reversal or counter-form which constitutes every boundary and which here is expressed in terms of play or freedom.

Zero-degree is thus a theoretical condition of no meaning, no form, of absolute disorder which one might call the primary source of form or organization, if the concepts of 'primary' and 'source' did not call to mind the sense of an absolute origin which was itself organized. The disorder of the zero degree is that which is essentially undecidable and it is this feature which energizes or motivates the call to order or organization. Order/organization, stemming as it does from undecidability, cannot in any ultimate sense be based on a natural 'logic' or 'rationality' but is realized only through an 'externally' imposed determination which effectively means 'force' or 'power' in one or more of its thousand guises.

## ORGANIZATION AND THE THERAPEUTIC FUNCTION

If zero degree is an excess, a surplus, a supplement, if it is always 'more than', then order and organization must necessarily be a reduction, a deduction, 'less than'. In a parenthetical remark in his article, 'Structure, sign and play I the human sciences', Derrida (1978) draws attention to this distraction in a specially interesting way. Commenting on Lévi-Strauss's use of the term *ration supplementaire* (supplementary allowance), the 'economic' reserve of the zero degree which has to be 'shared out among things according to the laws of symbolic thought' (Derrida, 1978: 95), Derrida suggests that this is the origin of the concept of ration itself (reason, reckoning, rationality).

The relevance of this remark for understanding social action may be grasped by retracing part of our earlier argument [. . .] which couched social behaviour in terms of the action of differences. We showed there that 'difference' was essentially a reversible structure which we illustrated through the 'reversible profile' of Figure 5.1 (page 85). The 'ratio', or 'sharing out', discussed by Lévi-Strauss and Derrida is here the reciprocal sharing (not specifically a 'sharing out', as we indicated) of the same space (actually the zero degree) which is intrinsically resistant to division, i.e. is undecidable. To solve this problem, social systems have to organize themselves as to deny the existence of undecidability by erecting systems of 'logical' and 'rational' action. Without elaborating this point, we believe that a related argument exists in the work of Herbert Marcuse. In his essay 'Industrialization and capitalism in the work of Max Weber', Marcuse reinterpreted Weber's concept of 'rationalization' so that, instead of rationality as calculable efficiency, it was seen as a form of unacknowledged political domination which serves to privilege the interests of particular groups (Marcuse, 1968). In an exemplary move, Marcuse also reveals the extent of Weber's own 'will to power' when he points out that Weber himself recognized his own commitment to the concept of 'rationality', thus admitting a limit (we would say a 'frame') to his conceptual scheme:

> [Weber] defined himself as a 'bourgeois' and identified his work with the historical mission of the bourgeoisie; in the name of this alleged mission, he accepted the alliance of representative strata of the German bourgeoisie with the organization of reaction and repression.
>
> (Marcuse, 1968: 208)

In declaring his frame of reference, his metastructural position, Weber invalidates rationality as a transcendent product of scientific thought and shows that it too 'takes sides'; in doing so, Weber implicitly recognizes the differential character of social structure in which formal rationality is further supplemented by the framework of domination:

> Precisely insofar as this formal rationality does not go beyond its own structure and has nothing but its own system as the norm of its calculations and calculating actions; it is as a whole dependent, determined 'from the outside' by something other than itself.
>
> (Marcuse, 1968: 214)

We would like to suggest (as Marcuse himself does in various writings) that rationalization as domination is dependent upon the mastering or control of the surplus or supplement that characterizes the zero degree in all social systems and that this essentially involves controlling the metastructure and the metalanguage. In another essay, 'Aggressiveness in advanced industrial society',[7] Marcuse recognizes this same process when he associates what he calls 'surplus-repression' (essentially, the incorporation of the supplement or excess of zero degree into a privileged and preferred point of view) with the 'management of language', providing examples of communicational domination that vividly demonstrate for our own time Plato's similar appropriation of the *pharmakon* (Marcuse, 1968). But all this can be summarized in the thesis that social power (authority, law, organization) is the forcible transformation of undecidability into decidability. We illustrate this thesis in the organizational context by means of a fictionalized account of several real-life incidents which occurred in the British and US navies nearly two hundred years ago, contained in Herman Melville's *Billy Budd, Sailor* (1970).[8] This is the story of a young sailor on a British man-of-war in the year 1797. Falsely accused of mutinous plotting by the devious master-at-arms, John Claggart, Billy, unable to answer the charge because of a stutter, impetuously strikes Claggart dead in front of the ship's captain, Vere. The captain, a just and honest man with much sympathy for Billy, convinces his fellow-officers that under the circumstances—Britain is at war with France and there have been other mutinies—Billy must hang. Undecidability constitutes the warp and woof of the story: Billy is fair, innocent and harmless but he kills; Claggart is evil, mendacious and pernicious but he dies a victim; Vere is wise and honourable but he is directly responsible for the hanging of a man whom he feels is blameless. Billy is a simple believer in manifest meanings and the transparency of signification: 'To deal in double meanings and insinuations of any sort was quite foreign to his nature' (Melville, 1970: 327). He cannot comprehend the possibility of there being a discrepancy, a perversion, between covert structure and overt meaning. Claggart, in contrast, a believer in the discrepancy between structure and meaning, personifies ambiguity and duplicity. Claggart accuses Billy of duplicity, of being other than he seems. Billy's denial of this through the striking of Claggart actually proves the very duplicity he denies. Action demands the resolution of this contradictory network and this of course is left to Captain Vere who makes his decision on the basis of political and historical circumstances (not unlike Weber's reasons for supporting formal rationality) to preserve the traditions of 'lasting institutions'. Melville clearly sees this organization problem in terms of the mastery of difference and in a short passage that recalls Saussure's equation of arbitrariness and difference ('arbitrary and difference are two correlative qualities') and Derrida's proposition that *différance*, especially in social life, is always attended by a certain 'violence', comes to the heart of the issue:

> Who in the rainbow can draw the line where violet tint ends and the orange tint begins? Distinctly we see the difference of the colours, but

where exactly does the one first blindingly enter into the other? So with sanity and insanity. In pronounced cases there *is* no question about them. But in some supposed cases, in various degrees supposedly less pronounced, to draw the exact line of demarcation few will undertake, though for a fee becoming considerate some professional experts will. There is nothing nameable but that some men will, or undertake to, do it for pay.

(Melville, 1970: 397)

Vere 'draws the line' with reference to the requirements of the established institution. Even the ship's captain is enjoined to render and thus to gloss the exercise of 'violence' in the name of a superior 'presence':

Bluntly put, a chaplain is the minister of the Prince of Peace serving in the host of the God of War—Mars. As such, he is as incongruous as a musket would be on the altar at Christmas. Why, then, is he there? Because he indirectly subserves the purpose of the cannon; because too he lends the sanction of the religion of the meek to that which practically is the abrogation of everything but brute Force.

(Melville, 1970: 398–9)

Melville shows that the undecidable can only become decidable through the practice of power and 'violence' and at the same time reveals authority as an institution which can only eliminate violence by elevating it into the ultimate authority. Domination occurs here in many guises, not least of which is the control and mastery of the metalanguage necessary to rationalize and justify the point of view of organized authority. Melville completes his story with a graphic example of the domination of *différance* through an account of the Claggart-Budd affair which supposedly appeared in a official naval chronicle of the time:

On the tenth of the last month a deplorable occurrence took place on board HMS *Bellipotent*. John Claggart, the ship's master-at-arms, discovering that some sort of plot was incipient among an inferior section of the ship's company, and that the ring leader was one William Budd; he, Claggart, in the act of arraigning the man before the captain, was vindictively stabbed to the heart by the suddenly drawn sheath knife of Budd.

The deed and implement employed sufficiently suggest that through mustered into service under and English name the assassin was no Englishman, but one of those aliens adopting English cognomens whom the present extraordinary necessities of the service have caused to be admitted into it considerable numbers.

The enormity of the crime and the extreme depravity of the criminal appear the greater in view of the character of the victim, a middle-aged man respectable and discreet, belonging to that minor official grade, the petty officers, upon whom, as none know better than the commissioned gentlemen, the efficiency of His Majesty's navy so largely depends. His function was a responsible one, at once onerous and thankless; and his fidelity in it the greater because of his strong patriotic impulse. In this instance as in so many other instances in these days, the character of this unfortunate man signally refutes, if refutation were needed, that peevish saying attributed to the late Dr Johnson, that patriotism is the last refuge of a scoundrel.

The criminal paid the penalty of his crime. The promptitude of the punishment has proved salutary. Nothing amiss is now apprehended aboard HMS *Bellipotent*.

(Melville, 1970: 407)

In this example—which, along with Plato's manipulation of the *pharmakon*, could claim to represent Orwellian 'Newspeak' apparently before its time—authority and reason work through language to marginalize that position which threatens their institutional sovereignty. At the same time an illusory unity of England is created which represses the conception of difference, the unitary system being sustained overall by the symbolic purging of corrupt forces from a 'pure inside'. Efficiency is aligned with good against evil, which at the same time is a stigmatum for undecidability. What constitutes the *apparent* logic of authority and reason is the figurative language of rhetoric at work in the metalanguage and it is the insidious movement of such language that carries out the 'force or 'violence' that is necessary to formally organized systems.[9]

Marcuse's most systematic critique of rationality is contained in *One-Dimensional Man* (Marcuse 1964) which focuses on the management of language as a significant process in the creation of systems of technological rationality. In this book there is much to suggest that Marcuse was aware of the undecidable character of social relations, especially in his suggestion that cognitive concepts have a transitive meaning, i.e. an excess of meaning over and above the particular, operational referent. The purpose of technological rationality is to repress the essentially ambiguous nature of social symbolism and appropriate it in the name of authority and reason by 'cleaning up' undecidables such as the *pharmakon*. Marcuse maps out a similar role for applied social science in industrial society, e.g. 'The elimination of transitive meaning has remained a feature of empirical sociology' (Marcuse, 1964: 114). Although not an issue which Marcuse addresses, we are inclined to suggest that the so-called elimination (one could also say domination) of transitive meaning is part of a more general urge for the elimination of the uncertain or undecidable and that this desire is most conveniently 'satisfied' through power.

In the social sciences, such certainty (i.e. decidability) would seem to be more realizable through social power, that is, the development of social science in society is likely to depend upon the development of a validating relationship between the social scientist and the dominant institutional power in the society. We believe that this suggestion is implicit in Marcuse's critical analysis, especially in his condemnation of 'operational thinking' in social science. Despite its claim to objectivity, operational thought is not in any sense different from any other means of generating 'information' since it is necessary to a selection process, i.e. something undecidable has to be made decidable. What enters the selection process and structures the decidable is of course power in some form or other. This essentially is Marcuse's thesis. He demonstrates it with several examples from sociological research, one of which is the 'classic' study of the Hawthorne Works of the Western Electric Company. In this study, says Marcuse, operational thinking served to manipulate workers' complaints against management by reducing the 'excess' meaning contained in such vague indefinite terms as 'the washrooms are unsanitary', 'the job is dangerous', 'rates are too low', etc.

A worker, 'B' complaints that the piece rates on his job are too low. An interview reveals that B's wife is in hospital and he is worried about the medical bills. Transitive statements of wide generality are thus translated into functional form. Marcuse details the general movement from undecidability to decidability:

1 'Wages are too low'. The subject of the proposition is 'wages', not the particular remuneration of a particular worker on a particular job. The man who makes the statement might only think of his individual experience but, in the form he gives his statement, he transcends this individual experience. The predicate 'too low' is a relational adjective, requiring a referent which is not designated in the proposition—too low for whom or for what? This referent might again be the individual who makes the statement, or his co-workers on the job, but the general noun (wages) carries the entire movement of thought expressed by the proposition and makes other propositional elements share the general character The referent remains indeterminate—'too low, in general' or 'too low for everyone who is a wage-earner like the speaker'. The proposition is abstract. It refers to the universal conditions for which no particular case can be substituted; its meaning is 'transitive' as against any individual case. The proposition calls indeed for its 'translation' into a more concrete context, but one which the universal concepts cannot be defined by any *particular* set of operations (such as the personal history of the worker B, and his special function in the plant W). The concept 'wages' refers the group 'wage-earners', integrating all personal histories and special jobs into one concrete universal.

2 'B's present earnings, due to his wife's illness, are insufficient to meet his current obligations'. Note that in this translation of (1) the subject has been shifted. The universal concept 'wages' is replaced by 'B's present earnings', the meaning of which is fully defined by the particular set of operations B has to perform in order to buy for his family food, clothing, lodging, medicine, etc.

The 'transitiveness' of meaning has been abolished; the grouping 'wage-earners' has disappeared together with the subject 'wages', and what remains is a particular case which, has been stripped of its transitive meaning, becomes susceptible to the accepted standards of treatment by the company whose case it is.

(Marcuse, 1964: 122–13)

Marcuse is at pains to show that the particularization involved in this brand of operational thinking is also the 'particularization' of the problem, that is, it involves the selection of a point of view which favours—is partial to— one of the parties. As such, it requires the suppression of *différance* and the substitution of 'presence'. Marcuse, in a most revealing phrase, describes the Hawthorne research as having a 'therapeutic function' in which an 'unrealistic' excess of meaning is abolished. This observation assumes a special trenchancy in the context of Derrida's analysis of Plato's similar 'therapeutic' operation on the *pharmakon* in which an undesirable 'excess' has to be excised. The therapeutic function is the purging of the 'bad' which threatens the system's internal purity and security and it is this function that Marcuse sees as fundamental to the conceptualization and practice of organization. The therapeutic function serves the process of rationalization in which social structures are ordered, organized and made decidable always at the boundary line between opposing forces, between inside and outside, good and bad. The redefinitions of 'problems' that Marcuse notes in the Hawthorne study are really reappropriations of the ambiguity which characterizes the boundary. But it is more than the simple idea of control of one party by another. Essential to it is the therapeutic function by which the 'controllers' can purge themselves of the 'bad' side of the *pharmakon* by locating it 'out there', in the 'other', leaving only the purified 'good' inside. Power thus assumes a kind of morality, the expression of the war between good and evil, between the essential and the parasitic, so establishing a hierarchy not merely of simple position but of worth and centrality. The struggle for the 'superior' position necessarily requires the 'support' of an 'inferior' position insomuch as the latter is what defines the former. The boundary as the line of *différance* is the combat zone between authority and non-authority; in itself, the undecidable. To appropriate the undecidable is to claim a certainty on 'information', which is to say that knowledge is power.

## ORGANIZATION AND THE NORMALIZING FUNCTION

In its most fundamental sense, organization is the appropriation of order out of disorder. In our analysis, we have tracked this process through the concept of information from which order is extracted as form and disorder refused as non-form. In Saussure and Bateson, order is a result of the directing function of the sign or frame which itself is an active and continuous process of selection based on the principle of inclusion/exclusion. In Derrida, the action of order in systems of communication is revealed as a struggle between the decidable and the undecidable. In other words, Derrida places the selection of order from disorder in a context of power in which language (by which we mean systems of communication in general) becomes the very object of the conflict. It is necessary to understand that, viewed in this way, language and speech are not merely the vehicles for the expression of conflict but become the objects to be appropriated, as our exposition of Marcuse's work suggests. Language is not rooted in the object *per se* but in the active subject which wills and energizes the object into existence. Derrida calls attention to this will-to-power as an antagonism between the pure and the impure,[10] between the certain and the uncertain; the selection of information is dramatized as a therapy of power.

To understand more clearly this conception of the 'active subject', let us recall Saussure's view of language as a 'system of differences' in which the speaking subject is a product of the language system rather than its producer; this is equivalent to saying that the subject is actualized by division or information and, far from being a self-sufficient and unitary structure, is identifiable only in terms of its differences from other terms in the system. Furthermore, these differences are inscribed as social marks upon the human subject's material body and property; this is how the subject is enabled to 'speak' to other differences in the system. Since the subject's realization of itself is so utterly dependent upon the mark of difference, it would be more correct to say that the subject *is* difference.

Now, we have seen (Figure 5.1 and related discussion) that differentiation includes an area of mutual parasitism from which the binary terms of difference have to disentangle themselves in order to gain the certainty of identity. Since these differential terms *are* the subject, the quest for certainty (or purity) of knowledge is also a quest for self-certainty and these two processes cannot be separated; hence the deep involvement of the subject in the act of knowing, for in purging the object of knowledge or 'error' or uncertainty the subject at the same time purges itself of any doubt about its own self-identity. The equivalence of subject and difference is thus distinguished by *order* in a dual sense: an 'external' order which organizes differences into a system of lawful relationships and an 'internal' order which is a command to the subject to rid itself of 'error'. Here we have the mechanism which explains Derrida's 'therapeutic' in which power emerges in the division of the subject and finds its *metier* in purification; thus power cleanses.[11]

A familiar objection may be raised that the concept of the therapeutic, whose aim is to heal and make whole, is appropriate only to the medical and physiological order and not to the social order which is an entirely different domain. But this misses the essential point that it is order *per se* and not its particular content that necessitates the corrective and restorative function of 'therapy'; it is an exigency of the process of understanding itself, necessary for the subject's own conceptualization.

In an incomparable study of therapeutics in biological and social systems, Canguilhem has shown how the concept of organization developed in the nineteenth century through the normal-abnormal opposition (Canguilhem 1978). The normal became an object of study initially through a concern, both practical and theoretical, with pathology, disease, and in a more general sense, with 'error' and the 'incorrect'. Both correct knowledge of the systems as well as their correct administration required an understanding of their correct norms and these were to be discovered only through their inversion in the abnormal. What is right and acceptable in a system is therefore based on an inclusive/exclusion principle which maintains the 'purity' of the inside by keeping out 'impurity'; understanding is really a curative process.

It would not be difficult to show that the scientific interest in norms and normalization which began in the nineteenth century was correlated with the problems of administering the large populations that accompanied the rise of industrial societies at that time. It was found that problems of great scale could only be effectively understood and managed through a systemization of linguistic, legal, sanitary, industrial and other norms as well as the deviations from these. The norm became a formalized tool for dealing with aggravated differentiation. Canguilhem traces the development of normalization in France from the formalization of rules for the correct usage of the language by the State's grammarians in the seventeenth century, which enabled the identification of linguistic mistakes in terms of difference from the norm, through the establishment of the metric system at the end of the eighteenth century, to the technological and administrative norms appearing in more recent times (Canguilhem, 1978: 145–88). The norm functions as the basis of order, not only ordering the system to restore normal state in cases of deviation but at the same time providing an order of knowledge for the system to conceptualize itself. The norm is therefore to be seen as a conceptual and perpetual necessity rather than a mere means of survival.

As a result of Canguilhem's analysis, the concept of formal organization has to be read in a new light and its component features of division of labour, administrative centralization, standardization and rational planning—now innocently understood as the rational expedients of modern administration—have to be seen as instruments of a process of *technological normalization* motivated by a therapy of power. It will help at this point to recall our earlier discussion of traditional approaches to social systems, especially Blau's functional view of organization as an 'instrumental order'; in that approach the emphasis is placed on the 'instruments' which enable effective goal attainment; for Canguilhem, the 'instruments' are secondary to the 'order' which they have to create. In other words, the nature of the 'object' is different in the two approaches: for Blau, the object of formal organization is a utilitarian product or service; for Canguilhem, normalization is the object in which the system must realize itself. Mass-produced items are perhaps the clearest examples of objects that are standardizing according to the system's norms; as such they are materialized expressions of the system's needs to conceptualize itself: adapting a conceit from Lévi-Strauss (1966) we may say that the mass-produced goods of industrial society are good to think with and not merely good to consume.[12]

In Canguilhem's analysis, objects do not have natural and translucent lives of their own but are products of intense and complex social labour, imbued with normalized meaning and value. In contrast to the functionalist coherence of traditional systems theory based on an implicit metalanguage which excludes the subject from knowledge of its own involvement in the production process, Canguilhem directs attention to an object-language which works on the boundaries of systems, revealing each boundary as a gap that resists order and where every object has to be earned against an anti-object, a norm against an ab-norm. Since we have seen that the boundary as a differential term *is* the subject, Canguilhem's analysis necessarily includes the human subject in the object-language where it acts through a 'will-to-cleanse'; in other words, information, subject and certainty are coterminous in every system of production. When we apply this consideration to the study of formal organization as a system of academic production we are obliged to recognize the same processes that Canguilhem notes in the making of an 'object', that is, the complex process of social labour embodied in the actual instruments of investigation and which *precedes* what is in this case a theoretical object. But the instruments of investigation are normally regarded as supplementary (in Derrida's sense) and therefore external to the object. The purity of the object's 'inside' can only be attained, says Derrida, if the 'outside' is branded as a supplement that is not necessary in itself. But Derrida also shows, as we have noted, that the supplement is added in order to complete and compensate for a lack in what is thought to be already complete.

It is this sense that the statements of that discourse which we call 'organization theory' are supplementary, for they represent the 'organization of organization', that is to say, that as texts *on* organization they are themselves 'organized' according to certain normalized criteria (often called scientific and/or academic) so that it becomes impossible to disentangle the content of organization studies from the theory or methodology that frames it. By this logic each statement about system or organization is not merely a piece of information about a particular subject matter but—significantly—the statement 'produces' what it denotes. As an agent of supplementary production, the text includes itself in the structure it seeks to analyse and understand, thus creating undecidability. In differential system, which by definition can guarantee no certainty, the lack of surety forces theory to invent the means of its own realization. It is this desperate insight that motivates the thought of the writers we have examined here and which links their varied approaches, from Gouldner's probing of the practice of theory to Marcuse's dissection of the theory of practice.

# NOTES

1 I am very grateful to Peter Manning of the Centre for Socio-Legal Studies, Wolfson College, Oxford, for extensive and constructive comments on a draft version of this paper.

2 Even in General Systems Theory, a discipline reputed to have laid bare the lineaments of a general theory of systems of any and every kind, one seeks in vain for a full and proper treatment of the boundary concept. In L. von Berta-lanffy's *General System Theory* (1971), widely recognized as an authoritative text on systems by a founding father of the subject, the concept of boundary is scantily dealt with and no definition is offered. The related idea of "differ-ence" is introduced in terms of its possible mathematization by means of dif-ferential equations—and then abruptly dropped. It therefore seems that the very concept which originates system—namely, boundary or division—is the one which is most neglected.

3 This bias is equivalent to the "imperative of selection" discussed earlier, i.e., the included/preferred vs. excluded/non-preferred structure of the frame ana-lysed by Bateson.

4 We may suppose that it is for this reason that theorists of social systems such as Parsons and Blau treat key social concepts such as "interaction", "differentia-tion", "representation" as taken-for-granted terms which do not require analysis.

5 The work of the semiologist Roland Barthes are also variously caught up with the distinction between free play and fixed meaning: in *Writing Degree Zero* (1967) and *The Pleasure of the Text* (1975), where the concept of zero degree is defined as that which is "deprived of fixed meaning"; in essays such as "From work to text" (where zero degree assumes the metaphor of the "text that plays with itself") and "The death of the author", both from Barthes (1977). In relation to Lévi-Strauss on myth, it is also instructive to read Barthes' (1972) essay on "Myth today", which offers a different defini-tion of myth—one based on signification of metalanguage—than the former's but which views the non-mythical stratum of communication (the object-language) in terms of zero degree.

6 Guy Oakes' careful introduction to Simmel's *Essays on Interpretation in Social Science* (1980) helps fill out the above overly brief sketch of Simmel as a theorist of the zero degree; see especially p. 84.

7 This essay pursues the thesis that aggression as a form of power is based on the "purity" of the "inside" against the "impurity" of the "outside". For a similar argument, see Ryan (1982), especially Chapter 7, which uses the work of Derrida, Habermas and Lacan as general background for a critique of "rationality" in capitalist society.

8 In an editorial introduction to this edition, Harold Beaver provides informa-tion on the factual background of *Billy Budd*.

9 Let us note, parenthetically, that "formal" and "pure" are conceptually related, with "formal" usually meaning methodical, systematic, punctilious, etc. The study of "formal organization" thus *predisposes* itself to the *exclu-sion* of the "non-formal" or "disorganized".

10 In the study of social life, *prestige* and *status* are ways of talking about "purity". Everett Hughes (1958) work in the sociology of occupations exemplifies this idea, especially in the hypothesis that occupational prestige is inversely related to "dirty" work.

11 The conception of struggle as a cleansing process is used by Gaston Bach-elard; see Canguilhem (1978).

12 For a similar argument, see Douglas and Isherwood (1979), especially Chapter 3.

(Excerpt from 'Interview with Robert Cooper' Robert C. H. Chia and Jannis Kallinikos, in Chia, R. (ed) (1998) *Organized Worlds: Explorations in Technology and Organization with Robert Cooper*. London: Routledge, 130–6.)

## REFERENCES

Bateson, G. (1972) "A Theory of Play and Phantasy", in G. Bateson, *Steps to an Ecology of Mind*. New York: Chandler Publishing Company: 177–93.

Bittner, E. (1974) "The concept of organization", in R. Turner (ed.) *Ethnomethodology: selected readings*. Harmondsworth: Penguin.

Blau, P. M. (1974) *On the Nature of Organizations*. New York: Wiley.

Buckley, W. (1967) *Sociology and Modern Systems Theory*. Englewood Cliffs, New Jersey: Prentice Hall.

Canguilhem, G. (1978) *On the Normal and the Pathological*. Dordrecht: Reidel.

Derrida, J. (1978) *Writing and Difference*. London: Routledge & Kegan Paul.

Derrida, J. (1981) *Dissemination*. London: Athlone Press.

Derrida, J. (1982) *Margins of Philosophy*. Hassocks, Sussex: Harvester.

Gouldner, A. (1959) 'Organizational analysis', in R. K. Merton, L. Broom and L. S. Cottrell (eds) *Sociology Today*. New York: Basic Books.

Gouldner, A. (1973) *For Sociology*. London: Allen Lane.

Johnson, B. (1980) *The Critical Difference*. Baltimore: The John Hopkins University Press.

Lévi-Strauss, C. (1950) 'Introduction', in M. Mauss, *Sociologie et Anthropologie*. Paris: Presses Universitaires de France.

Lévi-Strauss, C. (1966) *The Savage Mind*. London: Weidenfeld and Nicholson.

Lévi-Strauss, C. (1979) *The Raw and the Cooked*. London: Routledge & Kegan Paul.

Marcuse, H. (1964) *One-Dimensional Man*. London: Routledge & Kegan Paul.

Marcuse, H. (1968) *Negotiations*. London: Allen Lane.

Melville, H. (1970) *Billy Budd, Sailor and Other Stories*. Harmondsworth: Penguin.

Parsons, T. (1951) *The Social System*. London: Routledge & Kegan Paul.

Polanyi, K. (1969) *Primitive, Archaic and Modern Economies*. London: Hutchinson.

Saussure, F. de (1974) *Course in General Linguistics*. London: Fontana/Collins.

Simmel, G. (1950) *The Sociology of Georg Simmel*. New York: Free Press.

Simmel, G. (1968) *The Conflict in Modern Culture and Other Essays*. New York: Teachers' College Press.

Simmel, G. (1980) *Essays on Interpretation in Social Science*. Manchester: Manchester University Press.

Spencer-Brown, G. (1969) *Laws of Form*. London: Allen & Unwin.

Wilden, A. (1982) 'Semiotics as praxis: strategy and tactics', *Recherches Semiotique: Semiotic Inquiry* 1: 1–34.

(Excerpt from 'Interview with Robert Cooper' Robert C. H. Chia and Jannis Kallinikos, in Chia, R. (ed) (1998) *Organized Worlds: Explorations in Technology and Organization with Robert Cooper*. London: Routledge, 130–6.)

*Your paper 'Organization/Disorganization' (Cooper, 1986), published more than ten years ago now, is still for many a rather difficult read. Together with other papers such as 'Information, Communication and Organization: A Post-Structural Revision' (Cooper, 1987), it seems to mark the moment of your assimilation of the rise of post-structural thinking into your own concerns with the nature of human organizing. What affinities and differences do you see between your own intellectual concerns and those of post-structural writers such as Derrida, Foucault and Deleuze? How do you view their contributions in relation to others such as Heidegger, Olson and Whitehead who have influenced your thinking?*

The term 'post-structural' is of quite recent origin, having come into general usage only in the last twenty or so years. Post-structural ideas—by which we mean process, complexity, de-differentiation as opposed to structure, simplicity, categorization—have been of intellectual concern since the time of the pre-Socratic philosophers in Ancient Greece. My own systematic exposure to post-structural thinking—although we didn't call it that in those early days—was in the 1950s through the works of the American poet Charles Olson and—via Olson—the British philosopher Alfred North Whitehead. Shortly after, I discovered the works of the social anthropologist-cybernetician Gregory Bateson, the philosophers of science Gaston Bachelard and Alfred Korzybski, and the philosopher Martin Heidegger, all of whom complemented Olson's and Whitehead's concerns. The works of thinkers such as Derrida, Foucault and Deleuze did not appear on the Anglo-American scene until much later—around 1970. So it's not correct to suggest that I 'assimilated' post-structural writing with the publication of the 1980s papers you mention. In fact, I had already published some personal speculations on 'process thinking' in social science in my 'Open Field' essay (Cooper, 1976) which was written in 1973. It would be more accurate to say that I welcomed these post-structuralist writers because their approach augmented my own thinking and because they showed how 'process thinking' might be used in social theory.

I've come to recognize that three general themes run through my work, especially over the last twenty years: *systemness, interdisciplinarity* and *imagination*. I will try to show how these themes relate, in the first place, to the writings of Derrida, Foucault and Deleuze.

## Systemness

Let's define systemness as exaggerated order: a place for everything and everything in its place. Foucault's work could be described as perhaps the most comprehensive analysis of modern systemness *and* its transgression. The theme of systemness and its emergence in seventeenth-century Europe is first developed in Foucault's *Madness and Civilization* (1973) where he described the birth of the mental hospital and the workhouse as mechanisms of increasing social and psychological control by the modern state. *The Birth of the Clinic* (1975) continues this theme through the institutionalization of modern clinical medicine and the ways in which it 'carved up' (Foucault's term) the human body into separate, specialized spaces that could be 'understood' and controlled by separate, specialized terminologies. For Foucault, systemness emerges out of systematic *description*, for to describe something is to make it visible. The role of language in the creation of systems of knowledge—specifically, the human sciences—is explored by Foucault in *The Order of Things* (1970) where, again, 'spaces' are made visible through the 'describing' strategies of tabulation, representation and classification. *The Order of Things* reveals the complex ordering techniques devised by modern systems of administration in their drive towards systemness. In *Discipline and Punish* (1977) systemness is exemplified in the idea of the Panopticon, the instrument and symbol of all-seeing, centralized power. In Foucault's work, systemness is the end result of a long historic process of making people and things *visibly knowable* so that they can be more easily controlled. The essence of this process is the *inscribing, describing* and *prescribing* powers of language. For Foucault, language is the major device for making 'space/s' and hence for their systematization (See Chapter 4 on 'Speaking' in *The Order of Things*). But Foucault also knew that the systematization of space necessarily includes its own dislocation. This is the problem he analyses in his famous account of Velázquez's painting, *Las Meninas*, where he shows that Velázquez was working simultaneously with two competing spaces: the space of *speaking*, of discourse, and the space of *seeing* (see Cooper, 1993). Speaking designates and locates things in specific spaces. It rests on a logic representation which works according to a hierarchy of original and copy, so that the original is thought of as cause, and copy, effect. Speaking creates spaces of identity and identification. Seeing, on the other hand, works in a space that is 'outside' speaking and discourse, a space that denies the hierarchy of original and copy, not least because there can be no original without a copy, so that copy and original can be said to create each other. The space of seeing is what Mark Taylor (1995) has recently called the *mediatrix*, an undifferentiated confusion in which there is neither beginning nor end, neither here nor there, neither this nor that, in short, a space that seems to collapse upon itself. The space of seeing is always 'outside' systemness while at the same time being integral to it.

Systemness has long been recognized as a special feature of the modern world. The scientific determinism of Charles Darwin was a form of systemness. Despite the underlining of transformation in evolutionary development, everything was viewed as predetermined—even chance was thought to be subject to 'as yet unknown laws'. And for the Victorians more generally, determinism became a widely held way of thinking about the world in its social, economic and political forms: 'determinism represents a knowable order . . . an inherent and irreversible order capable of including all phenomena . . . The individual is directed into a restricted time, space, and activity' (Beer, 1989: 118). Like Foucault's space of saying, determinism depends on linguistic devices—words, syntax—to systematize its orders of knowledge. It place things in an all-inclusive narrative order of specified relations that are 'fixed in a succession which more and more acutely delimits and characterizes', so that 'the indeterminate, the reversible, the reality of that which might have been, the multiplicity of the future, the moment broken away from sequence, broken away from relations, fear without object, lack without 'object' is viewed as 'wish-fulfilment, impossibility, something freakish and fitful, something delusory'—a kind of 'second-order experience, doomed and negative' (Beer, 1989: 119).

Kant, too, wrote about determinism and its emergence in the modern university in *The Conflict of the Faculties* (1978). For Kant, the modern university was like an industrial machine which *produced* knowledge for students who simply became its passive consumers. Knowledge was divided into disciplines and departments, each with its own specialized way of *speaking*. Kant's argument is echoed in the recent governmental programme to formalize the knowledge system in British universities—what Marilyn Strathern (1995) has called the 'enhanced systematization' of the university or 'systematization gone mad . . . in the name of enhancing the system' (pp. 28–29). Here, systemness occurs in the forms of knowledge codification, strategic planning, concentration *within* fields of knowledge, measurement of quality output—all of which are imposed on the universities *from above*. Strathern reminds us that knowledge is never a product—it's a continuous and unfinished process whose intrinsic nature resists systematization. It's self-organizing, non-linear and multi-stranded. It grows from the *bottom up* and not from *top down*. To illustrate self-organizing, bottom-up knowledge, Strathern uses Deleuze's image of the *rhizome*, a botanical metaphor to describe growth that spreads in all direction, nomadically, without plan, spontaneously. The rhizome cuts across artificially imposed divisions. And it's this informal transgression of formal systematization that Strathern endorses as the real source of knowledge creation in the university—and elsewhere.

## Interdisciplinarity

Deleuze's rhizome (Deleuze and Parnet, 1987) is clearly another way of talking about the interdisciplinarity of the knowledge process. It summarizes the main concerns of Deleuze's later work—the need to understand the world as unfinished multiplicity and shifting heterogeneity. The rhizome lies beyond conceptual understanding—it can't be caught in a concept or arrested in a label. It's always on the move—*becoming*, as Deleuze has it. Becomings always work *between* binary terms—*between* question and answer, human-machine, man-woman, etc. Becoming is, therefore, the basic mechanism of interdisciplinarity—it's when *inter* becomes *between*. Organized knowledge comes to us in discrete packages or disciplinary fields that require an artificial homogeneity or unity to give them authority and credibility. Again, it's a version of simple location. But Deleuze's becoming asserts the heterogeneity of understanding, and it's this that Mark Taylor (1995) calls *interstanding*, in which 'understanding' loses its sense of revealing a permanent truth that lies *under* and instead reveals a forever open-ended, ambivalent and shifting process that can't be known in any formal sense. It can't be known formally because it can't be simply located: 'Its place is the dis-place of interstanding' (Taylor, 1995: 33). It's always *inter* or *between*. Taylor uses the new communication technologies to exemplify his idea of *interstanding* as a version of Deleuze's rhizome:

> Our medium is the *mediatrix* . . . which is constituted by the intersection of electronic media and compu-telecommunications technology. This mediatrix includes mediating structures ranging from television, radio, film and video to telephones, faxes, computers, and perhaps most important, the net.
>
> (Taylor, 1995: 25)

To grasp the significance of the mediatrix as *rhizome interstanding* we have to dispense with the conventional understanding of *the* media—the specific forms of mass communication such as TV, radio, newspapers, etc. These can be 'understood' in the conventional sense but the mediatrix—like the rhizome—is beyond formal comprehension: it can only be alluded to, indirectly sensed, improperly grasped.

Gillian Beer (1992) has caught this sense of interstanding in her characterization of interdisciplinarity as *over-interpretation*. While what she calls *underinterpretation* is the conventional way of understanding that determines its objects through simple location, over-interpretation rejects such scant attentiveness and specificity—instead, it avoids, deflects and even denies the supposed clarity of under-interpretation; instead of fixing and limiting the meaning or significance of an idea, it leaves it unresolved. Thus, a necessary feature of interdisciplinarity as interstanding is over-interpretation. Like interstanding, over-interpretation is always *dis-placed*, always *becoming*.

Beer exemplifies her understandings of interdisciplinarity as over-interpretation through the metaphor of the 'missing link', both in its evolutionary context and, more generally, as a way of thinking the experience of 'missing connections'. The Victorians became obsessed with the evolutionary implications of the missing link because it suggested that their 'humanness' was contaminated by their 'relationship' to the apes. But, as Beer makes clear, what underlies the Victorians' obsession is the peculiar logic of the 'missing link' as a general metaphor for division and boundary with its strange power to attract *and* repel *at the same time*: 'The idea of the missing link. . . . Was as much a way of reinforcing distance as it was of seeking out connection' (Beer, 1992: 37). As division, boundary, the missing link is an impossible site, a displacement rather than a placement, that haunts every aspect of human activity. And what we call *organizing* or *regenerating* is really the continuous contention or agonistics generated by the betweenness and heterogeneity of the missing link: 'The human psyche may need always the monstrous to reject, that other which lurks inside the self to be split off as enemy. The desire to expel, reify, and control' (Beer, 1992: 23–24). This, of course, is yet another way of expressing Samuel Weber's (1987: 33) argument that the conscious human subject is contextualized by forces which 'it can neither fully assimilate nor totally exclude'. But, for Beer, the significance of interdisciplinarity is that it keeps open the intrinsic tensions of the missing link—in other worlds, it keeps the link always missing. In this way, knowledge of our world is kept always alive, always irresolvable, transgressive. And, further, interdisciplinarity is more than a field of tensions— it reflects an intense human need to question, to problematize, to doubt. Or, as Beer has it, to *inauthenticate*: '*Inauthenticating*, keeping belief wavering, making monsters, or fictions . . . (may be) a more intense need than authentication or discovery' (Beer, 1992: 41, original emphasis); the need to *become*, to *interstand*.

## Imagination

Interdisplinarity as interstanding implies imagination—the relaxing of systemness with its divisions and disciplines, and the creating of more open, fluid fields of knowing. Imagination is Ehrenzweig's (1967) unfocused, de-differentiated form of knowing—a way of interstanding that 'sees' the indeterminate, the subliminal. The loosening up of determinate systemness was Samuel Butler's theme in his satirical novel, *Erewhon* (1970, but first published 1872). Butler was an active critic of Darwin's evolutionary biology—especially its deterministic bias and its distinction between the organic and the inorganic. Butler could not accept this distinction between 'life' and 'non-life', and argued for their equivalence. Instead, he posited the world as a dynamic, interactive *self-organizing* system that *becomes* in an indeterminate environment. It's this point that leads me to Butler's novel, *Erewhon*. *Erewhon* is the story of an English traveller, Higgs, who crosses a giant mountain range to discover the remote country of Erewhon. The inhabitants of Erewhon abhor systemness and simple location. For example, the Erewhonian institutions of higher learning—the so-called Colleges of Unreason—insist that Unreason is commutual with Reason: 'Unreason is a part of reason: it must therefore be allowed its full share in stating the initial conditions' (Butler, 1970: 188). The Professors of Unreason call the co-implication of Reason and Unreason a 'double currency', thus recalling the ambivalence and ambiguity of interstanding and over-interpretation. The static and the separate are the marks of Reason: 'Reason betrays men into the drawing of hard and fast lines. . . . Extremes are alone logical; but they are always absurd; the mean is illogical, but an illogical mean is better than the sheer absurdity of an extreme' (Butler, 1979: 187).

The Erewhonian educational system is based on 'hypothetics' which, briefly, is thinking in terms of *possibilities*. Education should not be limited to learning about things—that's merely factual knowledge. It should be about imagining contingencies and possibilities. Hypothetics is the science of possibilities, as opposed to the science of actualities. Hypothetics as the recognition and cultivation of possibilities is also basic to Butler's intellectual strategy in *Erewhon* itself. For Erewhon is almost literally the inverse of 'nowhere'—a place that *might be* or *could be*, a place that is a *potential* space but which nowhere actually exists. Butler's hypothetics is Deleuze's *becoming*, which always occurs in a potential space of multiple interactions: 'In a multiplicity what counts are not the terms or the elements, but what there is "between", the between, a set of relations that are not separate from each other' (Deleuze and Parnet, 1987: viii). For Butler, for Deleuze, imagination begins with the idea of *reflection* and the endless potential of relations for combinability and permutability, and continues as a rhizome of possibilities. There are, thus, only beginnings, becomings—and, therefore, no ends, no endings.

Butler's argument recurs in the more modern guise of information theory, especially in the way that this has been employed by Umberto Eco (1989) in the context of modern art analysis. Where Butler talks about 'nowhere' and Deleuze of the rhizome, Eco talks about the 'open work' with its stress on multiplicity and unfinished becoming. Eco's open work is the work of the indeterminate. And Eco expresses the openness of indeterminacy through the concept of information as used in information theory. (It's important here to recognize that, for information theory, information is also a definition of *organization*, i.e. the construction and maintenance of pattern out of chaos, dissipation). Information is defined by probability—information is what's *least probable*. The less likely a message of event, the more information it provides. Novelty and surprise thus constitute information. It's this point that Eco picks up as a feature of his concept of the open work. But Eco transforms the idea of improbability into *possibility*—information—organization becomes 'the dialectic between *form* and the *possibility* of multiple meanings' (Eco, 1989: 60). Possibility is a consequence of the indeterminate, while probability is a function of the determinate, of systemness. And just like Beer's (1992) stressing of the human need to *inauthenticate*, Eco says that modern culture is inherently attracted to the indeterminate, to 'all those processes which, instead of relying on a univocal, necessary sequence of events, prefer to disclose a field of possibilities, to create "ambiguous" situations open to all sorts of operative choices and interpretations' (Eco, 1989: 44). In other words, the imagination feeds unceasingly on the indeterminate, on possibilities and improbabilities. **Or,** better, the imagination *sees* possibilities and even *creates* them.

Finally, you ask how thinkers like Derrida, Foucault and Deleuze relate to other influences like Olson, Whitehead and Heidegger. It is well known that Derrida and Foucault were variously preoccupied with central aspects of Heidegger's thought, though there are no direct connections between their work and that of Olson and Whitehead (although Deleuze does sometimes call on certain features of Whitehead's process philosophy). But it is possible to see a fundamental community of thought among these writers if one approaches them through the philosophy of modern science. Not much attention has been given to the implications of quantum theory and Heisenberg's Uncertainty principle for the social sciences. But if we examine what these findings actually say, it does not take much imagination to see their relevance to certain themes highlighted in post-structuralist social thinking, including that of the writers discussed here. Ambiguity, ambivalence, duplicity, oscillation, heterogeneity, etc. are all features of modern science's revealing of reality as unstable and even illusory. Quantum theory in particular reminds us that there is no objective world, that the human agent *participates* in a construction of the world, that our representatives are simply convenient pictures that stand in for reality, so that the map is never the territory. Actor and acted-on are complicitous, inextricably intertwined. All this is strangely like Deleuze's *becoming* and Taylor's *interstanding*, where the *'between'* becomes the 'intertwined'. And it's also like the participation we've noted in Olson's 'projective art', where the actor's senses and organs participate in the field of action. The 'participative universe' of modern science is, again, reflected in Heidegger's ideas of *Ereignis* and the Open. *Ereignis* is participation in the sense of 'mutual reflecting' or the 'mirror play' of the world—Heidegger's way of saying interstanding and becoming. The German *Ereignis* is also another way of saying the English *origin, organ,* and *organize*. In this interpretation, *origin, organ* and *organize* are—like Eco's 'open work'—strategies and devices for opening up possibilities. Heidegger illustrates this with the example of the body and its organs. The body is *part* of—or *participator* in—a mutually reflecting field of possibilities. The mouth, for example, 'is not merely a kind of organ of the body understood as an organism—body and mouth are part of the earth's flow and growth in which we mortals flourish' (Heidegger, 1971: 98). The 'earth's flow and growth' is an infinite, unfinished process—it's Heidegger's concept of the Open, which is never closed. Mouth and body are *origins-organs* which *organize* continuous interstanding of the possible. The mouth reaches out to the world through language and its infinite openings and possibilities: 'Language is the flower of the mouth', says Heidegger (1971: 99).

The pliable, plastic, open and indeterminate character of modern science's reality offers us a way—perhaps a generic methodology—of bringing together (or interstanding) the other thinkers named in your question. Foucault's space of seeing and Derrida's space of writing are both translatable into the philosophical language of modern science. But this is a challenge that still remains to be taken up.

## Editors' Note

All the references for these interview sections can be found after the final interview extract, 'Main features of my approach . . .', in section 15.

# 6  Information, Communication And Organisation

## A Post-structural Revision

*Robert Cooper*

('Information, Communication and organization: a Post Structural Revision', 1987, *The Journal of Mind and Behaviour*, 8, 395–416. Grateful thanks to the editor of the journal for permission to reprint this piece.)

The concepts of information and communication are analysed in terms of "difference". The essence of difference is self-interference, a process in which terms contain their opposites and thus defy any *singular* grasp of their meanings. To illustrate this way of looking at difference, concepts from psychoanalysis, the logic of infinite sets, language, etc., are discussed. Social organisation is fundamentally motivated by the need to supress the self-interference intrinsic to difference and it does this through the creation of social objects/objectives. The specific function of the object/objective is to banish self-interference by separating its self-referential duality. This characterises a basic principle of human action: the principle of least effort. The function of modern organisation is the objectification of least effort in a codified order of information/knowledge which is designed to exclude self-interference from organised social systems. But since "organisation" and "object" are also information-based structures, they too are subject to self-interference. This means that the object/objective is compelled to repeat that which it suppresses and so creates a process in which intentional actions produce unintended as well as intended consequences.

Information, communication and organisation are terms that are fundamental to the thesaurus of modern systems theory (Buckley, 1967) but there is a developing debate as to their precise meaning. For systems theory, information is seen as a commodity which, when exchanged, serves the needs of both social actors and system, for whom it therefore has functional value. It is meaning and relevance of information *for the system* that is emphasised. In recent years, the critical interventions of post-structuralist thought have brought about a radical revision of the system-centered view of human discourse (e.g., Derrida, 1973; Foucault, 1970) substituting for it (1) a conceptualisation of language (the organisation of information and communication) as a process that actually originates and structures human experience in contrast to the functional view of language as a mere vehicle for human interaction, and (2) a characterisation of language as a structure of material marks or sounds which are in themselves "undecidable" and *upon which meaning has to be imposed*. I want to argue here that these conceptual displacements have significant implications for the way in which the social sciences understand social organisation and that the key concept for this analysis is information and its correlation of communication and organisation.

The current mobilisation in the field of information technology seems likely to be accompanied in the social sciences by a closer look at the nature of information itself. Already there are signs that this is happening, especially in that intellectual movement identified as "postmodernism" (a form of post-structuralism) which seeks to ground information and knowledge in a process of perceptual demurrage and instability (e.g., Lyotard, 1984). Of course, informational and cybernetic concepts are now part of the tradition in several areas of social science such the psychology of information-processing (e.g., Attneave, 1959) and social anthropology (e.g., Lévi-Strauss, 1966), as well as systems theory. What seems to be new in the present questioning is the recognition of an implicit and therefore hidden assumption in the traditional approaches: that of an origin or source which provides a legitimating order for the processing and understanding of information. In social science, this covert assumption is most evident in systems theory where the concept of an ordered system legitimizes everything that comes within its purview, to such an extent that "system" is deemed "natural". Postmodernism reveals that such systems are based on a metanarrative which privileges unity, simplicity and communicability (Lyotard, 1984). One could go further and suggest that the real object of systems theory is *systemness* per se—individuals, groups, and societies are simply media for the expression of systemness. This observation reveals a significant tautology: in taking systemness as such as its object, systems theory repeats what it sets out to understand. Repetition, as we know from psychoanalysis, is that process which presupposes itself (Lacan, 1977a) but which gives the impression of revealing that which is already objectively constituted in the external world. In systems thinking, a presupposition of systemness organises the world in its own image and this has important consequences for how we define information. Let us note that information theory itself defines information in terms of probability: that which is least likely gives the most information. Now, probability is the expression of an assumed pre-existing order which rests on the idea of the expected and the certain, i.e., the reoccurrence of that which is already known. Like repetition, probability is a form of prediction or prior awareness which defends the system against the strange and the unknown; the system is therefore incapable of dealing with information that is non-probabilistic and unpremeditated. Information in this latter sense has the character of surprise, of a sudden and involuntary seizure of the attention by a force beyond conscious control—such as the "in-flashing" of spontaneous insight that Heidegger (1949/1977) contrasts to the patient building-up that characterises rational-instrumental-knowledge and the similar instantaneous process of unconcealment-concealment through which the psychoanalytical unconscious reveals itself (Lacan, 1977a). The possibility of surprise is represented in the informational formula which reduces uncertainty to unpredictability. Prediction and control become definitive components in the transformation of information into systemized knowledge. As such systemized knowledge, systems theory is itself predestined to neuter and exclude the eruption of information that would spell disaster for its own reassuring certainty. Surprise as the deconstruction of a familiar order can only emerge if there exists an attitude which permits a degree of distantiation from the routinizing or normalising operations of the system.

Since such normalising pressures appear also to structure the sciences as producers or reproducers of "normal" information (e.g., Kuhn, 1970), one is tempted to ask to what extent the social sciences themselves are characterised by the very objects which they study and the degree to which their language and concepts are mobilised (perhaps at times unwittingly) in order to master the uncertainty intrinsic to information in its material aspect (i.e., the undecidability of the material marl referred to above). Much of Heidegger's work can be seen as an analysis of the suppression of surprise in modern life (including science) in which key ontological concepts have become "empty words and evanescent vapours" of a language that is worn out and used up and which is now merely "an indispensable but masterless means of communication that may be used as one pleases, as indifferent as a means of public transport, as a street car which everyone rides in" (Heidegger, 1935/1959, p. 51). In this process, language as the material expression of information has to be secured against the possibility of doubt and undecidability (Heidegger, 1949/1977, especially pp. 115–154). It would not be difficult to illustrate Heidegger's indictment from the literature of social science, especially that which is directed by the systems paradigm whose functional emphasis serves to expel the contrarieties endemic to social life and so to homogenize it. One outstanding common feature of systems-based thinking is its refusal to analyse the fine-grain of its key concepts, as though a hardening of the critical arteries afflicts the systemic mind when it observes its own fabric.

This recognition is reflected in certain well-known criticisms of systems-orientated sociology. In particular, the work of the sociologist Peter Blau has been censured for viewing social structure and social exchange in purely systemic-functional terms which gloss over the complexities intrinsic to social processes (Douglas and Isherwood, 1978). This glazing process can be clearly seen in Blau's (1964) work on formal organisation and perhaps especially in his glossing of the concept of "differentiation" in organisational structure. By differentiation Blau means the division of labour (specialisation) and authority. In the present context, the significance of Blau's approach lies in his attempt to pin down the concept of organisation through operational measures without actually understanding the full significance of the concept of differentiation which appears to be the mainstay of his theory of organisation. We know from the work of Derrida (1973) that the idea of difference has a dialectical character covering a spatio-temporal complex which includes "to differ" (in space) and "to defer" (postpone in time) and that what is deferred in difference is the function of an original, undifferentiated whole. All this is excluded from Blau's picture because he does not stop to examine the ontological structure of his basic terms. Blau appears not to realise that the informational pedigree of a particular social analysis first on a thorough understanding of the onto-logic of its basic concept. To the extent that one glosses over these, sacrificing the problematic in favour of systemic unity and ease of comprehension, then to that extent one leaves out a true understanding of social life.

Currently a new dimension is being added to this issue: systems theory seems headed for a new lease of life with the development of advanced information technology which enhances the possibility of actualising cybernetic models of "performactivity" (Lyotard, 1984). The significance of performativity in relation to information and knowledge is that it makes possible the more efficient suppression of the surprise factor of information since more or less everything is administered according to a principle of *pre-formance* (i.e., performance). This is already a feature of those modern institutions we call formal organisations; but whereas up until the present time these have been largely concerned with the application of know-how to the administration and management of physical commodities (labour, raw, materials), it seems likely that knowledge as an informational objective in its own right will chiefly characterise postmodern organisations. Already the instrument which structures and serves to maintain information as a domesticated and reassuring novelty, as opposed to information as the uncanny violation of the normal, organisation will increasingly become the pre-formation—and therefore routinisation—of system-relevant information on a world scale. In this context, information is not communicated but programmed—for what is already established through systematic pre-formation is unitary, simple and therefore comprehensive to all; the contradictions, paradoxes and other tropes that create surprise are ironed out and smoothed over; and dissensus as a feature of communication is illegitmated. It would appear that it is high time for the disinterment and resuscitation of information (and its components) as a pre-systemic possibility.

## INFORMATION AND DIVISION

The concept of information is well-known thought it is construed in different ways (e.g., Brown, 1969; Buckley, 1967). However, one can say with confidence that information is essentially a *binary structure*, based on the idea of division. The human world is constituted by such divisions, e.g., man-woman, teacher-student, day-night, summer-winter, etc. There are two ways of interpreting division: (1) by placing the emphasis on the two separate terms, or (2) by focusing on the actual process of division itself. Experience suggests that people tend to do (1) i.e., they perceive the world in the disjunctive mode of systemic-functionalism. To focus on (2) requires a conscious effort in order to see that division is not merely an act of separation but is also an undifferentiated state in which its terms are actually joined together, i.e., *division* both *separates* and *joins*. In fact, it is the act of separation which paradoxically, creates the perception of something that is also whole or unitary. This observation—of fundamental significance in understanding the nature of information—can be more clearly seen in reversible figure-ground patterns such as Rubin's (1921) double profiles which illustrate the separation-wholeness paradox of information: a rectangle is divided into two halves by a wavy line running down its middle. Either the right half can be seen as a human face looking to the left or the left can be seen as a face looking to the right. While the separate faces share the same profile, at the same time they repress each other in the sense that the perception of one face is always at the expense of the other.

No longer a simple binary structure, information now appears as the sharing or alternation of a whole between two terms. It is the idea of alternation or reversibility that distinguishes information. With this recognition we have gone beyond the commonly held definition of information as merely useful knowledge and have revealed its ontological structure. The reversibility of Rubin's profiles suggests a model of information which reveals the latter's essentially interactional, even dialectical, nature: a process in which form (each face) is wrested out of non-form (the shared line which fuses—and therefore confuses—the two profiles). Form is: bounded, framed, fixed, certain, finite, made firm. Non-form is: infirm, informed, vacillating, uncertain, infinite.

It is instructive to note how the form/non-form relationship is traditionally dealt with in information theory. Form is given privileged status, so that non-form is treated as a purely abject process. For example, in Attneave (1959, p. 1) we learn the "uncertainty" is tantamount to "ignorance" (i.e., not knowing the probability of an event) and that "shared information "(or "interaction") is defined as a problem in predicting the transmission of information from one or more variables to another in which the transmitted information predicates (stated beforehand) its own outcomes, i.e., repeats itself.[1] In other words, information is that which is added to what we *already know* and it is therefore the *already known*—the presupposition—which, as we have noted, repeats itself. Information becomes the exorcising of doubt through the apotheosis of certainty or the "solace of good forms" (Lyotard, 1984, p. 81). Information theory can offer no insight into the real nature of the uncertain, which requires that quality which the poet Keats (1947) called "negative capability"—"when a man is capable of being in uncertainties, mysteries, doubts, without any irritable reaching after fact and reason" (p. 72). To understand uncertainty in this latter sense it is necessary to turn to Freud's mapping of the unconscious in psychoanalysis.

## PSYCHOANALYSIS AND THE UNCERTAINTY OF INFORMATION

Psychoanalysis can be viewed as a complete reversal of information theory; whereas the latter, as we have seen, approaches the uncertain from the perspective of the certain, psychoanalysis maintains that the certain may only be understood as a derivation of the uncertain, i.e., the unconscious. The unconscious *causes* form not in any lineal, determination sense but as an originating void or chaos ("cause" comes from the Greek *chaos*[2]) which has to be covered over, as it were, to remain covert. Without elaborating the obvious complexities behind these brief points, some insight into the vacillatory and uncertain character of the unconscious can be obtained from Blanco's (1975) representation of it as a structure of infinite sets. Drawing on the mathematician Dedekind's definition of the infinite set, Blanco distinguishes the unconscious as that which treats relations as essentially "infinite" (unfinished, unformed, uncertain): in infinite logic, relations are symmetric, i.e., the converse of any relation is identical with the relation and therefore the part identical to the whole. The work of the painter Magritte provides some of the most striking examples of such infinite structures (see Foucault, 1982): the representation of a pair of women's shoes takes on the shape of the feet that they are meant to cover (*La Philosophie dans le Boudoir*); a ship at sea not only looks like a ship but its hull and sails are composed of the very waves it rests on (*La Seducteur*); the leaf of a tree assumes the shape of the tree so that one sees the tree as the leaf (*L'Incendie*). However, the fact that one normally sees Magritte's pictures in art galleries or books helps to neutralise their surprise or shock value for there they can be denied their uncanny, disquieting power by being dismissed as mere works of artifice.

It is precisely this infinite dimension of the unconscious that is responsible for the experience of surprise as a revelation of the uncanny. Such is the pervasiveness of the systems paradigm in those social science disciplines that deal with form, structure, uncertainty, etc., that it is necessary to go outside institutionalised social science in order to find that literature which has kept alive the tradition of information as the "infinite" source of surprise and shock; psychoanalysis (Freud, Lacan), philosophy (Foucault, Deleuze), art (Magritte, Rauschenberg), literary theory and semiology (Hassan, Barthes). But it is perhaps in the work of Freud that we find the richest source of enlightenment on the complex ramifications and dynamics of this facet of information. In his essay *Beyond the Pleasure Principle*, Freud (1920/1955) argues that the unconscious is characterised by a "compulsion to repeat" itself. In the example of repetition we have already used, the repetition compulsion is expressed in terms of the literature of systems theory which presupposes a system existing in its own right "out there." However, a basic uncertainty informs the relationship between systems theory itself and the systems it purports to talk about so that it is not possible to say *with certainty* which term is the actual system; a kind of vacillating interaction occurs between the two to produce an uncanny merging that causes surprise such as we also saw in Rubin's alternating profiles. The conscious mind functions as a protective shield against threatening stimuli from the outside world by ordering these in *certain* (i.e., "knowable") spatio-temporal arrangements; by this means consciousness reduces or completely neutralises the surprise or shock impact intrinsic to stimuli in much the same way that the uncanny content of a Magritte painting undergoes censorship.

In thinking of information as a reversible whole that vacillates between two terms, we highlight two forms of action: (1) a *primary process* which is a conflation and negation of the individual terms—the interactive mix of common line in Rubin's profiles, and (2) a *secondary process* which supresses primary activity by accenting the individual terms—the separate faces of Rubin's figure. Information can now be more formally conceptualised as a dynamic relationship *between* primary and secondary process. The significance of psychoanalysis—especially in the present context—lies in recognising that human action revolves around the primary/secondary complex as a subversion of that rational mode of thought which privileges conscious control; instead, consciousness is viewed as being subject to an autonomous and automatic force (Freud's *Treib*) which, already built into the very mark of difference as an alternating structure, impels the subject to come down on either one side or the other; paradoxically, choice itself, at this level, is forced on one, i.e., the subject has no choice but to be conscious.

The principle of the unconscious as a manifestation of the forces inherent in difference has been exhaustively articulated by Lacan (e.g., 1977a) who has also bought out the temporal uncertainty characteristics of primary process which reveals itself only through the sudden stealth of surprise. (The classic example here is the joke which takes us unawares in what Freud [1905/1060] describes as an automatism that is beyond rational control.) Information in the psychoanalytical sense, then, is uncertainty which reveals itself only in the unconscious moment of surprise where there is an unexpected experience of obstruction or failure in that which normally makes sense.

## COMMUNICATION AS THE DISCOURSE OF DIFFERENCE

Communication is normally understood as the transmission of information between two terms. But if information is defined as the division of a primary system (a reversible whole), then communication has to be understood as a process which is characterised by the division of that primary system. In fact, communication can be quite properly seen as a continuous attempt to fill in the gaps and holes (not the reversibility at work in the meanings of *whole* and *hole*) made in the primary process by the secondary process.

Social life is characterised by what many be called "taking on the differences." Difference is simply another way of talking about information (Bateson, 1972). The process of taking on the difference can be seen spelled out in Freud's work on sexuality, for one of the first and most significant differences in human life is the early recognition of the male and female signs. Taking on the difference then proceeds throughout social life: teacher-pupil, friend-enemy, producer-consumer, etc. Thus, entry into the social system occurs by taking on the difference. A difference, as we have also argued, structures a primary reversible whole (i.e., a non-difference) which, however, can never be directly and immediately known since its realisation depends upon its being differentiated or divided. In other words, the primary whole is always a lost whole, one which we can only see through the work of division. The recognition of male-female difference, for example, leads back to the idea of a lost androgynous state which can only be known mythically. Such lost states represent the "originary voids" that constitute the informational project of communication. Reference to Rubin's double profile will help in understanding this idea. One profile is necessarily always incomplete because it shares the same space as the other profile so that neither profile can share the same space *at the same time*, that is, the *other* is always lost; but since it completes the other *other* it must be found again, although the logic of the primary process has to deny this possibility. Communication is therefore always based in the experience of lack or loss (see also Cooper, 1983). Communication now becomes a process in which two partial terms are trying to find some sense of wholeness. It is no longer the mere functional transmission of information or signs.

This approach aligns communication with language. It is central to the anti-functionalist argument presented here that language itself is structured around the sense of a primal lost unity or originary void; it is not just a vehicle for social exchange. Etymologically, "language" is cognate with a series of words which derive from the Greek *logos*, whose rot gives *lack*, *link*, *linga*, etc. In semiology and structural linguistics, language is see as the communication of *signs*—but a sign is simply another name for a division, a difference, or a distinction. When one signifies one distinguishes, hence the act of signification is that of dividing a prior of undifferentiated whole. This is the basis of social organisation where people relate to each other (i.e., *signify* to each other) the needs or lacks created by the structural necessity of division. In short, a language is premised on some such conception of a lost whole or lack.

It is precisely this intuition of a relationship between language (or communication) and loss that the young Lukács (1974) brought out in his essay on "Longing and Form," especially in the idea that form is always a kind of longing or desire for completeness: "Longing and love are the search for one's own lost other half" (p. 92). Lukács was but a step away from linking the etymologies of "longing" and "language" for to long is to want to belong and belonging is a form of communication. Lukács idea that form is a desire for completeness is simply another way of expressing the psychoanalytic view of information uncertainty (the unconscious) in terms of infinite logic (see previous section): the infinite is complete by virtue of its mutuality between part and whole which is resistant to division and separation. Lukács image of form thus echoes the completeness of Rubin's shared profiles.

To help us formalise these general insights on the relationship between language and lack, we can draw on de Saussure's (1974) view of language as a system of differences in which the human subject is portrayed as an effect of the language system rather than its cause; this is the same as saying that the speaking system is realised through the mechanism of division or information and, far from being a self-sufficient unit in itself (i.e., a whole), is identifiable only through its differences from other terms in the system. What is more, these differences are inscribed as social marks upon the human subject's material body and property (in effect, the process of taking on the differences already mentioned); this is how the subject is enabled to "speak" to other differences in the system. Since the subject's actualisation of itself is so utterly dependent upon the mark of difference, it would be more correct to say that the subject is difference.[3] In other words, language is not rooted in the object per se, in the external and objective world, but in the act and process of division which inaugurates the active subject as a lack which seeks its completion in the lack of the other.

In his discussion of the function and nature of speech and language in psychoanalysis, Lacan (1977b) explicates a similar thesis, particularly in the dictum that language is the discourse of the other. Lacan expresses the essential process of repetition at work in language in the following lapidary sentence: "Human language . . . constitutes a communication in which the sender receives his own message back from the receiver in an inverted form" (p. 85). Thus, when a subject states "you are my wife" he marks himself with the seal of wedlock and designates himself as a husband. Speech always subjectively includes its own reply, says Lacan, and in this way repeats *itself*.[4] Implicit in his model of communication is the idea of *agonistic interaction* in which the active subject has to struggle (sometimes playfully, sometimes seriously) with the appropriating other. Agonistics is not a form of relationship which can be comprehended in the traditional information-theoretic conception of communication. As Lacan points out:

The more the function of language becomes neutralised as it moves closer to information, the more language is imputed to be laden with *redundancies*. This notion of redundancy in language originated in research that was all the more precise because a vested interest was involved, having been prompted by the economic problems of long-distance communication, and in particular that of the possibility of carrying several conversations at once on a single telephone line. It can be asserted that a substantial portion of the phonetic materials is superfluous[5] to the realisation of the communication actually sought.

(Lacan, 1977b, p. 86)

Thus, economic and technological exigencies cast in the systems mode expunge the factor of excess, on which agonistics rests, as a useless redundancy. Interestingly and in a different context, Lyotard (1984) makes a similar criticism: "the trivial cybernetic version of information theory misses out something of decisive importance . . . : the agonistic aspect of society"(p. 16). The cybernetic model of an informational system which epitomizes the performativity criterion of systems theory is aptly exemplified by Lacan (1977b) in the language system of bees as decoded by Karl von Frisch. When the bee returns to his hive from gathering honey it communicates to its co-workers the location and distance from the hive of the honey source by means of highly routinized dances which in are in effect signal systems. But these signal systems, precisely "because of the fixed correlation of their signs to the reality that they signify" (Lacan, 1977b, p. 84), do not include that property of unconscious repetition that especially distinguishes the language of human subjectivity as an activity of renewal and decline. What is respected is subject to the law of informational loss for what we already know cannot inform us; the joke said again loses its power of surprise. Repetition is therefore a demand for the new and unknown which results from the decline or decay of information into the customary and habitual;[6] the language of bees works precisely because it *excludes* the unknown; human language works for the reason that it *includes* the unknown.[7] Furthermore, while these stereotyped messages determine the behaviour of each bee as a locus in the network of performance, there is no retransmitting of the message to another bee. "This means that the message remains fixed (in its function as a relay of the action, from which no subject detaches it as a symbol of communication itself" (Lacan, 1977b, p. 85). In other words, there is no repetition from which agonistic interaction can emerge.

All this permits us to advance the idea of there being two basic (but here didactically exaggerated) models of information and communication underlying current conceptions of social organisation: (1) a *systemic-functional model* in which psychic and social energy is fast bound in a fixed system of signals which leaves no room for agonistic interaction and surprise; information is already constituted by the fixed relationship between signs and referent; performativity is the key criterion, which makes the system fit only for busy bees; it is though Freud's secondary system has been wrenched from its symbiosis with primary process and preserved in aspic (from the Greek *asphyxia*); and (2) an *agonistic model*, marked by the contestation of difference, in which psychic-social energy runs freely to subvert the idea of there being a permanent seal between sign and referent and hence to reject the idea of a fixed unchangeable totality or meta-system; information is see as an infinitude and therefore full of surprise; rules come *after* the event and not *before*; secondary system works with but follows primary process.

All information "can be stored and transmitted only by being inscribed on a matter-energy base" (Wilden, 1982, p. 2). Social organisation includes the transformation, use and exchange of matter and energy. It also includes the production, consumption, exchange and reproduction of information (Wilden, 1982, p. 2). Organisation, therefore, works at two levels: the material and the informational. But there is a sense in which the informational level is more basic than the material level: matter-energy can only be conceived and expressed through information, for in order to know it one must name it (as we do here, for instance). In other words, information subjects matter-energy to the process of division described earlier. Now, a definitive feature of social organisation is that human beings themselves constitute a significant component of the matter-energy base); that is, human beings constitute the raw material of their own organisation so that they too are subjected to the process of division that characterises information. They thus pose to themselves the paradox of self-identity which faces any subject that is compelled to take itself as its own object.

This question can be further elaborated in Brown's (1969) example of the physicist whose subject matter is the physical world. The world described by the physicist "consists of a number of fundamental particles which, if shot through their own space, appear as waves . . . and other wave forms called electromagnetic which (travel) through space with a standard velocity" (pp. 104–105). Now the physicist him or herself is made up of the very factors he or she describes and is bound together by and has to obey the very laws that he or she records. The world (i.e., the subject, subject matter) thus appears to be constructed in order to see itself. In this process, the world

> Must first cut itself up into at least one state which sees, and at least one other state which is seen. In this severed and mutilated condition, whatever it sees is only *partially* itself. We may take it that the world undoubtedly is itself (i.e., is indistinct from itself), but in any attempt to see itself as object, it must, equally undoubtedly, act so as to make itself distinct from, and therefore false to itself
>
> (Brown, 1969, p. 105).

The state of being indistinct from itself is equivalent to the unity or wholeness which we suggested earlier is basic to the communications process of social organisation and which, as Brown indicates, is lots in the subject's obligatory act of dividing itself from itself.

The logic of this position can be more clearly brought out through the example of the symbol. The symbol is essentially a material mark (such as these letter on this page) which is characterised by an intrinsic division;

Rubin's alternating profiles represent such a symbol. As a divided mark, the symbol is evenly informed i.e., it contains within itself is own opposite. Typographers, for example, recognise the same idea in the enclosed white backgrounds of printed letters which they call counters. The opposite or counter is really a "sub-version (turning under) of the surface upon which it is written" (Brown, 1969, p. 100) and is therefore a formation within (in-formation) of what it expresses. As such, the symbol "is thus informed in the sense of having its own form within it, and at the same time informed in the sense of remembering what has happened to it in the past" (p. 100). The symbol is thus the precursor of the more complex and varied forms of infor-mation that we find in social life. However, these latter may only be taken as tokens or expressions (the common understanding of symbol) of some other more primitive form whose sub-ject (since it lies under) they represent. From this perspective, information is intrinsic to and already contained within the symbol. Significantly, information is not a product of the social agent, rather the reverse since it is the agent who is produced by the symbol. More radically, we may say that in assuming the symbol (or taking on the differ-ences), it is not the agent who "thinks" but something more fundamental, namely the structure of the symbol itself. In this sense thought is automatic and the thinking agent repeats an over which he or she has no direct, con-scious control. The symbol thinks itself. In its thinking, the symbol follows, a double action: it censors (to cense, a now obsolete word but cognate with "sense", which meant "to think") or strike out its opposite or counter while at the same time necessarily hiding and thus preventing that which it cen-sors: moreover; it must do this continuously or repeatedly.

Information thus divides the subject onto an *active* state that sees, thinks, etc., and a passive state that is seen, thought, etc. The paradox of self-identity is that the state of seeing or thinking can never see or think itself, for when it tries to do so it must necessarily take itself as its own object and thus lose sight of its active subjectivity. It is appropriate, therefore, to distinguish two forms of the subject: the *primary subject*, unconscious and indeterminate, and the *secondary subject* which is in effect the object of con-scious, determinate thought. Human organisation is now more specifically the process of producing and reproducing the *objects* (which are also *objec-tives*) by means of which a group or society can see or think itself; for this reason, Lévi-Strauss (1966) defined social objects as "good to think with" rather than merely goods to use or consume.

It will be clear from this analysis of symbolic structure that the symbol is based on the infinite logic which, as we noted earlier, Blanco (1975) used to characterize the unconscious and in which relations are symmetric, i.e., the converse of any relation is identical with the relation and therefore the part is identical to the whole. This conception of the symbolic especially reveals its "self-interfering" character which also epitomizes Derrida's idea of undecidability: that which contains its opposite and thus refuses any *sin-gular* grasp of its meaning. Thus, this aspect of the symbolic is a refusal of thought since thought can only emerge in the perception of singularities. It is precisely this suppression of self-interference or undecidability which Zipf (1965) argues is constitutive of the *object* or *objective* in human action. Thought is always harried by the intrinsic opposition in Rubin's profiles so that, as Zipf notes, the perception or pursuit of one aspect precludes or frustrates the perception of the other aspect. The function of the object or objective is to close off the other or second aspect in order to attain what Zipf calls the singleness of the objective (p. 3). It is this that characterizes a basic principle of human action which Zipf terms the principle of least effort. The sophism here is that least effort is not an act of efficiency or even of laziness but is essential to the self's process of realizing itself by detaching itself from the vacillating duality of the symbol; in order to be and to act, one has to take the lesser part of the whole. Now, wholeness in this context is the same as Brown's condition of indistinctness noted above and this is also another way of thinking about Zipf's observation that the object's singularity can only be realised through the suppression of another potential object with which it is compounded. In other words, the object is the result of an activity that counters or strikes out its double; in this sense, the object is that which *objects*, otherwise it would be so entangled with *itself* that would be lost to knowledge. The subject (whether individual, group or system) is necessarily an object constructed out of the uncertainty of division in order to provide a stable identity which is lacking in the primary subject. The surprise and shock experienced at the uncanny character of the primary has now to be seen as a potential danger to the subject since, it its continuous vacillations (its doublings, splittings and fading), the primary's very appearance eludes perception and hence implies a crisis of cognition and of phenomenality. It is this crisis that organisation seeks to avert through the *construction* of objects of knowledge. Now, every construction is also a *perception* (Bachelard, 1934) and that which is prepared is a form of defence *in advance* against the uncertainty of the primary (see also the discussion of information and probability), Lacan (1977a, p. 214) reminds us that that the *par* of "prepare" means to defend, to be vigilant. Conscious knowledge is not now merely fixed and certain information but a structure for deferring surprise; one must take surprise, as it were, and not to be *taken* by it, and one does this by *pre-venting* (i.e., coming *before*) it. Thus, the object of organisation is never just a utilitarian product or service as it is conceived in the naïve interpretations of the systemic functional model but rather the preparation of objects by means of which the system can distinguish itself from its primary subject and, therefore, be certain of itself.

## MODERN ORGANISATION AND PERFORMATIVITY

It is said that industrial societies are entering a new phase in the social-economic process in which the commodity as the discrete object of production is being displaced by systems of information and knowledge. In *The Coming of Post-Industrial Society*, Bell (1973) charts the case for the new social forms based on information and knowledge. In the first instance, the change is from a goods-producing to a service economy, especially in the areas of health, education, research and government. The knowledge that characterizes these areas is essentially *theoretical* and it is this fact that mars off post-industrial society from previous societies. Of course, earlier societies depended on knowledge, as all societies must, but the nature of that knowledge was non-theoretical, intuitive, know-how, often handed down from generation to generation. The chemical industry is cited as the first of the truly modern industries to illustrate the intricate linking of science and technology: it is necessary to have a theoretical understanding of the macro molecules being manipulated in order to bring about chemical synthesis (the recombination and transformation of compounds).

Post-industrialism tends towards a more systemised society in which people live increasingly communal existences, bound together by their dependencies on organised systems which run on information. This entails the need to master "scale" or the distribution of information over space and time by means of new technological devices such as real-time computer information or new kinds of quantitative programming (Bell, 1973). The general effect is to reduce differences by making everything instantaneously present and therefore, unitary. But performance rather than size is the distinguishing feature of post-industrial systems. The defining feature of performance is what Bell calls the economizing mode, most clearly seen in the idea of productivity: more for less effort and/or less cost. The special significance of the modern corporation is that it has created and universalized the idea of performance as *a mode of ordering social relations*.

It would be wrong to limit the analysis of functional rationality to the simple pursuit of efficiency per se, for what is really presented here is a *modus vivendi* as well as a *modus operandi*. It is not the mere fact that modern organisations are mechanisms for pursuing their objectives efficiently that is significant but rather that they have created, maintained and indeed universalized the idea of efficiency as a way of life and thought. In short, they *objectify* the systemic-functional model. In this conceptual switch we see that functional performance has been raised to a principle of performativity (Lyotard, 1984). Performativity may be superficially concerned with systemic efficiency and rationality but its latent purpose is to authenticate its own solidarity through the suppression of difference. Let us recall Derrida's (1973) definition of difference as that which—divided in space and time—has no unity. Lyotard's point is that the optimization of the relationship between the system's inputs and outputs is really the optimization of unity and the suppression of *difference*. In speech act theory (Austin, 1962) the performance is a statement that executes the act to which it refers; it represents the translation of words into action *without* delay; sign and act are bound as one and *affirm* each other; they are thus beyond question.

In this sense, performativity is concerned with the optimization of a set of imperatives which, since they are "already constituted" (i.e., pre-formed), are experienced less as commands and more as exigencies of the natural order of things.

Conceived as the suppressor of difference, performativity is a major theme in the work of the culture analyst Walter Benjamin (1973), especially in his criticism of the mechanization of modern life: "The invention of the match around the middle of the nineteenth century bought forth a number of innovations which have one thing in common: one abrupt movement of the hand triggers a process of many steps" (p. 176). The telephone and the camera are also cited. Taylorism, which popularised the slogan "Down with dawdling!", represented the early formalisation or performativity in the modern factory through the discovery of "laws" of work governing the most economical motions on the shortest possible time. In the same terms, Benjamin quotes the poet Valéry, who prefigured the human and social consequences of post-modern information technology: "just as water, gas and electricity are brought into our houses from far off to satisfy our needs in response to a minimal effort, so we shall be supplied with visual or auditory images, which will appear and disappear at a single movement of the hand, hardly more than a sign" (p. 221). Performativity contributes to the totalising tendencies of the system in that it reduces the differences (or delay) between human effort and production, thus glossing and smoothing over the uncertainties and paradoxes that constitute the very process of difference. However, as we have noted, it is a feature of human language that it must repeat that which it represses so that it is more correct to view the systemic-functional and agonistic models as alternative movements of the same process, which close and open on each other. We can picture the movement in terms of the repetition compulsion.

## FROM PERFORMATIVITY TO ORDERABILITY

Let us note that the compulsion to repeat is a call to *order*. The order in this case is the division that the subject must assume *in order* to know itself. Let us also recall that Freud's term for the repetition compulsion is *Widerholungzwang*. It is significant for us that *Wiederholung* (repetition) draws together several separate ideas: "again," "against" (*wieder, wider*) and "collect" (*holen*), thus identifying repetition with recollection. Now, *wieder* is also cognate with the English "wide" and "wider" and thus suggests the sense of expanding in order to contain more; the repetition here is not mere reoccurrence of the same but invokes the idea of "least effort" in which an undecidable "double" is objectified into the "singularity" of a wider frame. We can illustrate this operation through Rubin's profiles where the instability created by the oscillation of the shared faces is held in place by the *wider* frame of the page; without the support of the page's frame the observing subject would be lost in a vertigo of continuous vacillation. The act of recollection thus involves the subject in an act of division which entails two steps: (1) the *prior* preparation of an object (only) through which the subject can *later* appear to itself—"a retroversion effect by which the subject becomes at each stage what he was before and announces himself—he will have been—only in the future perfect tense" (Lacan, 197b, p. 306); (2) the attenuation and simplification of the ambiguous and contradictory structure of difference, i.e., the finitizing of the finite. All this occurs, moreover, through a call to order which is a compulsive force (*Zwang*) and which operates automatically and without our conscious knowledge. Thus, order is peremptory.

Using a conceptual framework similar to that of repetition, Simmel (1950) shows how the social collective comes about through the suppression of individual differences. As with the vacillations intrinsic to division, the individual is subject to chronic uncertainty and indeterminateness. In contrast, "the mass does not know the dualism of egoistic and altruistic impulses, a dualism that often renders the individual helpless and makes him embrace a vacuum" (p. 27). The function of the collective is to constrain these vacillations into a communal structure through the fixing of an average or mean value. Simmel tells us that this averaging process is not the same as the statistical:

> It is . . . misleading to designate the level of a society that considers itself a unit and practically operates as a unit, as an "average" level. The "average" would result from adding up the levels of the individuals and dividing the sum by their number. This procedure would involve a raising of the lowest individuals, which actually is impossible. In reality, the level of a society is very close to that of its lowest components, since it must be possible for all to participate in it with identical valuation and effectiveness. The character of collective behaviour does not lie near the "middle" but near the lower limits of its participants. (p. 37)

Simmel expresses this a principle of community or social mass: "what is common to all can be the property of only those who possess least" (p. 37). This is clearly another way of thinking about the repetition compulsion, especially in the attempt by the collective to recollect itself as a subject through the containment of more with less cost and effort. In other words, simplicity is gained at the cost of lost complexity, which is precisely the function of the object in social organisation, a *function that is inversely proportional to the degree of difference in the subject*.

We thus see that Simmel's analysis is an extension of Zipf's principle of least effort into the social world where it enables us to connect the ordering process with communication since the social collective calls itself into a communicative order through the creation of objects which can be transmitted with minimal social effort. In this state, the objects must take on the appearance of the *common* and the *ordinary* (i.e., the mean-ness of meaning). Order thus slips into the ordinary (let us also note that "object" slips metonymically into "abject," the mean and worthless).

The objectification of least effort is also analysed by Heidegger (1927/1978) in his phenomenological study of time and being, in a way which both complements and supplements Simmel's analysis of the development of collective discourse. In particular, Heidegger's concept of the "they" helps fill out the collective work of averaging down. The "they" is not any specific group or person; in fact, it is not any "one" at all, rather it is the neuter or the fictional "Others." By 'Others' we do not mean everyone else but me—those over against whom the 'I' stands out. They are rather those from whom, for the most part, one does *not* distinguish oneself—those among whom one is too" (Heidegger, 1927/1978, p. 154). In other words, "one" is also included in the "they" or the "Others" as an indistinguishable "average" value which pre-empts any possibility of distinction.

> In this averageness with which it (the "they") prescribes what can and may be ventured, it keeps watch over everything exceptional that thrusts itself to the fore. Every kind of priority gets glossed over as something that has long been well known. Everything gained by a struggle becomes something to be manipulated. Every secret loses its force. (p. 165)

The "they" exerts an automatic force of exclusion on the remote and the strange by simply bringing them close. The modern world is especially prone to this form of closure in its concern with speeding things up and conquering vast distances by electronic and other means. Exclusion and closeness become aspects of the same process, for that which is closest to us is that which we are normally least aware of. "When, for instance, a man wears a pair of spectacles which are so close to him distantly that they are 'sitting on his nose' they are environmentally more remote from him than the picture on the opposite wall" (p. 141).

The language of the anonymous and instantaneous "they" averages down in a process of idle talk. (Heidegger intends nothing pejorative by "idle"—rather, it should be understood in the sense of idling or taking things easy as one does with the instantly simple and effortlessly comprehensible). In idle talk, the collective achieves the suppression of the infinite and unpredictable, the uncertain and ambiguous, the strange and remote, so that collective talk with its basis in common (i.e., communal) meanings is also that which already knows:

> Idle talk is the possibility of understanding everything without previously making the thing one's own. If this were done, idle talk would founder; and it already guards against such a danger. Idle talk is something which anyone can make up: it not only releases one from the task of genuinely understanding, but develops an undifferentiated kind of intelligibility . . . (p. 213)

In the concepts of the "they" and "idle talk," we see represented the subject/object dialectic whose terms, as noted earlier, complement each other *inversely* i.e., the undecidable characteristics of the primary subject are curtailed in the collective in the direction of the communal properties of simplicity, clarity and stability (i.e., finitude). Moreover, as Heidegger's analysis reveals, the language of the collective "they" knows what it knows *in advance* and therefore can never be open to doubt and uncertainty.

We have said that the subject has to posit itself as an object in order to know itself, i.e., the object has now to be seen as the result of a realization technique (Bachelard, 1934). As Bachelard argues, the subject "instructs itself by what it constructs," i.e., the process of production feeds back to tell the subject what it is and it is in this sense that the subject has to re-collect itself. Bachelard calls the methods by which objects are created for scientific investigation, *phenomena-techniques.*

It is central to the present argument that all knowledge (not just scientific) in society is subjected to *phenomena-techniques.* What Bell (1973) describes as the priority given to information and theoretical knowledge in post-industrial society is in effect the development and application of phenomeno-technique to large-scale systems, i.e., the subject or system tells itself what it is by what it constructs and, therefore, embodies or realizes itself by means of the objects it makes.

Bell also states that performance and certainty are the dominant behavioural and cognitive modes which structure information and theoretical knowledge in post-industrial society. The argument presented here leads us to suggest that performance and certainty are logically related in the sense that performance expressed as a principle of performativity is a guiding and legitimating criterion for post-industrial systems, i.e., it pre-forms that certainty which realizes the system as a subject. When Bell says that the rationalization and codification of information is *the* major problem for post-industrial systems, he neglects to include in his analysis the fact that this is essentially the problem of the system objectifying itself through its performance.

The object is the end result of a process of objectification in which the object is prepared for us as a perceivable and meaningful thing or event. In other words, the object is the product of a particular *way of seeing,* i.e., the creation of phenomeno-techniques. Heidegger (1949/1977) addresses the same problem in his essay on technology. For Heidegger, technology is not merely a set of techniques for accomplishing a specific purpose: it may be that for the functionalist but for the thinker it is more radically, a way of both ordering and revealing the world. Modern technology makes active demands on the properties of nature (and human nature) which are then reinscribed as *resources* which are everywhere made to stand by, on order and ready for use. The earth is now reinscribed as a constant source of coal and ore. The field, formerly in the care of the peasant, now receives a technological meaning because of its place in the mechanised food industry. A hydro-electric plant is set into the current of a river. The plant orders the river to supply its hydraulic power, this then energizes the turbines which then activate the electric current for the power station which then dispatches electricity to factories, offices and homes. Here, the river is revealed as displaying the specific characteristics of an object that is for even on order, and which no longer appears to us as a landscape that provides a natural habitat. The object of modern organisation must always be already constituted for immediate and constant use, i.e., the real objective of organisation is orderability. In such ordering people must necessarily include themselves as raw material that serves as standing reserve: they are reinscribed as human resources, e.g., as the supply of patients (i.e., raw material) for a clinic (Heidegger, 1949/1977). Through modern technology, modern organisation becomes the "making secure of a constant reserve" (p. 86) in order to calculate in advance and thereby make certain.

Heidegger's message is that organizing or ordering the world is no mere functional process but a form of *revealing*. This is what Bachelard means when he says that the objects of scientific research are the products of a phenomeno-technique. Such revealing is aimed at the securing of certainty through the making secure of a constant reserve. Furthermore, this process tends towards finality through the construction of large-scale systems of certainty which seek to master what remains of uncertainty: a continuous chain of terms is forged which must reinforce each terms certainty. Heidegger calls this process "the gigantic" (p. 135). The gigantic annihilates vast distances by airplane; through radio and television it casually sets before us "foreign and remote worlds in their everydayness" (p. 135). But the gigantic harbours within itself the seeds of uncertainty in so far as the striving for large-scale (even world) systems makes everything smaller. Heidegger quotes atomic physics in evidence. Today, he might also have instanced modern computers which calculate in billionths of a second. This is Heidegger's way of expressing what we earlier called the self-interfering character of the symbolic: that which contains its opposite and thus refuses any *singular* grasp of its meaning. Since organisation and object are also symbolic structures, they too are subject to self-inference. In essence, this means that the object or objective is fated always to repeat that which is censors and is thus paradoxically a process in which intentional actions produce unintended consequences. We can state this more formally in the language of modern physics and mathematics which tells us that: (1) all decision-making has consequences which cannot be predicted because each decision has the character of amplification, i.e., it creates *more* choices and uncertainty rather than less, and (2) it is *not* true that uncertainty (lack of control) decreases as accuracy of information goes up—uncertainty actually increases with accuracy (Lyotard, 1984; Peitgen and Richter, 1985). To the extent that post- structuralist information and organisation is thus contradictory and agonistic, it represents the anti-model of a predictable, stable system.

## NOTES

1  A related argument is that of the economist Shackle (1969) who poses the problem of uncertainty in terms of possibility rather than probability. *Probability* is foreknowledge based on a complete list of hypotheses as to the future state of a thing or event; probability is thus closed to possibilities which are not included in the list. Shackle's characterisation of probability is therefore similar to the logic of repetition we have noted in systems theory. Possibility is similar to the post-structuralist conception of information and language as essentially "undecidable".

2  In early Greek thought chaos was defined as a gap of *infinite* space; it is the infinitude or uncertainty (see discussion of infinite logic below) of *chaos* that *causes* (i.e., urges or forces) the subject into a state of conscious certainty. Lacan (1977a, especially Chapter 2) discusses the concept of cause as a "gap" of the unconscious that *drives* the subject to fill its "hole" with the orderly work of consciousness. It is this sense of cause which leads me to suggest its relationship with *chaos* as a state of incompletion that impels the actor towards a state of completion.

3  To say that the subjects is different is to locate the origins of its actions in the vacillations and automatisms of informational uncertainty as defined above: this denies the common conception of the self as a subject that is relatively self-sufficient, more or less in control of its own actions and capable of exercising rational choice.

4  The pronoun "it" comes from the Latin *idem*, which means the "same", and, *as idenudem*, "repeatedly."

5  Lacan no doubt refers here to the work of the telecommunications engineer R. V. L. Hartley in the 1920s on which was founded the later development of the mathematical theory of information

6  The again (or repeated) is a gain in the sense of interest added to information in decline. Information theorists intend this meaning then they define information as "that which adds to a representation" (MacKay, 1969, p. 163) but the terms "again" and "gain" also imply a contestaory relationship such as we find in the Greek *agon*, meaning a struggle of interests (see also related discussion of form as that which is wrestled out of non-form for undecidability.

7  The argument here is more complex than space permits but it is taken further by Lacan (1977a) in, for example, the ideas the human structure is caused by that which "does not work" (p. 22 and passim), i.e., the undecidability by Wollheim (1968, Section 36) is the distinction between code and language; and at a much earlier period by the Italian philosopher Giambattista Vico (1668–1744) in the view that one's relationship to the world has its fundamental motivation in uncertainty *(homo non intelligendo fit omnia)* rather than in a fixed and stable certainty *(homo intelligendo fit omnia);* see Brown (1973) for an elaboration of Vico's view.

## REFERENCES

Attneave, F. (1959) *Applications of Information Theory to Psychology*. New York: Holt.

Austin, J. L. (1962) *How to do things with words*. Oxford: Oxford University Press.

Bachelard, G. (1934) *Le Nouvel Esprit Scientifique*. Paris: Alcan.

Bateson, G. (1972) *Steps to an Ecology of Mind*. London: Intertext.

Bell, D. (1973) *The Coming of Post-Industrial Society*. New York: Basic Books.

Benjamin, W. (1973) *Charles Baudelaire: A Lyric Poet in the Era of High Capitalism*. London: New Left Books.

Blanco, I. M. (1975) *The Unconscious as Infinite Sets*. London: Duckworth.

Blau, P. (1964) *On the Nature of Organisations*. New York: Wiley.

Brown, G. S. (1969) *Laws of Form*. London: Allen and Unwin.

Brown, N. O. (1973) *Closing Time*. New York: Random House.

Buckley, W. (1967) *Sociology and Modern Systems Theory*. Englewood Cliffs, New Jersey: Prentice Hall.

Cooper, R. (1983) The Other: A model of human structuring, in G. Morgan (ed) *Beyond Method: Strategies for Social Research* (pp. 203–218). Beverly Hills, California: Sage.

Derrida, J. (1973) *Speech and Phenomena*. Evanston: Northwestern University Press.

Douglas, M., and Isherwood, B. (1978) *The World of Goods*. New York: Basic Books.

Foucault, M. (1970) *The Order of Things*. London: Tavistock.

Foucault, M. (1982) *This is Note a Pipe*. Berkeley, California: University of California Press.

Freud, S. (1955) 'Beyond the Pleasure Principle', in *Standard Edition* (Vol. 18, pp. 1–64). London: Hogarth Press. (Original work published 1920).

Freud, S. (1960) 'Jokes and their Relation to the Unconscious', in *Standard Edition* (Vol. 8). London: Hogarth Press. (Original work published 1905).

Heidegger, M. (1959) *An Introduction to Metaphysics*. New Haven: Yale University Press (Original work composed 1935).

Heidegger, M. (1977) *The Question Concerning Technology*. New York: Harper and Row. (Original work composed 1949).

Heidegger, M. (1978) *Being and Time*. Oxford: Blackwell. (Original work published 1927).

Keats, J. (1947) *The Letters of John Keats*. London: Oxford University Press.

Kuhn, T. S. (1970) *The Structure of Scientific Revolutions*. Chicago: Chicago University Press.

Lacan, J. (1977a) *The Four Fundamental Concepts of Psychoanalysis*. London: Hogarth Press.

Lacan, J. (1977b) *Ecries: A Selection*. London: Tavistock.

Lévi-Strauss, C. (1966) *The Savage Mind*. London: Weidenfeld and Nicholson.

Lyotard, J. F. (1984) *The Postmodern Condition: A Report on Knowledge*. Manchester: Manchester University Press.

Lukács, G. (1974) *Soul and Form*. London: Merlin Press.

MacKay, D. M. (1969) *Information, Mechanism and Meaning*. Cambridge, Massachusetts: MIT Press.

Pietgen, H. O., and Richter, P. H. (1985) *Frontiers of Chaos*. Bremen, West Germany: Forschungsgruppe Komplexe Dynamik, Univeristat Bremen.

Rubin, E. (1921) *Visuell Wahrgenommene Figuren*. Copenhagan: Gyldendalska Boghandel.

de Saussure, F. (1974) *Course in General Linguistics*. London: Fontana/Collins.

Shackle, G. L. S. (1969) *Decision, Order and Time in Human Affairs*. Cambridge: Cambridge University Press.

Simmel, G. (1950) *The Sociology of Georg Simmel*. New York: The Free Press.

Wilden, A. (1982) 'Semiotics as Praxis: Strategy and Tactics', *Recherches Semiotique Inquiry I*, 1–34.

Wolheim, R. (1968) *Art and its Objects*. Baltimore: Penguin.

Zipf, G. K. (1965) *Human Behaviour and the Principle of Least Effort*. New York: Hafner.

(Excerpt from 'Interview with Robert Cooper' Robert C. H. Chia and Jannis Kallinikos, in Chia, R. (ed) (1998) *Organized Worlds: Explorations in Technology and Organization with Robert Cooper*. London: Routledge, 156–159.)

*You have worked with ideas from information theory. Can you tell us why you consider the concept of information to be important for social analysis?*

Social science seems to me to suffer from two major intellectual vices: *objectification* and the *naturalization of order*. Objectification frames the social world as a collection of divided, self-identical objects such as the 'individual', the 'group', the 'society'. We even tend to think of these as structures with physical properties. The naturalization of order is the assumption that order and regularity are somehow congenital to social action and that disorder and disturbance are unnatural distortions of an original state of harmony. The significance of the concept of information lies in its capacity to problematize these convenient simplicities and to radicalize the structural tendencies of social analysis.

Let's start with the basic ideas of information theory. Information theory works in terms of probabilities: information is inversely proportional to its probability, so that information is what's *least probable*:

> To calculate the amount of information contained in a particular message, one must keep in mind that the highest probability an event will take place is 1, and the lowest 0. The mathematical probability of an event therefore varies between 1 and 0. A coin thrown into the air has an equal chance of landing on either heads or tails; thus, the probability of getting heads is ½.
>
> (Eco, 1989: 45)

This, or course, is the common sense version of the *binary digit*—the 'bit'—which is the technical definition of information in computer science. The significance of the binary digit is that it forces us to see information as the product of probability *and* improbability *in combination*.

To say that information is what's least probable is the same as saying that it's least predictable. If an event is complete predictable, it simply doesn't provide us with information. We already know it. Information derives its significance from its unpredictability. Information is thus novelty and newness—*news*, in fact, something that we didn't previously know. In cybernetics, information is also a measure of organization or order. Organization and order are forms of predictability. But since information is related to improbability, organization and order are also dependent on disorganization and disorder. Communication (i.e., the transmission of information) in social systems is bound up with predictability-disorganization-disorder. The system is defined as much by what it does *not* know as by what it knows. In fact, unpredictability-disorganization-disorder is what makes ordered systems possible. Information helps us to understand why this is so. Information occurs on the cusp of probability—improbability. It's always momentary, tentative and transient. This is what Lyotard (1991:105) means when he writes that 'information is by definition a short-lived element. As soon as it is transmitted and shared, it ceases to be information, it becomes an environmental given, and "all is said", we "know". It is put into the machinery memory. The length of time it occupies is, so to speak, instantaneous.' Information thus occurs in that imperceptible moment between the known and the unknown. It lasts but an instant and is quickly gone. For this reason it has to be repeated, otherwise knowledge, probability, prediction would also come to an end. Lyotard is telling us that information must never be concluded; by definition, it must remain unfinished, infinite, indeterminate. Information in this sense is what per-*forms* the forms of social life. I would like to suggest that the technical definition of information as the *binary digit* (the measure of the probability—improbability of an event) can now be extended to social analysis as the *binary act*. The binary act not only draws attention to the constitutive role of the probability-improbability relationship in social action but also suggests the human agency is defined by the informational act which is compelled continually to recreate itself out of the infinite and indeterminate. In short, the binary act redefines social action as (1) the making of something out of nothing; (2) never complete; (3) a compulsion to repeat; (4) instantaneous; (5) evanescent.

The general significance of these features of the binary act is discussed by Lyotard in the context of techno-scientific research and social practice. Techno-scientific research, according to Lyotard, is motivated primarily by informational possibilities—by the infinite and indeterminate. It responds to the challenge posed by the post-industrial recognition that there is no objective, true reality but only an infinity of possible 'realities' which have to be realized as the probabilities of predictabilities of 'knowledge'. Lyotard describes how this occurs in the social and organizational context through the example of photography. Photography has to be understood as both expression and product of techno-scientific culture. 'Science, technology and capital, even in their matter-of-fact style, are so many ways of actualizing the infinity of concept' (Lyotard, 1991: 123). Techno-scientific knowledge is a complex *making over* of the unknown into the known. But this making over hides its real nature by presenting its products as 'ready-made' and owing nothing to the infinite and indeterminate. Photography as a product of industrial techno-scientific and as per-formed on a mass scale by the so-called amateur photographer is also the construction and consumption of objects and knowledge out of the informational possibilities of the infinite. The amateur photographer, ostensibly utilizing the camera's capacity to personal image-making, is really part of this wider complex that constructs performable knowledge out of the indeterminate: 'The amateur (photographer) is in this way in the service of experimentation carried out by laboratories and ordered by banks' (Lyotard, 1991: 123). The social subject is thus caught up in a techno-scientific field of binary acts that represents 'the concretization of an anonymous infinite that ceaselessly organizes and disorganizes the world, and of which the individual subject, at whatever level she be in the social hierarchy, is the volume or involuntary servant' (p. 123). It's not only that techno-scientific organization insinuates itself into all levels of the social system but that its general elaboration of the principle of information (in the way I have defined it here) subjects all social relations to what Lyotard calls 'the management of infinite research', which effectively means information as the endless transformation of spectral 'realities'.

To appreciate the general significance of this 'information revolution', we have to remind ourselves of the philosophy and objectives of traditional science which sought to ground knowledge in a rational system of cause and effect and in which 'all things are reduced to the level of pure presences that can be measured, manipulated, replaced and therefore easily dominated and organized' (Vattimo, 1992: 8). This is an interpretation of knowledge that stresses predictability, order and probability. It marginalizes the unpredictability and improbability that defines information as infinite possibility. It says that laws and regularities constitute scientific knowledge. But information as improbability reminds us that 'it is necessary to rethink the world . . . in terms of perturbations and turbulences, in order to bring out its multiple forms, uneven structures, and fluctuating organizations' (Harari and Bell in Serres, 1982: xxvii). The new techno-science overturns the traditional conception of science as objective law and order and substitutes the idea of a 'founding disorder' in which informational improbability becomes the infinite source of ever-changing social forms. It's no longer the conventional view of technology as the technical means of mastering nature but of the generalized organization of techno-science and is 'primarily and essentially defined by systems collecting and transmitting information' (Vattimo, 1992: 15). This is what the Italian philosopher Gianni Vattimo calls 'the society of generalized communication', which is sustained by the continuous creation and circulation of new information—news, images—through a techno-scientific complex which relies centrally on the mass media. As we've noted, information is by definition momentary and transitory. Its special character is that *it does not last*. This is what makes Vattimo's society of generalized communication seems so destabilized, so liquid: 'The advent of the media enhances the inconstancy and superficiality of experience ' (p. 59). It's Lyotard's argument that techno-scientific organization can only actualize itself via the *production*—which is also the *prediction*—of the infinite or 'unfinished'. Vattimo vividly illustrates the transience of technologized information though Walter Benjamin's social and cultural analysis of cinema. Cinema, says Benjamin, was constructed to disorient, to destabilize—'the rapid succession of projected images whose demands on a viewer are analogous to those made on a driver in city traffic' (Vattimo, 1992: 51)—in order to keep the infinite or 'unfinished' continually alive. Cinema reveals the special character of information as *instantaneous*, as imperceptibly transient, must like Deleuze's insight that 'movement always happens behind the thinker's back, or in the moment when he blinks' (Deleuze and Parnet, 1987: 1). Information happens between the *not yet* and the *no longer*. It suggests that time (as *tense*) is a *tension* between the *not yet* and the *no longer*—a tension that has to the iterated otherwise information will not last and will be lost. This is why Vattimo cites films like *Blade Runner* and *Planet of the Apes* in which the future is seen in 'the light of ruins'. In *Blade Runner*, for example, the example, the techno-scientific action of the film takes place against a background of urban ruin and decay which serves to remind us not only of the transient of so-called techno-scientific progress but also of the need or compulsion intrinsic to the binary act of information to repeat that strange complicity between the *not yet* and the *no longer*.

These comments are intended to introduce information as a process that is fundamental to social practice. The concept of the *binary act* in particular draws attention to the significance of the mutually defining interaction between probability and improbability in everyday social action, and, as I've tried to show, the society of post-industrial techno-science not only foregrounds information as an operation and ontological principle but demands its understanding and analysis in information-theoretic terms.

## Editors' Note

All the references for these interview sections can be found after the final interview extract, 'Main features of my approach . . .', in section 15.

# 7 Modernism, Postmodernism and Organizational Analysis
## An Introduction

*Robert Cooper and Gibson Burrell*

(*Organization Studies*, 1988, 9/1: 91–112)

## ABSTRACT

The paper introduces the current debate in the human sciences between the opposing conceptual positions of 'modernism' and 'postmodernism' and discusses its implications for organizational analysis. The debate focusses on the nature of 'discourse' (information, knowledge, communication) and its role in social systems. The discourse of modernism rests on transcendent yet anthropocentric criteria such as 'progress' and 'reason' which are varyingly exemplified in the work of Bell, Luhmann and Habermas. In contrast, post-modern discourse (represented here mainly by the work of Lyotard, Derrida, Foucault, Deleuze and Guattari) analyses social life in terms of paradox and indeterminacy, thus rejecting the human agent as the centre of rational control and understanding. The paper then considers two contrasting views of the organizing process which follow from these opposing approaches to discourse. In the modernist model, organization is viewed as a social tool and an extension of human rationality. In the postmodern view, organization is less the expression of planned thought and calculative action and a more defensive reaction to forces intrinsic to the social body which constantly threaten the stability of organized life. The implications of the latter view for orthodox organizational analysis are discussed in some detail.

## PREAMBLE

This paper is the first in a series for *Organization Studies* in which we attempt to outline some of the key concepts and methodological insights which a number of European social theorists have developed in recent years and which are of direct relevance to organizational analysis. The work of these thinkers is seen here as being inextricably tied up in a major ongoing debate concerning what have been called Modernism and Postmodernism. In this first, long article we have attempted to do justice to many of the issues raised in the course of this debate pointing to the battle positions which have been drawn up on both sides. The language used in this introductory paper may prove to be out of the ordinary for many readers of the journal. This is because we have tried to be true to the positions of those involved and also to respect their phraseology, conceptualization and forms of expression. In doing this, we are conscious of the space we have taken up and do not make this claim upon the reader's time lightly. We have struggled to provide an introductory piece which is neither inaccessible to those unfamiliar with the modernism-postmodernism debate nor so naïve and oversimplistic as to disgust those readers who do have a degree of familiarity with the issues at contention. The penalty we have paid for aiming at this intermediate position is length. The present paper provides an overview of the debate and makes passing reference to the work of Modernists such as Bell, Luhmann and Habermas. We also speak here of Nietzsche, Derrida, Lyotard and Foucault to all of whom the epithet 'postmodernism' has been attached. In our second article, we will turn to the work of Michel Foucault and discuss his direct relevance to the world of organizational analysis. Following this, in later issues of *Organization Studies*, the work of Derrida, Habermas and Luhmann will be subjected to precisely the same critical investigation. The present paper then has to be seen as pointing the way into what may be, for some, a new area of intellectual endeavour and confrontation. It is to be followed up by more detailed, substantive considerations of individual social theorists whose work is relevant to organization studies and who are important figures in the modernist-postmodernist confrontation.

## INTRODUCTION

The human sciences are currently undergoing one of their periodic bouts of self-analysis and self-doubt in which certain traditionally prized shibboleths of liberal academic discourse such as 'reason' and 'progress' have come under the microscope of a renewed critical reflection. The debate is polarized around two apparently conflicting epistemological positions: modernism with its belief in the essential capacity of humanity to perfect itself through the power of rational thought and postmodernism with its critical questioning, and often outright rejection, of the ethnocentric rationalism championed by modernism. Apart from the radical revaluation of the whole process of modernization which this dialogue evokes, there are significant implications for how we understand the role and nature of organizations in the modern world. Not least of these is the shift away from the prevailing definition of organization as a circumscribed administrative-economic function ('*the* organization') to its formative role in the production of systems of rationality. This is clearly a return to the grand concerns that Weber introduced into the study of modern social systems, in which bureaucratic organization had created the 'iron cage' of the modern economic order and whose significant effect had been to purge the world of the auratic and magical. In other words, Weber made us se modern organization as a process which emblemized the rationalization and objectification of social life, and it is to this process that the current debate returns us, but with a fresh twist which directs our attention to the concept of *discourse* and its place in institutional structures.

Weber's work holds a significance that has been generally submerged in contemporary organizational analysis: the object of his analysis was modern bureaucratic organization as a *process* in the continuing mastery of the social and physical environment rather than organizations *per se*. Rational organization is a response to forces that we cannot really understand and it is as much a progression of 'errors' as it is of rationality (Smart 1983). In fact, rationality in Weber's analyses shades into 'rationalization', a form of discourse in which logically consistent or ethically acceptable reasons are presented for ideas and actions whose true motives are not perceived. Rationality thus becomes a concealment of its own inner workings. Since it is partly grounded in the 'unknown' or the unconscious, it also appears to have a life of its own, an automaticity that is beyond direct human control. All this was part of Weber's project in analysing the development of modern bureaucratic organization.

In contrast, the object of contemporary modes of organizational analysis is the organization as a discrete system which subordinates bureaucratic logic to its own hypostatized needs. What is privileged here is the idea of organization as a quasi-stable collection of things or properties, whereas for Weber the very concept of organization was placed in question as an uneasy fabrication. What defines this concept of organization is its prior and implicit self-classification as a formal system of work; its capacity to 'produce the goods' precludes any other possible conception (see, e.g. Hall 1972; Perrow 1972). This mode of organization thus emerges as a product of 'spontaneous sociology' in which we merely see reflected the images that the organization tends to offer of its own functioning and functions (Bourdieu and Passeron 1977).

This historical displacement in the nature of the object of organizational analysis adduces the tasks of the present paper: the identification and analysis of two general forms of organization—the one, automatic and autonomous in operation, defying logistical closure; the other, calculative and utilitarian in intent, reassuring in its substance—within the wider context of the discourses of modernism and postmodernism, with special reference to the implications of this contextualization for the social science of organizations.

A similar distinction is drawn by Varela (1979) in his analysis of the two major forms of knowledge used in the study of natural and social systems. Varela's work is significant in the present context because it directly relates forms of discourse to the cybernetic concept of organization (Morgan 1986). Varela distinguishes two basic themes of organization: *autonomy* and *control*. The two themes entail two different discourses of information/ knowledge. In the autonomous approach, information is 'always relative to the process of interactions of the domain in which they occur, and to the observer-community that describes them' (Varela 1979: 267). Consequently, autonomous information is a process of interaction between terms which specify *each other* and, since therefore it cannot be located in any one particular term, it denies the tendency to see the world in terms of simple substances or things. In contrast, information in the control sense is referential (mapping one set of terms onto a corresponding set), it restricts the point of view to fixed interactions and observational positions, it is 'instructive' (i.e. it tells us how to act in regard to a particular goal), and does not explicitly include the observer, an elision which runs the risk of denying the active role the observer plays in the construction and maintenance of information/ knowledge systems.

The discourse of modernism can be said to be referential in the sense that it sees language as a means of expressing something other than itself. More specifically, it is a *metadiscourse* which legitimates itself by reference to 'some grand narrative, such as the dialectics of the Spirit, the hermeneutics of meaning, the emancipation of the rational or working subject, or the creation of wealth' (Lyotard 1984: xxiii). It posits the idea of a criterion which *already* exists, an already-made-up mind—often of extra-historical and universalistic content—which necessarily implies an already existing answer to questions. It puts the answer before the question and in this sense may be said to be 'instructive'. In the sense that it 'already knows', modernism is totalizing and controlling.

Postmodern discourse begins with the idea that systems have lives of their own which make them fundamentally independent of human control. Systems express only themselves and we may understand them only through analysis of their own self-referential workings. For the postmodern thinker systems do not have meanings or purposes; these are human projections in which we uncritically assume that the world exists only for us and by which we locate ourselves at the controlling centre of things. Since the world is basically self-referential, it is neither pro-human nor anti-human; it just *is*. Postmodernism therefore decentres the human agent its self-elevated position of narcissistic 'rationality' and shows it to be essentially an observer-community which constructs *interpretations* of the world, these interpretations having no absolute or universal status.

## MODERNISM

Modernism is that moment when man invented himself; when he no longer saw himself as a reflection of God or Nature. Its historical source lies in the eighteenth-century philosophy of the Enlightenment which chose Reason as the highest of human attributes. Reason, according to Kant, is when we think for ourselves and cease depending on an external authority to make up our minds for us; it thus implies a *critical* sense in which we have both to develop our powers of rational discrimination and have the courage to express them when appropriate; *Aude sapere*, said Kant: 'dare to know'.

Also at this time the expediencies of Reason were appropriated by social thinkers such as Saint-Simon and Comte whose concern was their application to the increasingly weighty problems of government, administration and planning brought about by the industrialization of society. We thus find the rudiments of organizational thinking in the Enlightenment philosophy. But at this historical point there occurs a schism within Reason itself, showing that it too is subject to the displacements intrinsic to self-reference: Reason is appropriated by an early form of systems thinking which subverts its critical edge to the functional demands of large systems. The followers of Saint-Simon drew up a blueprint for the *systéme de la Mediterranée*, a projected 'universal association' of the peoples of Europe and the Orient through a comprehensive network of railways, rivers and canals. The Suez Canal, begun in 1854 and completed in 1869, represented part-realization of this dream. Comte, perhaps the first philosopher of organization, saw industrial organization (the scientific organization of labour and knowledge for the production of wealth) as the source of human unity and progress. His was a theory of organization applied to the administration of society as a whole, but which laid down detailed specifications at the level of the micro-function: the precise roles of politicians, industrialists, bankers: the optimum number of men in each city, etc. The spirit of this functional reason was well captured at the time by Goethe in the character of Faust who translated passive reason, mere thought, into active reason, the accomplished deed, through the technological transformation of the entire world (Berman 1983). Modernization thus appeared early on as the organization of knowledge expressed in terms of the needs of large-scale technological systems. The Victorians celebrated this achievement in the Great Exhibition of 1851.

Modernism thus has two versions: *critical modernism*, a reanimation of Kant's programme of enlightenment, and *systemic modernism*, the instrumentalization of reason envisioned by Saint-Simon and Comte.

Systemic modernism is currently seen to the dominant form of reason, now more usually expressed as 'instrumental rationality'. This is well brought out in Bell's (1974) thesis that modern (or post-industrial) society differs from previous societies in relying on knowledge that is essentially theoretical. Bell cites the chemical industry as the first of the truly modern industries because its origin lies in the intimate linkage between science and technology: it is necessary to have a theoretical knowledge of the macro molecules being manipulated in order to create chemical synthesis (the recombination and transformation of compounds). Bell's vision of how theoretical knowledge is used in the post-industrial era reveals its technocratic and systematic character. 'Post-industrial society is organized around knowledge for the purpose of social control and the directing of innovation and change. . . .' (Bell 1974: 20). The point is further elaborated in the argument that theoretical knowledge offers a 'methodological promise' for the management of the complex, large-scale systems which distinguish from the modern world. The major social, economic and political questions of the post-industrial era centre around the problem of 'organized complexity': large scale systems with many interacting variables, 'which have to be coordinated to achieve specific goals'. The new intellectual technologies now available for this endeavour are: information theory, cybernetics, decision theory, game theory, utility theory, etc. The distinctive function of this technical armoury is the definition of rational action and the identification of the means for achieving it. Problems are formally defined in terms of certainty/uncertainty, of constraints and contrasting alternatives. 'Certainty exists when the constraints are fixed and known. Risk means that a set of possible outcomes s known and the probabilities for each outcome can be stated. Uncertainty is the case when the set of possible outcomes can be stipulated, but the probabilities are completely unknown' (Bell 1974: 30). In this context, rationality is that action which can yield the preferred outcome, given several competing alternatives.

Bell indicates the urge to determinacy and firm foundation in systemic modernism in the suggestion that social 'progress' is motivated by the human quest for a 'common tongue and a unity of knowledge, for a set of "first principles" which, in the epistemology of learning, would underlie the modes of experience and the categories of reason and so shape a set of invariant truths' (Bell 1974: 265). This leads to an increase in the *scale* of institutions which, among other things, creates a vast interlocking network of relationships, more and more thickly integrated through the 'revolutions on communication and transportation'—the spread of cities, the growth of organizations, etc. The major social revolution brought about by modernism is the attempt to control 'scale' by new knowledge technologies such as real-time computer information and new kinds of quantitative and qualitative programming.

Added to the concept of the large-scale unitary system is the concept of 'performance'. In Bell's view, is it performance rather than size that distinguishes post-industrial systems, The definitive feature of performance is what Bell calls the 'economizing mode', most clearly seen in the idea of productivity: 'the ability to gain a more than proportional output from a given expenditure of capital, or given exertion of labour or more simply, society could now get more with less effort or less cost' (Bell 1974: 274). The significance of the modern corporation lies precisely in its invention of the idea of performance, especially in its economizing mode, and then creating a reality out of the idea by *ordering social relations* according to the model of functional rationality. Thus corporations, as the dominant social subsystems, become the paradigmatic organizations of systemic modernism. This conception or organization has been identified as an exigency of modern social systems by the German sociologist Niklas Luhmann. Luhmann's work represents a formalization as well as a justification of the developments charted by Bell. In what is sometimes called the 'new systems theory', Luhmann spells out the inexorable rationality of systemic modernism in which Kant's notion of the critically rational subject is completely repressed in the interests of a machine-like system of social functionality. Society itself becomes a gigantic organization: 'The true goal of the system, the reason it programmes itself like a computer, is the optimization of the global relationship between input and output—in other words, performativity' (Lyotard 1984: 11). Now performativity in systemic modernism assumes a more fundamental function than the performance criterion noted by Bell; it becomes a generalized capacity to 'produce the goods' effectively and hence *it is also a principle of realization and objectification*. It therefore takes precedence over thought itself in the social mind. Luhmann recognizes this point when he says that in post-industrial societies the normativity of laws is superseded by the legitimation of performativity. More specifically, the source of legitimation becomes the system's capacity to control its context (a form of contingency theory) by reducing the complexity external and internal to it; individual aspirations must therefore take a subordinate role. In fact, Luhmann argues that the system must make individual actions compatible with its own overall goals through a process of 'disturbance-free apprenticeship'. Administrative procedures should make individuals "want" what the system needs in order to perform well' (Lyotard 1984: 62). We have come a long way since Saint-Simon and Comte, and Kant has been thoroughly expunged.

Critical modernism stands opposed to the cybernetic-like monolithism of systemic modernism. Its chief exponent in contemporary social science is Jürgen Habermas whose project has been to reclaim the spirit of enlightened rationalism for late modernism. Again, discourse is the object of analysis. For Habermas, language is the medium of reason: 'All ordinary language allows reflexive allusions to what has remained unstated' (Habermas 1972: 168). This sets ordinary language, with its origins in the spontaneous activities of the common life-world, against the instrumental-calculative language of organized systems. Hidden but still active in ordinary language is a 'natural' kind of reason which speaks to us with the instinctive wisdom of an ancient oracle, thus guiding our communal works. The contemporary fate of this 'communicative rationality' has been its repression by the discourse of systemic modernism. For Habermas, the discourse of the ordinary life-world is the basis of his critical modernism and it is through the 'language of the community' that we may refind that lost sense of enlightenment which Kant first revealed to us. More-over, the need for such critical reason is now more urgent that ever precisely because of the colonization of the life-world by systemic reason. Kantian reason takes on an added significance; it is no longer a measure of human 'maturity' but has become a *sine qua non* for emancipating individuals from the totalizing control of systemic logic.

Despite the difference between the systemic and critical forms of modernism—the one bent on the mechanization of social order; the other, on the liberation of the life-world—they share the belief in an intrinsically firm foundation. This takes two forms: (1) that discourse mirrors the reason and order already 'out there' in the world, and (2) that there is a thinking agent, a subject, which can make itself conscious of this external order. In the case of systemic modernism, the rational subject is the system itself which works according to the cybernetic discourse of 'control and communication in the animal and machine' (Wiener 1948); this discourse has its own laws which can be discovered through the application of scientific and mathematical techniques. In this context, reason is a privileged property of the system as distinct from its parts. For critical modernism, the thinking subject is the human individual or, more precisely, a network of interacting individuals who, through the commonsense of ordinary discourse, can reach a 'universal consensus' of human experience. There is thus a presumption of unity which legitimates (i.e. provide an authoritative 'logic') to the critical position, so that what is critiqued are the forces that fragment the ideal of this unity or prevent its emergence as a possibility. It is such legitimating meta-positions to which postmodernism objects.

## POSTMODERNISM

The key to understanding the discourse of postmodernism is the concept of *difference*: a form of self-reference in which terms contain their own opposites and thus refuse any *singular* grasp of their meanings, e.g., the paradox of the 'global village' in which the enlargement of the world through modern communication techniques actually makes it smaller. Difference is thus a unity which is at the same time divided from itself, and, since it is that which actually constitutes human discourse (Derrida 1973), it is intrinsic to all social forms. At the very centre of discourse, therefore, the human agent is faced with a condition of irreducible indeterminacy and it is this endless and unstoppable demurrage which postmodernism thought explicitly recognizes and places in the vanguard of its endeavours. In this context, Lyotard has defined postmodern discourse as 'the search for instabilities' (Lyotard 1984: 53). Lyotard notes that modern science is based on indeterminacy: quantum theory and microphysics demand a redefinition of our ideas of determinate, predictable systems because their data reveal the world as a network of self-referential structures, e.g., it is found that far from uncertainty decreasing with more precise knowledge (i.e., greater control), the reverse is the case: uncertainty increases with precision.

Lyotard elaborate an argument of considerable seductive power which is mounted against the 'grand narratives' that legitimate the two major positions of modernism. Their drive towards determinacy—in the systems case, expressed as the mechanical harmony of interacting functional actors; in the critical case, as the agreement of men in bondage to emancipate themselves—is also a drive towards *consensus*. But we have seen that modern science poses a dialectic of difference and self-reference whose logic must thwart convergence. Lyotard argues that this applies to consensus—the more one reaches for it, the farther away it seems to be: 'Consensus is a horizon that is never reached' (Lyotard 1984: 61). Instead of consensus being the powerhouse of social action, it is dissensus which continually compels our attention.

In another text, Lyotard (Lyotard and Thébuad 1968) analyses some of the less obvious aspects of this typically postmodern approach to discourse via the concept of the 'game'. He has already viewed social action as a 'language game' in which the participating actors made various 'moves' according to recognized rules (Lyotard 1984). This time he extends the idea of a language game to include the idea of 'agonistics' or contest and it is this which gives 'drive' to social life. As soon as the element of struggle goes out of the game, it loses its power to motivate human action. Thus mastery and domination obtain their vitality not from the complete annihilation of one player by the other but through maintaining a state of continuous difference and provocation. The triumph of consensus is thus similar to the destruction of opposition, for it negates the very thing, dissensus, on which it rests. In an afterword to Lyotard, Samuel Weber interprets the dissensus of the game as a '*tension* between unity and disunity' (Lyotard and Thébaud 1986: 113) and thus gives to difference and self-reference the function of an ordinary and irreducible *force* which pervades all social encounters as raw 'feelings of envy, jealousy, and rancour' (Lyotard and Thébaud 1986: 106). Difference is thus more than a theoretical concept since it takes on the force of elemental passion, a kind of prime energizer. Human action is thus seem to stem from drives beyond direct human control; behaviour, individual or institutional, is essentially a reaction to an originary force. The idea that we are controlled by forces that lie beyond us is fundamentally repugnant to modern rational thought which has constructed, over the centuries, a discourse more or less deliberately aimed at denying this possibility. We now know that organizational society set out to tame man's impulsive passions by attenuating them into social and economic 'interests' (Hirschman 1977). Passions as 'determining movements whose composition organized social life. . . . Were forgotten by the productivist economy of the nineteenth century, or rejected into the sphere of literature. The study of passions thus became a literary specialization in the nineteenth century; it is no longer belonged to a political philosophy or economy (Certeau 1986: 25).

We have to turn to Nietzsche (perhaps *the* major influence on postmodern thought) to understand what underlies this particular insight into the nature of modernist rationality. For Nietzsche, the force of difference is *the active*, that which possess power of self-transformation, i.e. self-reference; opposing it is *the reactive*, a form of action which is at once inferior to and dependent on the active. These opposed forces, the active and the reactive, constitute the basis of Nietzsche's concept of 'genealogy'; 'the art of difference or distinction' (Deleuze 1983: 56). Genealogy is Nietzsche's way of showing how the superior force of the active becomes inverted in the inferior force of the reactive. The reactive denies its origin in the active' . . . it is characteristic of reactive forces to deny, from the start, the difference which constitutes them at the start, to invert the differential element from which they derive and to give a deformed image of it' (Deleuze 1983: 56). In this way, the reactive reduces all knowledge and discourse to mere representation, to 'talking about', and, ultimately, negation. In the sciences of man especially we see that passive, reactive and negative concepts are everywhere dominant: 'utility', 'adaptation', and 'regulation' serve as the major explanatory motifs.

The work of another postmodern thinker, Jacques Derrida, extends Nietzsche's analysis of differential forces but turns it in an unexpected direction. Starting from the position that meaning and understanding are not naturally intrinsic to the world and that they have to be constructed, Derrida develops a *deconstructive* method which, in reversing the process of construction, shows precisely how artificial are the ordinary, taken-for-granted structures of our social world. Derrida's purpose is to show that rationality and rationalization are really processes that seek to hide the contradictions at the heart of human existence. What motivates the call to organize is the recognition of a discursive 'gap' which organization serves to cover up. Derrida's analysis is focused on the processual, as opposed to structural, character of human institutions. He wants to show that the world of commonsense structures is the active product of a process that continually privileges unity, identity, and immediacy over the differential properties of absence and separation; in this active privileging there emerges the element of contestation in which the logic of unity and identity is pitted against the forces of difference and undecidability. Modernist reason now becomes more like Lyotard's conception of a contest in which reason is aligned against unreason, truth against error, etc.

Nietzsche's genealogical method leads to another feature of postmodernism: the idea that the knowledge is the result of a force that compels us to render the world unthinkable, i.e., determinate. As we have seen, the world is not already there, waiting for us to reflect it. It is the result of a complex process of a *will to know* which orders and organizes the world because it cannot tolerate not knowing; contradiction and ambivalence are forms of abnormality which have to be exorcized. What Luhmann identifies as the need as modern systems to run smoothly is seen in postmodernism as a gigantic social version of the 'haste of wanting to know'. What modernism considers 'rational', postmodernism sees as the attempt to canonize the discourse of the normal over the abnormal. Rorty (1980) captures the spirit of these conflicting interpretations in his distinction between 'systemic' and 'edifying' discourses. The former serves to justify and ground everyday actions and beliefs by making them seem logical, even natural; it provides an order of reassurance. 'Edifying' discourse helps us break free from outworn vocabularies and attitudes' (Rorty 1980: 12); it seeks to auraticize (i.e., eroticize) discourse and knowledge, to show the extraordinary within the ordinary, the active within the reactive.

Now for Nietzsche the forces surrounding the active-reactive opposition are focussed on the body—biological, social, or political—and it is the materiality of the body, the lived social organism in its physical expression, that provides the *perpetuum mobile* of social life. The body is self-referential in the sense that every social action originates it in and returns to it: '. . . the animal body is the great central ground underlying all symbolic reference . . . Every statement about the geometric relationships of physical bodies in the world is ultimately referable to certain definite human bodies as origins of reference' (Whitehead 1929: 198). The immanence of the body in social life, universally neglected by social scientists, is taken up as a pervasive critical theme by postmodern thinkers and its institutional and organizational implications worked through perhaps the most thoroughly by Michel Foucault (e.g., Foucault 1980). For Foucault, the body is the locus of the auratic and not merely a physiological structure; it is the place of passion, will, 'desires, failings and errors . . . and a volume in perpetual disintegration' (Foucault 1977a: 148)—in short, the body is the organ of *difference*.

In Foucault's work, the auratic dimension appears as a form of 'estrangement' in which the normal and familiar come to be seen in a novel and sometimes disturbing way. In order to see the ordinary with a fresh vision, we have to make it 'extraordinary', i.e. to break the habits of organized routine and see the world 'as though for the first time'; it is necessary to free ourselves of normalized ways of thinking which bind us to the strangeness of the familiar. Hence, Foucault's use of provocative images and tropes to stop the reader's understanding in its tracks: the hypothesis that the idea of man is a modern invention, scarcely two centuries old; the grotesque description of Damiens, the regicide, whose body was publicly tortured, fleeced and dismembered as a symbol of penal repression (i.e. legalized violence) in the eighteenth century; the idea that modern medicine, far from having its origin in altruistic humanism, developed out of the State's concern for the management of the 'bio-mass', i.e., the population of bodies, Foucault remind us that all discourse has an inbuilt censoring function which represses the intrinsic strangeness of symbolism and that the first step in analysis is to recognize this as a way of 'enlightening' ourselves. Thus enlightenment takes on a new aspect here. For Kant, enlightenment was a rational but still normalized mode of critical thought. For Foucault, enlightenment is the experience of sudden and spontaneous insight when one is seized by a power beyond rational, conscious thought, i.e., by the auratic. Foucault reveals the experience of estranging enlightenment most notably through his adaption of Nietzsche's method of genealogy (Foucault 1977a: 139–164). Genealogy is opposed to the search for pure and ideal forms which pre-exist our profane, everyday world. Instead, the genealogist finds that ideal essences, essential truths, are fabrications taken from 'alien forms'. What we find at the so-called origin of things is not a reassuring state of perfection, now lost but still reclaimable; instead there is disparity, difference, indeterminacy. Foucault's genealogical method is therefore similar to Lyotard's agonistics and Derrida's deconstruction: all deny the concept of a perfect origin and substitute for it a process of differential contestation. For this reason, Habermas criticizes Foucault (and the postmodernists in general) for being 'irrational'. Habermas (1984) considers reason to be conditional on a concept of the perfect origin; his 'communicative rationality' presupposes just such an ideal state. But the logic of postmodern thought starts from a different understanding of reason, one that appears at times more veraciously argued than that of rival positions. It is a rationality that is based not on finding answers but of 'problematizing' answers. This is entirely consistent with the genealogical position which says that disparity (and not parity) is the source of human structures: answers are merely temporary inversions of problems. Whereas Habermas is looking for *the* answer (or at least an approach to it), Foucault can only see answers as ways of short-circulating problems, as expressions of the 'haste of wanting to know'. His analysis always proceeds from the complex process of how thoughts are structured so as to give a solution. In the human world, this is always subject to the work of power, inevitably because power is intrinsic to the agonistic logic of disparity. Discourse is the expression of power that is centred on problems. Power precedes the answer through its subtle and covert prior structuring of the problem. This is why Foucault is so concerned with 'problematizing', since the proper understanding of a solution can only be got from seeing how the problem was structured in the first place. All of Foucault's work deals with this issue in one way or another: the development of the problem of madness in medieval times, the origin of modern medical discourse with the organization of specialist clinics and hospitals in the eighteenth century; the rise of the social sciences as devices for structuring problems so as to market them more amenable to management and administration.

Discourse is no longer a neutral means for communicating about the world. Instead, it is the discourse of difference and self-reference. It is no longer an extension of human organs or faculties; it is the latter that are extensions of discourse.

## ORGANIZATIONAL ANALYSIS

The object of orthodox organizational analysis is *the* organization: a bounded social system, with specific features and goals which acts more or less rationally and more or less coherently. Within this context, the concept of organization itself functions as a metadiscourse to legitimate the idea that organization is a social tool and an extension of the human agent, an 'auxiliary organ' by which 'man has . . . become a kind of prosthetic God' (Freud 1961: 92) in pursuit of the *idea* of anthropocentric order. Bell's

(1974) account of the modern corporation represents the apotheosis of this idea. Now the cognitive mode of this form of organization is based on what Varela (1979) calls the 'control' image of the 'computer gestalt' which, like Lyotard's systems of performativity, programmes itself in order to optimize its overall input-output ratio (Lyotard 1984). Since inputs must 'correspond' to outputs, the computer gestalt is a referential model of organization which employs information/knowledge (discourse) in a fixed, operational and 'instructive' sense. However, Varela reminds us that referentially is merely a special or limiting case of self-referentiality so that the latter has to be seen as the more encompassing (Varela 1979: 265–267). Varela wants us to see organization as a product of self-reference and thus decentre the role of rational purpose.

It is common for social scientists to think about social systems, and perhaps especially organizations, from the referential point of view, even when their explicit purpose is understanding rather than social engineering. This of course is a recognized criticism of the systems paradigm whose function emphasis serves to supress the action of difference and self-reference (Cooper 1986). We see such suppression at work in Blau's theory of organization which relies centrally on the concept of 'differentiation' (Blau 1974). By 'differentiation', Blau means the divisions of labour (specialization) and authority. Since he is predisposed to viewing organizations within the functional (i.e., referential perspective of the computer gestalt—the 'defining criterion of formal organization . . . is the existence of procedures for mobilizing and coordinating the efforts of various, usually specialized, subgroups in the pursuit of joint objectives (Blau 1974: 29)—Blau is then led to place the emphasis on *specialization and authority rather than on differentiation*, i.e., the perceptual centring on 'control' seduces him into defining structure in terms of *static* difference, the *active* nature of difference becoming hidden from awareness and therefore unavailable to analysis. Like most theorists, Blau begins his analysis from a position which omits the originary step of differentiation or division in social organization. Organization therefore appears *already formed*.

It is exactly this issue that is raised in Mayntz's criticism of the dominant models of organizational decision-making for being *normatively rational*: goals are set by the organization and this step is followed by a search for the best solution from competing alternatives (Mayntz 1976). Thus, 'action appears to be touched off by preconceived goals or purposes' (Mayntz 1976: 119). Mayntz reverses this order of decision analysis by suggesting that organizational processes are in reality *reactions* to 'local' perturbations: 'organizational activity in general and policy-making in particular is primarily triggered by situational factors which constitute a *pressure to act*, rather than being generated by deliberations on how certain abstract values can be achieved' (Mayntz 1976: 119). This criticism also significantly emphasizes the 'interactive' or 'agonistic' nature of organizational activity for Mayntz reminds us that, in contrast to the normative-rational model, decisions are rarely, if ever, taken by individuals but are invariably embedded in an active network of people within a *division* of labour.

Mayntz's criticism is reflected in similar analyses by writers in field as diverse as economic development, technological research and development, and policy-making (Hirschman and Lindblom 1962). This gist of this work is that there are no perfect theoretical solutions to problems which we can prepare in advance and that decisions have to be made as *remedial* moves in situations marked by uncertainty, disorder and imbalance. In these analyses, practice usurps theory, and organization, far from being a structure of calculated, deliberate actions, is in reality the *automatic* response to an impending threat. The analyses thus suggests that rational control subserves a more fundamental process which acts autonomously in much the same way that Varela suggests that referentiality subserves self-referentiality (Varela 1979). In short, the process of organization is self-originating and automatic.

Insights into this alternative way of thinking about organization may be sporadically discerned in the literature of social and organizational analysis. Gouldner's concept of 'functional autonomy', which states, among other things, that organizational activity is focussed on the boundaries or divisions *between* system parts, is an early recognition of self-reference at work in formal organizations (Gouldner 1959). Specifically, Gouldner argues that organizational divisions exert an autonomous pressure on organizational activities because they are the source of paradoxical interactions constituted by the mutuality of 'separation' and 'joining'. The theme of self-reference also pervades Merton's analyses of social systems: the formal rationality of bureaucracy paradoxically produces 'dysfunctions' alongside its 'functions' (Merton 1968: Ch. 8); social beliefs may function as 'self-fulfilling prophecies' (Merton 1968: Ch. 13); intentional social actions may lead to unintended consequences (Merton 1976: Ch. 8). Despite Merton's recognition of the interplay between the referential and the self-referential, his bias (as a self-confessed functionalist) is towards the former so that a fuller understanding of self-reference itself is left, finally, in mid-air. Nonetheless, these brief references to the social science literature do indicate an awareness of two opposed ways of thinking about organization: (1) a 'control' model which is referential, instructional and conceived as the expression of human rationality; (2) an 'autonomy' model which is self-referential, processual (i.e., without fixed location) and which acts automatically, i.e., independently of external (human) control. The 'control' model approximates the modernist view of the world, especially in the idea of the ultimate rational subject who can 'meta-organize'. In contrast, the 'autonomy' model approximates the arguments of postmodernism, especially the rejection of the omniscient, rational subject.

Postmodern thought begins with the insight that all discourse suffers from an intrinsic *reactivity* and this has to be addressed as a problem before the epistemological possibilities of the 'autonomy' model can be properly realized. Hirschman and Lindblom characterize the reactivity problem as the tendency of rational actions to be *remedial*, i.e., 'they move *away* from ills rather than *toward* known objectives' (Hirschman and Lindblom 1962: 216). If this diagnosis can also be applied to academic discourse, we can perhaps begin to see that the dice are already loaded against the development of postmodern methodology in the social sciences. Postmodern analysis confronts this issue with Nietzsche's genealogical method. As we have noted, genealogy defines difference in terms of the *active-reactive* distinction. The active and reactive are, respectively and roughly, Varela's (1979) concepts of 'autonomy' and 'control', except that in Nietzsche's formulation the former are regarded as forces, sources of power, rather than just intellectual concepts. The active is the 'essential priority of spontaneous, aggressive, expansive, form-giving forces that give new interpretations and directions' (Deleuze 1983: 41) but which must be tamed, even denied, by the countervailing forces of the reactive which thus function *remedially*.

The genealogical displacement of difference from mere concept to active force is effectively the inversion of the traditional (i.e., referential) understanding of difference as a *static effect* of separation (such as we saw in Blau's use of 'differentiation') to an awareness of difference as active codependence; from simple division to unitary flow, from isolated term to interactive process. A definitive feature of autonomous systems is their intrinsic resistance to division, partialization and classification. Viewed in this way, an organization is a unity or coherence of forces which we lose sight of when we apply the accepted academic specializations (sociology, psychology, economics, political science, etc.) and methodologies. In the latter, we merely *represent* the *structures* of social systems, the representations being representations for a subject who (or which) attempts to appropriate and master the system as a field of knowledge. A genealogy of system and organization begins with the recognition that representations and structures derive from a more fundamental process of materiality and energy. Ideas, images, discourse itself, are now to be viewed as a material force that dissolves the conception of the human world as a series of divisions. This view is elaborated in a key postmodern text by Deleuze and Guattari in which social 'bodies' are defined as productive 'machines' which are continually engaged in the processing of matter (Deleuze and Guattari 1983). The unitary point of view taken by Deleuze and Guattari rejects the representation of separate social terms, which means that the concept of the productive machine applies to everything in the human (and natural) world: machines are individuals, groups, organizations and whole societies. This approach also means that we have to reject the usual conception of machines as extensions of human power; in fact, Deleuze and Guattari argue that man is actually an appendix of machines. This is because machines are powered by the irresistible force of the active. In effect, machines produce remorseless flows of matter-energy; they then divide the flows, codify them, and finally, inscribe the codifications on the 'body' (the material source of the flows) in order to establish boundaries. A simple illustration of this process is the animal which uses its flow of bodily secretions to mark out its territory; the animal is thus a machine which produces a habitable territory. By the same token, organizations are social machines which produce elaborate discourses of information/ knowledge in which human subjects are a necessary part of the material flow on which the discourses are inscribed. Organizations operate either directly or indirectly on the world of nature and, because of the self-referential logic of autonomous systems, this necessarily includes 'human nature'.

The conception of the 'body' as material flow has two important consequences for organizational analysis. First, the idea of 'flow' draws attention to the essential instability of the human environment, including the human body itself. There are no absolute constraints in life or nature. 'Nothing in man—not even his body—is sufficiently stable to serve as the basis for self-recognition or for understanding other men' (Foucault 1977a: 153). Second, the role of the human subject in traditional organizational analysis has been shaped by certain functional requirements: the subject is a 'decision-maker' or a 'worker', for example: that is, the definition of the subject is dependent on the prior acceptance of a normative-rational model of organization. In contrast, the genealogical conception of the subject as a body in material flow leads to think of it as a machine that produces itself; it thus places the subject at the origin of the organizing process instead of seeing it as an adjunct. These points demand a radical revaluation of the traditional concept of organization as a circumscribed administrative-economic unit as well as the methodologies that go to define it. Instead, we need to see organization as a *process* that occurs within the wider 'body' of society and which is concerned with the construction of objects of theoretical knowledge centred on the 'social body': health, disease, emotion, alimentation, labour, etc. In other words, to understand organizations it is necessary to analyse them from the outside, as it were, and not from what is already organized. It becomes a question of analysing, let us say, the production of organization rather than the organization of production. Hence the importance of starting from genealogy rather than from organization itself: organization as an object of knowledge emerges out of the contestation intrinsic to the logic of difference and self-reference—as we saw, for example, in Hirschman's study of the reactive origin of modern organization in the eighteenth century as a devise to subject and harness man's impulsive nature to social and economic production (Hirschman 1977).

Perhaps the first step towards a postmodern interpretation of organization is the recognition that all organized human activity is essentially reactive or defensive. This would then logically imply recognition of the active, especially as the superior force. These fundamentals are universally absent from orthodox organization theory. It is difficult, for example, even to catch a glimpse of the active-reactive dynamic at work in the static picture of organization drawn in terms of the bureaucratic paradigm (e.g., the dimensions of authority, structuring of activities, standardization of procedures, etc.) A massive shift in theoretical perspective would be needed to translate the

bureaucratic model into the active-reactive model, especially to do justice
to the insight that all institutional and organizational activity is basically
self-referential. Postmodern thought begins with the latter thesis and always
comes back to it. We see it constantly at work in Foucault's analysis of organizational processes where 'organization' is viewed as a series of interrelated
rationalities of *programmes, technologies* and *strategies* which are forever
beset by the problems of recursion endemic to self-reference (Gordon 1980).
A programme is, minimally, a set of instructions for achieving a goal. Less
obviously, it *presupposes* a knowledge of the field on which it is to operate by rendering reality 'in the form of an object which is programmable'
(Gordon 1980: 248). The programme is therefore a version of Mayntz's
(1976) normative-rational model of organization as well as invoking Bell's
(1974) protypical post-industrial organization which runs on theoretical
knowledge. Built into the programme are 'mechanisms of correct functioning' which in social systems appear as *norms* of appropriate behaviour for
individuals and collectives. Now the norm itself is a product of techniques
of normalization which structure discourse in terms of the correct-incorrect,
the desirable-undesirable, etc. In fact, the programme becomes actual to the
extent that it is supported by a technology. There is thus a co-dependent (i.e.
self-referential) relation 'between the programmatic and the technological,
the normal and the normative' which 'is in turn the outcome of the conceptualization within the discursive form of the programme itself of an ineluc-
table discrepancy between discourse and actuality' (Gordon 1980: 250).
This is because the peculiar logic of self-reference dictates that terms necessarily contain their own opposites, as we have seen, and this means that for
every programme there is an un-programme, for every norm there is an ab-
norm. Deviations and errors are no longer to be thought of as adventitious
effects of imperfect rationality for they are built into the very instruments
which seek to annul them. Programmes and technologies are therefore, in
this odd sense, anti-functional. Among other things, this means that 'every
programme caters in advance for the eventuality of its own failure' (Gordon
1980: 250). Foucault instances prisons as organizations which, while continually besieged by their failure to attain their planned goals as reformato-
ries, have sought just as continually to reorganize themselves of the model
of their original but failed programme:

> 'One should. . . . Recall that the movement of reforming the prisons, for
> controlling their functioning, is not a recent phenomenon. It does not
> even seen to have originated in a recognition of failure. Prison "reform"
> is virtually contemporary with the prison itself: it constitutes, as it were,
> its programme. From the outset, the prison was caught up in a series of
> accompanying mechanism, whose purpose was apparently to correct it,
> but which seem to form part of its very functioning, so closely have they
> been bound up with its existence throughout its long history'.
>
> (Foucault 1977b: 234)

It would be hard to find a more telling example of organization as *remedial reaction* which, as it were, thinks on its feet. Here we have the works of *strategies* which, in contrast to the normative rationality of the programme, are pragmatic, instinctive and improvisational. Strategy operates at the level of practice rather than theory. This is because its action occurs in a complex and heterogeneous field of instantaneous forces where it exploits 'possibilities which it itself discerns and creates . . . strategy is the arena of the cynical, the promiscuous, the tacit, in virtue of its general logical capacity for the synthesis of the heterogeneous' (Gordon 1980: 251). Strategy operates at the labyrinthine core of organization—the eye of the vortex—where difference and self-reference reign. In emphasizing this level of institutional action, postmodern analysis wishes to draw our attention to the central role of autonomy (in Varela's sense) or the machine (in Deleuze and Guattari's sense) in social systems. It is this primary force which, via the level of strategy, animates programmes and technologies rather than the reverse.

Lyotard (1977) provides an illuminating analysis of strategy at work in his concept of the *mise-en-scène*, the complex play of operations which make the basic components of social organization 'come alive'. In the organizational context, we are faced with a set of primary data constituted by programmes and technologies. These are essentially groups of discourses belonging to different systems of rationality (legal, economic, scientific, etc.) They thus represent a heterogeneous field with two noteworthy features: it is 'inert' and, because of its diverse origins, it has a potential for 'disorder'. The *mise-en-scène* lays hold of this intractable space and 'gives it life'. To 'give life' means to transcribe the inert discourses or programmes and technologies onto living bodies. The transcription involves the translation of the inert and heterogeneous into the elementary unit of the 'polyesthetic' human body considered as a 'multi-sensory potentiality' with its 'capacity to see, hear, to touch, to move . . .' (Lyotard 1977: 88). It involves a movement from the referential register of programmes and technologies to the self-referential register of the *mise-en-scène*, which now has to be understood as the active origin of organization. Organizations do not first pre-exist and then create their relationships; they *occur* in existential gaps which lie beyond knowledge discourse. These gaps are the loci of operation of *mise-en-scènes* and strategies which focus their attentions on, and emerge out of, the unprogrammable and non-discursive. Organized rationality, far from originating in *beau*-ideals and consummate logics of efficiency, is founded on sleight-of-hand, vicious agonisms and *pudenda origo* ('shameful origins'). This is the revisionary lesson that postmodernism brings to organizational analysis.

## Post Scriptum

Let us remind ourselves that the subject of organizational analysis is *formal* organization. It is not organization as such that demands analysis but its 'formal' character, though this is often forgotten. Ordinarily, the word 'formal' signifies what is proper, methodical, and punctilious. In the context of formal organizations and institutions, the 'formal' is not just the proper and methodical but also the 'official'; it becomes raised to the level of law and public truth. What is formally organized takes on the virtue of a moral order. Hence the emphasis in modernism on the search for 'rational authority' as the basis of the *good* social order. But the logic of human discourse insists that every symbol carries within its own opposite, so that the 'formal' is continually shadowed by the 'informal'. Douglas (1970: 100) develops this opposition within the context of social organization: 'Formality signifies social distance, well-defined, public, insulated roles. Informality is appropriate to role confusion, familiarity, intimacy'. In other words, the 'formal' has all the characteristics of classical reason as conceived by the Enlightenment: it is referential, transparent, closed, monumental. 'These are the terms of Foucault's *"regimen"* and Weber's *"rationalization"*, the strong forms of functional purity which, certainly by the eighteenth century in England, led to the great age of "institutionalizing"—asylums, hospitals, schools, barracks, prisons, insurance and finance houses—which, as Foucault has suggested, embody and assure the maintenance of classical bourgeois reason' (Stallybrass and White 1986: 22). As Douglas' definition suggests, the 'informal' is that which threatens to transgress the 'formal', it is the local and immediate, that which resists categorization and rationalization. In short, the 'informal' is the self-referential and as such it is the special province of postmodern analysis.

We have already noted that modernism puts the answer before the question and thus acts on the principles that it 'already knows'. It thus privileges the idea of formal organization (i.e., the organization of the 'formal') while at the same time rationalizing away the existence of the 'informal'. It is not difficult to see this process at work in the literature of contemporary organizational analysis which unknowingly repeats the formalized structures of organization in its own methodology. Various studies of organizations have identified 'formalization' as a major feature of organizational structure (e.g., Hall 1972: 172–199). To simplify, these studies indicate that formalization is concerned with the definition and maintenance of 'correct' behaviour or what we here call the 'formal'. As we noted, behind the idea of the 'formal' is a moral imperative (i.e., an 'order') which demands the total exclusion of the 'informal' (which now becomes the 'immoral'). It is this process of exclusion that constitutes the already-made-up-mind of formalism and of course it is present in all formalizations, including those that make up the methodologies of organizational analysis. Let us briefly illustrate this idea with the concept of 'uncertainty' which has received extensive treatment in various areas of organizational analysis (e.g., decision-making, technology, environment). In these analyses, the indeterminateness intrinsic to uncertainty (by definition, an aspect of the 'informal') is viewed in terms of the 'formal', e.g., the well-known framework that reduces task uncertainty to the 'non-routine', thus defining uncertainty from the point of view of the 'routine', i.e., the certain (see, e.g., Perrow 1972: 166–167). The same tendency to formalize the unformalizable can be seen at work in Luhmann's (1976) analysis of uncertainty in complex, organized systems where, among other things, the concept of self-reference is discussed entirely in referential (i.e., determinate) terms. In short, formal organization is characterized by an inveterate urge to supress its own opposite in such a covert way that we remain unaware of its censoring function.

The task of postmodern thought is to expose the censoring function of formalization and, what is more, to show that the 'informal' actually constitutes the 'formal'. The 'formal' and 'informal' reflect each other like the obverse and reverse sides of a coin; to the extent that they can never be separated, they are not just mutually-defining but can be said to be the 'same' or self-referential. It is from this point of view that writers such as Foucault and Derrida view and analyse the 'formal', so that it is no longer a privileged and unassailable site in social discourse. The purpose of Foucault's analysis of the emergence of formal organization at the time of, and subsequent to, the Industrial Revolution is to show how the 'formal' was constructed out of the 'informal' through the processes of discipline and normalization. Significantly, the style of discourse he employs to do this itself 'informal', e.g., the modern reader's understanding of 'organization' is turned upside down by Foucault's depiction of it as a 'disciplinary technology'. The normalized world of formal institutions becomes part of the grotesque side of life. The concept of power is similarly reversed when one is forced to view it from an 'informal' or self-referential perspective. Formal views of power are centred on such formalized units as 'individuals' or 'organizations' and one is led to think of power as a kind of property that is owned and manipulated by such social units. The 'informal' perspective makes us see power as an autonomous system of compulsion which *works through* formal systems of discipline and organization. One consequence of this is that social science disciplines such as psychology and sociology themselves become formal discourses that normalize and anaesthetize us to the 'informal' substrata of human life. Postmodernism reveals formal organization to be the ever-present expression of an autonomous power that masquerades as the supposedly rational constructions of modern institutions.

These considerations lead us to the general observation that two radically different systems of thought and logic are at work in the modernist-postmodernist confrontation. There is some reason to believe that they are fundamentally irreconcilable because they derive from that basic split in the structure of human logic associated with the 'formal'-'informal' distinction which has been exacerbated by the extension of formal organization into so many facets of modern life. In fact, it may be more appropriate to view these competing views organized systems less as competing conceptual positions and more as symptoms of the problematic that they aim to analyse and understand. It is this angle that we shall pursue in taking the work of Foucault, Derrida, Habermas and Luhmann as subjects for more detailed and systematic exposition of the modernist-postmodernist debate in relation to the study of organized systems in subsequent issues of *Organization Studies*. On the postmodern side, Foucault and Derrida have dealt, in their different ways, disabling body blows to the traditionally unquestioned pillars of modern institutionalized thought, centering their analyses on the organized and even manufactured status of the discourse used to support these pillars. On the modern side, Habermas has been vigorous in his criticisms of Foucault and Derrida, defending particularly the concept of critical and responsible human agency (which postmodernism puts in question) against the massive, machine-like instrumentalization of social life by large-scale formal systems; Luhmann's response to the progress of complex, organized systems is more benign, for he is the cartographer of modern, instrumental systems whose analyses tell us how to find our way about them. The significance of these four thinkers in the present context lies in their counterpointing of issues and concepts that lie at the heart of the organizing process, for they deal essentially with the same themes—differentiation, power, authority, discipline, etc.—but produce radically different interpretations of them. It is this agonistic rivalry—sometimes overt, sometimes mute—that in our view brings out the relevance of the modernist-postmodernist debate for the reinvigoration of analysis of social systems in general and organizations in particular.

## REFERENCES

Bell, D. (1974) *The coming of post-industrial society*. London: Heinermann.

Berman, M. (1983) *All that is solid melts into air: the experience of modernity*. London: Verso.

Blau, P. (1974) *On the nature of organizations*. New York: Wiley.

Bourdieu, P., and J. C. Passeron. (1977) *Reproduction in education, society and culture*. London: Sage.

Certeau, M. de. (1986) *Heterologies*. Manchester: Manchester University Press.

Cooper, R. (1986) 'Organization/Disorganization'. *Social Science Information* 25/2: 299–335.

Deleuze, G. (1983) *Nietzsche and philosophy*. London: Athlone Press.

Deleuze, G., and F. Guattari. (1983) *Anti-Oedipus: capitalism and schizophrenia*. Minneapolis: University of Minnesota Press.

Derrida, J. (1973) *Speech and phenomena*. Evanston: Northwestern University Press.

Douglas, M. (1970) *Natural symbols*. London: Barrie and Jenkins.

Foucault, M. (1977a) *Language, counter-memory, practice*. Ithaca, NY: Cornell University Press.

Foucault, M. (1977b) *Discipline and punish: the birth of the prison*. London: Allen Lane.

Foucault, M. (1980) *Power/Knowledge*. Brighton: Harvester Press.

Freud, S. (1961) 'Civilization and its discontents' in *The standard edition of the complete psychological works of Sigmund Freud*, Vol. XXI, 57–145. London: Hogarth Press and Institute of Psycho-Analysis.

Gordon, C. (1980) 'Afterword' in *Power/Knowledge*. M. Foucault. Brighton: Harvester Press.

Gouldner, A. (1959) 'Organizational analysis' in *Sociology today*. R. K. Merton, K. Broom and L. S. Cottrell (eds), 400–428. New York: Basic Books.

Habermas, J. (1972) *Knowledge and human interests*. London: Heinermann.

Habermas, J. (1984) *The theory of communicative action. I: reason and the rationalization of society*. Boston: Beacon Press.

Hall, R. H. (1972) *Organizations: structure and process*. Englewood Cliffs, NJ: Prentice-Hall.

Hirschman, A. O. (1977) *The passions and the interests*. Princeton, NJ: Princeton University Press.

Hirschman, A. O., and C. E. Lindblom. (1962) 'Economic development, research, and development, policy-making: some converging views'. *Behavioural Science* 7: 211–222.

Luhmann, N. (1976) 'A general theory of organized social systems' in *European contributions to organization theory*. G. Hofstede and M. S. Kassem (eds.), 96–113. Amsterdam: Van Gorcum.

Lyotard, J. F. (1977) 'The unconscious as *mise-en-scéne*' in *Performance in postmodern culture*. M. Benamou and C. Caramello (eds.) 87–98. Wisconsin: Center for Twentieth Century Studies and Coda Press.

Lyotard, J. F. (1984) *The postmodern condition: a report on knowledge*. Manchester: Manchester University Press.

Lyotard, J. F., and J. L. Thébaud. (1986) *Just gaming*. Manchester: Manchester University Press.

Mayntz, R. (1976) 'Conceptual models of organizational decision-making and their application to the policy process' in *European contributions to organization theory*. G. Hofstede and M. S. Kassem (eds.), 114–125. Amsterdam: Van Gorcum.

Merton, R. (1968) *Social theory and social structures*. New York: Free Press.

Merton, R. (1976) *Sociological ambivalence*. New York: Free Press.

Morgan, G. (1986) *Images of organization*. Beverly Hills, Cal.: Sage.

Perrow, C. (1972) *Complex organizations*. Glenview, Ill.: Scott, Foresman.

Rorty, R. (1980) *Philosophy and the mirror of nature*. Oxford: Blackwell.

Smart, B. (1983) *Foucault, Marxism and critique*. London: Routledge and Kegan Paul.

Stallybrass, P., and A. White. (1986) *The politics and poetics of transgression*. London: Methuen.

Varela, F. J. (1979) *Principles of biological autonomy*. New York: North Holland.

Whitehead, A. N. (1929) *Process and reality*. New York: Macmillan.

Wiener, N. (1948) *Cybernetics, or control and communication in the animal and the machine*. New York: Wiley.

(Excerpt from 'Interview with Robert Cooper' Robert C. H. Chia and Jannis Kallinikos, in Chia, R. (ed) (1998) *Organized Worlds: Explorations in Technology and Organization with Robert Cooper*. London: Routledge, 125–9.)

*It would not be too far wrong to suggest that many writers and readers in the more conventional mould of organization theory think of you as a 'postmodern' organization theorist. A central reference point here is the 'modernism/postmodernism' series of articles written for the journal* Organization Studies, *beginning with the introductory piece written jointly by yourself and Gibson Burrell (Cooper and Burrell, 1988). Given the vastly different side of thinking you bring to the study of organization, how does 'postmodern' organization theory, as you understand it, differ from the kind of writing produced by more conventional organization theorists?*

We should be careful of labelling, I feel. It can be *too* convenient, and, in the extreme, intellectually unhealthy. All labels tend to arrest critical thought. This is what has happened with the term 'postmodern'. As we know, Lyotard (1991) has questioned the 'postmodern' as a label that distinguishes it from—and even opposes it to—the 'modern'. It's not a case of the postmodern coming *after* the modern. For Lyotard, the modern is already conflated with the postmodern, 'modernity contains the promise of its overcoming' (p. 25), it's already at war with itself. For this reason alone, it becomes difficult to call oneself a postmodernist. In my own case, I have always thought of the modern-postmodern connection as a mutually constituting complicity, or better, as Lyotard (1991) has it, a 'general agonistics', in which you can't have one without the other. And, by the same token, I have never thought of myself as an organization theorist but rather as an intellectual interrogator of the modern condition in which organization, technology and information all call into play their agonistic complicity with disorganization, disorientation and 'un-formation'. This means that I don't consciously practice 'postmodern organization theory', despite the label that others may apply. Instead, I employ a *generic* methodology which stresses general process rather than then particularized details of *specific* methodology. The generic approach underlines the *sameness* rather than the difference of things. The lack of specific difference or detail means that one's intellectual strategy is forced to face a world that lacks intrinsic identity and certainty. Applied to organizational analysis, generic methodology means that one analyses *organizing as a general process* rather than organizations and their specific features. In generic analysis, there are no natural distinctions between 'individual', 'organization' and 'society', for example. Rather, there are only interlocking and intertwining associations that are continually on the move and that thus deny the idea of fixed entities with separate insides and outsides. Generic analysis does not recognize the self-contained human actor with its intentions and objectives. In the conventional view, intention is read as a mental event, a purpose 'in' an actor's mind. In generic analysis, intention is the tensional traction of a *field* of heterogeneous events, 'intention means "in tension", a pattern of actions that is distributed throughout such a field and which serves to *maintain* it or hold it together. The intention is no longer "in the head" of the actor—it is the actor that is "in "the happening of the field' (Cooper and Law, 1995: 246). Generic analysis subordinates the intentional object and the specific part in order to reveal organization in its most general sense. It's this sense of the generic that's implied by organization as the regeneration of general processes of 'survival' or 'living-on' rather than organization as the specialized pursuit of specific goals . . .

Generic knowledge is scattered, flexible and undivided. In contrast, specific knowledge divides and categorizes, locates 'things' in simple spaces, and linearizes its subject matter. It's a product of what the philosopher Whitehead (1925: 72) called *simple location*: the translation of raw matter into 'things' that get their definition by being placed in 'definite finite region(s) of space and definite finite durations of time'. Specific knowledge answers the specific questions of: What? Where? When? It precasts its questions in a way that demands they be answered in the specifiable space—time terms of simple location. This is the knowledge that modern organization has constructed in its pursuit of modernity—the knowledge of things in specific, self-contained spaces. Michel Foucault's work is mainly about the development of simple location as a major strategy of modern organizing. His analysis of the *gaze*, for example, is also a story about the suppression of the generic and its supersession by a form of knowing that specifies the world in terms of increasingly particularized structures and grids. We see the same story in the development of the modern professions in the nineteenth century, which used the principle of simple location to 'place' knowledge in *knowable* (i.e., coherent, self-contained) spaces (Bledstein, 1976). And, of course, it's a story that repeats John Wilkin's 'analytical language' as the basis for (a form of) scientific knowing in the sixteenth century. From these observations, we begin to see that modern organization is much more than an administrative—economic convenience. Organizations are the social *organs* through which society's members know, think, remember, etc. They are the social-cultural *organs* by which society renews the life-world of its members. But it's also in this sense that we have to understand organization as the reproduction of a society's population, where organization as regeneration takes as its objects the individual bodies of the populace: members' bodies always necessarily included as raw material—human resources—in the production and reproduction of organization. As agents of production, organizational members are also necessarily included as agents of consumption. We can see this recursive process in one of its more dramatic versions in the production of 'urban man' in early Victorian Britain, especially through the training of the excretory functions: 'If man could be forced to yield to interference in such a sensitive domain, he could be made to acquiesce in any kind of control; he could be made to learn many ways of binding his energy, he could be pressed into modernity' (Schoenwald, 1973: 675). Not least, this meant that the organization of orderly private habits could be generalized to the performance of orderly public roles: a version of Michel Foucault's (1977) 'docile bodies'. But there's more to it than productive effort and orderly comportment. The creation of 'urban man', of the producing consuming agent, is the translation of the human body (together with other raw materials) into *generic* organization. By this, I mean the making abstract and interchangeable of bodies and other objects into a pool of generalizable and transmutable resources. This, of course, is Marx's view of modernity, especially his characterization of the 'social human being' as the 'most total and universal possible social product'. It's also Deleuze's and Guattari's (1983) idea of 'deterritorialization'—the de-localizing of matter or raw material from 'simply located' bodies and objects for purposes of general transmutability (and hence transmissibility). But Deleuze and

Guattari also remind us that the deterritorialization of forms is simply the excuse for their 'reterritorialization' in new 'simple locations', hierarchies and institutional structures. Behind every example of modern production lurks the ghost of generic organization.

In the idea of deterritorialization-reterriorialization we meet a yet further feature of generic organization—*general agonistics* (Lyotard, 1991). Territorialization is the divisioning and compartmentalization of a territory or field—academic, administrative, cultural, social, etc.—into *simple locations*. It's agonistic in the sense that the setting up of divisions demands their continuous maintenance, since divisions are always *internally* constituted by undivisions, insides by their outsides. Generic organization explicitly recognizes this agonistics or struggle. This is, again, Samuel Weber's (1987) argument that the concept of the Self is never just a simple difference from others but is an effect of a continuously maintained contestation *with* others . . . As Bledstein (1976) shows, the organization of American universities in the nineteenth century was formally and consciously based on the divisioning and compartmentalization of fields of knowledge. The divisions thus constituted served not only to found individual 'disciplines' in the conventional academic sense but—like the anally disciplined 'urban man' of Victorian Britain—also served to discipline individuals by excluding the very things that recursively constituted them, that is, by setting *apart* those things of which they were *apart*. Both subject as agent *and* as subject matter are co-implicated in a tensional field of (apparently) discrete elements that *neither fit nor do not fit together*. It's in this sense that agonistics is the continuous regeneration of generic organization.

Another way of saying generic organization is *cyberorganization*. Cyberorganization is short for cybernetic organization. Briefly, cybernetics is the science of communication and control in humans, animals and machines. And, for cybernetics, organization means communication and control. Cybernetic organization is always *on the move*, it's organization as the continuous regeneration of patterns—patterns that perpetuate themselves through changing circumstances. In this sense, organization is really *information*, or rather *re*information, the active making of forms. Cybernetic organization is *generic* in at least two senses: (1) it reads the world according to an abstract and generalizable language like Deleuze and Guattari's (1983) *deterritorializationreterritorialization*; and (2) it reveals the world as series of *circuits of differences* (Bateson, 1972) or *becomings* in which 'things' or 'states' are secondary to process or continuous movement. Donna Haraway's (1991) notion of the *cyborg* (short for cybernetic organism) illustrates these two features of cybernetic organization. The cyborg is a 'hybrid of machine and organism' which relativize 'the difference between living and mechanical systems' and radically challenges 'the line of demarcation drawn between the natural and the artificial' (Johnson, 1993: 105). It expresses itself through the 'plasticity' of informational patterns (e.g., databases, electronic money)' which make 'possible the combinatorial play of matter and thus the continuous disassembly and reassembly of new forms and patterns' (Cooper and Law, 1995: 268). In stressing *information on the move*, cyberorganization stresses *translation* as the modus operandi of social life: the translation of patterns, ideas, programmes *between* systems rather than the individual systems themselves. For, in cyberorganization, it's not the systems—the individual, the organization, the society—that count but the patterns of information that move between them and which constitute them as *repeated punctualizations*. It's these features of cyberorganization that we meet in Haraway's (1991: 164) description of biotechnology as information. Biotechnology is the exemplary science of the cyborg because it *translates* living organisms into 'problems of genetic coding and readout . . . In a sense, organisms have ceased to exist as objects of knowledge, giving way to biotec components, that is, special kinds of information processing devices'. Here, cybernetic information surpasses the conventionally recognized separation between biology and technology to form a new punctualization. In this sense, cyberorganization eliminates the old labels and categories of thought.

In several recent publications, the philosopher Mark Taylor (Taylor and Saarinen, 1994; Taylor, 1995) has discussed similar 'collapsings' bought about by the new *underlying*—and therefore largely neglected—nature of information in his notion of the *mediatrix*. The mediatrix is 'that which constituted by the intersection of electronic media and computelecommunications technology' (Taylor, 1995: 25). The mediatrix is not a stable form—in fact, it's more like 'un-form' because its complex, fleeting, unstable connections and multiplicities defy conventional logic and analysis. For this reason, the mediatrix is beyond formal comprehension—it can only be hinted at, alluded to, because it's *medium-media* in the most literal sense of being in the *middle* or *between*. All this suggests a radically different vocabulary of thinking than conventional methodologies provide. And this alternative vocabulary is exactly what Taylor and Saarinen (1994) offer in their *Imagologies* book, where they discuss the implications of the new electronic technologies for various organizational and institutional processes. In effect, they provide a genetic methodology for the new cyberorganizational 'forms'—a methodology which says that in our late-modern world of electronic interaction 'everything is everywhere at all times' (Whitehead) and where, instead of organizations, we have '*organizings*' as ongoing actions in heterogeneous field of tension, as happenings—on the wing, so to speak' (Cooper and Law, 1995: 271–272); a world of collage, mergings and mixings; a world that is always in the *middle*, always *in-between*. Taylor and Saarinen's *Imagologies* introduces us to a range of cyberorganization-relevant ideas and terms to reflect this electronically mediated world of the *in-between*: Interstanding, Netropolis, Net Effect, Electronomics, Shifting Subjects, etc. This is the vocabulary of generic knowledge—scattered, flexible, undivided.

Your question asks how my why of thinking *organization* differs from conventional organization theory. I have answered you in terms of how

I think the subject of modern organizing, rather than how others think the field of organization studies. For me, modern organizing has to be understood (1) by means of a *generic methodology* which underlines the scattered and heterogeneous nature of organization as distinct from the study of organizations and their specific features; (2) as a repeated process of *social-cultural regeneration* in which society recursively includes its members as raw material for organizing; (3) as a *general agonistics* of differentiation-de-differentiation in which organizing defines and recognizes itself through *setting-apart* that which it needs to exclude; and (4) as the *cyberorganization* interpretation of organization-information in terms of translation and the transitional space of the mediatrix.

## Editors' Note

All the references for these interview sections can be found after the final interview extract, 'Main features of my approach . . .', in section 15.

# 8  The Visibility of Social Systems

*Robert Cooper*

(From M. C. Jackson, P. Keys, and S. Cropper (eds) 1989, *Operational Research in the Social Sciences*, New York: Plenum, 51–59. Copyright © 1989 by Plenum Press. Reprinted by permission of Spinger-Verlag GmBH.)

## INTRODUCTION

The role of the senses in social life is a neglected theme in social analysis. Despite the philosopher Whitehead's (1938) early call for systematic study of the 'organization of the sensorium' in human communication, it is only recently that this has been taken up as a serious challenge by the human sciences. Much of this work has focused on the dominance of vision, especially in modern social systems subjected to 'bureaucratization' and the processes of formal organization more generally. As Rorty (1980) has reminded us, modern thought has privileged the eye as the sense organ by which we may represent the world to ourselves most effectively. Yet it was not always like this. The historian Lucien Febvre (1982), in a study of 16th-century social life, comments on the underdevelopment of sight in that period:

> Like their acute hearing and sharp sense of smell, the men of that time doubtless had keen sight. But that was just it. They had not yet set it apart from the other senses. They had not yet tied its information in particular in a necessary link with their need to know. (p. 437)

Consequently they lived in a fluid world 'where nothing was strictly defined, where entities lost their boundaries and, in the twinkling of an eye, without causing much protest, changed shape, appearance, size . . .' (p. 438). The stabilization of the world required a specialized training of the visual sense and its elevation over the other senses. The process of stabilization called from quantification and calculation and this necessarily involved the eye: 'The passage from the qualitative to the quantitative is essentially linked to advances in the predominance of visual perception' (Rey quoted in Febvre, 1982, p. 432).

It is customary to view the careers of societies in terms of the division of labour where the emphasis is placed on the specialization of skills and occupations in an hierarchical framework. The social analysis of the human sensorium suggests an alternative way of viewing this process: instead of the 'division of labour', the differentiation of the senses draws attention to the complex processes at work in actively shaping the human agent as a perceiving organism in the social system. This differentiation process we may more accurately call the 'labour of division' since it not only highlights the act of division itself (as opposed to the specific agents of 'labour') but it also suggests that the 'division' in this context is significantly bound up with the act of 'seeing'—that is, 'vision' is an intrinsic component of 'division'. We can take this analysis further through the work of the philosopher Jacques Derrida (see, for example, Norris, 1987) who views the logic of 'division' in terms of (1) *hierarchy* and (2) *interaction*. (These are not Derrida's terms— I have retained his ideas but used a more familiar terminology.) In hierarchy, it is recognized that systems, social or otherwise, are structured around binary oppositions (e.g., good-bad, male-female) in which one of the terms dominates the other. As Derrida (1981) writes: '. . . we are not dealing with the peaceful co-existence of a *vis-à-vis*, but rather with a violent hierarchy. One of the two terms governs the other (axiologically, logically, etc.), or has the upper hand' (p. 41). In interaction, as Derrida reminds us, there is a continuous double movement *within* the binary opposition so that the positively-valued term (for example, good) is defined only by contrast to the negatively-valued second term (for example, bad). In fact, the relationship between the apparently opposing terms is really one of mutual definition in which the individual terms actually inhabit each other. In other words, the separate, individual terms give way 'to a process where opposites merge in a constant *undecidable* exchange of attributes' (Norris, 1987, p. 35). Interaction describes precisely the fluid, changing forms of perception characteristic of the human agent in the 16th-century, as noted by Febvre (1982). The conversation of this state of perpetual ambiguity into a more determinate structure necessitated the hierarchical step of raising the status of sight over the 'primitive' senses of touch, taste and smell in favour of the *visualization* of perception. In this way, the general process of the 'labour of division' enables greater control over the social and material world through enhanced clarity, transparency and visual certainty *at a distance*.

## VISIBILITY AND THE DEVELOPMENT OF MODERN SOCIAL SYSTEMS

The first widespread attempts to organize and systematize the social world occurred in the 16th century. As Foucault (1979) points out, the 16th century saw the emergence of an increasing concern with the 'art of government' and political economy, that is, with the management of people, territory and raw materials. Perhaps for the first time, people began to be defined in terms of their relationship with 'wealth, resources, means of subsistence, the territory with its specific qualities, climate, irrigation, fertility, etc.' . . . as well as in their relation to 'accidents and misfortunes such as famine, epidemics, death, etc.' (Foucault, 1979, p. 11). In short, the management of social-economic systems began to take shape in men's minds. The creation of visibility, the harnessing of a precise visual bias to the control of people and things, was a necessary component of this development.

In his study of hospitals and medical practice at the end of the 16th century, Foucault (1973) identifies a new phenomenon of organized perception—the 'gaze'—which subjected the individual to the definition of a new social practice, i.e., medicine, that assumed the authority of a 'science'. The concept of the gaze as a technique for ensuring the maximum visibility of individuals is further elaborated in Foucault's (1977) study of the prison system in which the gaze finds its special pedigree as a power (here the significance of the French '*pouvoir*', with its inclusion of the verb 'to see', underlines the imbrication of power, knowledge and visibility) that 'must see without being seen' (p. 171). The necessary role of surveillance in the construction and maintenance of visibility is perhaps best exemplified in Jeremy Bentham's architectural concept of the Panopticon, 'the polyvalent apparatus of surveillance, the universal optical machine of human groupings' (Miller, 1987, p. 3). The Panopticon was a circular building with a central tower from which continuous surveillance could be unilaterally exercised on inmates housed in perimeter cells. The Panopticon represented a more general idea—the Panoptic principle—in which Bentham dreamt 'of a transparent society, visible and legible in each of its parts' (Foucault, 1980, p. 152) which would expurgate 'the fear of darkened spaces, of the pall of gloom which prevents the full visibility of things, men and truths' (p. 153) that haunted the second half of the eighteenth century. Hence the need to elaborate that compendious theoretical system of administration which absorbed so much of Bentham's life in the pursuit of the criteria of visibility: transparent knowledge *at a glance* through surveillance at a distance.

The pursuit of visibility was advanced, as Foucault (1977) notes, through the introduction of the 'examination', a technique which combines the power of an 'observing hierarchy' with that of a 'normalizing judgement'. The examination 'is a normalizing gaze, a surveillance that makes it possible to qualify, to classify and to punish. It establishes over individuals a visibility through which one differentiates them and judges them' (p. 184). In the eighteenth century, the hospital emerged as one of the first modern examples of an 'examining apparatus'. It regularized the form and frequency of the medical inspection and made it 'internal' to the hospital. Formerly a religious hospice, the hospital became subject to medical authority and the physician, hitherto an external element, displaced the religious staff into a subordinate role in the technique of examination. The hospital became a place of training and of the development of a form of knowledge which had as its object the subjection of the patient through techniques of surveillance and the normalizing gaze. The medical examination exemplified the logic of division: it hierarchized individuals into the categories of 'normal' and 'abnormal' and, just as importantly, it served to prevent the 'interaction' or intermixing of these categories. Ultimately, it enabled everyone *to see more clearly* the difference between 'good' and 'bad' physical and mental health.

In the same way, the early schools became a sort of examining apparatus. 'The Brothers of the Christian Schools wanted their pupils to be examined every day of the week: on the first for spelling, the on the second for arithmetic, on the third for catechism in the morning and for handwriting in the afternoon, etc.' (Foucault, 1977, p. 186). The school examination made the pupil subject to a 'discipline' of continuous surveillance and visibility: 'it guaranteed the movement of knowledge from the teacher to the pupil, but it extracted from the pupil a knowledge destined and reserved for the teacher' (p. 187).

There are three specific ways, according to Foucault (1977), in which the examination promotes visibility while at the same time linking the latter to knowledge and power. First, *'the examination transformed the economy of visibility into the exercise of power'* (p. 187). In contrast to traditional forms of power whose efficacy rested on the full display of the power holder (e.g., king, general) and the passive invisibility of its servitors, the new examination-based disciplinary power revers this process by imposing a 'compulsory visibility' on its servitors while it itself remains invisible. 'In discipline, it is the subjects who have to be seen. Their invisibility assures the hold of the power that is exercised over them. It is the fact of being constantly seen, of being able always to be seen, that maintains the disciplined individual in his subjection' (p. 187). Second, *'the examination . . . introduces individuality into the field of documentation'* (p. 189). The examination not only locates individuals in 'a field of surveillance' but it 'also situates them in a network of writing: it engages them in a whole mass of documents that capture and fix them' (p. 189). Through administrative writing it became possible to describe, identify and record in precise form the visibility of individuals according to the logic of division. Through what Giddens (1985) has called 'textually mediated organization' (p. 179), the examination made it possible to develop a system of accountability for 'normal' and 'abnormal' behaviour: it enabled 'the constitution of the individual as a describable, analysable object, not in order to reduce him to "specific" features, as did the naturalists in relation to living beings, but in order to maintain him in his individual features, in his particular evolution, in his own aptitudes or abilities, under the gaze of a permanent corpus of knowledge' (Foucault, 1977, p. 190). Third, *'the examination, surrounded by all its documentary techniques, makes each individual a "case"'* (p. 191). Through writing, the examination documented the individual as a 'case', made him visible as an object of 'normalizing' management or, more precisely, 'an object for a branch of knowledge and a hold for a branch of power' (p. 191). The management and control of social systems finds its leverage increasingly at the level of the bio-scopic individual 'case'.

Against this background of the visible insinuated within the lisible, Hoskin and Macve (1986) have traced the history and development of accounting out of the technology of the examination. Accounting is that branch of modern management which has capitalized most on those two characteristic features of writing's visibility—*instantaneity* and *distance*; in other words, writing enabled information to made available *at a glance* and in a *depersonalized* form (i.e., free from the possibility of 'contamination' by social 'interaction', in Derrida's sense). Writing within the general context of Foucault's analysis of 'knowledge-power', Hoskin and Macve argue that 'examination, discipline and accounting are historically bound together as related ways of writing the world (in texts, institutional arrangements, ultimately in persons) into new configurations of power' (p. 107). These new ways of re-writing the social world date conceptually from antiquity but their influence is limited until medieval times when a 'new knowledge elite appears, centred around the nascent universities' (p. 109). The new elite of clerks and masters 'produce a vast new range of pedagogic re-writing of texts, i.e., techniques which grid texts both externally and internally in the service of information-retrieval and knowledge-production' (p. 109). Hoskin and Macve note that 'the scholars of the cathedral schools and universities began to use visualist metaphors both to denote reading (e.g., *videre, inspicere*) and composition (*scriber* for *dictare*)' (p. 110). Above all, the gridding of texts—the use of alphabetical order, a visually-orientated layout, systems of reference—and the substitution of read-easy Arabic numerals for the more clumsy roman numbers created by a new ordering of knowledge and understanding based on visibility. The new techniques were first perfected in the universities, especially those of Paris and Bologna, but later the exponents of these methods took their places as 'professionals' either in the church or at court. They included men like Thomas á Becket, who began his career, after qualifying in Paris, as a clerk-accountant in London in the 1140s. Double-entry book-keeping appeared in the thirteenth century as a particularly sophisticated form of the new examination-based writing. Significantly, as Hoskin and Macve point out, 'double-entry' was based upon the visualist metaphor of the Mirror—it was a mirror-book that reflected the 'equal and opposite signs of debit and credit' (p. 121). This too, owed its emergence to a university teacher and cleric—Pacioli. Despite its relative sophistication 'double-entry' was limited to 'financial examinatorial control' and therefore could not make 'human accountability' more visible. Hoskin and Macve argue that the accounting of human behaviour in terms of the debit-credit system had to await the introduction of the examination mark into the educational system in the 19th century (pp. 129–130).

## VISIBILITY, KNOWLEDGE-POWER AND PROFESSIONALIZATION

The point of Hoskin and Macve's analysis is to reveal the power of accounting to create a specific form of knowledge (knowledge-power) which subjects individuals to a fixed and determinate visibility. As such, it is a specific example of a more general trend in modern society—the development of knowledge-power by means of professionalization. In fact, Hoskin and Macve characterize accountancy as a profession that is squarely founded on the knowledge-power of accounting technology. The implication here is that the professions are those groups in society that are accredited with the task of creating and maintaining the appropriate 'visibility' of social agents through such techniques as the examination. This view of the professions is clearly at odds with the prevailing general and academic understanding of the professional's contribution to society as being both benevolent and selfless. As Goldstein (1984) points out, the sociological definition of a profession rests on four criteria: (1) it is a body of highly specialized knowledge which has to be formally mastered before it can be practised; (2) it is a monopoly, i.e., the body of knowledge is recognized as the exclusive competence of those who practise it; (3) it is autonomous, i.e., the professionals control their own work and how it should be done, and (4) it embodies a service ideal, i.e., 'a commitment of ethical imperative to place the welfare of the public or of the individual client above the self-interest of the practitioner, even though the practitioner is earning a living through the exercise of the profession' (p. 175). This is essentially a 'theory' about certain kinds of occupational groups. When Foucault's ideas about 'disciplines' and knowledge-power are applied to the professions a totally different picture emerges. In fact, as Goldstein argues, the sociologist's professions turn out to be none other than Foucault's 'disciplines'. Like disciplines, the professions are now seen to be not only bodies of esoteric knowledge but also social practices. As social practices, disciplines/professions institute and maintain procedures for 'disciplining' individuals in the sense of subjecting them to the new forms of theoretical knowledge that epitomize the major professions. Human subjects become 'framed' in a 'picture' that is meticulously drawn in the practice of the professional's knowledge-power. Hence they can be made operationally visible.

Another version of this argument has been presented by Frug (1984) who has identified professionalism with bureaucratic legitimation. In an exemplary analysis which uses Derrida's idea of 'interaction', Frug shows that the central problem of bureaucracy (as studied by organization theorists and scholars of corporate and administrative law) is that of reconciling the relationship between *subjectivity* and *objectivity*. Derrida's notion of 'interaction' means essentially that no division can ever realistically be made between these concepts since they are 'confused' within each other. But the visual imperative that orders the social world means that (somehow) they must be kept apart—otherwise they could not be 'seen'.

> All the stories of bureaucratic legitimation . . . share a common structure: they attempt to define, distinguish, and render mutually compatible the subjective (and objective) aspects of life. All the defences of bureaucracy have sought to avoid merging objectivity and subjectivity— uniting the demands of commonness and community with those of individuality and personal separateness—because to do so would be self-contradictory. Moreover, it has never been enough just to separate subjectivity and objectivity; each must also be guaranteed a place within the bureaucratic structure.

(Frug, 1984, p. 1287). In this case, the process of making bureaucratic structures clear and legible is self-deceiving for while the 'objective' qualities of professionalism are seen 'as something outside the individual to which he must adapt, they are qualities that the professional himself helps to define' (p. 1331). Such interweaving of objectivity and subjectivity necessarily undermines the 'transparent' or 'obvious' features of bureaucratic logic—the lack of division of distinctness between the two making it difficult to see either. The answer to the problem is the creation of a 'fiction' of objectivity. The suspicion that this 'fiction' may be vision-based is suggested in a study by Weinstein and Weinstein (1984) of what they call 'the visual constitution of society'. Briefly, Weinstein and Weinstein base their study of Sartre's famous analysis of the 'look' (*le regard*)—essentially, Foucault's gaze—which functions to *objectify* the social world by fixing or freezing individuals in a determinate framework from which they cannot escape since they are held (and, of course, *beheld*) by 'eyes that must see without being seen' (Foucault, 1977, p. 171). Because it cannot be seen, the 'look' cannot be questioned—this is its lethal, invisible power; vision and objectivity are thus mutually-defining. The significance of the 'look' is not only that it objectifies but also that it is the prototype form of visual interaction in formal social systems such as bureaucratic organizations.

It would be myopic to assume that the visual bias of the 'objectifying gaze' is limited to the examples of the disciplines/professions—medicine, accountancy, etc.—we have discussed here. The definitive feature of modern society is not so much the presence of 'undisciplined vision' in formally-recognized institutions but its unobtrusive diffusion in the least expected places. For example, Bové (1986) has recently shown how the institution of modern Anglo-American literary criticism was 'professionalized' by the famous Cambridge critic, I. A. Richards, beginning in the 1920s. Significantly, Richards was a follower of Jeremy Bentham and Bové shows in some detail how Bentham's Panoptic principle—Foucault's gaze again—shaped Richards' model of literary worth as well as his teaching practice. Literary criticism became less concerned with novels and poetry as an expression of human endeavour and emotions but was turned into a 'project for the production of knowledge, the exercise of power, and the creation of careers' (Bové, 1986, p. 48) on the model of 'the other positive disciplines such as economics, psychology, medicine, and anthropology' (p. 48). Richards' project was concerned with the training (i.e., 'disciplining') of teachers and readers as part of a wider programme which would 'manage (the) larger forms of sociocultural and political different between men and women, various classes, and competing ideologies and nations' (p. 53) . . . 'reducing the complex function of modernist literature to an ahistorical training school for teacher education in cultural management' (p. 55). His purpose was to develop a *way of seeing* the world and its literature according to a 'normalized' and 'transparent' perception. Like the early constructors of the objectifying gaze studied by Foucault in the fields of medicine, prisons, education and the human sciences, Richards succeeded in applying the same normalizing vision to a body of expression traditionally valued for its explanation of precisely those areas of human sensibility which lie beyond the 'gaze of discipline': the spontaneous, the erotic, the uncanny, etc.

The analysis of knowledge-power and the 'labour of division' in social systems has two important critical functions: (1) it reorients analysis away from the static picture of social structures produced by the division-of-labour perspective to reveal 'division' as a central force in the social production of 'visibility', and (2) it underlines the cardinal role of the discipline-professions as social practices which create and maintain 'division' through 'visualization' techniques.

# REFERENCES

Bové, P. A. (1988) *Intellectuals in Power: A Genealogy of Critical Humanism*, New York: Columbia University Press.
Derrida, J. (1981) *Positions*, Chicago: University of Chicago Press.
Febvre, L. (1982) *The Problem of Unbelief in the Sixteenth Century*, Cambridge: Harvard University Press.
Foucault, M. (1973) *The Birth of the Clinic*, London: Tavistock.
Foucault, M. (1977) *Discipline and Punish*, London: Allen Lane.
Foucault, M. (1979) 'Governmentality', *Ideology and Consciousness*, 6.5.
Foucault, M. (1980) *Power/Knowledge*, Brighton: Harvester.
Frug, G. E. (1984) 'The ideology of bureaucracy in American law', *Harvard Law Review*, 97: 1276.
Giddens, A. (1985) *The Nation-State and Violence*, Cambridge: Polity Press.
Goldstein, J. (1984) 'Foucault among the sociologists: the "Disciplines" and the history of the professions', *History and Theory*, 23: 170.
Hoskin, K. W. and Macve, R. H. (1986) 'Accounting and the examination: a genealogy of disciplinary power', *Accounting, Organizations and Society*, 11: 105.
Miller, J. A. (1987) 'Jeremy Bentham's panoptic device', *October*, 41: 3.
Norris, C. (1987) *Derrida*, London: Fontana/Collins.
Rorty, R. (1980) *Philosophy and the Mirror of Nature*, Oxford: Basil Blackwell.

Weinstein, D. and Weinstein, M. (1984) 'On the visual constitution of society: the contributions of Georg Simmel and Jean-Paul Sartre to a sociology of the senses', *History of European Ideas*, 5: 349.
Whitehead, A. N. (1938) *Modes of Thought*, New York: Macmillan.

(Excerpt from 'Interview with Robert Cooper' Robert C. H. Chia and Jannis Kallinikos, in Chia, R. (ed) (1998) *Organized Worlds: Explorations in Technology and Organization with Robert Cooper*. London: Routledge, 149–152.)

*In your paper 'The Visibility of Social Systems' (Cooper, 1989) you reverse the classical concept of the 'division of labour' and speak instead of the 'labour of division' as an essential process through which rationality is sustained in social systems. How are we to understand this evocative reversal?*

The division of labour is, of course, an historic part of social scientific thinking and goes back to Adam Smith and Karl Marx. It was memorialized by Durkheim (1933) in his classic study, *The Divisions of Labour in Society*, which today still provides the general framework by which we understand the concept as a force in modern society.

Durkheim saw modern society as occupationally differentiated in a complex division of labour in which the various specialized functions contributed to the moral and economic maintenance of the social whole. The division of labour was a general principle which applied to all organic part-whole systems, including the biological organism. The parts existed for the benefit of the whole, as though divisions existed for the sole purpose of creating unity. And this was the way that Durkheim viewed the role of occupational division—each social function had a moral obligation to work for the grater whole through the creation of harmony and order. Implied here, of course, was the existence of forces antagonistic to social unity, but Durkheim's explicit emphasis was always on the moral duty of occupational incumbents to heal the divisions. Durkheim's book sometimes reads more like diagnosis and prescription than social analysis.

In inverting the traditional locution of the division of labour to the *labour of division*, I was trying to express certain features that traditional analyses had seemed not to notice. In particular, I wanted to reveal the *visual* nature of the social world, to draw attention to the role of *vision* in the constitution of social knowledge and to the role of *labour* in the construction of social objects. In other words, I wanted to expose the hidden depths in the term 'division'. Instead of accepting its conventional glossing as simple *differentiation*, I saw 'division' as a much more basic ingredient in *how we come to see* our world and in *how are perceptions are constructed*. This was the significance of the vision of *di-vision*.

The general idea that the social world is a construction is by no means a novel one, of course. Berger and Luckman's (1967) *The Social Construction of Reality* makes the same argument and also, interestingly, reminds us how we constantly deny our part in the construction of the ordered world of social reality by claiming that it exists independently of us, that it is somehow there 'naturally'. We simply represent the social order that is already there. But the labour of division emphasizes a special aspect of the construction process—the construction of *visible spaces and times*. This is how Bledstein analyses the development of the professions in mid-Victorian America:

> Space and time were the most elementary categories in everyday experience . . . Mid-Victorians turned their interest toward identifying every category of person who naturally belonged in a specific ground-space: the woman in the residential home, the child in the school, the man in his place of work, the dying person in a hospital, and the body in the funeral parlor.
>
> (Bledstein, 1976: 56)

Here, the labour of division represented by the professions was clearly focused on the construction of specific spaces and specific times. And a necessary feature of this process was the filling of these structured, self-contained spaces with special terms that helped to secure them against the vagaries of chance and fleeting impressions. But more important for my argument is Bledstein's account of the increasing miniaturization of space through the labour of the professions: division was an endless process that segmented life into smaller and smaller spaces. Bledstein records the early development of the medical professions around increasingly particularized parts of the human body: the specialized knowledges of the eye, the ear, the nerves, the skin, the womb, the bones, etc. 'As professionals, they attempted to define a total coherent system of necessary knowledge within a precise territory, to control the intrinsic relationships of their subject by making it a scholarly as well as applied science' (Bledstein, 1976: 88). We are reminded of John Wilkin's and Thomas Sprat's programme for the development of science in seventeenth-century England, with its knowledge based on discrete spaces and discrete words . . . American universities in the nineteenth century pursued a similar programme of specialization-spatialization by reducing problems to scientific and technical amenability, and thus hoped to reduce the influence of ambiguity, chance and transience on public knowledge. The labour here is clearly the labour of making spaces and times easily and 'naturally' visible by including the simple and excluding the complex. Academic knowledge is still today largely a product of the same labour of division described by Bledstein in nineteenth century America. It follows the distinction made by Maurice Blanchot (1982) between work as *le travail* the labour of purposeful action, productive organization—and as *l'oeuvre*, the work of negative space that resists purpose and production. The anthropologist Clifford Geertz (1975) notes a similar distinction in the academic discipline of social anthropology when (borrowing from the philosopher Gilbert Ryle) he talks about two approaches to ethnography—'thin' and 'thick' description. Thin description glosses its accounts of the social world in basic operational terms, presents social events as isolation phenomena and neglects their contexts (e.g., the abstracted definition of intelligence by standardized intelligence tests). In contrast, think description recognizes 'a multiplicity of complex conceptual structures, many of them superimposed upon or knotted into one another, which are at once strange, irregular and inexplicit' (Geertz, 1975: 10). Thick description seeks to reflect the labyrinthine nature of social life. (Hidden here is a connection between *labour* and *labyrinth*. For example, Penelope Reed Doob, 1990, notes that *labour* comes from the medieval *labor intus*, the Latin origin of 'labyrinth', which means 'difficulty going in', and which is also associated with lack of vision, blindness.) Geertz's interpretation of 'thickness' as 'knotted, strange, irregular, and inexplicit' suggests an uncanny connection with Heidegger's (1971) concept of *Dichtung*, normally translated as 'poetry' but literally translatable as 'thick language'—not unlike Geertz's characterization of 'thick description' as a 'confusion of tongues'. Now, what's 'thick', 'confused' or 'mixed up' is clearly difficult to see and, in the extreme, must remain invisible. The function of the labour of division is to make the invisible visible, to sort out what's confused. This is the 'vision' of *di-vision*. But for Heidegger, what's invisible in *Dichtung* is the unnameable origin of things, a negative space which serves as a divided source for the positive spaces of everyday life and work. It's the *void* of '*di-vide*' (in passing, let's note that the French *vide* means 'empty') and which the labour of division has to exclude in its construction of positive spaces and times—otherwise *nothing* (literally) could be *seen*. But Heidegger's point is that the positive spaces and times depend on the *void*, the negative space, of *Dichtung*. It's their ontological ground. Heidegger calls it *Being*, the source of the acts of *being*. And 'Being is not to be found as a harmonious whole, but is always already split, divided' (Melberg, 1995: 163). The void is *already* divided, which another reason why we can never see it. It 'retreats' in the very act of division. This is why Heidegger says that *Dichtung* is primordial, by which he means pre-linguistic, unnameable, unspoken. It can never be made explicit but only *hinted* at, like the *hinterland* (i.e. the 'underland', 'interland' or 'underground') of Being. This sense of the void can be inferred from the form of the word *vision* itself when it's seen in its lateral versions of *fission* (division, thinness) and *fusion* (unity, thickness)—the three words, superficially different hint at a common sense which is itself pre-linguistic, unnameable. In other words, the common source of the three words 'retreats' behind the simple terms that *already* divide it.

This way of thinking the labour of division is strangely similar to the old idea that negative space acts like a hidden common ground to the varied productions of positive space. It's like Lao Tzu's famous image of the holes between the spokes that make the wheel. In recent years, the same idea has been articulated more formally in the mathematics of fractals in chaos theory (Gleick, 1988). Fractals are a way of seeing infinite division and the 'retreat' of the void. Imagine a line. Divide it by removing the middle section—you have two lines and the space between them remaining. Then divide the two remaining lines—you are left with four lines and three spaces between them. Repeat the division on the four lines, then on the next eight lines, and so on. The lines get smaller while the spaces between increase in frequency. But the size of the initial space—the first line—does not itself change; there's neither more nor less of it. The significant changes lies in the *acts* of division—it's they that divide and redivide in a continuous labour of division. As Gleick (1988) points out, developments in the technology of human vision such as telescopes and microscopes were really technologies of infinite and repeated division. They didn't increase or decrease the actual size of the world—they simply served to increase its divisions. All this, of course, is strikingly similar to Bledstein's (1976) account of the professions in nineteenth-century America where the labour of division was an endless process that divided society into smaller and smaller spaces. We need to also recall that these divided spaces were made to be unquestionably visible. And, by implication, what lay outside these visible spaces was more difficult—and sometimes perhaps impossible—to see. The labour of division thus works to 'thin out' social space and to exclude (or, better, *avoid)* the 'thick' complexities of the *void.* But this is an endless process because the void is a 'debased, lateralized, repressed, displaced' force that exercises a 'permanent and obsessive pressure from the place where it remains held in check' (Derrida, 1987: 270). Here we are back with Taylor's (1995) idea of the mediatory that 'resists reflection' because its complex, fleeting, unstable connections and multiplicities defy conventional logic and analysis. The labour of division thus reveals itself to be much more than that process of occupational specialization which keeps society functioning. We can now perhaps begin to see it as a constitutive feature of social form itself, as that compulsive force that repetitively and literally per-*forms* social forms.

## Editors' Note

All the references for these interview sections can be found after the final interview extract, 'Main features of my approach . . .', in section 15.

# 9 Formal Organization as Representation
## Remote Control, Displacement and Abbreviation

*Robert Cooper*

In recent years, organizations have come to be seen as organizers of information. An early stimulus to this way of thinking was Simon's (1955) famous criticism of the theory of rational choice: that the latter imputes to the rational actor exaggerated capacities for processing information. In reality, human rationality is severely bounded. Formal organization was seen as an instrument for solving problems specifically deriving from bounded rationality. Williamson's (1975) theory of transaction costs is one attempt to explain bounded rationality in terms of the supply of information and its effects on the organization of the market. Two factors are salient: the cost or difficulty of acquiring necessary information about the market, and the number of firms in it. If information is freely available and firms are numerous, then, because transaction costs are low, the profit advantage goes to the individual who is self-employed. On the other hand, where information is costly and where there are few firms, transaction costs become too high and it therefore pays the individual to take employment with a big firm that can control information and thus reduce transaction costs.

Extending Williamson's analysis, Schotter (1981) has reworked the relationship between rationality and organizations in the language of information theory. Information is no longer a commodity that is more or less available; it is now that which has surprise value. If an event can be predicted or is already known, it carries little or no information. Information increases with unpredictability. Schotter views organizational structures as forms of informational complexity. Past experience becomes sedimented in an organization's structures where it functions as a guide to future events. The more completely organizational structures encode information, the less unpredictability or uncertainty there is likely to be.

Williamson and Schotter both underline the boundedness of individual rationality and then go on to say that by constructing organizations individuals extend the limits of their capabilities for processing information. For Williamson, organizations augment bounded rationality by controlling the flow of information, so reducing transaction costs for individual actors. For Schotter, organizations augment the limits of rationality by encoding as much information as possible in their structures and rules. But both Williamson and Schotter overlook a fundamental and mandatory act in the processing of information: representation. Information theory begins with the construction of a representative (pattern, picture, model) of some aspect of the world (MacKay, 1969). The representation must exist before we can go on to think about information in the Williamson-Schotter sense. When Williamson, for example, talks about the effects of information on the organization of the market he is really talking about *changes* in a representational construct of that market. The representation comes first; information is that which augments or reduces the power of the representation. On this analysis, organizations are not merely organizers of information; they also construct the forms in which information appears.

This insight has been taken up by Zuboff (1988) in a study of the effects of information technology in various commercial and manufacturing organizations. Zuboff distinguishes two functions of information technology: it *informates* as well as *automates*.

The automating function of technology refers to the machine's appropriation of human skills and effort; its informating function is its power to translate activities, events and objects into visible information. In manufacturing, for example, microprocessors enable robots, programmable logic controllers and sensors 'to translate the three-dimensional production process into digitized data. These data are then made available within a two-dimensional space, typically on the screen of a video display terminal or on a computer printout, in the form of electronic symbols, numbers, letters, and graphics' (Zuboff, 1988: 10). Informating is in effect a process of representation. The function of representation is to translate difficult or intransigent material into a form that facilitates control. As Zuboff shows, information technology does precisely that: it absorbs and substitutes for the debriefed, implicit knowledge and skills of workers and managers; it impersonalizes the authorship of the system and so makes control less vulnerable to criticism; it makes information transparent and 'instant'; when information is uncoupled from its action context and represented symbolically, events can be manipulated and combined in new ways, so enabling greater control. In short, information technology encapsulates a general function of all formal organization: the need to make transparent what is opaque, to make present what is remote, and to manipulate what is resistant. It is not just a question of information or symbolization but of technologies which enable us to represent information and symbols in a convenient form. This is how the Voyager II spacecraft can bring the planet Neptune on to the computer screens of the Houston space centre, how geologists can probe the depths of the earth for minerals and oil, and how medical doctors can see inside the human body by means of X-ray tomograms. All rely on specific technologies of representation.

In Zuboff's analysis, three specific features of the informating process can be singled out as having special relevance for understanding the role of representation and its technologies in organizations: (1) symbols and electronic devices substitute for direct human involvement with the raw material and thus abstract thought from action: 'Absorption, immediacy, and organic responsiveness are superseded by distance, coolness and remoteness' (1988: 75); (2) organizational activity becomes less a structure of discrete acts coordinated in space and time and more a series of displacements or transformations along informational networks: 'The electronic texts exists independently of space and time . . . the contents of the electronic text can infuse an entire organization, instead of being bundled in discrete objects, like books or pieces of paper' (1988: 179–80); (3) information technology abbreviates complexity: a three-dimensional world is reduced to a two-dimensional representation on a terminal screen which can be read instantly. These three themes—remote control, displacement, abbreviation— are by no means unique to information technology; they are simply hyperbolized there. They define all techniques of representation, however ordinary and unobtrusive. Ironically, their constitutive ordinariness has led to their neglect in organizational analysis.

These features of representation help us to understand the relationship between bounded rationality and organizations as organizers of information. Unfortunately, the literature on bounded rationality gives the impression that rationality is a cognitive process which takes place 'in the brain' and that its boundedness is a function of the limited capacity of the human mind:

> The capacity of the human mind for formulating and solving complex problems is very small compared with the size of the problems whose solution is required for objectivity rational behaviour in the real world— or even for a reasonable approximation to such objective rationality
> (Simon, 1957: 198).

When we view the question of bounded rationality in terms of techniques of representation, both rationality and boundedness take on a wholly different meaning. To illustrate the difference, let's take two simple examples of human technology: chair and glove (Scarry, 1985). Both chair and glove represent (that it, replace or stand in place of) specific aspects of the body in its dealings with the world. The chair represents the general shape of the human skeleton and compensates for the body's tendency to tiredness. Likewise, the glove (let's say an industrial glove) represents the hand; while the natural hand is frail (for example, it can be easily burnt), the industrial glove is robust and refractory. Whereas the body and its parts are limited by a natural fragility, it is precisely these limiting conditions that enable and promote the process of representation. In these examples, we see that human 'rationality' is not characteristically cognitive but is intrinsic to the general field of action of the body and its parts, and that boundedness, far from being a restriction, is a required stimulus for representation. As representations, techniques and artefacts are *embodied* (note, not just 'enacted'[1]) processes that remedy and compensate for the body's deficiencies and, at the same time, extend, magnify and make more durable its power. In short, representations embody a principle of economy which turns losses into gains.

It is this principle of economy which makes the logic of representation more fundamental to the understanding and analysis of organizations than the traditionally more limited concept of information. This is an economy of convenience in which the affairs of the world are made pliable, wieldable and therefore amenable to human use through technologies of representation. It turns a boundary or limit from a privation into profit.[2] Remote control, displacement and abbreviation are the mechanisms by which representation realizes this economy of mental and physical motion. In the case of remote control, such economy is made possible by substituting symbols and other prosthetic devices for direct involvement of the human body and its senses. Administrators and managers, for example, do not work directly on the environment but on models, maps, numbers and formulae which represent that environment; in this way, they can control complex and heterogeneous activities at a distance and in the relative convenience of a centralized work station. Events that are remote (that is, distant and heterogeneous) in space and time can be instantly collated in paper form on the desk of a central controller. This has the paradoxical effect of bringing remote events near while, at the same time, keeping them at a remote through the intervention of representations. In other words, the power of representation to control an event remotely is a form of displacement in which representation is always a substitution for or re-presentation of the event and never the event itself.

Remote control underlines the economy of convenience intrinsic to representation: one may not be able to move the mountain itself but it is easy to move a model or map of it. This mobility of representation helps us to understand why paperwork of all kinds is so essential to organizations: mobility is central to control. Representation displaces the intractable and obdurate; it denies the idea of fixed location and emphasizes movement. Displacement, therefore, means mobile and non-localizable associations. It therefore becomes inappropriate to talk, for example, about the organization and its environment since this gives the impression of distinct domains separated in space and time. In terms of displacement, organizing activity is the transformation of boundary relationships which are themselves continually shifting. Again, the concept of the boundary comes into its own.

The organization's inside and outside are correlative: 'no inside is conceivable . . . without the complicity of an outside on which it relies. Complicity mixed with antagonism . . . no outside would be conceivable without an inside fending it off, resisting it, "reacting" to it' (Starobinski, 1975: 342). In this way, inside and outside, organization and environment, continually displace each other. But neither remote control nor displacement are thinkable without abbreviation. Abbreviation makes possible the economy of convenience that underlies representation. It simplifies the complex, makes the big into the small, converts the delayed into the instantaneous. It works according to a principle of condensation in which as much as it is needed is condensed into as little as is needed so as to enable ease and accuracy of perception and action. Through abbreviation, representations are made compact, versatile and permutable. The development of the computer in recent years perhaps best exemplifies the abbreviation process: 'The power of ten cubic meters of 1965-vintage computer can now be held in the palm of the hand. Thanks to telephone hook-up, the mini-computer presently affords us access to millions of data' (Bertin, 1983: x). In these examples, representation combines with electronics to provide increasingly powerful means of 'abbreviating' the world.

This schematic characterization of the components of representation—remote control, displacement, abbreviation—clearly needs amplifying with the organizational context and it is to this that we now turn, with two specific objectives in view: (1) to illustrate the operation of the three components in terms of concrete examples; and (2) to show how they can augment more conventional dimensions of organizational analysis, such as formulization and centralization.

## REMOTE CONTROL: THE CASE OF PORTUGUESE EAST INDIES COMPANY

We illustrate the workings of remote control with the story of how the Portuguese created and extended the organization of their East Indies Company at the end of the fifteenth century (Law, 1986). The basic question is how the Portuguese were able to set up a large organization based on *control at a distance*. The main technology in this story is the ship. The medieval European sailing vessel's range and endurance were limited and its carrying capacity small; it was also unable to cope well with adverse weather conditions and it was not very effective in navigating out of sight of land or without regular soundings. Clearly, such vessels could not deal with the challenge of controlling the Indies spice markets which the Portuguese were keen to exploit. What was required was a ship (with associated technology) that was both mobile and durable enough to match the uncertainties and rigours of long-distance sailing in unknown territories. The development by the Portuguese of new vessels that were more mobile and more durable placed them in a better position to control not only the sea and weather (for example, new types of sail enabled the extraction of more power from the wind), but more discipline was required of everyone involved—seamen, masters, envoys—in order to comply with the greater demands of the new technology. All this was realized through the development of more powerful technologies of representation.

As we have seen, representation is really a reversal process in which a disadvantage is turned into an advantage—for example, chair and glove embody this power. This is essentially now the Portuguese extracted compliance from the heterogeneous elements—social, technological, natural—that constituted the maritime organization of their East Indies Company. In the larger context, this meant that some centre in Lisbon could dominate activities on the other side of the world. But the success of this enterprise was built on the patient accumulation of many small technical advances arranged in an interlocking series. Each small advance was a triumph of remote control. Long-distance control became possible through a sequence of short-distance achievements of remote control, all of which embodied the following steps: (1) the substitution of a symbol or technical device for direct human involvement; which led to (2) the curious effect of bringing the remote—that which is cut off by a limit or boundary—near, while at the same time keeping it at a remove.

Among the major technical advances of remote control developed by the Portuguese were new forms of sail and new navigational devices. Natural forces such as winds and sea currents became prevalent dangers as soon as the Portuguese left the relative safety of European waters for the uncertainties of the African and Eastern seas. The technical task facing the Portuguese was how to represent these natural forces in their own maritime organization and thereby turn potential hazards into benefits. This was a case of extracting compliance from the natural forces by incorporating them into the ship's sociotechnical organization so that these forces would augment rather than hinder the voyage. In the case of the winds, smaller sails at bow and stern made the vessel more manoeuvrable; smaller sails needed fewer crew, which further increased the ship's mobility and durability since less crew meant less sickness and mortality, common problems on such long voyages. By means of increased geographical knowledge and improved navigational competence, ocean currents were also harnessed. The navigational advances of the Portuguese were even more dramatic. In 1484 King John II of Portugal set up a prototypal research and development group and charged it with the task of developing a system for navigating outside European waters. The system developed by the group, the *Regimento do Astrolabio et do Quadrante*, 'not only fulfilled the expectations of the king but it also laid the foundations of modern astronomical navigation' (Law, 1986: 248). The *Regimento* was essentially a comprehensive representation of the new navigational contexts being charted at that time by the Portuguese vessels; it modelled not only the seas and land but also the heavens. It used written or printed inscriptions based on the positions of the North Star, the Sun and its declinations, and so on. In short, the new system represented the wider world and the heavens in models, tables, rules, and their possible permutations; it reproduced a complex astronomical and geographical framework in a portable and manipulable system, as Law (1986: 252) illustrates

> Consider one case, that of the table of solar declination. This represented the distillation . . . of many years of astrological expertise, of correspondence, of argument and of innovation . . . this created a kind of surrogate astronomer. It was not necessary to take along the inventors and designers of the new system. Their force, and the work of their predecessors, was being borrowed, converted onto a highly transportable and indefinitely reproducible form, and being put to work on every ship. The production of tables of solar declination for the purpose of navigation may thus been seem as a way of reducing the relevant aspects of a weighty astronomical tradition to a form that, in the context of the vessel, was more mobile and durable than the original. It seems . . . to have been a way of capitalising on generations of astronomical work by converting this into a nicely simplified black box that might be carried anywhere within the Portuguese system of long-distance control and which would contribute to this when posed the right questions.

Here we have all the elements of remote control: build a reduced model of the original, bring the distant to the here-and-now, make a visual representation of that which defies physical contact. The solar table not only represents the sun's declinations but it also represents the work of countless predecessors, which remains ever present in the sociotechnical organization of the Portuguese vessels. Both the heavens and history may be distant but they are nevertheless actively present in the remote control capacities of representation. Remote control in this case borrows power from astronomical, geographical, natural and historical sources. By incorporating significant features of the environment into representational forms, by appropriating environmental powers through models, data and instruments and turning them back on their sources, remote control ensured independence from external forces, freedom of mental and physical motion and, ultimately, secures a position from which it is able to dominate the world and not be dominated by it.

## DISPLACEMENT: LOUIS PASTEUR AND THE MANAGEMENT OF MICROBES

As we have just seen, the whole Portuguese enterprise was built on many small technical advances arranged in an interlocking series. Viewed in this way, the total organization of the Portuguese East Indies Company is best understood as a sociotechnical network of displacements or translations; for example, the appropriation of the powers of wind and sea currents by the various technologies of representation on board ship are really displacements or borrowings of power and energy from one point to another. Organizing thus becomes a network of mobile and non-localizable associations instead of the static distinction between organization and environment. Organizing, as we have noted, is the transformation of boundary relationships which are themselves continually shifting. It is this theme of organizing as displacement or transformation that we now turn to in a brief discussion of the work of the microbiologist Louis Pasteur on the development of an antidote to the anthrax bacillus (Latour, 1983, 1988).

In the early 1880s, Pasteur's laboratory, situated in the Ecole Normale Supérieure in Paris, turned its attention to finding a preventative to the disease anthrax, which at that period was proving excessively damaging for the French cattle industry. The variable and unpredictable nature of the disease made it difficult to study, especially in terms of one single cause. This made the disease unnameable to traditional laboratory investigation. Pasteur's laboratory and French cattle, at this point, are worlds apart. But, in order to get nearer the source of the disease and to stimulate its own milieu more accurately, Pasteur takes his 'laboratory' to a farm in the French countryside. Pasteur is now out in the 'field' and so confuses the usual distinction between the laboratory and the outside world. He and his colleagues learn from the veterinarians' and the farmers' knowledge of the anthrax bacillus and how it affects the cattle. After a period, Pasteur returns to his main laboratory in Paris and takes with him a significant part of the field, the cultivated bacillus. Back in the laboratory, he is able to grow the bacillus in isolation and in large quantities. The bacillus, formally invisible because of its microscopic size and its admixing with millions of other organisms, now becomes visible and therefore amenable to investigation. The cause of the anthrax disease can now be *seen* at the Ecole Normale Supérieure, while back at the farm it remains invisibly lethal. This is a major displacement, but bigger ones are to come. Pasteur is now able at will to simulate anthrax outbreaks in his laboratory by inoculating animals with the anthrax culture he has specially created. This makes it possible to chart and record—that is, represent—all the important features of the controlled simulation. Pasteur scales down the problem and reduces it to its essentials: his animals die from being inoculated with anthrax microbes and from no other cause. The nature of this displacement is obvious: by representing the disease on a small scale (a form of remote control), by isolating its cause and developing an effective vaccine, Pasteur and his colleagues increase their own power while reducing the power of the microbes. Still weak in relation to the microbes, the veterinarians and the farmers are forced to go to Pasteur in order to become strong, so further enhancing the power of his laboratory.

But it was still necessary to make a further displacement: to return the anthrax (now in the form of a vaccine) to the farm in order to demonstrate its effectiveness, otherwise it would simply remain a micro level achievement under the artificial conditions of the laboratory. The next step, therefore, was to organize a field trial on a larger scale. This displacement is also a representation since Pasteur has to re-present relevant features of his laboratory in the French countryside in order to ensure that his experimental work can be repeated effectively. Veterinarians and farmers then see that, provided they reproduce certain basic laboratory practices such as disinfection, inoculation technique, timing and recording they too can practice Pasteur's power. Through its portable knowledge and techniques, the laboratory is simulated or represented in every French farm. The displacements, when added up, describe a reversal: first, the power of the invisible microbe that decimates the population of cattle on the farms of France; second, the overturning and incorporation of the microbes' power in the laboratory vaccine; third, the return of the domesticated microbe as vaccine to the farms where, supported by appropriate laboratory practices, it serves to neutralize the population of 'wild' microbes.

Pasteur's displacements begin to make us see the artificiality and limitations of thinking in terms of discrete terms such as laboratory and agriculture, organization and environment, since they also displace the traditional static distinction between 'inside' and 'outside'. As we have noted, inside and outside are not separate places; they refer to a correlative structure in which 'complicity is mixed with antagonism. . . . No outside would be conceivable without an inside fending it off, resisting it, "reacting" to it (Starobinski, 1975: 342). Pasteur reproduces inside his laboratory 'an event that seems to be happening only outside—the first move—and then. . . . Extend[s] outside to all farms what seems to be happening only inside laboratories. As in some topological theorem, the inside and outside world can reverse into one another very easily' (Latour, 1983: 154). This is what we meant earlier when we described displacement as a series of mobile and non-localizable associations. It is difficult to think of associations as having insides and outsides; for example, the inner spaces of the human body—mouth, stomach, and so on—are really pockets of externality folded in. Organization as an active process of displacement or transformation denies and defies such categories as inside and outside; it is more like a process that travels along sociotechnical networks. This is what Pasteur discovered when he first tried to extend the anthrax vaccine to the farms of France: the vaccine would only work on the farms if the necessary laboratory conditions were set up beforehand.

The displacement of the inside-outside problem also has consequences for Simon's (1957) idea of bounded rationality, discussed earlier, and its suggestion that rationality is somehow located 'in the brain'. The argument from displacement denies the existence of special cognitive or personal qualities intrinsic to individuals or organizations. Pasteur is not necessarily more rational or more cognitively gifted than the veterinarians and farms he has come to help. Pasteur's advantage is that he has a laboratory and the others don't. In the laboratory, Pasteur works on small-scale representations of large outside problems which are then made easy to control; during the experimental period he is insulated from the outside world, so that the mistakes he makes do not go beyond the laboratory walls and are therefore hidden from public view. Each mistake is carefully recorded and cumulatively built on until 'certainty' is gained. It is not Pasteur's cognitive, social or psychological dispositions nor even his unbounded rationality that make him more 'certain' than the veterinarian or farmer, but the special sociotechnical organization of the laboratory which enables Pasteur to reverse the power of the microbes and to extend this capacity by re-presenting it in farms throughout France. By this means, the farmers of France become Pasteur's representatives.

## ABBREVIATION: THE ECONOMY OF REPRESENTATION AND THE BIRTH OF MODERN ADMINISTRATION

Neither remote control nor displacement are thinkable without abbreviation. To achieve remote control, the Portuguese abbreviated the magnitude of the heavens to a set of tables and a clutch of astronomical techniques. Pasteur abbreviated France's anthrax epizootic to a single bacillus and a micro level representation of the larger farm context. Abbreviation is intrinsic to the economy of convenience and control that representation embodies.

Behind every act of representation lies the urge to minimize effort; the economy of convenience works according to a principle of least effort (Zipf, 1949). Representation reproduces the events and objects of the world in a curtailed and miniaturized form so that they can be more easily engaged by mind and body. Representation in its abbreviation mode is a tactics of micropractices; it displaces the molar for the molecular. Abbreviation economizes space and time in two ways: by close packing and the reduction of size and mass (Zipf, 1949). By arranging the elements of representations—tools, techniques, symbols, models—as closely together as possible, close packing reduces the amount of time and effort involved in manipulating them. For example, information in a computer database is more closely packed than the equivalent information in a printed book or written record and thus can be more easily retrieved. The principle of close packing is important because it implies the abbreviation of size and mass: the smaller in size and mass the elements are, the closer together they can be packed. The miniaturization of computer parts, especially the silicon chip, illustrates the significant advantages of abbreviating size and mass to facilitate close packing.

The degree to which technologies of representation contributed to the historical development of the practical disciplines of administration and management is not widely appreciated. One aspect of this development was the tendency from the seventeenth century onwards to think in terms of the economy of convenience—instant information, knowledge 'at a glance', was what administrators demanded. In effect, this required a radical restructuring of the administrative and governmental process towards strategies of abbreviations. These strategies were directly mainly to the sense of vision—for good reasons. It is know that vision is the most efficient of the sensory systems: it can take in a far wider range of information in a much shorter span of time (Bertin, 1983). For this reason, optic-friendly technologies of representation began to emerge systematically with the increasing complexity and range of administrative problems that accompanied the population explosion in Europe in the eighteenth century[3].

Foucault (1979) tells us that the arts of administration and government in the modern sense arose out of the demographic expansion of the eighteenth century. Before this period, government was conceived on the model of the family and governors and administrators, like good fathers, viewed their roles in terms of the management of the household where the common welfare of all was uppermost. The word 'oeconomy' in this context was limited to the benign control 'of the head of a family over his household and his goods' (Foucault, 1979: 10). With the population increases of the eighteenth century, the interpretation of government, administration and 'oeconomy' underwent radical change. From now on, one managed a large amorphous mass whose sheer magnitude kept it at a distance, and which one could only understand in terms of statistical representations—statistics being 'the science of the State'—of population density, rates of birth and death, epidemics, cycles of scarcity, and so on. Government and administration no longer dwelt on citizens as members of a large 'family' but on the 'complex unit constituted by men and things' (1979: 11)—men in their relation to resources, to territory, means of subsistence, work, accidents, death. In short, the management of social-economic systems began to take shape in men's minds. A new metaphor takes the place of the family in the minds of the administrative theorists of the time—that of the ship. What does it mean to govern or manage a ship?

> It clearly means to take charge of the sailors, but also of the boat and its cargo; to take care of the ship means also to reckon with the winds, rocks, and tempests, and consists in that activity of setting in relation with one another the sailors who are to be taken care of with the cargo which is to be bought safely to port, and with all these events such as winds, rocks and tempests, etc. This is what characterizes the government of a ship.
>
> (Foucault, 1979: 11)

The family is no longer the model of good government; it is now the ship as a sociotechnical metaphor that forces itself on the attention of administrators. Whereas the members of the family have to be *cared for*, the ship has to be *managed*. And this of course is exactly the problem encountered on a smaller scale by the Portuguese East Indies Company three centuries before. For the new art of administration and for the Portuguese, it is the same question of how to extract maximum productive compliance from all elements—people, technical devices, printed documents—of the 'ship'. Just as the Portuguese were forced to develop more effective technologies to represent and control the distant heavens and the refractory natural forces of sea and weather, so the new breed of administrators were forced to develop more effective ways of representing and thus controlling the new urban masses of the eighteenth century. Almost by definition, a human mass defies formal knowledge and representation. Any mob or mass, simply because it lacks classification and resists calculation, is 'already seditious' (Miller, 1987: 17). In this sense, the masses were remote; their sheer numbers also made them physically unmanageable. Before they could be organized and managed, the masses had to be re-presented in the form of remote control, displacement and abbreviation. No one understood this better than Jeremy Bentham (1748–1832), the utilitarian and father of administrative theory.

Bentham's extensive writings on various aspects of government, administration and management are marked throughout by a combative concern to tame the mass and its aberrations: the mass 'evades taxonomies, makes enumerations indeterminable. Instead of regulated relationships, confusion reigns, fomenting unrest, excluding reflection; change is constant in a mob, giving rise to impressions as varied as they are striking' (Miller, 1987: 17). Bentham's answer was to divide and rule; the spatial and temporal division of workers at their benches, pupils at school, prisoners in their cells, enabled classification and counting, the rudiments of representation. The next major step of control was the abbreviation of the physical disposition of organizational incumbents in their architectural contexts in the form of written records. 'Books must be kept. "Bookkeeping" is a science. . . . Chronological entries will be made daily, methodological entries—products, population tables, stock inventories, health records, moral conduct records, requests, punishments (with a black cover), rewards (with a red cover) . . .' (Miller, 1987: 19). By this 'methodization' (Bentham's term), large numbers of people distributed over a large area can be represented in the small space of a book and inspected 'at first glance'. Bentham had begun to systematize a principle that is fundamental to modern cybernetics and information technology: representation is not the reproduction of *things* or *meanings* but their organization in space and time and this is why representation (as Bentham so clearly saw it) deals with factors such as 'ordering, listing, display, hierarchy of arrangement, edge and margin, sectioning, spacing, contrasts . . .' (McArthur, 1986: 23). Just as a series of numbers is distributed over a page in, say, an accounts book, so people and things are distributed in space and time. This correspondence between the world 'out there' and techniques of representation is essential to the construction of management 'at first glance'; in Bentham's eyes, all factories, schools and prisons are materialized classifications, lists, hierarchies, and statistics. Through representation, the big and the small become interchangeable.

The principle of abbreviation is 'much condensed into little'. It is the fulcrum of Bentham's theory of management. Bentham brought it to perfection in his architectural concept of the Panopticon, 'the polyvalent apparatus of surveillance, the universal optical machine of human groupings' (Miller, 1987: 3). The Panopticon was a circular building with a central tower from which continuous surveillance could be unilaterally exercised by one inspector on many inmates individually housed in perimeter cells. In effect, it was a technological eye which capitalized on the natural efficiency of the visual sense. The function of the Panopticon was part of Bentham's economy of division: what can be divided, kept separate yet closely packed in physical space, can be more easily transferred to the smaller space of the record book. The purpose of the Panopticon was not only to guarantee managerial control and the efficiency of working but to facilitate the abbreviated representation of the physical world in classes, numbers and names; to enable administrators to see more clearly and more quickly: 'To procure for a small number, or even for a single individual, the instantaneous view of a great multitude' (Foucault, 1977: 216).

The whole idea of the Panoptic principle was to connect abbreviated representations—models, signs, summaries, and the like—with a many-layered imbrication of social, political, architectural and other factors in a kind of *semio-technical hierarchy* where the simplest term could represent the most complex series, where the most intricate details of institutional behaviour could be orchestrated to respond to the briefest command, the most peremptory signal[4]. Today, this programme is being dramatically advanced by means of information technology. Zuboff (1988) shows how the informating function of information technology reveals the organization as the managing of 'electronic texts' (that is, representation) in which the major aspects of the organization's work (behavioural, technical, and so on) can be centrally summarized as real-time data on terminal screens; and in which Bentham's criterion of 'at-a-glance' management becomes doubly instantaneous because organizational processes are re-presented as they actually happen.

## REPRESENTING ORGANIZATION: FORMALIZATION AND CENTRALIZATION TRANSFIGURED

Institutional approaches to information view it as either a commodity (for example, Williamson, 1975) or as an event that has surprise value (for example, Schotter, 1981). When information is placed in the context of representation, it takes on a different meaning. Representation is the more fundamental concept simply because information must first be represented in some way. 'By a representation is meant any structure (pattern, picture, model) whether abstract or concrete, of which the features purport to symbolize or correspond in some sense with those of some other structure'

(Mackay, 1969: 161). Information is what which contribute to the efficiency of a representation: 'Information may be defined in the most general sense *as that which adds to a representation*' (Mackay, 1969: 163). Information thus provides *advantages* or *gain*. This is the same as saying that representations embody a principle of economy which turns losses into gains, as argued earlier. As we noted, the principle of economy revolves around the concept of boundary or limit. The boundary is simultaneously a constraint and an advantage, where complicity is mixed with antagonism (Starobinski, 1975); it is a site of struggle. Representation and information are therefore always preoccupied with the struggle for representational and informational gain, since this what enhances power and control. We saw this struggle in the case of the Portuguese navigators who incorporated the external powers of nature and the heavens into a range of shipboard technologies of representation, in Pasteur's successful attempt to displace the anthrax microbe's power through various techniques of laboratory representation, and in the efforts of the early administrative theorists to represent complex organizations in the abbreviated techniques of statistics, optical models and the like.

At this point it is appropriate to ask how the representational view of organizing relates to more traditional approaches to the analysis of organizations. It is certainly possible to suggest points of contact with Weber's (1947) characterization of bureaucracy: the reliance on written documents, the cultivation of 'depersonalization', and the 'concentration of the means of administration' all clearly imply remote control and abbreviation. But Weber was more interested in developing a general picture of bureaucratic organizations as a political-economic structure than in understanding the pragmatic and mundane logic that lies behind the techniques he identified. More recent analyses of organizations have summarized much of Weber's account of bureaucracy in the organizational dimensions of *formalization* and *centralization* (see, for example, Hall, 1987). Formalization is traditionally defined in terms of rules and procedures that are written down in official documents—that is, formalized. Centralization is the degree to which power and decision-making are located within one individual or group in the organization. Again we see in these definitions only tenuous echoes of representation. The active logic of the representational process is of course lost here. The reason for this would seem to be the prior assumption that there is a 'natural' entity called '*the* organization' which, like bounded rationality, is already constituted for us, and it is this spontaneously supposed structure that requires detailed definition. The definitions of formalization and centralization follow on from this supposition. The argument from representation makes no assumptions; instead, it poses the more fundamental question of how representation processes serve to construct organizations. Again, representation comes first. Let's see how this reversal of the question helps us to get closer to the formalization-centralization issue in organizations.

Conventional definitions of formalization and centralization can be reduced to two basic ideas: *objectification* and *control*. The function of formalization is the objectification of structures so as to make them appear external to the subjective of the participating actors (Scott, 1987). Centralization (which is also controlization) is the control of events in space and time; it realizes this control by incorporating the power of external objects and events into its own structures (usually called *centres)*. It is exactly these functions that representation makes possible; technologies of representation convert the inaccessible, unknown and private in the accessible, known and public; they convert the deferred and faraway into the instantaneous and immediate; and their portability or mobility makes them easy to manipulate and control. Viewed in this way, formalization and centralization are less like static structures and more like active conversion processes.

Formalization makes structures clear, visible, transparent; its aim is to make the 'organization' *see able*. Bentham saw this as the first problem of administration: to give written substance to the complex matrix of interacting factors that was otherwise impossible to see. For Bentham, the first step was to re-present the multi-dimensional world of administrative events, objects and people in two-dimensional paper forms—'bookkeeping'. Hence, the initial step of dividing organization incumbents in architectural and administrative space in order to apply classes, numbers, names, job descriptions, incentive schemes, which served as the content of the written representations. As we have seen, this is the logic of remote control, which reduces what is distant and resistant to what is near, clear and controllable; at the same time, the significance of representation through remote control is that it takes precedence over the event it represents. This means, for example, that we no longer see a 'picture of the organization' but the organization grasped as a formalized picture. Transparency and visibility in two-dimensional media became significant factors in management by formalization. As Zuboff shows, these factors become exaggerated with the introduction of information technology: 'In each of the organizations I studied, information technology had textualised [that is, formalized—R.C.] not only the content of work but also the task-related behaviours of the men and women who engaged with the data interface' (1988: 319). In a telecommunications company, 'Computerization meant that the work itself . . . had become transparent. The [new system] meant that the workers' behaviour was now almost as visible as their work. Gone were the bins filled with paper "trouble tickets"; gone were the ledger books and files. All of the information was "at your fingertips" in a moment' (1988: 331). The computer made formalization instantaneous and certain: 'I can know everything in an instant': 'Now we have it in black and white' (1988: 331).

Zuboff's (1988) case studies also show how the computer is able to centralize the textualized work structures through the instant collation and integration of information on terminal screens and printouts. The computer becomes a mechanized centre which is not only continuously registering and displaying (that is, formalizing) system behaviour but is also able to condense data from many sources and focus it at one point. This, of course, is the conventional definition of a centre. But the concept of a centre (and the centralization processes that go with it) has another and less obvious aspect: it displaces power from its peripheral sources in order to augment its own power. This enables the centre to dominate its world and not be dominated by it. The computer only becomes a centre when the systems designer appropriates the skills and knowledge that reside in people and books and then, as Zuboff (1988) shows, uses this appropriated power to dominate the very sources it borrows from. This is what happened with the Portuguese navigators and their techniques of representation when they borrowed the powers of such distant factors as the heavens, the winds and currents of the Atlantic Ocean and turned these powers against their sources; the Portuguese vessels became centres able to dominate an environment which formally dominated them. Ultimately, of course, the Portuguese vessels became subcentres of the main centre of the Portuguese East Indies Company in Lisbon which not only dominated in turn the vessels, the heavens, and winds and ocean currents but also the spice industry of the East Indies. A site becomes a centre to the extent that incorporates relevant features of its periphery and makes those features work for it.

In addition to the appropriation of space, the centre ideally has to appropriate time. The power of the computer is that it can collate and integrate complex data from various sources in real time. A centre is powerful to the degree it can predict or know in advance. It is easy show that prediction is a result of efficient technologies of representation. When Pasteur announced the field demonstration of this anthrax vaccine, he was in effect making a prediction that all the vaccinated animals would live and all the non-vaccinated animals would die. Of course, Pasteur had already successfully performed this prediction in his laboratory; its successful extension to the farm required, as we saw, the transformation of the farm into the laboratory. The prediction was fulfilled but it was really a *retrodiction* that relied both on prior work and on physically extending this prior work to the farm in the form of specific laboratory techniques. In other words, Pasteur's prediction would not have worked outside the specific practices *previously* developed in the laboratory. When Pasteur demonstrated that he could 'predict' the outcome of the field trail, his laboratory became a centre for interested farmers and the agricultural business.

Conventional organizational analysis typically views its field in terms of separate categories, which are assumed to inhabit insulated and singular spaces. The traditional division between organization and environment is an example of this mode of analysis. Formalization and centralization are also traditionally understood in this way. Formalization creates a set of structures which occupy an objective space separate from the subjective space of individuals. Centralization creates singular and specific locations of authority in the organization. Simon's (1957) concept of bounded rationality is a further example of an insulated and singularized space: the 'rationality' is located *within* the limited cognitive capacities of individual decision makers. Serres (1982) has called this mode of thinking 'Euclidean': it casts everything into single spaces, displacements without change of state, disconnected morphologies.

> Euclidean space was chosen in our work-orientate cultures because it is the space of work—of the mason, the surveyor, or the architect. . . . My body lives as many spaces as the society, the group, or the collectivity have formed: the Euclidean house, the street and its network, the open and closed garden, the church or the enclosed spaces of the sacred, the school and its spatial varieties containing fixed points, and the complex ensemble of flow-charts, those of language, of the factory, of the family, of the political party, and so forth. Consequently, my body is not plunged into one space but into the intersection or the junctions of this multiplicity. (1982: 44–5).

Serres goes on to argue that a topology of movement is required which recognizes that human actions occur not *in* spaces but *between* them. As we have seen, this is exactly what the logic of representation offers. It works on the boundaries or intersections of the inside and the outside, between here and there, this and that. It displaces space (and time) through remote control and abbreviation; it traverses a mobile space of non-localizable relationships.

If we look back at our examples of representation in action, we get a good idea of how this new topology works. Since it is not a space of singularities but of intersections or interactions, it always works in terms of *folds* or *doubles*—for example, the complicity—antagonism fold if the inside-outside relationship. The Portuguese navigators were able to displace the Atlantic winds when they saw their sails as folds in which an *inside* (the protective sociotechnical system of the vessel) was doubled with an *outside* (threatening winds). This simple example of the topology of the fold also shows that the inside is an interiorization of the outside, a kind of doubling of the outside. Pasteur's laboratory became a fold of the infected farm, his anthrax vaccine doubled the anthrax bacillus.

Formalization is also a topological fold: its objectivity is the double of its subjectivity, just as Bentham's institutional formalizations were mirror images of the wayward and intransigent behaviour of the eighteenth-century masses. The centre, too, is a fold; it doubles itself around a periphery whose power it borrows and simulates. Representation also shows that the inside is always doubling *of* the outside, that the inside is always an inversion of the outside, and never the other way round. In remote control, representation displaces the outside of the remote and 'beyond' into the inside of the near and familiar. In abbreviation, it displaces the outside of the dispersed and macroscopic into the inside of the compact and manageable. Representation displaces the outside inside. In contrast, bounded rationality, as a singularity, must always be an inner resource which acts on an outer problem; it is allied to intentions and goals which are also presumed to be integral to the organizational decision-making apparatus directed from the 'inside' of the individual. For representation, however, intentions and goals are themselves displacements in the topological folds of organizational space.

Finally, representation enables us to see formal organization and information in a new light. Information is no longer commodity or surprise. Representation shows it to consist of a spatial and temporal fold where an inside of familiar and manageable forms is constructed, re-presented, from an outside of restraint and retroactive non-forms or forces. Representation becomes the conversion of force or power into information. Conventional organizational analysis is still generated in a Euclidean space that prevents it from understanding the outside of its object[5]. Representation offers a way out of this conceptual impediment.


## NOTES

1 Weick (1979) on 'enactment' and organizing.
2 O'Hara (1988) uses the oxymoron 'enabling constraints' to describe this phenomenon.
3 Foucault (1977) analyses a range of vision-orientated administrative technologies that were constructed or perfected during this period: for example, hierarchical observation, normalizing, judgement, the examination, the Panopticon.
4 Again, Foucault (1977: Part 3, Chapter 1) provides some details of this technique; for example the association between 'signalization' and the 'precise system of command'.
5 These final comments (as well as borrowed turn of phrase) rely heavily on Deleuze (1986) who has analysed the fold and the inside-outside relationship in some detail.


## REFERENCES

Bertin, J. (1983) *Semiology of Graphics: Diagrams, Networks, Maps*. Madison, Wisconsin: University of Wisconsin Press.
Deleuze, G. (1986) *Foucault*. Minneapolis, MN: University of Minnesota Press.
Foucault, M. (1977) *Discipline and Punish: The Birth of the Prison*. London: Allen Lane.
Foucault, M. (1979) 'Governmentality', *Ideology and Consciousness*, 6: 5–21.
Hall, R. H. (1987) *Organizations: Structure and Process*. Englewood Cliffs, NJ: Prentice-Hall.
Latour, B. (1983) 'Give me a laboratory and I will raise the world', in kn. Knorr-Cetina and M. Mulkay (eds), *Science Observed: Perspectives on the Social Study of Science*, London: Sage.
Latour, B. (1988) *The Pasteurization of France*. Cambridge, MA: Harvard University Press.
Law, J. (1986) 'On the methods of long-distance control: Vessels, navigation and the Portuguese route to India', in J. Law (ed), *Power, Action and Belief: A New Sociology of Knowledge?* London: Routledge & Kegan Paul.
McArthur, T. (1986) *Worlds of Reference: Lexicography, Learning and Language from the Clay Tablet to the Computer*. Cambridge: Cambridge University Press.

MacKay, D. M. (1969) *Information, Mechanism and Meaning.* Cambridge, MA: MIT Press.

Miller, J. A. (1987) 'Jeremy Bentham's Panoptic device', *October*, 41: 3–29.

O'Hara, D. T. (1988) 'What was Foucault?', in J. Arac (ed.), *After Foucault: Humanistic Knowledge, Postmodern Challenges.* New Brunswick: Rutgers University Press.

Scarry, E. (1985) *The Body in Pain: The Making and Unmaking of the World.* New York: Oxford University Press.

Schotter, A. (1981) *The Economic Theory of Social Institutions.* Cambridge: Cambridge University Press.

Scott, W. R. (1987) *Organizations: Rational, Natural and Open Systems.* Englewood Cliffs, NJ: Prentice-Hall.

Serres, M. (1982) *Hermes: Literature, Science, Philosophy.* Baltimore: The Johns Hopkins University Press.

Simon, H. A. (1955) 'A behavioural model of rational choice', *Quarterly Journal of Economics*, 69: 99–118.

Simon, H. A. (1957) *Models of Man.* New York: Wiley.

Starobinski, J. (1975) 'The inside and the outside', *The Hudson Review*, 28: 333–51.

Weber, M. (1947) *The Theory of Social and Economic Organization.* Glencoe, IL: Free Press.

Weick, K. (1979) *The Social Psychology of Organizing.* Reading, MA: Addison-Wesley.

Williamson, O. E. (1975) *Markets and Hierarchies: Analysis and Anti-Trust Implications.* New York: Free Press.

Zipf, G. K. (1949) *Human Behaviour and the Principle of Least Effort.* Reading, MA: Addison-Wesley.

Zuboff, S. (1988) *In the Age of Smart Machine: The Future of Work and Power,* New York: Basic Books.

# 10 Organization
## Distal and Proximal Views

*Robert Cooper and John Law*

(From Samuel B. Bachrach, Pasquale Gagliardi, and Bryan Mundell (eds) 1995, *Research in the Sociology of Organizations: Studies of Organizations in the European Tradition*, 13, Greenwich, Conn.: JAI Press, 275–301. Thanks to the editors for their permission to republish this piece.)

## INTRODUCTION

Sometimes sociology is accused of being too presumptuous: for assuming that its objects of study are already constituted, and are simply waiting for the sociologist to come along to analyse and describe them. This kind of sociology comes in various forms. For instance, "spontaneous" sociology takes it subject-matter at face value, and "understands the system as the system asks to be understood" (and Passeron 1977, p. 159). Again, there is the "idealized" sociology of static states and homeostatic social systems. In this, the "state of rest" is viewed as normal and change as accidental, even malfunctional. A basic criticism of these *fait accompli* sociologies is that they deal with *results* rather than the *processes* that lead to the results.

Elias (1978) captures the essence of this criticism in his analysis of Talcott Parson's work. In particular, he notes that Parson's sociology is *retrospective, jumping* to its conclusions by putting its ends before its beginnings. Elias says of Parson's work that it is a "systematic reduction of social processes to social states, and of complex, heterogeneous phenomena to simpler, seemingly homogeneous components" (p. 228). It uses key terms like "individual" and "society" uncritically, unproblematically, as though they were part of the natural order of things. But, Elias continues, "individuals" and "society"—along with other concepts such as structure, function, norm, and role—are *preconceived* notions; they are conclusions that efface their origins. And what is preconceived here is the idea of a complete, finished, self-contained social unit of the kind described by Elias in his concept of *homo clausus*: the human actor (though it could just as well be the organization) closed around itself divided from others by an "invisible wall."

This idealized inclosure is accepted as a natural state of being, part of the order of things:

> But the nature of this wall is hardly ever considered and never properly explained. Is the body the vessel which holds the true self locked within? Is the skin the frontier between "inside" and "outside?" What in man is the capsule, and what is the encapsulated? The experience of "inside" and "outside" seems so self-evident that such questions are scarcely ever posed; they seem to require no further examination
>
> (Elias, 1978, p. 249).

Like Elias, we want to say that such taken-for-granted states of being—human or organizational—are products or effects of complex social processes. And that if we want to understand them, then we need a sociology of *becoming*. Parson's work is thus a sociology of *being*, while Elias's is a sociology of *becoming*. The one sees social terms as self-contained ends; the other, as continuously renewed becomings and beginnings. This, then, is the rudimentary opposition: between being and becoming; or result and process. And it is an opposition roughly equivalent to the distinction which we make in what follows between the *distal* and *proximal* modes of thinking in organizational analysis. Like Elias, we argue for a proximal approach to the analysis of social institutions. At the same time, we recognize that the distal and proximal are *both* complementary *yet* different ways of looking at human structures.

This chapter has the following plan. In the first section we characterize the distal and the proximal, and in particular seek to distinguish between a distal focus on "organizations", and an alternative proximal concern with the nature of "organization." As a part of this concern with the proximal, we consider the uncertain processes which produce planning and prediction, the boundary between inside and outside, and the relationship between parts and wholes. In the second section, we outline a proximal theory of organizing, and illustrate this in considerable empirical and conceptual detail. Moving from a concern with process, we explore the relational character of organization, its material heterogeneity, and the way in which this is recursively implicated in representation. In the third and final section, we briefly consider some broader implications of our argument. We do this by linking the proximal theory of organizing to two quite distinct intellectual traditions. First we look at cybernetic writing on information theory. There are, we suggest, strong affinities between this and the proximal: each implies that people and organizations are better seen as coding effects or products rather than as objects in their own right. Second, we touch on feminist writing in science, technology and society. This, like the proximal theory of organizing, emphasizes the importance of material heterogeneity, and argues that people and organizations are "cyborgs"—a promiscuous mix of biology and technology. But they are also (or so runs the argument) partial, decentered and political in character. This is because, *pace* cybernetics, there is no perfect information or code. Instead there are endless partial and discrepant codes which generate dispersed organizational (and political) assemblages. In the final section we thus press the logic of the proximal one stage further by dissolving intellectual boundaries; first, between organization theory and other social science traditions; and second, between the descriptive and the normative.

## THE DISTAL AND THE PROXIMAL

The distinction between distal and proximal thinking has a long history in intellectual enquiry (e.g., Heider 1959). Distal thinking privileges results and outcomes, the "finished" things or objects of thought and action. It privileges the ready-made. So the distal is what is preconceived, what appears already constituted and known, what is simplified, distilled; it's a bit like fast food—packaged for convenience and ease of consumption. Proximal thinking deals in the continuous and "unfinished"; it's what is forever approached but never attained, what is always approximated but never fully realized. The proximal is always partial and precarious, forever fated to repeat itself in an effort to reach (but never attain) completion. The distal is constituted by *action at a distance;* the proximal, through *action by contact* (Korzybski, 1958). The distal stresses boundaries and separation, distinctness and clarity, hierarchy and order. The proximal manifests implication and complicity, and hence symmetry, equivalence and equivocality. The distal reflects "a *universe* of a finished, explicit totality in which the relations are those of reciprocal determination, "whereas the proximal reveals "a *world* that is an indefinite and open multiplicity in which relations are relations of reciprocal implication" (Merleau-Ponty 1962).

Applied to organizations, the distal and proximal modes yield the following rough profiles. The distal organization is a definable system with a strong boundary. For instance, the traditional distinction between organization and environment is distal conception. So is the idea that organizations are "things" that can be measured. By contrast, proximal thinking views as mediating networks, as circuits of continuous contact and motion—more like assemblages of *organizings*. What we call (in the distal mode) the boundary between organization and environment becomes (in the proximal mode) an intervening medium, a point, or line of passage for action, movement. When we say, distally, that organizations are structures that can be measured, the proximal mode reminds us that organizations so conceived are really *effects* created by a set of mediating measuring instruments. Whereas the distal mode talks in terms of insulated individuals, groups, and organizations, thus underlining the separateness of these terms and the distances between them, the proximal mode talks about their permeation and interpenetration.

But notice that our title refers to "organization" and not to "organizations." To talk of "organizations" is somehow to suggest that we are studying specific systems that are already set up for us, and that we know (more or less) what they are. To talk of "organization" is to introduce a more general referent, to loosen the distal preconception implicit in "organizations". The dictionary defines "organization" as "the state of being organized" *and* "the act of organizing." The first definition tells us that organization is an *effect*, while the second suggests it is an active process of organizing that has not yet solidified into an effect. Together, these definitions focus the central issue we address here: the nature of the relationship between effect and process, between distal and proximal. Let's recall our earlier discussions of Elias's (1978) criticism of Parson's work, namely, that it's a *retrospective* sociology, one that trades in effects rather than processes. Implicit in this criticism is the idea of the so-called "retrospective illusion," a kind of sleight-of-mind by which *we covertly convert after-effects into pre-existent cause of thought and action* (Merleau-Ponty, 1962) or where, in another formulation of the same idea, "the meaning of a structure exists only to the extent that it is constituted after the event" (Johnson 1993, p. 170). A proximal sociology seeks to disclose such legerdemain by expressly analysing forces and agents that order relatively stable effects (such as organizations, societies) out of intrinsically partial and precarious processes.

One consequence of the critique of the "retrospective illusion" is the idea that nothing should be presumed or privileged in advance; in the first instance, everything should be given equal weight. An expanded version of this is the *principle of symmetry* which says that distinctions in the human world are not naturally given: again, they are products or effects of ordering or organizing (Matte Blanco 1975; Law 1993). To talk of symmetry is to draw a methodological stance from the contemporary sociology of science. It is not to imply anything about orderliness or tidiness. Instead it is to say that when we study organizations—or any other social phenomena—we cannot set out by assuming the presence of prior ordering or distinction (either spatial or temporal). Neither can we take it for granted that there are hierarchies or sequences given in the order of things. Instead, it is to work on the assumption that oppositions such as before/after, inside/outside, or simple/complex do not preexist analysis, but (like other such orderings and distinctions) are condensed or collapsed into each other. And it is also to assume that instead of unambiguous difference there is equivalence, equivocality, uncertainty. Thus to talk of symmetry is another way of talking about Elias's idea that social terms are not separated from each other by "invisible walls" but are *interpenetrative*. It also underlies his point that we should not assume that organization, ordering, direction have already taken place. So the task of a proximal sociology s to show how what was symmetrical has been translated into the asymmetrical. And a proximal sociology is necessarily symmetrical, once that does not take its objects of study as taken for granted effects or products.

To illustrate the implications of these ideas for the analysis of organization and organizing, we will now consider three themes: (1) organizing as programming, planning and predicting; (2) the distinction between organization and environment; and (3) the issue of differentiation-integration.

## Programming, Planning and Predicting

Programming, planning, predicting—all are terms that could stand in for the act of organizing. In the present context, their significance lies in the fact that they lead us to think of organization as the *anticipation* of action in space and time. Perhaps counterintuitively, we want to argue that to talk of *anticipation* is merely another way of talking about *retrospection*. How do we make this argument? The answer is that the factors of *time* and *tense* are all-important here. We have said that the distal is about products and effects. Or, more precisely, about how these are generated. But the logic of symmetry can be extended. It is possible to say that time and tense are also products, effects, or outcomes. Or to put it a little differently, and to play with the etymology (and the intrinsic relations) of the words, in the logic of symmetry/asymmetry, *production* is also *prediction*—an attempt to *anticipate*; that is *products* (or effects) are really *pre-dicts* or anticipative actions.

Let us explore this thought by considering for a moment, the character of action. Our view of action is that it is primitive. It *precedes* thought, ordering, or organization. Thus, in its most callow sense, an action is a *happening;* before anything else—before meaning, significance, before it's fitted into any schema—*it simply happens.* Any happening—action, event, occurrence—

> is infinitely simple, but this simplicity can only be approached through a state of privation. That which we call thought must be disarmed. . . . Thought works over what is received, it seeks to reflect on it and overcome it. It seeks to determine what has already been thought, written, painted or socialised in order to determine what hasn't been
>
> (Lyotard 1991, pp. 90–91).

Thus, in this way of thinking, a happening is a proximal and symmetrical experience whose indeterminacy provokes a state of tension, of agitation. This is because it always remains "unfinished." For the proximal never arrives, it's always "next:"

> this agitation is only possible if something remains to be determined, something that hasn't yet been determined. One can strive to determine this something by setting up a system, a theory, a program or a project— and indeed one has to, all the while anticipating that something
>
> (Lyotard 1991, p. 9).

So there is the *happening* of action. And then there is the question of what will come "next". And the problem about what will come "next" is perhaps the fundamental problem of ordering and organizing. For an obvious (but neglected) feature of formal organization is that it has to repeat itself in time, to renew its actions every working day. In this sense, we can say that formal organization is never finished. Again, it's a question of after-effects. "After" this day, "after" this thought, "after" this sequence, this word, comes another, and so on. . . . The program, the plan, the prediction are all contingent on the imperative to keep on going, to forbid "the possibility of nothing happening, of words, colours, forms, or sounds not coming; of this sequence being the last, of bread not coming daily" (Lyotard 1991, p. 91). The happening is "nothing"—or, rather, "no thing," no object, no form— because it is symmetrical and equivocal; it's not yet properly articulated, ordered, organized, not yet been converted into a product or effect. In other words, the happening is a heterogeneous process that has no before or after, no start or finish, no cause or effect. Only when it takes place in the network of what has *already* happened does it become ordered and organized, translated into an effect. Hence the significance of retrospection. Anticipation resides in retrospection. Without retrospection there is no anticipation, no ordering, no organization.

We are saying here that retrospection is really the *engineering* of time. It is a matter of constructing the future so that it looks like it's always been here. We get some idea of how this works by studying the case of the first U.S. astronaut in space (Latour 1987). This was a program or "prediction" which depended on the patient accumulation over a period of years of significant features of outer space and then incorporating them into the Space Center at Cape Canaveral. The astronaut's final success was really a repetition of many earlier strategic moves—unmanned flights, trials with monkeys, flight simulations on earth and so forth—which, when added up, converted the unknown (or symmetrical) into the known (or asymmetrical). With the help of the many previous steps in the program, the astronaut had already been in outer space many times. What *seemed* to be the *first* time was really the $(n+l)th$ time. Retrospection thus depends on repetition, where a first time is revealed only by its being repeated. "The first time we encounter some event, we do not know it; we start knowing something when it is at least the *second* time we encounter it, that is, when it is familiar to us" (Latour 1987, p. 219). The second time represents the point where proximal becomes distal, where process becomes effect, where retrospection has worked to produce anticipation.

## Organization/Environment

The story of the space programme also raises the old question of where the organization stops and where its environment starts. But the question "where?" is a distal question; it asks for a specific and stable location; it implies a sharp boundary between what lies "inside" the organization and what's "outside." As we've seen in Elias's proximal sociology, this question makes no sense since social terms are not bounded by "walls;" there are no containers and no contained in the social world. There are only interpenetrating networks. This is certainly the case with the Space Center at Cape Canaveral and its relations with outer space, both of which are constituted by a continuous and interlocking network of people, monkeys, simulators, computer terminals, control tower, spacecraft—not to mention such phenomena as the density of the atmosphere, the equations of thermodynamics, and the forces of gravity. What's striking about the programme is the heterogeneity of the physical components that make up its ordered network. But does this mean that the organization and its environment are separate and specific domains? The answer, we suggest, is "no." Rather, "outer space" and "inner space" interpenetrate, interlock, within a single sociotechnical network. Instead of the distal view of organization as locatable structure, proximal organizing involves mobile and non-locatable associations and, as we've said, such organizing is always partial and precarious. Distally, the boundary is an effect; proximally, it's a happening, a process. An organization's insides and outside are symmetrical and correlative: "No inside is conceivable . . . without the complicity of an outside on which it relies, complicity mixed with antagonism . . . No outside would be conceivable without an inside fending it off, resisting it, 'reacting' to it" (Starobinski 1975, p. 342). Some sense of the dynamics of this mutuality can be gleaned from the story of Louis Pasteur's development of an antidote to anthrax in the early 1880s (Latour 1988).

Pasteur's laboratory, situated in the center of Paris, begins a program of research to find a remedy for anthrax, a scourge of the French cattle industry at that period. Difficult to study because of its unpredictable nature, the disease could not be investigated by traditional methods. So, Pasteur first transplants his laboratory to a farm in the French countryside, thus confusing the usual distinction between the laboratory and the outside world. Pasteur learns from the farmers and the veterinarians how the anthrax bacillus affects the cattle, and then returns to his laboratory with the cultivated bacillus. He's now able to grow the bacillus in isolation and in large quantities. The cause of the disease can now be *seen* and therefore be more easily investigated, while back at the farm it remains invisible and deadly. Pasteur can now simulate anthrax outbreaks in his laboratory by inoculating cattle with the anthrax culture he's created. He's able to chart and record all the significant features of the controlled simulation. His next step is to organise a field trial. In effect, this means that he translates relevant features of his laboratory to the French countryside so as to ensure that his experimental work is reproduced properly. Veterinarians and farmers then see that, provided they reproduce such laboratory practices as disinfection, inoculation, recording, and so forth, they too can practise Pasteur's power. The laboratory, finally, is simulated and reproduced in every French farm.

Pasteur's translations underline the artificiality and limitations of thinking in terms of distal concepts such as laboratory and agriculture, organization and environment. This is because they also question the traditional static distinction between "inside" and "outside." As we have seen, inside and outside are not separate places; they refer to a correlative structure in which "complicity is mixed with antagonism. . . . No outside would be conceivable without an inside fending it off, resisting it, 'reacting' to it (Starobinski 1975, p. 342). Pasteur reproduces inside his laboratory "an event that seems to be happening only outside—the first move—and then extend(s) outside to all forms what seems to be happening only inside laboratories. As in some topological theorem, the inside and the outside world can reverse into one another very easily" (Latour 1985, p. 154). The inside-outside relationship now takes on the un-ordered logic of the principle of symmetry, a kind of continuous oscillation in which neither one side nor the other has the upper hand. What arrests this oscillation (at least temporarily) is the retrospection at work in Pasteur's extension of the anthrax vaccine to the farms of France: the vaccine would only work on the farms if the required laboratory conditions were set up *beforehand*. It's this move which links Pasteur's laboratory and the U.S. space program.

## Part/Whole

A definitive problem of organization is the balance between *differentiation* and *integration* (e.g., Scott 1987) or what is more called the part/whole question. Organizational writers typically deal with this question in a distal way. To illustrate, we refer to Lawrence and Lorsch's (1967) widely-quoted study, *Organization and Environment* (not a work of sociology but of management theory, it is perhaps worth noting in the present context). Lawrence and Lorsch view organization as a system characterized by differentiation and integration. Differentiation here refers to the range of cognitive and emotional differences among the organization's managers. Integration is a state of unity in which these cognitive and emotional differences have to be taken account of in the "conflict resolution" required for the "achievement of organizational collaboration." The approach of Lawrence and Lorsch to the differentiation/integration problem is distal. Like Parson's, they privilege the (managerial) actors as relatively self-contained units with psychological "insides" (cognitions and emotions) who *then* relate themselves to other actors to achieve unity. In other words—and this is also Elias's (1978) criticism of Parson's—interaction or interdependence is *secondary* to the individualized self-containment of the actors. Of course, Lawrence and Lorsch as management theorists are predisposed to seek answers to *functional* questions and this is (one reason) why they emphasize functional parts—managers, jobs, departments—and their integration rather than the more problematic question of interdependence as *interpenetration* (Elias 1978). Their analysis is distally simplified around the *polarity* of parts *and* whole.

The complex processes that actually constitute what is *between* parts and whole are elided. But for the proximal thinker, what is *between* is where the real action is. And, significantly, it is the logic of the *between* that mediates parts and wholes, differentiation and integration. Again, it is a question of the boundary. Proximal theory sees the boundary as a surface that *at the same time* divides *and* joins. It is not a question of simple polarity—part and whole, inside and outside—but of partial and precarious connection. In the language of chaos theory, we find that contacts of whatever kind are always *intermittent*:

> Contacts between surfaces have properties quite independent of the materials involved . . . One simple but powerful consequence of the fractal geometry of surfaces is that surfaces in contact do not touch everywhere . . . it is why two pieces of a broken teacup can never be rejoined, even though they appear to fit together at some gross scale
> (Gleick 1988, p. 106).

So, parts do not unproblematically turn into larger wholes. Instead, the idea of the boundary—or the *between* condition—compels us to see parts and wholes as *tensions* that hold incompatible things together (Haraway 1991). "Things hold together," as Strathern (1991, p. 35) says, but only as "working compatibilities" and certainly not as pure, unitary wholes. Proximally, the part/whole relationship is always approximate, never complete.

In the proximal approach it is not the interdependence of functions that constitutes organizational differentiation/integration. Rather, it is the connections between material elements—human actors, plans, accounts, machinery, telephones, buildings, and all the rest. The proximal thus differs from the distal in the way in which it emphasizes *materials* rather than functions. And also in the way it concerns itself with the *specificity* and *indeterminacy* of links. For connections occur, but they are endlessly and uncertainly produced at the *surfaces* of objects. For the surface—as a boundary—is intrinsically unordered and directionless. Such distinctions as inside and outside, or part and whole, are not given in the order of things but are rather products or effects of organizing activity. In other words, there are no natural distinctions between the heterogeneous elements that make up systems and organizations. There are no preconstituted functions which then require integration. The parts and wholes of systems—*before* they are distally understood as parts and wholes—are all equivocal and uncertain. And any reduction in their uncertainty, their indeterminacy, is an effect or a product. So it is that part/whole relationships may be seen as *tensions* of incompatible things that are held together. To sum up, we are saying that to hold together the incompatible and heterogeneous is precisely the function of *productions* as *pre-diction* or the anticipation of the future as retrospection. And here we see retrospection *in action*, so to speak, and not merely as a distal accomplishment. As we have noted, the distal is about time and tense. In the proximal analysis of the part/whole relationship, *time* and *tense* have to be understood as *tensions* that hold incompatible and heterogeneous elements together in space as well as time.

It is this proximal character of the part/whole relationship that helps elucidate a further definitive feature of organization—*intention* or purpose. In conventional organizational analysis, intention is usually read as a mental event, that is, it is distally conceived as a plan or program "in" an actor's mind. In the proximal approach, intention refers to the tensional traction of a *field* of incompatible and heterogeneous events. In short, *intention* means "in tension," a pattern of actions that is distributed throughout such a field and which serves to *maintain* it or hold it together. The intention is no longer "in the head" of the actor—it is the actor that is "in" the happening of the field, whether this be an artist's studio, or the even more visibly heterogeneous assemblage put together by an architect when she designs a house (Baxandall 1985; Deleuze and Guattari 1988, Ch. II; Jameson 1991, Ch. IV). Intention is, therefore, definitively bound up with the continuously partial and precarious character of the part/whole relationship.

In discussing the themes of: (1) programming, planning, predicting, (2) organization/environment, and (3) part/whole, our point as been to illustrate the ideas of the distal and proximal in the context of certain enduring concerns of organization theory. At the same time, we have argued for a proximal sociology of organizations, that seeks to understand organizing as an interpenetrative and continually recursive process (Elias 1978) instead of the conventional view of organization which rests of a set of distal and static concepts and categories (e.g., plans, structures, technology, environment). Whereas the distal view rests on a conception of organization as a set if self-contained effects, the proximal view discloses *emergent* organization—or, better, *organizings*—which has (have) to be understood as a seamless web of interconnecting yet heterogeneous actions (Hughes 1983).

## PROXIMAL ORGANIZING

So what might a proximal theory of organizing look like? In this section we explore this question by telling some empirical stories about organizing and ordering. The first of these takes us quite a long way from the formal organization, but not so far as it might appear. For it has to do with imperialism—Portuguese imperialism—and for our purposes imperialism maybe seen as another mode of organizing, albeit one that plays itself on a world scale. We start, then, by considering how the Portuguese built up their empire and (this will be the particular focus of the first story) how they managed to travel all the way from Lisbon to the shores of India and back again. For our second example we draw on material that is more recognizably organizational by looking at a laboratory and exploring certain aspects of the process of scientific research. Finally, with our third example, we approach the question of organization or organizing more directly by applying and developing what we have learned from the first two examples to the process of management.

## Relations and Processes

In the thirteenth century a few brave Italians tried to open up a sea passage to India (Law 1986a). They rowed in their galleys through the Straits of Gibraltar and set out across the Atlantic. And they never came back. Two hundred years later, at the end of the fifteenth century, a Portuguese expedition under the command of Vasco da Gama set sail in three vessels. It travelled from Lisbon south-west, sailing in a huge loop that first took it close to the shores of Brazil before crossing the South Atlantic to round the Cape of Good Hope. From there the expedition sailed in a north-easterly direction past Madagascar to the Indian Ocean, from which, blown by the seasonal monsoon winds, it sailed eastwards to India. The Portuguese traded with the local ruler and they fell out with him—for he was used to richer gifts from his Arab trading partners. So they departed, tracing a somewhat different course through the trade winds, and arrived back in Lisbon. But for the Samorin of Calicut it was only a brief respite for the Portuguese returned with a well-armed expedition. One morning the unfortunate Samorin looked out of his window to see the little fleet that was to bombard him into submission. In this way, then, started both the Portuguese empire and its hugely profitable trade in spices.

This is the story of organization—organization, as we have indicated, on a world scale. But what is it about? To answer this question proximally we have to look at *details*. Details for instance, to do with vessels and techniques of navigation. Let's talk a little about those details. Let's note, for instance, that in the 200 years between the failed Italian attempt to row across the Atlantic and the successful Portuguese attempt to sail round the Cape of Good Hope sailing technology had advanced out of all recognition. For instance, the ships used by the Portuguese—they were called caracks— were sailing vessels. Unlike galleys, they were not rowed. And unlike the sailing vessels used for trade in Europe in the Middle Ages, they were relatively manoeuvrable and (more important still) they didn't have to wait for a following wind, but were able to sail across it. Furthermore, since they borrowed the power of the wind to reach their destination, they didn't need a large crew of oarsmen. These, then, were some of the reasons why the Portuguese were able to navigate to India while the Italians were not.

So here is the first difference. As we've seen, distal theory tends to concern itself with outcomes and results. It has a bias towards a general overall perspective. But a story that is proximal concerns itself with "detail." Important "details." It says that all structures, political, economic, technical, and organizational, are effects or products. And it says that it is important to look at the way in which those structures are produced.

How, then, are structures or organizations generated? What we have said about the Portuguese suggests a way of thinking about this question, and this is our second point. *It is a matter of relations* between surfaces, of uncertainties that are, for a moment, domesticated. In the proximal view we achieve a structure—no, better, let's say that a structure *performs itself*—to the extent that a somewhat stable set of relations is brought into being through the generation of anticipated by means of retrospection. Think, again, of the carrack and its crew. Compare this with the galley. Each may be pictured as a set of relations. People, oars, provisions, sails and all the rest—these are viable vessels so long as all the different relations hold in place: so long as there are the surfaces of sails to catch the edge of the wind: so long as there are the hands of seamen ready to raise and lower those sails; so long as there are barrels of food and water for the crew; so long as the crew, through fear or sense of duty, follows the orders of the navigator; so long as the navigator reads the surface of his charts, and so manages to direct the vessel away from the rocks; so long as the course that it sets is drawn by the winds and currents; so long as the great waves of the Atlantic do not swamp the vessel, battering on the surface of its hatches and flooding into the compartments below.

So proximal theory is concerned with detail. It's concerned with relation. It's concerned with specifics. It's concerned with the interactions between surfaces. But, and this is the third point, it is also concerned with *processes*. We've noted that relations and the objects they produce don't exist in and of themselves. They are not secure, and *there is not order of things*. Everything is a momentary *effect* (Callon 1980; Latour 1987). There are no natural divisions and distinctions. And everything may change. For instance (this is the proximal suggestion), the vessel and its crew is a fairly precarious set of relations that reinforces and braces itself to perform a viable vessel *if all goes well*. Indeed, it is more than this, for it is a set of interactions that extends into and incorporates its environment (as it does for the case of the winds); but it is a set of relations that is easily overwhelmed and destroyed if things go wrong; which is, presumably, what happened to the Italians. For in their galleys they could not have rowed very far. Quite apart from the question of exhaustion, vessels with such a large crew would have needed to stop for provisions and fresh water within a few hundred miles. In the middle of the Atlantic! Unless, of course, they chose to sail down the coast of Africa with its dangerous reefs, its diseases, and its unhelpful indigenous peoples. Which means, in the proximal view, that what we call "organization" is shorthand for an (pretty precarious and reversible) effect generated in the patterning of relations, of interactions between surfaces.

## Material Heterogeneity

So far we have made three suggestions. Proximal theory, we have said, concerns itself with "detail." It concerns itself with relations. And it tries to treat those relations as processes, rather than assuming that they are secure. This means that it tries to resist the distal view which assumes that objects or organizations are given in the order of things, but, instead, explores the processes that *generate* such effects. Now, however, we want to press the argument one stage further by considering the *material* character of those relations.

Let's tell another story, this time about navigation. Again, to say it quickly, it is a matter of before and after. Before the middle of the fourteenth century European mariners made little use of celestial navigation. They used the magnetic compass and portolan charts which laid out compass courses. Or, more often, they used the *rutter*, a kind of guidebook to the sea, which described prominent landmarks, distances elapsed, the colour of the water—anything that would allow the navigator to direct a vessel from A to B along a predetermined route that was usually within sight of land. However, after the middle of the fourteenth century, and under the impetus of the Portuguese, matters started to change. And by the time of Vasco da Gama's expedition to India, navigators were being drilled in the basics of celestial navigation.

This revolution, vital to the Portuguese Empire because it allowed the carracks to sail thousands of miles from land without getting lost, was (or so the story runs) set in train by the Portuguese monarchy which established a Royal Commission which was charged with finding a way of transferring the expertise told that the world was a sphere and that the heavens look different at different latitudes: that, for instance, the pole star falls in the night sky as one moves south. This meant that in principle the latitude could be calculated, though there were many practical complications. For instance, near the equator the pole star disappears below the horizon, so the sailor has to use the positions of other heavenly bodies. But this is more complication because these move around the sky. Again, if you want to measure the altitude of a heavenly body you have to be able to see the horizon—but this is difficult at night. But using sun sightings (which gets round the problem) is even more complicated because this moves through the sky annually as well as daily. And then there was another kind of complication: the fact the people doing the navigating wouldn't be sophisticated astronomers standing on dry land, but relatively untutored mariners standing on the heaving deck of a carrack many thousands of miles from any advice. What, then, was to be done?

The Commission proposed the creation of what we may think as a *network of different materials*. First, there was a technology. Thus mariners were to be equipped with very simple instruments for measuring the altitude of the sun—instruments derived from astronomy and astrology but shorn of every unnecessary complication. Second, there were texts. Mariners would have a down-to-earth manual to tell them, step by step, how to measure the altitude of the sun, and convert that measurement into altitude. In addition, they would have a set of tables giving the altitude of the sun at noon for every day of the year. And third, there was the matter of converting unskilled mariners into celestial navigators. Here the proposal was that the apprentice navigators should be drilled in the art in a special school.

We are making an argument about navigation similar to that about the carrack—or indeed, about Pasteur in his movement from the laboratory to the farm. We are saying that it is pattern of relations. But we are also saying that is it a pattern of *materially diverse relations*. We are looking then, at a process which we might call *heterogeneous engineering* (Law 1987), a process which, at least in the first instance, ignores the distinctions between people, technologies, text and natural objects, and combines them all together to create an effect or a product. This is a move crucial to proximal theory. The assumption is that the relations making us (what we call) the social are *continuous*. They don't stop, as a distal perspective tends to assume, with the great ontological barriers which (we tend to think) stand between nature and culture, or between agency and structure (Latour 1993; Law 1993: Callon 1986a). Or, indeed, between organization and environment (Cooper 1992; Malavé 1992). For the networks spill over such categories. They form a seamless web (Hughes 1986). And (this is the proximal claim) if we want to understand the process of ordering and patterns which result, then we too need to ignore these divisions. To note, for instance, that the position of the sun, the astrolabe, the mariner, the charts, the Royal Commission and the training school—all these and many more—came together in the ordering that generated the Portuguese system of navigation and so the Portuguese imperial adventure.

So the proximal theory of organizing stresses material diversity. It says that both the navigator *and* the position of the sun form part of the networks of the social. But now we want to explore the character of these materials in a little more detail by considering the role of representation in this process. Which means (since all is relational, all is a matter of surfaces) that we need to look at the methods within which materials form and tie themselves together.

Let's start with another story about heterogeneous engineering. This time it's a modern-day story. We are in a laboratory, and we are with a scientist who we will call Rose (Law 1986b, 1986c). She is a successful scientist. She heads a group that works on drug targeting, and her work is generously supported by a number of grant-giving bodies. So she spends a lot of her time writing grant applications, organizing patenting and giving conference papers. Today, however, she is doing one of the things that she likes best: she is working at the lab bench on an experience, testing a new compound. The compound is a polymer, one that might be used to carry drugs to particular organs in the body.

Note before going further that we are also describing a field of intention: a pattern of heterogeneous elements, that is also, and recursively, a retrospection. What, then, is the intention? The answer: to test a particular polymer. To see if it will "work." And in particular, to see whether it is actually attracted to any organs. Rose cannot check on this directly, so what she's done is to attach it to a radioisotope. Then she has injected it into a rat. The radioactivity means that she will be able to measure where it has gone in the body of the rat. Is it simply excreted, in which case it isn't going to be much use. Or perhaps it is attracted to the liver? Or the spleen? The purpose of the experiment is to answer questions such as these.

Rose doesn't like killing laboratory animals, and she is very careful not to inflict unnecessary pain on them. But to measure the level of radioactivity in the different organs she has to "sacrifice" the rat. After doing so she dissects it, isolating, washing and weighing each of the organs. Then she "blends" each, adds distilled water, and puts the resulting suspensions in a test tube, one for each organ. She is very careful to label each of the test tubes. She doesn't any to get confused and mix up the results. Now, with all the test-tubes labelled, it is time to start measuring the level of radioactivity so she puts the test tubes—lots and lots of them, because there are lots and lots of rats—in a radiation counter. This is a large machine which will work right through the night measuring the radioactivity level of each sample, and typing the result on a printout. Rose closes the top of the machine, presses the button that turns it on, and leaves it to get on with the job.

This, then, is another relational story. It is about how a lot of different material bits and pieces—people, animals, machines, texts—come together in a continuous network. But there is something special about this network. It is going, if all goes well, to produce a set of figures which stand for something else. For when Rose goes to the radiation counter in the morning she is going to tear off the printout. And then she is going to paste it in her lab book. Then she is going to work on those figures. She is going to "correct" them because the organs differ in weight. The liver, for instance, is larger than the spleen, which means that is everything else is equal it will have taken up more of the polymer and given off more radioactivity. So she is going to divide the figure given by the counter by the weight of the organ to arrive at a corrected figure which will tell her about the level of "uptake" of the test compound per unit of organ weight. And then she is going to combine these figures for a whole lot of rats to arrive at an average figure for the different organs—a figure which will be reported as a "result" in the scientific paper that she expects to write about the experiment.

All of this is commonplace: thousands of such experiments are carried out in laboratories around the world every day. It is a mundane form of ordering, one that is almost clichéd in character. But look at it from a proximal perspective. First, we are dealing again, to be sure, with a relational process. Bits and pieces, surfaces, are being assembled and bought into being. Second, those bits and pieces come in a range of material forms. Heterogeneity is the name of the game. But, third, some of the bits and pieces bought into being have this peculiar feature: that they "stand for" others. That they *represent* those others, or their relations. It is important, here, to see behind the distal concern with "results." This is because what we are observing, if we think about it proximally, is a delicate process of *translation*. What is happening is that the structure of certain relations generated in one material is being transposed to another: the material form is being altered, but the patterning is being held stable. Or at any rate, it is being held stable if all goes well (Latour and Woolgar 1979; Latour 1987; Callon 1986a).

So what is the process? What is going on? The distal offers us an answer. It says that a scientist like Rose is able to make predictions. That in the course of experimenting she has learned something important about the natural world, something which may turn out to be useful, for example, in chemotherapy. This is right, but it hides the *process* that makes it possible. Such, at any rate, is the proximal view. For if the figures generated in the experiment represent certain processes to do with rats and compounds, if the pattern depicted in the figures is the same as the pattern in the rats and compounds, then they are also the relational effect or product of the interaction of a million other bits and pieces. The radiation counter, Rose's pocket calculator, the conventions of statistics, the procedures involved in using a chemical balance, the interaction between chloroform and the rate, an uninterrupted power supply, the delivery of radioisotopes—all of these and endless more come together in a heterogeneous process of patterning, to generate the experiment and its "result." And they come together, as we've noticed, again. And again.

Rose's figures are indeed representations. They are representations because they take a pattern created in one set of materials and recreate it on or in another material form. On the surface of a sheet of paper. Or in the place between that sheet of paper and the body of the scientist. But in the proximal account norms are turned into verbs. So the transposition of pattern becomes a process of "patterning." And repetition. And that process is extremely complicated since it takes up, forms and reforms all the bits and pieces that we have just mentioned. Which has several implications. One is quite straightforward. This is that since it is borne in—indeed created in—a complex process, representation is precarious. Which means in turn that all sorts of things may go wrong. Repetition may cease. This, to be sure, is a finding that can easily be incorporated into the distal. However, its significance is different and, as it were, more comprehensive in the proximal. This is because what is treated as a technical matter prone to technical faults and (and in principle) equally technical correction in the case of the distal, is converted into a complex, comprehensive, and relational whole in the proximal. Pre-diction may break down. Retro-spection may have to hunt wildly through novel possibilities searching for a future. Or, to put it differently, in the proximal, the realisation of a successful representation is an astonishing and materially heterogeneous effect rather than a technical accomplishment to do, for instance, with scientific method.

The proximal picture of representation also emphasizes that the interpretation of a representation is highly *selective*. That, to be sure, its character as a representation, whether good, bad or indifferent, is not given in the order of things. Indeed, the fact that this is not obvious is an example of the tidiness of the distal at work. Thus if everything else is equal, the distal view (which is indeed Rose's view) suggests that the figures created in the experiment represent something about a very specific set of circumstances, the relationship between a particular compound and the body-organs of a rat. *But this is not obvious* because everything else that they might be said to represent has, somehow or other, been deleted. Or (as we will suggest shortly), in some cases it has not been bought into being. So, for instance, it does not occur to us (or indeed Rose) to treat the figures as an expression of her skill, let alone the character of her pocket calculator or the laws which govern the decay of radioisotopes, despite the fact that these are perfectly plausible interpretations. Our point is this. The character of representation rests upon an heroic process of deletion. Or, perhaps better, an heroic process in which possibilities are *not* developed. Almost everything that one set of materials might be said to be telling of another is not actually said. And the particular character of the representation—the fact that Rose's figures are said to speak of rats, body organs, and chemical compounds rather than, say, the presence of a mains electricity supply—is an effect generated by a process of "non-representation," a process in which the myriad other possible representative connections that might be built up are not bought into being.

## Representation and Material Ordering

Thought they look so different, what happens in Rose's laboratory isn't so very far removed from the Portuguese system of navigation—or, indeed, the "Pasteurisation" of French agriculture. All have to do with the ordering and organizing of heterogeneous materials. Of surface phenomena. Or the interactions between surfaces. For the astronomers, it was a matter of assembling the tables, the sun, the astrolabe, the rules laid out in the manual, the skills to be learned by the mariner. If these were all combined together in just the right way then a particular figure emerged—a figure, the latitude, which represented the position of the vessel on the surface of the earth. But now we want to take the argument a further stage forward by considering how representations relate to heterogeneous engineering. So let's return to Rose and her laboratory.

We've noted that Rose's laboratory is rather successful. It produces good science and is generously supported by a number of grant-giving bodies—which two factors, to be sure, go together. But what is the character of the link? One rather Machiavellian but not entirely inappropriate way of talking of this is to say that the laboratory gathers information about the world which it then uses to control or influence its environment. In this view, then, knowledge is power, and the two go together to form a virtuous circle from the standpoint of the laboratory.

This way of speaking captures an important truth, but it does so in a distal manner. So what would be the proximal version of this truth? A brief reminder. Any answer to this question will insist not only on the material heterogeneity of the laboratory and its works (which is covered by the distal account) but will also press the relational and processual character of that material heterogeneity. It will suggest, then, that the bits and pieces assembled together are *themselves* relational products, surface effects, rather than being given in the order of things. Which means, in turn, that distinctions—for example between the scientific and the social, and the social and the natural—will be treated as products or consequences rather than having the a priori status preferred in a distal approach. The proximal account, then, will try to uncover the processes which create both knowledge *and* power. And it will say that, notwithstanding the fact that we experience them differently, these are effects generated in a common process.

The first step toward the proximal argument takes us into counter-intuitive territory. Radically, we need to say that the process of representation doesn't describe something that existed beforehand, but that it also *produces* what it describes (Derrida 1976; Foucault 1979; Latour and Woolgar 1979). That, for instance, scientific research doesn't simply report on natural objects that were there all along, but rather creates those objects in the process of describing them. The heart of the argument is difficult, but there is a straightforward and matter-of-fact way making a part of it. This is to observe (if we may go back to Rose's laboratory again) that the relationship between a particular, manufactured and quite esoteric polymer on the one hand, and a set of body organs on the other, is something that has been nought into being in the course of the experiment itself. That relationship simply didn't exist before. So the experiment *produces* the relationship. And then it produces a representation of that relationship.

Perhaps this looks like solipsism. Perhaps, that is, it sounds as if we are saying that there is no "outside world," so we may dream up valid worlds as we sit in our armchairs. But this is not the case. It is it not the case because the process of experimenting isn't primarily to do with thinking (though it, to be sure, includes this) so it does not take place primarily inside the head. Rather, it is materially heterogeneous. It is a matter of ordering elements, of assembling them into a pattern, a pattern that is recursively intentional. And then it is a matter of keeping that pattern stable enough so that it may be translated into another material form. So we are *not* saying that Rose invented her data. She wasn't imagining her findings. Not at all. Her data were good and reliable. But they were good and reliable because the ordering of the laboratory and its materials was patterned in a very particular way. Or, to put it somewhat differently, it was reliable because the various materials were brought together and induced to act in specific ways. They were, as it were, shaped by virtue of the fact they stood in relation to one another—and that process of reshaping generated a pattern that was translated into the figures collected by Rose.

This, then, is why proximal theory insists that representation is a process which creates its objects as well as their representations or depictions. It is, as it were, a process of engineering as well as description. But the engineering stretches out beyond the walls of the laboratory—and it is this fact that starts to explain, in proximal terms, why it is that what we call truth is so inextricably mixed up with power. And why it is that advantage might accrue to those locations which successfully create representations.

We have said that Rose's laboratory is rather successful. It wins large grants, and the work that comes out of it is generally considered to be of high quality. That is a distal summary of the facts. But if we look at it proximally what it means is that the laboratory can persuade others—perhaps in the first instance of other scientists—that (for instance) its descriptions of the relationship between rat body organs and polymers are to be taken seriously. That they are, to put it distally, true. But what does it take to persuade such other scientists that these descriptions are true? We already touched on the proximal answer in our discussion of Pasteur and the search for a vaccine for anthrax. It is that *the ordering patterns in Rose's laboratory have to be recreated elsewhere* (Latour 1988). All the bits and pieces assembled on the one site have to be reassembled—or at any rate mimicked—on another site. What this means is that Rose's truths are, at least in the first instance, only truths within the network of laboratories that goes about producing representations in broadly the same way. They aren't truths outside that narrow network. It means, then, that scientific truths are truths only where science has already spread itself. They don't exist, or are not truths, elsewhere.

There's a kind of circularity here—though it's not a vicious circularity. For if a representation is to be taken seriously—if it is to be validated—it must needs to be inserted into other places where there is the same ordering of heterogeneous materials, the same juxtaposition of surfaces. *Which means that other places must be persuaded to order themselves in the same way*. Truth, then, is integrally linked to (what we may, for the purposes of brevity, call) power. And power depends on truth. That is the character of circularity. What we are witnessing is a form of self-validation in which heterogeneous engineering generates truths which in turn underpin the need for (and the wisdom of) that heterogeneous engineering (Foucault 1979; Latour 1987).

We have stressed that the materials which are being ordered are, indeed, heterogeneous, and that we are not, therefore, advocating a form of solipsism. Now we need to extend this point by noting that neither are we subscribing to the peculiar perversion implied by certain extreme political doctrines—namely the view that the natural world is simply a reflection of political prejudice or will. Proximal theory is not an excuse for Nazism or Stalinism (Star 1988; Law 1991). It offers no such *apologia* precisely because it takes the heterogeneity of materials so seriously. For the world isn't endlessly malleable. It cannot be bent endlessly to arbitrary political will. This is because successful heterogeneous engineering has to cope with the resistances put up by that world whether these be "social" or "natural." Indeed, it needs to find ways of incorporating both into its ordering arrays.

## Representation, Tractability and the Obligatory Point of Passage

So what is the advantage of building material representations? What is the advantage that accrues to a place such as a laboratory that translates the world? Our discussion points to an answer, albeit one that grows out of the circularity mentioned above. To the extent that other locations in the world (let's call them "clients") mimic the ordering generated by the laboratory, they find that what this says helps *them* in turn to order the world. In other words, the engineering tools and truths from the laboratory become useful to its clients if the latter order the world in exactly the same way. If, in other words, they turn themselves in clients.

But the argument doesn't simply apply to laboratories. It works for any location that creates or deploys representations. For instance, it applied to the process that generated the Portuguese ability to navigate the oceans. The navigational system worked (stage one) because there was a patterning of materials in the observatories which established itself by incorporating and rubbing together parts of both the heavens and the earth. And then it worked (stage two) because the vessels were in turn translated, in the way we have described, into miniature observatories, observatories that drew on the procedures of astronomy and the position of the sun to generate an ordering figure, one relevant to navigation, that of the latitude. In analytical terms, the different between this and the case of Rose's laboratory is small. The latter, as we have observed, grows in a virtuous cycle. Its truths and its procedures of heterogeneous (social and natural) engineering spread, but as they spread, its truths become more truthful, and its engineering procedures more effective. It becomes, to coin a phrase, an *obligatory point of passage* (Callon 1986a). Which means that anyone who wants to work in drug targeting—indeed, anyone who is interested in chemotherapy—needs to keep abreast of work being done in the laboratory.

This, then, is a matter of "truth" and "power." Though we are cautious about such distal nouns—remember that proximal theory treats such objects as precarious surface effects or outcomes—one shorthand way of summarising our argument is to say that the processes of representation generate effects of truth and power together. Or, to put it slightly differently, they are not simply epistemological in import, but also *ontological* (Law and Mol 1994). But there is a further important consequence of representation that has consequences of power. This has to do with the fact that *representations tend to be relatively tractable* (Latour 1990; Law 1986d). But why is this? What is happening? To answer these questions we need, at the risk of some repetition, to look at Rose's experimental work again.

1  Note, first, that like the Portuguese navigational system, it is a process of heroic *miniaturization*. All sorts of relatively large-scale objects and relations—rats, machines, and all the rest—are reduced in size. Or, more precisely, the materials that are said to represent those

objects and relations are smaller than the original objects and relations themselves.

2 It is not, however, simply a matter of scale, but also one of *concentration*. For the traces that represent the series of experiments are brought together in one place, passed as they are into Rose's laboratory notebook (which, we might note, has its precise analogue in the manual and the tables used by the Portuguese navigators). Those traces represent objects and relations distributed through time and space. This, then, is what we mean by concentration.

3 It is also a matter of relative *homogenization*. Before and during the experiment there is a diversity of materials—rats, machines, people and the rest. After the experiment, that material heterogeneity has been reduced. Indeed, perhaps the process of creating representations has precisely to do with the reduction of material heterogeneity. It has to do (as again is the case for the Portuguese) with traces on sheets of paper. Or other, materially simple if relationally complex, symbolic forms.

4 In addition, bits and pieces, or the relationships between bits and pieces, that were previously spread through time, space and material form are all juxtaposed and rub up together. We have already touched on this, but in different terms, for it is in this process of *juxtaposition* that new "facts" and (as we argued in the last section) new objects come into being. It is the process of juxtaposition that creates relationships by, as we might say, making them visible. Visibility, then, is the essence. It is the noticeability of links that is at stake. For Rose, as it is for the Portuguese mariners (though the latter were clients, having concentrations made visible for them in the juxtapositions of the tables that had already been made visible elsewhere).

5 Visibility and the creation of objects and representations are also a function of *simplification*. Thus, as we have already noted, almost everything that might be said about the rats, the experiments, the method and the circumstances, isn't formulated in the traces that appear in the laboratory notebook. Or it is not treated as so appearing. And exactly the same may be said of the Portuguese navigation.

These movements, miniaturization, concentration, homogenization, juxtaposition and simplification, are all effects of the process of translation. But they have a further consequence: this is that they generate *tractability*. They tend to make matters manageable and orderable. Or, to be more precise, they tend to generate materials and they *focus* these at a particular location of ordering—let us say a *center of translation* (Callon 1986b). This is because the process of representation is one in which obdurate materials are replaced by those that are more malleable. Malleable materials which come (if all goes well) to re-present their obdurate cousins. Malleable materials which enrol all those others at second hand. Malleable materials which are bought together in a single location, a special kind of space, the kind of space which we are calling a center of translation.

A center of translation, then, is a space or a location of representation which enjoys a series of privileges. It is an obligatory point of passage, one through which others find they have to pass, a space with many clients of all sorts. But it is, in particular, an obligatory point of passage which works—and tends to generate clients by creating and exploring ordering patterns which reach by proxy across time, space and material variety. Clients, then, are created through the manipulation of their representatives. It is a space where ordering essays may be carried out on a small scale, as it were, quickly and cheaply, to see if they will work. It is therefore also a space in which these patterns that don't work out—patterns in which the link between the representative and what it represents breaks down—may be discovered, as it were, in private rather than in public. Accordingly, it is a space in which it is possible to collect workable patternings, while discarding others (Latour 1990). One in which the retrospective sources of anticipation, the repetitions which permit pre-diction, are for the moment sustained in a pattern of intention.

So, to repeat, it is a space which hopes to enrol clients by creating representatives and binding them. So it is a space which borrows materials of all sorts and subsumes them to its ordering pattern. But it is also a space which adopts and performs the shape of those materials as it generates representations—for representatives have, as it were, to speak for what they are said to represent, or they are no longer representatives and they lose their legitimacy. To say otherwise would be to court solipsism. Let's remind ourselves: there is all the difference in the world between the real Napoleon Bonaparte and all those poor souls living in retreats in the country who simply believe themselves to be Napoleon Bonaparte. Though, at the same time, we should also remind ourselves that the difference is one of degree rather than kind. The "real" Napoleon orders more, reaches further, has more faithful representatives, and a larger number of clients than the others. But it might in principle be different—as the "real" Napoleon no doubt reflected in the leisure of his retirement on St. Helena.

## Organizing Patterns and Material Gradients

We now have all of the elements in place for a proximal theory of organizing. To summarize, this will concern itself with details, relations, and surfaces. It will concern itself with material heterogeneity, and in particular with the patterning translation that occurs when one set of materials comes to represent, and so stand for another. It will concern itself with the tensions that generate purpose in the dialectic between retrospection and prediction. It will, in other words, concern itself with ordering and organizing. For in the proximal the focus is on process rather than outcomes. Or, more exactly, it is on the way in which outcomes are achieved. The proximal, then, is a sociology of verbs rather than nouns. Confronted with something that appears to be a noun, something that appears to reside in the order of things, it asks about the processes through which it manages to look and be that way.

So what would a proximal theory of organizations look like? A part of the answer is to insist that the question be rephrased. For in the proximal perspective, organizations are outcomes, verbs and patterings, rather than structures in the stable distal sense. So *organizations* as nouns are transmuted into *organization*—or *organizings* which are verbs (Cooper 1987, 1992, 1993; Cooper and Burrell 1988; Foucault 1979; Law 1993; Malavé 1992). Proximal theory suggests, then, that we might look for heterogeneous patterings. Patterings in which the bits and pieces which make up "an" organizing somehow or other hold themselves in place. Patterings which, somehow or other, feed upon and continue to perform themselves.

For instance, a proximal view of Rose's laboratory might treat it as a set of self-bracing, self-supporting interactions between surfaces which, somehow or other, cycle back and feed upon themselves. Perhaps we might start by saying that it "borrows" rats, polymers, machines, human skills and the current from the electricity company and assembles them together to create a pattern in the form of some scientific results. But those bits and pieces are only borrowed. They might disappear if things went wrong. So how come they are borrowed? What holds them in place, as clients of the laboratory? The empirical answer is straightforward: it is money. But where does that money come from? The answer is that it comes, in the form of grants, from a range of funding agencies. But that flow of money might dry up as well. Like the rats and the technicians, it is "borrowed" from the funding councils. So how is that achieved? To answer this we move to the next set of clients—this time in the form of other scientists and laboratories which referee the applications for grants favourably. But how are these clients held in place? Why are they so favourable to Rose's requests for money? The answer is that they have been impressed by the scientific results generated by the laboratory—which brings us back, to be sure, to the findings which borrowed from those clients, the rats and all the rest (Latour and Woolgar 1979).

Self-feeding organizings, patterns of intention, are thus likely to take the form of cycles. Indeed of virtuous cycles (otherwise they would vanish, and we wouldn't detect them as "organizations" at all). As the example we have just cited suggests, they are likely to ignore what are usually taken to be the boundaries of "the organization." Inside and outside—in the proximal theory of organizing the distinction, like others, is treated as an effect or a product, rather than something that is given in the order of things (Malavé 1992). And, in the way that we mentioned earlier, they are also likely to take the form of virtuous cycles which simultaneously generate representative "knowledges" and heterogeneous orderings and so produce centers of translation. We would like to conclude this section by exploring this point a little further, this time by drawing on our third empirical study which has to do with an organization and its management (Law 1993).

We will call him Andrew, and he is a manager of a medium-sized formal organization—in fact a large scientific laboratory. Andrew is sitting in his office, and he is puzzling over a set of statistics. The statistics have to do with what they call "manpower bookings." That is, they report the "effort" committed in the previous months and the previous year, to a series of major scientific and technical projects. Andrew is puzzling over the statistics because he thinks that he has seen a problem. This has to do with the amount of effort put into a particular project, the so-called "Second Wiggler." It looks to Andrew as if the amount of effort being put into it is far too low. "We aimed to use nineteen in-house man years [last year]" he tells his colleagues, "but we [actually] used seven . . ." This may mean that there is a problem. A problem, we might say, of ordering. But what is the character of that problem?

The answer is that the "Second Wiggler" project is going to suffer delays. In effect, the figures suggest that it might be up to a year behind schedule. But any such delay would be a disaster because this is the "flagship project" of the laboratory. Everyone believes that the future of the laboratory depends on it. All sort of scientists want to come to the laboratory to use it in their experimental work. And the funders—for this is a government laboratory—have chosen to put scarce resources into the project because they judge it to be important, but they are certainly keeping a close watch on what goes on, and how well the laboratory performs. So Andrew is concerned. Deeply concerned. He knows that his neck is on the block if things don't work out. But he also knows that the reputation—and perhaps, as we have mentioned, the future—of the laboratory depends on its successful completion to time and budget. So he wants to know what his management team is doing about the apparent difficulties—and he learns that they have already had a crisis meeting. He asks what happened at that meeting and he learns that they had decided that they needed to shift effort off other projects, even if the latter suffered as a result. Andrew observes that he is much relieved. "You are," he notes, "addressing priorities." "Okay," responds one of his subordinates, "but *you* have to take the decisions!"

This laboratory isn't very different from the one headed by Rose—except that it is nearly a hundred times larger. But the principles are the same. It may be seen, in conformity with the proximal account of ordering, as a self-ordering cycle of heterogeneous materials and relations. That heterogeneity is visible here, embracing this complex machine, the "Second Wiggler," the scientists who hope to be able to use that machine in due course, and the government department that is paying for it. And the laboratory will retain these clients only if it keeps the project on schedule. But the ordering is not just heterogeneous. It takes the form of a set of self-feeding cycles. Thus the process of organizing the funders depends on the business of ordering the machine—while ordering the machine is not possible unless money is "borrowed" from the funders. But holding the scientists in place is only achieved by borrowing against the promise of a future machine, which depends on both funders and the project itself—though the ordering of the funders was originally achieved in turn by borrowing on the support of the scientists!

Such, then, are some of the complexities of organizing in the current case. But look, now, at the way in which representation fits into this cycle. For Andrew and his managers know that there is a problem. They know that the flagship project is at risk. And they know that this is the case long before the problem is likely to surface in the form of delays or cost-overruns visible to outsiders. They know this because the sexist manpower booking system generates figures that are printed on sheets of paper. We have, to be sure, been here before. We have looked at the way in which representations are derived from a complex of heterogeneous materials, and we have considered the precarious character of that process of translation. We have also considered some of the ways in which these representations feed back into the ordering of those heterogeneous materials—a point particularly pertinent to the present example where, as is obvious, the manpower booking system is both a product of, and helps to produce, the organizing cycle of the laboratory. However, the point that we want to stress is complementary to these: we want to note that there is an important sense in which Andrew and his fellow managers are *themselves* materially heterogeneous effects generated in the self-feeding organizing process of the laboratory. They aren't units. Examples of *homo clausus*. Not at all.

To see this we have to ask what it is that makes Andrew an effective manager. The question seems to call for answer in terms of his personality: that he is tough-minded, clear-thinking, personally attractive, thinks strategically. Note, however, that like the notion of "personal responsibility"—the notion which we mentioned above that if things go wrong Andrew's neck is on the block—this is a response in the distal mode. It says that Andrew "is," or at any rate possesses, a series of attributes. And that "he" succeeds, or fails. But the proximal tack is quite different. It says that Andrew may be seen as the somewhat stable outcome of a relational and in-tentional pattern of heterogeneous materials. It suggests, for instance, that if Andrew sees far (as indeed he does) then this is because he is well-informed. He is, for instance, well-informed about the seeming lack of progress on the Second Wiggler project because he knows about the manpower booking figures. But these don't drop onto his desk out of thin air. Like any set of representations, they are themselves the product of complex and heterogeneous processes. So this is the proximal version of the argument. Andrew's strategic foresight cannot be understood apart from the manpower booking system. It is, in part at least, an *effect* of that system. Or, to put the point a little more precisely, it is (in part) *an expression of the difference in tractability between the figures generated by that system and the materials which they claim to represent.* The very possibility of strategic foresight, of pre-diction, is opened up by that gradient in tractability. The fact that Andrew can "see" what others cannot, the fact that he can "see" into the *future*, this is possible because he sees farther, or differently, into the *past*. And this in turn occurs because the figures have been manipulated and reported to him. And, to be sure, because he is in a location which can borrow materials as part of an ordering response to that foresight.

The same point may be made in other ways. For instance, Andrew spends a good deal of time outside the laboratory, sitting in committees of the body that funds the laboratory, wheeling and dealing, and gathering intelligence in the corridors and saloon bars of power. It is possible to press the distal view: that Andrew "is" good at gathering and acting on intelligence. But the proximal analysis points in the alternative relational direction, suggesting instead that he is the *creature* of a set of other materials and the way in these interact together: the telephones and the fax machine; the electronic mail; the postal system with its constant flow of papers and reports; the Pullman express train which runs from near the laboratory to London; the club in London where he can buy the influential a glass of malt whisky and trade the confidential news of the day; the secretary who acts like a semi-permeable membrane, allowing through only important papers, visitors and calls; the office, with its conference table and its secretarial anteroom. All of these end and many more help to constitute Andrew (and to be sure, a group of his senior subordinates) as a center of translation. They help to perform him as a place or set of roles, which join together, participate in, and profit from the simultaneous creation and interaction of the processes of representation and those of heterogeneous orderings. Andrew, then, is a particular location in the self-ordering cycle of organizing. He is that location which, more than any other, profits from and so helps the gradient of malleability that is generated out of the formation of representations (Elias 1983; Law 1993).

## POSTFACE: ORGANIZATION, INFORMATION AND HETEROGENEITY

Here is the crucial distinction: between a theory of organizations and a theory of organization. The theory of organizations is distal. That is, it works on certain assumptions: that organizations have relatively clear boundaries; that they have a series of more or less discrete parts or functions; that the problem of the organization is to manage a series of functional interdependencies and so to achieve specific and more-or-less well-defined goals; that it does this through appropriate programming, planning and prediction. Change is not necessarily undesirable in this view, for it may suggest new organizational goals, or better means for achieving existing goals. So a certain kind of dynamism is possible within the distal, but it is the dynamism of the more-or-less preconstituted organism reacting to its environment.

We've tried to show what happens if we dissolve the core assumptions of the distal theory of organizations; what happens if we dissolve its presuppositions about relative stability, the discrete character of functional components, and the notion that there is, at the end of the day, a relatively unproblematic boundary between the organization and its environment. Our argument is not that such distinctions are never achieved. Often, indeed, they are. It is possible to point to IBM or the U.S. Air Force and say "Look: there's an organization." And, indeed, it's also possible to point to boundaries for they can be *made* to exist, as prisoners in particular know only too well. So the distal exists—but (or so we have suggested) *it is a proximal effect*. So our argument has been that the theory of organizations privileges the distal, and tends to repress, displace, or forget the proximal. And that a theory or organization might, with profit, attend to what has been forgotten, and explore the proximal processes that generate the possibility of the distal.

In the major part of this paper we have thus sought to outline such a proximal theory of organization. We've considered what we take to be the *relational* character of the components that go into organization—the fact (or so we believe) that they are effects or products generated in interaction, rather than existing in the order of things. We've argued that organization is a *process*, a verb rather than a noun; that it is a verb which sometimes generates more or less stable noun-effects or distal products. We've also explored (what we believe to be) the *material heterogeneity* of organization: the notion that it is a seamless web of different materials, human, un-human, technological, organic, natural, and all the rest. Throughout we've argued that matters are fluid: and that if they do not appear that way, then this is a precarious and reversible achievement; we've stressed, in other words, that we are concerned with ordering, rather than with order (Cooper and Burrell 1988; Law 1993). So the argument is that processes of organization are fluid and flexible; that everything is mobile and malleable; that everything could be otherwise; that everything is incomplete; that everything is in a state of both tension and motion; and that if matters are more or less stable for a moment, then this is, indeed, an achievement; an outcome achieved in a series of reversible translations.

This, then, is the outline of a proximal theory or organization. It is a theory quite unlike the distal approach widespread in the sociology of organizations. And neither is it so specific—for we take it that it is a way of thinking about social ordering both within and outside the area of formal organizations. Accordingly, in this final section we want briefly, and more controversially, to explore the way in which it might link with two other traditions in contemporary social thought which have little to do with organizations but much to do with organization. The first of these is cybernetics, and we make the argument that this is similar to the proximal theory of organization in its concern with information; and in particular with information; and in particular, we consider the way in which both treat people and organizations as coding effects or products rather than as prime movers. Second, we touch on a theme in feminist writing. Like the proximal theory of organization, certain feminists press the materially heterogeneous and relational character of social life by talking of cyborgs. But they also point to the partial character of such relations and codings, and in so doing point the way to a need for a politics of partiality. And it is on this controversial note that we conclude.

What, then, of the link between organizations and cybernetics? First, observe that it's commonly assumed that organizations exist to create order out of disorder. That (to use *our* language) order is a distal effect of proximal organizing. Much of our discussion has pressed this view. We've spoken of the way in which patterns of relations are produced by the processes of miniaturisation, concentration, homogenization, juxtaposition, and simplification. But something much more basic is going on here. Cybernetics says that organization is a process in which instability and fluctuation are primary. It is not order that motivates the system but disorder, disruption. This is what we meant when we said earlier that the proximal is forever incomplete, unfinished. Proximal organization seeks always to disrupt its own distal tendencies to equilibrium and finitude by *creating* novelty, indeterminacy, heterogeneity, complexity. Our reinterpretation of intention as a heterogeneous field "in tension" was based on this idea. Our concept of material heterogeneity is now not merely the patterning of materially diverse relations, as we suggested, but is also something more: the active generation of diversity and complexity *in order to make distal patterning possible*. In short, it is not simplification but complexification that generates organization (Atlan 1974).

The study of complex systems is the special domain of cybernetics (Wiener 1950). The latter is the discipline that has sought to develop a generalized universal language for talking about systems of any and every kind. And as it sought to do this, it has made no distinction between people, animals and machines. Here, then, it is like our theory of proximal organizing. Its practice is symmetrical. In its concern with control and communication *between* systems it is indifferent to the material character of the objects which carry these communications. Accordingly, it challenges the tidy anthropomorphic view that communication and control processes are ideally human. In fact Lyotard suggests that there is something strangely "inhuman" about the cybernetic approach to communication and control (Lyotard 1991)—though perhaps "un-human" would be a better word to use. Representation and translation are "un-human" processes that *enable* communication and control between heterogeneous elements like actors, machines, texts, buildings and all the rest. And human actors—like non-human actors—are simply points in a system that acts through and beyond them.

If the loss of an anthropomorphic order of things is the first complexity of cybernetics, then a second has to do with the character of information. For information is a measure of order or organization; it's what *results* from ordering disorder or equivocality. It is, in short, a distal effect. But this implies that information (and organization) is only possible if it colludes with disorder. It implies, in other words, that information and noise are dependent on one another. That they exist *in* and *off* each other. That there is no information without noise. That to generate information is also to generate noise; to generate things, words, signals, symbols that don't fit in. Anti-signals, anti-words. Non-symbols that threaten the system, while at the same time creating the conditions of its possibility. The argument, then, is that information represents the precarious intertwining of order/disorder, asymmetry/symmetry, in "the constant struggle 'de l'ordre et de l'aventure' " (Eco 1989, p. 65). And that every ordering, every attempt to be finite, to predict, is countermanded from within by its mutually defining opposites of disorder, infinitude and uncertainty.

The end of anthropomorphism, and the intimate embrace of information and noise—these are two proximal products generated by cybernetics. They undermine the anthropomorphic interpretation normally given to social systems and organizations. The *humanized* organization is said to be purposeful, it exists for the benefits of its members, it develops technology, it contributes to society, and all the rest. But nothing could be farther from the cybernetic view of organization as information-processing. In the cybernetic view neither organizations nor their members can be said to process information. It's rather that they are processed *by* information. And it's the same with technology—"technology wasn't invented by us humans. Rather the other way around" (Lyotard 1991, p. 12). Looked at in cybernetic terms, information technology exists *for itself*. It exists for its own perpetuation and survival. Thus the Portuguese navigators and Rose's laboratory work are cybernetic patterns of ordering that perpetuate themselves through (partly human activities of) representation and translation.

Perhaps this is a somewhat depressing conclusion. Perhaps it sounds "unhuman," not only in intellectual but also in political or ethical terms. But is this really the case? The answer we're going to have to give is conditional. For those committed to humanism the answer will be yes. But there is another, post-humanist answer too, which is the one we will press.

What, then, of the humanist view? One thing is clear: cybernetics and the proximal theory of organizing remove us far from the Western and Enlightenment view of "man." "Man" is no longer pictured as a reasonable, substantially autonomous, and more-or-less centered actor. He is not seen as an agent who gathers information in order to make more-or-less rational decisions. The collapse of the distinction between the human and its context—and the analogous annihilation of the distinction between the organization and its environment—takes us far from this humanism of classic liberalism. In this view there is not *homo clausus*, just as there is no contemporary version of the Athenian *polis* with its assumptions about the power of rationality and human-centered discourse. But this is not all, for concern with proximality and the cybernetic understanding of information remove us just as effectively from the Romantic reaction to the Enlightenment. Versions of humanism that seek to locate the essence of humanity in genius and creativity—or special access to divinity or beauty—are no more consistent with the proximal than their Enlightenment counterparts. Which means that those who are committed to theoretical humanism (or its political expression), whether in an Enlightenment or a Romantic form, will indeed conclude that our tale is dark one.

But for those who are not so sure, those who are not so committed to one version or another of *homo clausus*, the prospect is more interesting. For these stories of orderings, of information, of proximal and distal—these stories start to suggest new post-humanist and post-liberal intellectual and political possibilities. Consider, for instance, the autonomy of cybernetic organization/information. This isn't consistent with a liberal understanding of human nature—just as it isn't easily reconciled with a distal theory of the organization. As we have noted, this is because it suggests that people and organizations- there is no important difference between them in this view—both speak the code of—are products of—information. That they are, indeed, little more than coding effects. That, at any rate, is one of the implications of the turn to information that is detected by many. Perhaps this again sounds pessimistic, but we don't believe that this is the case. For cybernetic organization/ information has one feature that is most interesting: it remains forever "unfinished." *It remains forever unfinished precisely so that it can keep on going.* We've said this already: we are dealing with patternings which, somehow or other, feed upon and continue to perform *themselves.* And this happens despite, or even because, of our distal divisions and effects. For we may attempt to lock things up in organizational boxes and throw away the key. But what does this mean? The answer, one that is proximal both intellectually *and* politically, is this. That, contrary to what is distally professed, it is *not* the *goal* or the *effect* or organizing that is significant. It is not, in other words, the *ends* that matter. But rather it is the *means*: the means that are always displaced, always moving, but never achieved. Except that to talk of "means" is already to give too much away to the distal: it is to subordinate process to a distal account of being, one in which it does not exist for itself, but rather for something else.

But there is more complexity still. For what should we say of goals in a proximal account? What should we say about the formal charters of organizations? The mission statements? Or, for that matter, about the statements of belief or purpose by individuals? The *credos*? The answer we'd offer is this: that there are rationalizations or excuses. No, not excuses in the cynical sense that will have occurred to some readers—those who think of that phenomenon well-known to organizational sociologists, the "displacement of goals" (Selznick 1949; Becker 1963)—though even that is not completely wide of the mark. They are rationalizations in the sense that they are distal necessities to the *perpetuum mobile* of the proximal. That is, they are crucial distal grounds for the indeterminacy of organization. They are important points that are fixed, albeit for a moment only, which thereby render possible the perpetual interplay, the perpetual tension, between on the one hand what (is said, told, in-formed) *has* happened. And, on the other, what *will* happen. The perpetual tension—that is also the in-tention—between retrospection and anticipation. The tension that performs "the" organization, and is reflexively performed in the process of organization (Baxandall 1985).

Let's try to illustrate all this with a simple example—Andy Warhol's well-known paintings of Campbell's soup cans. A distal interpretation would say that a soup can is merely an industrial object—a product or effect—intended by the factory for human consumption. Warhol comes along and transforms an object of the commercial-utilitarian world into a work of art. Campbell's soup cans are exhibited in art galleries, reproduced in art books, and lectured on in art colleges. They now inhabit an entirely different world. But Warhol's point is that the distal soup can is much more than the Campbell company intends, for it carries proximal "unfinished" possibilities within itself. This is the real point of Warhol's exercise. He's not concerned with making art, for that's just another distal effect. His real concern is to show that distal objects are patterns of possibilities that are also proximally "open." The soup can is never just a consumer object nor an art object but is always "more." It exceeds the boundaries in which it is distally organized.

Warhol's story has analogies with the stories of the Portuguese navigators and Rose's laboratory work, for these were also caught up in crossing boundaries, in reproducing and transmitting the "same" patterns across different worlds. Like Warhol, the Portuguese "painted" the contents of the heavens on their manuals and tables, and then on to translate he latter into yet farther and different action-spaces. Again, it's all a question of patterns of information, but patterns that are also mutable and, and therefore, transmittable across distal spaces.

What we see in Warhol's painting practice is the dematerialization of the recognizable object. Distalization gives objects a specific enduring place and function in place and time. We understand the soup can in this way as well as the art work which occupies its place and function in the art gallery. Warhol deliberately weakens our perception of these as objects. They become dematerialized as patterns of relations which can "travel" almost anywhere. This is also the point of cybernetics inasmuch as its generalized, universal language seeks to represent the continuous movement and mutability of patterns of relations rather than the static and distal form of the physical object.

So cybernetics is about excess. It is about dematerialization. It is about making matters complex and proximal. And its proximality works more and more visibly in a world that is increasingly structured around techno-scientific institutions. In weakening the distality of objects and trading increasingly in the plasticity of informational patterns (e.g., data bases, electronic money), cybernetics makes possible the combinational play of matter and thus the continuous disassembly of new forms and patterns. The world becomes progressively unfinished, approximate, open and, indeed, infinitely analysable. But proximality also works in another way. It works through the *cyborg*. There's a celebrated essay by the feminist writer Donna Haraway (1991) which calls for (what we're calling) proximal ways of knowing. So what is Haraway's point? Her answer comes in two parts. The first is a version of what we've argued above. It has to do with *unfinished heterogeneity*. But the second is also proximal—though this is our language rather than hers. It has to do with *incompatibility* and *partiality*.

In order to make her argument, Haraway doesn't talk of people at all, but rather of *cyborgs*. The cyborg—and, by extension, the "cyberorganization"—is a "cybernetic organism, a hybrid of machine and organism." And, because it is partly the stuff of dreams and visions of what has not yet been, it is also a "creature of social reality as well as a creature of fiction" (Haraway 1991, p. 149). So the cyborg obliterates a series of distal dualisms: mind and body; nature and culture; animal and human; and human and technical. Instead, it exists in a world that is "multiple, without clear boundary, frayed, insubstantial" (Haraway 1991, p. 177). And this is a world of coding:

> A search for a common language in which all resistance to instrumental control disappears and all heterogeneity can be submitted to disassembly, reassembly, investment and exchange
>
> (Haraway 1991, p. 164).

The cyborg thus engenders a space of infinite analysability and combinability through telecommunications technology, computer design, and database construction. Likewise, biotechnology translates living organisms into "problems of genetic coding and read-out . . . in a sense, organisms have ceased to exist as objects of knowledge, giving way to biotic components, that is, special kinds of information processing devices . . . The world is subdivided by boundaries differentially permeable to information" (Haraway 1991, p. 164). Microelectronics facilitates the transformation of labor into robotics and word processing; it mediates the so-called homework economy in which organization reaches out into the home, thereby blurring another formally distal boundary: "The homework economy does not refer only to large-scale deskilling . . . Rather, the concept indicates that factory, home and market are integrated on a new scale" (Haraway 1991, p. 166). In this context, deskilling is not simply the reorganization of workers' skills in favour of management control, as traditional organization theory would read it. It now becomes the cyberorganizational of workers' bodies.

This, then, is the first part of Haraway's argument: the uncertainty and indeterminacy of the proximal understood in terms of unfinished heterogeneity. But at the same time, in talking of cyborgs, of what we've called cyberorganization, she is pressing a second proximal point, one that has to do with incompatibility and partiality. Thus, though her argument draws deeply on cybernetics, in the end this is a model that she (albeit implicitly) rejects. She rejects it, not because the world, the person, or the organization cannot be seen as a matter of coding—for they can. Rather, she rejects it because it assumes that there is the possibility of a *single* code.

> Cyborg politics is the struggle for language and the struggle against perfect communication, against the one code that translates all meaning perfectly, the central dogma of phallogocentrism. That is why cyborg politics insist on noise and advocate pollution . . .
>
> (Haraway 1991, p. 176).

So a cyborg is not simply a heterogeneous assemblage in the process of becoming—a set of proximal "means" rationalized in terms of a distal "end." It is also about a multiple and heterogeneous assemblage—a set of processes of becoming- that weave around and through a series of quite inconsistent distal "ends." In other words, the cyborg is another way of expressing our earlier point that organization actively generates diversity and complexity. There is no organized unity or singularity: Haraway's concept of cyborg politics rests centrally on recognizing the intrinsically unfinished and incompatible heterogeneity that characterizes politics, where "poly" literally means "diverse" and "complex." For the cyborg is an ironic metaphor:

> Irony is about contradictions that do not resolve into larger wholes, even dialectically, about the tension of holding incompatible things together because both or all are necessary and true. Irony is about humour and serious play. It is also a rhetorical strategy and a political method . . .
>
> (Haraway 1991, p. 149).

Processes that *could* not fit together, that somehow live together in the same cyberorganization: this is Haraway's second point in talking of the cyborg. The message is that we will only ever know partially. We will only ever know incompatibly. We will only ever *be* partial, a series of parts, proximal—a possibility that is explored at length by Strathern (1991) in her analysis of the formation of complexity, partiality—that of both her own account and her objects of study—and their relationship to phenomena of scaling.

So Haraway's argument is about heterogeneity in a double sense: the cyborg is materially heterogeneous, a process rather than an entity. This is the first source of indeterminacy, the first source of the proximal, the first reason for rejecting a picture of the cyborg as a technologically updated version of the *homo clausus*. But it is heterogeneous in a second way as well. This is because it is also inconsistent, multiple, oxymoronic, in a state of tension. It is, in other words, an assemblage that holds together what which cannot be held together. It is something that expresses, speaks and acts a series of different and discrepant codes. It is a *set* of wildly different distal images which somehow in the processes of the proximal, form an assemblage (Deleuze and Guattari 1988).

Looked at from the standpoint of the Enlightenment, this is a doubly frightening prospect. On the one hand, it looks as if the object—person or organization—has been turned into a robot: a device which expresses a program that comes from elsewhere. On the other, it looks at the same time like fragmentation, dissociation, the loss of coherence, such that the cyberorganization speaks, expresses, and performs, not one but multiple codings. But to put it this way is to put it distally. Looked at proximally, the gestalt switches, and it looks quite different. In two quite different ways. First, cyberorganization is a process of *becoming*. It is an indeterminacy which, like the can of soup, uses the distal to exceed and transgress it. But second, it is also a diversity—*not* a fragmentation—of possibilities and processes, a set of processes in which partial alternatives which exceed any particular alternative, partial codes that exceed any particular code, are endlessly played out.

It is indeed, possible to resist this image of organization. It is possible to insist that there are organizations—and, for that matter, that there are people. It is possible to insist that there are boundaries between inside and outside, and that what goes on inside is more or less coherent. It is possible to argue that such incoherence as there is is best seen as a problem—something to be resolved by better organizational design, or (in the case of people) more effective means of therapy. This is the distal view. But we've been arguing proximally. We've been saying that organization may be seen as an outcome—a more or less precarious outcome—of fuzzy and indeterminate processes. Processes that are uncertain. Processes that are heterogeneous. Processes that do not add up. And that this is not a cause for lament, but rather, both intellectually and politically, it is a cause for celebration.

Intellectually, in organization studies, it makes it possible for us to explore how it is that relative stability, relative specificity—what we've called the distal—are actually produced. That is, it allows us to study the production of organization (Cooper and Burrell 1988), with its boundaries, divisions and hierarchies, without having to assume from the outset what which we are seeking to explore. And politically? Well, it is a matter of your policies, to be sure. But the notion that diversity is properly to be understood as fragmentation, or encoding as a form of robotic programming—these are both notions which draw their strength and appeal from a particular and distal idea of the proper person and the rational organization—a notion that assumes that these are properly centered, discrete, and internally consistent. But, or so, we believe, if this was ever so, then it is certainly no longer the case.

A final thought. We began this chapter by talking about the distal and the proximal as if they were simple oppositions. But, in this detour through cyberorganization, we have tried to show that they depend on each other.

We have argued for a way of thinking that gives primacy to **proximal organizings** rather than **distal organization**, that would capture the sense of organizings as ongoing actions in the heterogeneous fields of tension, as happenings—on the wing, so to speak. We have also argued that our modern world of cybernetic organizings—cyberorganization—foregrounds the proximal in its tendencies to dematerialize and complexify. By implication, we have argued that the new sciences of cybernetics, information theory and chaos theory provide an appropriate conceptual vocabulary for thinking proximally. Modern organizing is no respecter of distal spaces. The lesson of cyberorganization is that we should begin to think cyberorganically—and that also means proximally.

## REFERENCES

Atlan, H. 1974. "On a Formal Definition of Organization." *Journal of Theoretical Biology* 45:295–304.

Baxandall, M. 1985. *Patterns of Intention: On the Historical Explanation of Pictures.* New Haven, CT: Yale University Press.

Becker, H. S. 1963. *Outsiders.* New York: Free Press.

Bourdieu, P. and J. C. Passeron. 1977. *Reproduction in Education Society and Culture.* London: Sage.

Callon, M. 1980. "Struggles and Negotiations to Define What is Problematic and What is Not: The Sociology of Translation." In *The Social Process of Scientific Investigation: The Sociology of the Sciences Yearbook*, Vol.4, edited by K.D. Knorr-Cetina, R. Krohn, and R.D. Whitely. Dordrecht and Boston: Reidel.

1986a. "Some Elements of a Sociology of Translation: Domestication of the Scallops and the Fisherman of St. Breiuc Bay." In *Power, Action and Belief: A New Sociology of Knowledge? Sociological Review Monograph* 32, edited by J. Law. London: Routledge and Kegan Paul.

1986b. "The Sociology of an Actor-Network: The Case of the Electric Vehicle." In *Mapping the Dynamics of Science and Technology*, edited by M. Callon, J. Law, and A. Rip. London: Macmillan.

Cooper, R. 1987. "Information, Communication and Organisation: A Post-Structuralist Revision." *The Journal of Mind and Behaviour* 8:395–416.

1992. "Formal Organization as Representation: Remote Control, Displacement and Abbreviation." In *Rethinking Organization*, edited by M. Reed and M. Hughes. London: Sage.

1993. "Technologies of Representation." In *Tracing the Semiotic Boundaries of Politics*, edited by P. Ahonen. Berlin: Mouton de Gruyter.

Cooper, R. and G. Burrell. 1988. "Modernism, Postmodernism and Organisational Analysis: An Introduction." *Organizational Studies* 9:91–112.

Deleuze, J. 1976. *Of Grammatology.* Baltimore and London: John Hopkins University Press.

Eco, U. 1989. *The Open Work.* London: Hutchinson.

Elias, N. 1978. *The Civilising Process: The History of Manners.* Oxford: Basil Blackwell.

1983. *The Court Society.* Oxford: Basil Blackwell.

Foucault, M. 1979. *Discipline and Punish: The Birth of the Prison.* Harmondsworth: Penguin.

Gleick, J. 1988. *Chaos: Making a New Science.* London: Heinermann.

Haraway, D. 1991. "A Cyborg Manifesto: Science, Technology and Socialist-Feminism in the Late Twentieth Century." In *Simians, Cyborgs and Women: The Reinvention of Nature*, edited by D. Haraway. London: Free Association Books.

Heider, F. 1959. "On Perception and Event Structure, and the Psychological Environment." *Psychological Issues* 1–123.

Hughes, T. P. 1983. *Networks of Power: Electrification in Western Society*. Baltimore: John Hopkins University Press.

1986. "The Seamless Web: Technology, Science, Etcetera, Etcetera." *Social Studies of Science* 16:281–292.

Jameson, F. 1991. *Postmodernism, or, the Cultural Logic of Late Capitalism*. London: Verso.

Johnson, C. 1993. *System and Writing in the Philosophy of Jacques Derrida*. Cambridge: Cambridge University Press.

Korzybski, A. 1958. *Science and Sanity*. Lakeville, CT: Society for General Semantics.

Latour, B. 1985. "Give me a Laboratory and I will Raise the World." In *Science Observed: Perspectives in the Social Study of Science*, edited by K. D. Knorr-Cetina and M.J. Mullkay. London: Sage.

1987. *Science in Action: How to Follow Scientists and Engineers Through Society*. Milton Keynes : Open University Press.

1988. *The Pasteurization of France*. Cambridge, MA: Harvard University Press.

1990. "Drawing Things Together." In *Representations in Scientific Practice*, edited by M. Lynch and S. Woolgar. Cambridge, MA: MIT Press.

Latour, B. and S. Woolgar. 1979. *Laboratory Life: The Social Construction of Scientific Facts*. Beverly Hills, CA: Sage. [Repr. Princeton, NJ: Princeton University Press, 1986]

Law, J. 1986a. "On the Methods of Long Distance Control: Vessels, Navigation and the Portuguese Route to India." In *Power, Action and Belief: A New Sociology of Knowledge? Sociological Review Monograph* 32, edited by J. Law. London: Routledge and Kegan Paul.

1986b. "Laboratories and Texts." In *Mapping the Dynamics of Science and Technology*, edited by M. Callon, J. Law, and A. Rip. London: Macmillan.

1986c. "The Heterogeneity of Texts." In *Mapping the Dynamics of Science and Technology*, edited by M. Callon, J. Law, and A. Rip. London: Macmillan.

1986d. "On Power and its Tactics: A View from the Sociology of Science." *The Sociological Review* 34: 1–37.

1987. "Technology and Heterogeneous Engineering: The Case of the Portuguese Expansion." In *The Social Construction of Technical Systems: New Directions in the Sociology and History of Technology*, edited by W.E. Bijker, T.P. Hughes, and T.J. Pinch. Cambridge, MA: MIT Press.

1991. "Introduction: Monsters, Machines and Sociotechnical Relations." In *A Sociology of Monsters? Essays on Power, Technology and Domination, Sociological Review Monograph* 38, edited by J. Law. London: Routledge.

1993. *Organizing Modernity*. Oxford: Blackwell.

Law, J. and A. Mol. 1994. "Semiotics, Strategy and Materiality." Keele and Limburg Universities (Mimeo).

Lawrence, P. R. and J. W. Lorsch. 1967. *Organization and Environment: Managing Differentiation and Integration*. Boston: Graduate School of Business Administration, Harvard University.

Lyotard, J-F. 1991. *The Inhuman*. Cambridge: Polity Press.

Malavé, J. 1992. "Systems, Networks and Structures." Unpublished Ph.D. dissertation. Lancaster: University of Lancaster.

Merleau-Ponty, M. 1962. *Phenomenology of Perception*. New York: Humanities Press.

Scott, W. R. 1987. *Organisations: Rational, Natural and Open Systems*. Englewood Cliffs, NJ: Prentice-Hall.

Selznick, P. 1949. *TVA and the Grass Roots*. Berkeley: University of California Press.

Star, S. L. 1988. "Introduction: The Sociology of Science and Technology." *Social Problems* 35:197–205.

Starobinski, J. 1975. "The Inside and the Outside." *The Hudson Review* 28:333–351.

Strathern, M. 1991. *Partial Connections*. Savage, MD: Rowman and Littlefield.

Wiener, N. 1950. *The Human Use of Human Beings*. Boston: Houghton Mifflin.

# 11 Cyborganization
## Cinema as Nervous System

*Martin Parker and Robert Cooper*

(Part two, from J Hassard and R Holliday (eds) (1998) *Organization—Representation: Work and Organization in Popular Culture*, London: Sage, 219–228.)

In the first part of this chapter, Parker spends a lot of time exploring what cyborg films 'mean', and then tries to conclude that they 'mean' 'nothing'. He explores the theme of body horror and the paranoia about the large corporation that is often a sub-text of these films. This textual analysis then gives way to a discussion of what cyborgs are, and how cyborganization takes place. Parker concludes by romanticizing the cyborg and demonizing the capitalist organization at the same time as he doubts his own judgement. In Part II, Cooper explores a range of ideas—*cyborg*,[1] *cybernetics*,[2] *nervous system*,[3] *cyborganization*[4] and *cinema* that help us to understand the intellectual sources of our fascination with filmic-literary science fiction and its real-life expression as science fact-ion. His Contingent Supplement is a series of brief essays on the theme of the human-machine relationship and the increasingly unstable reality produced by contemporary information-communication technologies, including cinema. In effect, Cooper provides a vocabulary of ideas that constitutes a background discourse to the developing techno-scientific-industrial complex of our late-modern world.

[. . .]

## PART II

### Contingent Supplement

**1 Cyborg** Manfred Clynes (Clynes, 1995; Clynes and Kline, 1995) neologized the term cyborg from 'cybernetic organism' in 1960. Clynes, a neurophysiologist and space scientist, researched the development of 'artefact-organism systems'—cyborgs—in order to free astronauts from routine flight-maintenance, so 'leaving man free to explore, to create, to think, and to feel' (Clynes and Kline, 1995: 31). Clynes saw the cyborg as human prosthesis, as a device for augmenting human powers.

While Clyne's cyborg was a tool devised for humanistic goals, Donna Haraway (1991) portrays the cyborg as 'a *hybrid* of machine and organism' in which the separate terms of machine and organism dissolve into a miscegenation that is 'multiple, without clear boundary, frayed, insubstantial' (1991: 177). Less of a thing and more of a process, Haraway's cyborg realizes itself through the 'plasticity of informational patterns (e.g., databases, electronic money)' which makes 'possible the combinational play of matter and thus the continuous disassembly and reassembly of new forms and patterns' (Cooper and Law, 1995: 268). Haraway's cyborg thus engenders a space of infinite patterning through telecommunications technology, computer design and database construction. Biotechnology is the exemplary science of the cybernetic organism because it translates living organisms into 'problems of genetic coding and read-out . . . in a sense, organisms have ceased to exist as objects of knowledge, giving way to biotic components, that is, special kinds of information processing devices. . . . The world is subdivided by boundaries differentially permeable to information' (Haraway, 1991:164). In contrast to Clyne's anthropomorphic cyborg which perpetuates the traditional subject-object dichotomy, Haraway's cyborg relativizes 'the difference between living and mechanical systems' and radically challenges 'the line of demarcation drawn between the natural and artificial' (Johnson, 1993: 105).

**2 Cybernetics** Briefly defined, cybernetics is the science of communication and control in humans, animals and machines. Where communication and control means *organization*. Cybernetics views organization as a measure of structure, pattern. The practice of organization is thus understood as the construction and maintenance of pattern out of chaos, dissipation. It's the *continuous* work of maintaining pattern or order in a continually dissolving world. Or, as Norbert Wiener (1954: 86), the founder of cybernetics, puts it:

> Our tissues change as we live: the food we eat and the air we breathe becomes flesh of our flesh and bone of our bone, and the momentary elements of our flesh and bone pass out of our body every day with our excreta. We are but whirlpools in a river of ever-flowing water. We are not stuff that abides, but patterns that perpetuate themselves.

So, organization is the reproduction of patterns, stability, in a context/contest of permanent change, instability. But Wiener means more than this. Cybernetic patterns move across different domains; they are acts of ordering which translate food into flesh and bone, flesh and bone into working bodies, bodies into machines, and so on. Cybernetic organization as stabilities-in-movement denies the fixed term, the specific location, the subject-object dichotomy.

> The effect of cybernetic explanation, the modelling of human mental processes on mechanical control systems and vice versa, is to relativize the difference between living and mechanical systems, pointing towards a theory of complex systems in general. The philosophical implication of cybernetic theory would therefore tend to be a certain parenthesis of the anthropological of the anthropomorphic . . .
>
> (Johnson, 1993: 105).

As the cybernetic thinker Gregory Bateson (1973: 454) argues, 'The mental world—the mind—the world of information processing—is not limited by the skin'. Human agents are not simply minds or 'bodies that inhabit the universe' (Virilio, 1994: 27). Instead, according to the cybernetic view, agents 'become *bodies inhabited by the universe, by the being of the universe*' (Virilio, 1994: 27). Thus, human agents do not simply live *in* the world, they do not simply *use* tools, nor do they simply *consume* food and air. To be 'inhabited by the universe', by its 'being', means that the agent is a temporary term or position in an ever-active matrix of order-disorder. So, to summarize: cybernetic organization means three things: (a) ordering, patterning; (b) patterning or organizing *between* apparently different systems, e.g., body-tool-environment; and (c) the continuously active and never-ending process of ordering.

Two further points need to be made about the order-disorder relationship. The first concerns the general bias to think order and disorder as *separate* forces in opposition to each other, as if the act of separation, of thinking biplicitly, were itself a form of reassuring order and control. The second point—and more important to our argument here—concerns the historical privileging, especially in the development of modern sciences, of order over disorder, as if order were somehow 'naturally' primal and transcendent, as if disorder were the degradation of a pristine and originary state of harmony. In a related discussion, Ilya Prigogine (1989) has noted a similar fate in the history of the concepts of stability and instability. In modern science, says Prigogine, 'The notion of instability has been ideologically suppressed' (1989: 396) and glossed in favour of determinism and control. But recent work in science has supported the cybernetic view that stability/order and instability/disorder are mutually constituting forces: 'order and disorder are created simultaneously' (1989: 398). Such systems are called *strange attractors*, where stability and instability are mixed. Living can only be understood by means of strange attractors—complex systems whose complexity is characterized by a correlative stability-instability. And, as we shall later argue, it is this complexity, this complicity that describes such man-machine systems as modern cinema.

There's another way of framing the order-disorder relationship—through that branch of cybernetics called 'information theory'. Cybernetic information is defined by the idea of probability: information is what is *least probable*. In other words, information is inversely proportional to its probability. The less likely a message or event, the more information it provides. Novelty and surprise thus constitute information. As Wiener (1954: 105) puts it: 'a piece of information, in order to contribute to the general information of a community, must say something substantially different from the community's previous stock of information.' There's also the implication here that information as novelty or surprise is vital to a community's life; as if the community as an information system would die without the stimulation of the new. From this, an important general principle emerges: all human agents are 'open', they necessarily depend on unpredictability and surprise.

Wiener's (1954) coupling of information with community is further illustrated in Umberto Eco's (1989) essay, 'Openness, information, communication', which discusses information theory in relation to the communal role of art. Eco argues that unpredictability and novelty are vital to the artistic experience and will. The artist, especially the avant-garde artist is compelled to contravene convention in order to provide artistic power—or informational vitality—both to him/herself and the community. But the community is also pulled in the direction of order and control. Order is necessary and what's necessary comes to be seen as the 'natural order of things'. Yet openness to information and disorder is not merely just as 'natural' as the closure of order but *logically constitutes the order-disorder of things*. Like Prigogine, Eco asserts the *necessity* of novelty and surprise to openness. New life, the possibility of sur-vival is, *necessarily* the creation of new information.

Cybernetic organization/information is thus 'living form in the making' (Goodwin, 1994), where *making* is the continuous mixing of order-disorder. Equally, we might call it 'self-organized criticality', 'an excitable medium', or even the 'edge of chaos' (Goodwin, 1994), all terms that dramatize the transitional *in-betweenness* of the order-disorder nature of organization/information.

3 **Nervous System** Michael Taussig (1992) introduced the metaphor of the Nervous System to describe the restless and even restive nature of the modern world: a system of *nervousness*, in fact. Taussig's Nervous System is an extension of the idea of cybernetic organization to the complexities of the social-economic-political world. Like Prigogine (1989), Taussig underlines the *mutuality* of order *and* disorder:

> I am referring to a state of doubleness of social being in which one moves in bursts between somehow accepting the situation as normal, only to be thrown into a panic or shocked into disorientation by an event, a rumour, a sight, something said, or not said—something that even while it requires the normal in order to make its impact, destroys it.
>
> (Taussig, 1992: 18)

This mutuality or doubleness of social being is a 'desperate place between the real and the really made-up' (Taussig, 1993: xvii), between fact and fiction, stability and instability. It's a place of biplicit thinking (2) where we have to act as if conventional order were the norm: 'we dissimulate. We act and have to act as is mischief were not afoot in the kingdom of the real and that all around the ground lay firm' (Taussig, 1993: xvii). So, the Nervous System problematizes the normal, makes us see it as a strange attractor, (2) a place of correlative stability-instability where—and this is the significance of Taussig's argument—instability is culturally and cognitively *censored* just like Prigogine's (1989, 396) critical observation on modern science in which 'the notion of instability has been ideologically suppressed'. But Taussig goes further: what we *normally* think of as fact or the real is a state of fictions or 'dream-images'—'hopelessly hopeful illusions of the intellect searching for peace in a world whose tensed mobility allows of no rest to the nervousness of the Nervous System's system' where 'immerse tension lies in strange repose' (Taussig, 1992: 10).

The nervousness and fictionality of the Nervous System is also Gianni Vattimo's (1992) theme in his analysis of the late-modern *society of generalized communication* in which the proliferation of the mass media and information technology stimulates a perpetual condition of 'oscillation' and 'shock'. The society of generalized communication is a society of cybernetic organizations, (1) (2) centrally defined by a range of technologies (including cinema) (5) constructed to transmit information: 'it is primarily and essentially defined by systems collecting and transmitting information' (Vattimo, 1992: 15). And, significantly, information itself is subject to the same dissembling logic that characterizes Taussig's doubleness of 'the real and the really made-up': for 'in-formation' is both what which *informs* or *enfirms* and that which *un-forms* or *in-firms*. Mutual stability-instability. Information thus becomes an 'excitable medium', a process at 'the edge of chaos' (Goodwin, 1994), expressing the nervousness of the Nervous System. We see the emergence of such collapsing and condensing forms in Vattimo's (1992: 16) idea of the 'contemporaneity' of the contemporary world. Contemporaneity doesn't just mean events that happen at the same time. It suggest both compassion and interlacing—a co-involvement in space *and* time. For Vattimo, the special nature of late-modern technologies of communication and information transmission is their production of 'contemporaneity'. Vattimo's 'contemporaneity' is a version of Walter Benjamin's (1970: 225) portrayal of modern methods of mechanical reproduction: 'Every day the urge grows stronger to get hold of an object at very close range by way of its likeness, its reproduction.' As Taussig (1993: 36) points out, this is another way of expressing Benjamin's 'insight into mimesis as the art of becoming something else, of becoming Other', mimesis as the 'sensuous connection with things', where the body and its senses blur with their objects of contact. Such continuous merging and dissolution of subject and object is Taussig's way of calling attention to the 'nervousness' of contemporaneity' and which, for Vattimo, eventually leads to the 'unfounding' of what Taussig (1993) calls the dissimulated firmness of reality. 'The advent of the media enhances the inconstancy and superficiality of experience . . . it allows a kind of "weakening" of the very notion of reality' (Vattimo, 1992: 59)—the nervousness of the Nervous System.

Benjamin's (1970) characterization of mimesis emphasizes the process of '*becoming* something else'. It's not the 'something else', the other term, that needs to be understood but the very act of mimesis itself. And to show us how this works, Taussig (1993) draws on an early paper by the French sociologist Roger Caillois (1984, but first published 1935) which discusses mimesis in terms of the simulation of space, i.e., Vattimo's 'contemporaneity'. Caillois notes a general tendency for living organisms to simulate aspects of their environment; for example, leaf insects resemble leaves. But it would be better to say that *space simulates* organism and environment. Or, following Virilio (1994), that organisms are 'bodies inhabited by the universe, by the being of the universe' rather than 'bodies that inhabit the universe'. (2) On this view, space is not simply a distance between two points but a *beckoning-becoming void*—a 'temptation by space', as Caillois (1984: 70) calls it. In humanistic terms, there is a loss of self: 'Then the body separates itself from thought, the individual breaks the boundary of his skin and occupies the other side of his senses . . . He feels himself becoming space, *dark space where things cannot be put*. He is similar, not similar to something, but just *similar*. And he invents spaces of which he is "the convulsive possession"' (Caillois, 1994: 30). He becomes *nothing*, no thing, in this assimilation to space. Mimesis is the dispossession of identity by similarity. It's when the 'informing' of information becomes 'unforming'. Built into the Nervous System itself, mimesis *compels* the agent to invent 'spaces of which he is the "convulsive possession"'. As though abducted by space. Not just a 'nervous' idea but a 'scary' one, as Taussig (1993: 34) notes. And, what's more, an idea that helps us see Haraway's (1991) *cyborg* in a different light. The miscegenation of machine and organism that characterizes the cyborg now becomes interpretable in terms of Benjamin's 'insight into mimesis as the art of becoming something else, of becoming Other' (Taussig, 1993: 36), as well as expressing Vattimo's (1992) '"weakening" of the very notion of reality'.

Nervous System, society of generalized communication, mimesis, cyborg—all, in their different ways, draw attention to the *medium/media* of technology. Not medium/media in the popular sense of the specific forms of communication media—TV, radio, cinema and so on—but the 'un-form' of what Taylor (1995) calls the *mediatrix* or media matrix: the complex, fleeting, unstable connections and multiplicities that defy conventional logic and analysis. Ostensibly, the mediatrix is 'that which is constituted by the intersection of electronic media and compu-telecommunications technology' (Taylor, 1995: 25). Latently, the mediatrix is beyond formal comprehension, can only be alluded to, precisely because it is literally *medium/ media*, literally in the middle, between: 'the mediatrix is nothing but the middle' (Taylor, 1995: 32). And, significantly, the middle is a *muddle*, a confusion: 'The structure of the real is indistinguishable from the structure of the medium. In more familiar terms, the medium is not only the message but is nothing less than reality itself' (Taylor, 1995: 26). Neither beginning nor end (but *both* beginning *and* end), neither here nor there (but *both* here *and* there), neither this nor that (but *both* this *and* that), the medium as middle is the hybridism of the cyborg, the de-definition of form wrought by mimesis, the collapsing forms of 'contemporaneity', and the 'excitable medium' of the Nervous System.

**4 Cyborganization** Short for cybernetic organization. (2) Where organization is the construction and maintenance of pattern, form, out of chaos, dissipation, the *continuous work* of maintaining pattern in a continually dissolving world.

Cyborganization is the complicity/complexity between human agents and machines that makes continuous pattern-making possible. The historical development of human cognitive systems reflects this cyborganizational complicity/complexity. As the neuropsychologist Merlin Donald (1991) shows, the modern mind is a hybrid of organism and external 'cognitive architectures' such as the alphabet, writing, calendars, clocks, maps, and so on: 'We act in cognitive collectivities, in symbiosis with external memory systems' (Donald, 1991: 382). In this sense, cyborganization is the *externalization* of mind through what Donald (1991) calls External Symbolic Storage devices, which include cinema and computers: 'the individual mind has long since ceased to be definable in a meaningful way within its confining biological membrane' (1991: 359). Moravec (1988) calls this a 'postbiological world': Humans evolved from organisms defined almost totally by their organic genes. We now rely additionally on a vast and rapidly growing corpus of cultural information generated and stored outside our genes—in our nervous systems, libraries, and, most recently, computers' (Moravec, 1988: 3–4). Clearly, the culture of External Symbolic Storage and the 'postbiological world' are also versions of Vattimo's (1992) society of generalized communication. (3) In these hybrid systems, what does hybridism mean? What does cyborganization mean by the hybrid? First, we must note that the cyborganizational hybrid is *not* anthropomorphic; it is not an extension of the human agent. We might just as readily say that the agent is an extension of the machine: 'it becomes immaterial whether one says that machines are organs, or organs, machines. The two definitions are exact equivalents' (Deleuze and Guattari, 1983: 285). Equivalence and non-distinction is the first feature of the cyborganizational hybrid. The hybrid is the *middle* of the mediatrix (Taylor, 1995). (3) The hybrid as middle is never a locatable place or term; we can't say it's *in* the middle. It's always *on its way* somewhere, always in movement, always *becoming*. 'To become is never to imitate, nor to "do like", nor to conform to a model . . . There is no terminus from which you ought to arrive at . . . For as someone becomes, what he is becoming changes as much as he does himself' (Deleuze and Parnet, 1987: 2). This is how we are meant to understand Haraway's (1991) cyborg—not as a thing-like structural 'hybrid of machine and organism' but as a process of becoming in which the cyborg is 'multiple, without clear boundary, frayed, insubstantial' (Haraway, 1991: 177). The cyborg moves at 'the edge of chaos' where it is 'living form in the making' (Goodwin, 1994), sur-viving, living-on, becoming: 'In a sense, organisms have ceased to exist as objects of knowledge, giving way to biotic components, that is, special kinds of information processing devices' (Haraway, 1991: 164). Hence, it's not the objects nor the components but *information as becoming* that marks the cyborganizational world: a 'world subdivided by boundaries differentially permeable to information (Haraway, 1991: 164). And not *merely* 'permeable *to* information, for information as process, as becoming, it itself constituted by 'subdivision', 'boundary', and 'difference', terms which are not only different ways of saying information but implicitly contain the idea of informational order-disorder as a doubly or mutually composed *interfold*, i.e., the mimetic hybridism of Caillois's notion of the 'similar'. In other words, subdivision, boundary and difference are versions of mimesis and hybridism; spaces where similarity and difference are knotted together, strangely doubled, in an 'unfinished heterogeneity' (Cooper and Law, 1995: 269) of parts and whole. Cyborganization is the re-production of such 'unfinished heterogeneity': 'cybernetic organization/information has one feature that is most interesting: it remains forever "unfinished". *It remains forever unfinished precisely so that it can keep on going*' (Cooper and Law, 1995: 267). Information as *becoming*. Viewed thus, information has no destination; it doesn't go anywhere since it has nowhere to go; it simply keeps on moving, all the time maintaining its differences, its spaces of mimetic division. Division is *always* unfinished. This is the point of Jacques Derrida's (1987) well-known study of the postal system, in which he subjects the 'postcard' and its transmission to an informational-mimetic analysis. The conventional understanding of the postal system is that is transmits information—letters, postcards, and so on—from sender to addressee; it supposes a direct line between the two and thus a perfect system of communication (although admitting that occasionally letters may *accidently* go astray). The postal system thus occults the significance of the space of division between sender and addressee. For the postal system, the sender and addressee constitute the communication process and division is simply a barrier to be overcome; for Derrida, the space of division constitutes communication, out of which sender and addressee form/firm their identities. Derrida's version of the postal system is a Nervous System, an 'excitable medium', whose space has the same character as Taylor's (1995: 34) *mediatrix*: 'Within the mediatrix, things neither come together nor fall apart. Circuits are not closed but open, constantly changing, and repeatedly shifting. Governed by neither the inclusive logic of both/and nor the exclusive logic of either/or, (the middle) apprehends that which stands between'. (3) Such a space 'resists reflection', says Taylor, precisely because of its unfinished heterogeneity, or, in the cybernetic language of Bateson (1973: 419), 'the cybernetic nature of self and the world tends to be imperceptible to consciousness' because consciousness, like the postal system, works in terms of linear purpose and identity whereas cybernetics recognizes the latent agency of the hybrid, interlacing 'circularities of the self and the external world' (1973: 420). So the postal system is that cultural and cognitive system of censoring noted by Taussig (1993) and Prigogine (1989), (3) a place of dissimulated reality, of 'immense tension . . . in a strange repose', where the unfinished heterogeneity of information as division is 'a debased, lateralized, repressed, displaced theme, yet exercising a permanent and obsessive pressure from the place where it remains held in check' (Derrida, 1987: 270). Mutual stability-instability again. All this makes the postal system a site of 'self-organized criticality' on 'the edge of chaos' (3), a site that is permanently divided from itself, in the divisions between the printed and written letter, words and sentences on the postcard between the artist's design and the printer's impress, between the manufacturer's production run and the public's purchase, between the sender and the addressee—a series of points marked by the struggle between order and disorder, stability and instability; where possibilities of deviation, drift errancy, of things going wrong, *interfold* with the requirements of direction, plan and rectitude. Derrida's reinterpretation of the postal system reveals it as a divided state of being, a collection of discrete elements that *neither fit nor do not fit together*, parts that must remain apart so that they can *suggest* (but not realize) completeness. And where the transmission of information is the repetition and iteration of this divided space, this unfinished heterogeneity.

It's this sense of information—information as division—that Italo Calvino (1987) conveys in an essay, 'Cybernetics and ghosts', in which the late-modern world is seen as a cybernetic space of 'discontinuity divisibility, and combination' (1987: 9), where discrete elements—letters, words, numbers—can be endlessly permutated and combined. As if to recall Taylor's mediatrix as a space that 'resists reflection' and Bateson's cue that cybernetic processes are 'imperceptible to consciouness', Calvino links the possibilities offered by the infinite (i.e., unfinished) permutability and combinability of elements to the unconscious. The unconscious is the 'unexpected meaning or unforeseen effect'—Taussig's (1992) 'nervousness of the Nervous System' and Vattimo's (1992) 'oscillation' and 'shock' (3)—'which the conscious mind would not have arrived at deliberately' (Calvino, 1987: 21). Here, Calvino puts his finger on the sub-versive character of cyberorganization: the repetition and iteration of divisions as discrete parts that differentially combine to create new, unfinished 'wholes'. Again, it's *information as becoming*. Calvino's cybernetic machine is also Haraway's cyborg which realizes itself through the 'plasticity of informational patterns (e.g., databases, electronic money)' which make 'possible the combinational play of matter and thus the continuous disassembly and reassembly of new forms and patterns' (Cooper and Law, 1995: 268). (1)

5 Cinema From the Greek *kinema*, movement. Conventional approaches to cinema distinguish between *film* (the screen and the moving images projected on to it) and *cinema* itself, which covers the economic, technological

and cultural system of production and reception that serves to realize film. In its filmic sense, cinema is viewed as a visual medium or art form which simply serves to represent something—reality, a story—for someone, and which, like Derrida's postal system, assumes a model of communication based on identity. But, as we've already hinted, cinema can also be viewed as a cybernetic technology in which the human agent and the machine form a hybrid in an informational complex of stability-instability. (2) (3)

This is how Merlin Donald (1991) understands cinema: as a form of *cyborganization*, a hybrid of organism and external 'cognitive architectures', which, along with TV and computers, constitutes the 'machinery' of 'the hybrid modern mind' (Donald, 1991: 382, 355). And, in the different intellectual context of late-modern ontology, it's also how Gianni Vattimo (1992) sees cinema in his society of generalized communication: as a technology of information transmission that *performs* the social and cultural mind, nor just the communication of reality but its expression and performance: 'The structure of the real is indistinguishable from the structure of the medium. In more familiar terms, the medium is not only the message but is nothing less than reality itself' (Taylor, 1995: 26). This, too, is the philosopher Gilles Deleuze's (1986, 1989) interpretation of cinema: reality as medium, medium as motion. Cinema, for Deleuze, is 'the machine assemblage of movement images' (Deleuze, 1986: 59). But it's more than that—it's a technological version of human life and culture: represents life, life re-presents itself as cinema, i.e., as movement. Cinema, body, brain and thought together constitute a cybernetic organism, a technological nervous system, 'a cinema of the brain' (Deleuze, 1989: 204). It's not the conventional idea of the film-goer viewing a film for the purpose of entertainment. For Deleuze, the film-goer wants to *become* part of the cinematic environment in which cinema, body and brain make up a cyborganizational experience.

One way of becoming a machine is to hook yourself up to one: video games, media, television, the new nonumbrical telephones (that transmit through walls), etc. This technology is described by some as an external nervous system connected to us by a variety of devices that radically change our sense of time and space (Jardine, 1987: 155)

The conventional view of cinema is that it is a window on the world: it's assumed to *represent* some aspect of the world. In Deleuze's view, cinema is not about representation; it's not *what* we see but that *with which, according to which*, we see: 'The structure of the real is indistinguishable from the structure of the medium. In more familiar terms, the medium is not only the message but nothing less than reality itself' (Taylor, 1995: 26). Cinema is thus *medium* in the most literal sense and as such is beyond formal comprehension, can only be alluded to because it is literally in the *middle*, between, and so without intrinsic order or direction. (3)

Deleuze interrogates the representation/medium distinction in cinema through the *audiovisual* character of film: 'There is a distinction between speaking and seeing, between the visible and the articulate: "What we see never lies in what we say", and vice versa . . . the audiovisual is disjunctive . . . it is not surprising and the most capable examples of the disjunction between seeing and speaking are to be found in cinema' (Deleuze, 1988: 64). Speaking articulates the *meaning* of a figure or event; it represents it in a systemic or narrative form. Seeing reveals only the visual form of the figure, without the help of words that name the structure. A hidden tension lies here: can we read the words *and* look at the letters that constitute them *at the same time?* Deleuze's answer is no: representation and medium, the articulable and the visual, are in necessary conflict: 'the audiovisual battle, the double capture, the noise of words that conquered the visible, the fury of things that conquered the articulable' (Deleuze, 1988: 112). This is cinema as Nervous System, or Taussig's (1993) doubleness of social being and its dissimulated firmness of reality. Taylor's (1995) contrast between the specific forms of media—TV, radio, cinema—and media as mediatrix also helps to us understand Deleuze's antagonism of the articulable and the visible. The *specific* media *represent;* the mediatrix simply *mediates* without any necessary order or direction.

Cinema as representation-articulation works according to a hierarchy of original and copy where the original has both a temporal and a 'truth' value over the copy, so that the original is thought of as cause, and copy, effect. But the argument from the medium-visible perspective denies such cause-effect direction:

> There can never be an original until there is a copy, which retrospectively creates the 'originalness' of the original. There can never be an original until there is a copy of it. In a sense, then, the original can be said to be constituted by the copy, just as cause and effect . . . can be reversed, from a temporal perspective, once we realize that it is always the effect that comes first, causing us to look for its cause.
>
> (Brunette and Willis, 1989: 74)

Nor does this mean that the copy creates the original, since that would be just another form of representation-articulation and the positing of yet another hierarchy: 'Rather, the relation between reality and, say, a documentary on it, would be displaced and redefined such that the two terms came to see as mutually constituting each other. The relation between them would thus be an intertextual one' (1989: 75). It's the equivalent of Deleuze's (1986) idea of meta-cinema: while cinema represents life, life re-presents itself as cinema. And this, of course, is also Taylor's (1995) mediatrix whose *middle* is a *muddle* since it has no one direction, no hierarchy. (3)

The dissolution of direction, order, is a definitive feature of cyborganization. As we've said, equivalence and non-distinction comprise the first feature of cyborganizational hybrid. It's what Vattimo (1992: 59) calls 'oscillation' and 'disorientation' in the society of generalized communication where the proliferation of media technologies creates 'a kind of "weakening" of the very notion of reality' which now 'presents itself as softer and more fluid'. Vattimo cites Walter Benjamin's diagnosis of cinema as the technical reproduction of an increasingly inconstant and superficial reality. What's more, says Vattimo, modern cinema draws attention to its own deconstructive role in the production of such cyborganizational 'nervousness'. He cites Ridley Scott's *Blade Runner* as a film that foregrounds the sense of 'contemporaneity' (3) and representational necrosis created by the new cyborg technologies. For Vattimo, *Blade Runner* is not so much a science-fiction *story* but more a disclosing of Deleuze's (1988) antagonism of the articulable and the visible in which the 'combinational play of matter and thus the continuous disassembly and reassembly of new forms and patterns' dominates (Cooper and Law, 1995: 268).

The cultural historian Mark Poster (1990) captures Vattimo's sense of representational necrosis in his analysis of human-computer interaction: 'Computer science . . . is a discourse at the border of words and things'—hence it illustrates Deleuze's articulable-visible conflict:

A dangerous discipline because it is founded on the confusion between the scientist and his or her object. The identity of the scientist and the computer are so close that a mirror effect may very easily come into play: the scientist projects intelligent subjectivity onto the computer and the computer then becomes the criterion by which to define intelligence, judge the scientist, outlines the essence of humanity.

(Poster, 1990: 148)

And Poster reports the anxiety of one computer scientist that 'we run the immense risk of being unable to recognize when we are becoming the subjects of the instruments we created to be our subjects' with the comment that: 'Artificial intelligence and human intelligence are *dopplegängers*, each imitating the other so closely that one scarcely can distinguish them' (Poster, 1990: 148-9). Here again we meet Benjamin's (1979) idea of *mimesis*, the process of '*becoming* something else', where it is not the 'something else' that needs to be understood but the very act of mimesis itself as 'a science of mediations—neither Self nor Other but their mutual co-implicatedness' (Taussig, 1992: 450, mimesis as mediatrix. (3) Neither the scientist nor the computer, neither the film-goer nor the film, but their mediation. When Haraway (1991) defines the *cyborg* as 'a hybrid of machine and organism' it's not the machine or the organism that specially interests her but their *hybrid* mediation. (1) This is a different space from the ordered representations of the articulable where every image or copy has a meaningful referent or original. It's space without order or direction, in which terms constitute each other as equals; it's the space of the visible that refuses articulation, where figure cannot precede ground nor subject dominate object. Together, the two spaces—the articulable and the visible—add up to Deleuze's (1988) 'audiovisual battle'.

The space of hybrid mediation, of the visible, of the cyborg, differs in another significant way. Unlike the space of the articulable, ordered by the speaking subject, the space of mediation is preconscious, primitive. This is what Calvino (1987) and Bateson (1973) mean when they say that the cybernetic organism/machine works at the level of the unconscious and when Taylor (1995) describes the mediatrix as a space that 'resists reflection'. (4) It's also Benjamin's (1970) way of understanding the mimetic nature of modern methods of mechanical reproduction (including cinema) which reply upon the synthesis of vision and touch—the 'optical unconscious', as Benjamin calls it, where the eye (as bodily organ) merges mimetically with the cinematic images: 'not merely our sensous blending with filmic imagery, the eye acting as a conduit for our very bodies being absorbed by the filmic, but . . . the eye grasping . . . at what the hand cannot reach' (Taussig, 1992: 146). Hence tactile version, which is unconsciously compulsive as in Caillois's (1984) exposition of mimesis as the loss of the self through 'temptation by space'. (3) Both hand and eye are seemingly incomplete and so compelled to make connections beyond themselves—another version of the idea that the transmission of information is the repetition and iteration of divided space. (4) Unfinished heterogeneity again but with a difference, for Benjamin's optical unconscious portrays the body as part of a more general process of the transgression of boundaries, distinctions. The eye does not merely *see* the film image—it merges with it (and takes the body with it). It's when *vision* becomes *fusion*, where vision-fusion is the space of the visible that refuses articulation. And it's this that prompts Vattimo to cite Benjamin's analysis of cinema as the technical reproduction of an increasingly inconstant and superficial reality. At the level of the visible, Benjamin's reproduction technologies con-fuse the real and its representation-articulation. For precisely this reason, cybernetic organization has to be understood as the reproduction of pattern, stability, in a context/contest of permanent change, instability. As we've seen, cybernetic organization denies the fixed term, the specific location, the subject-object dichotomy and insists that the human agent is a temporary-tentative term or position in an ever-active matrix of order-disorder. (2) Deleuze (1988) expressed the same idea in his image of the 'audiovisual battle' where representation-articulation is a *contesting* of the real.

Poster's (1990) computer scientists are also caught up in a *contest* to preserve their sovereign human agency from 'contamination' by the machine (just as realist cinema insists that the film-goer 'sees' film as the conventional representation of a real event or story). At stake here is perhaps the ultimate *test*: are machines human (and, inversely, are humans no more than machines)? In one sense, Haraway has already answered this question: 'The machine is not an it to be animated, worshipped and dominated. The machine is us, our processes, an aspect of our embodiment' (1991: 164). But the question will never be answered that simply, not least because it contains a necessary and intrinsic contest between the unitary identity claimed by representation-articulation and the unfinished heterogeneity of the medium-visible. The contestatory aspect of this incompatibility is raised in the computer scientist Alan Turing's (1950) famous question: Can machines think? For Turing, the answer lies in the act of *imitation* (we would say mimesis, or even becoming) and not in trying to understand the intrinsic properties of 'machine' and 'thinking'. In other words, the test of whether a machine can think like a human being lies not in the specific nature of human intelligence (whatever that is) but in the extent to which the machine can initiate human behaviours. This is why Turing is careful to devise a way of operationalizing the question so as to reveal the work of imitation *per se* rather than the subject and object of the imitation. Like Deleuze (1988), Turing wants to escape from the space of representation-articulation so that the space of medium-visible can emerge.

Turing's test consists of what he calls the 'imitation' game, which is played with three people: a man, a woman, and an interrogator (of either sex). The interrogator's task is to identify, through strategic questioning, who is the woman; the man's task is to confuse the interrogator by imitating the behaviour of a woman. The interrogator's only contract with the other players is through their typewritten responses to the questions. The Turing test then substitutes a computer simulation (imitation) for the man. If the computer can successfully simulate the man's task by completely refusing the interrogator, then the computer can be said to think like a human being. In effect, the Turing simulation tests (and con-tests) the representational-articulation view of the world, which assumes the existence of more-or-less stable identities, by subverting conventional categories (of intelligence and human-ness), by denying the distinction between practice and thought (theory), and by 'pushing the boundaries of the known and familiar almost to destruction' (Wood, 1988: 221). Thus Turing enables us to see cyborganization in a different lift: that of *test* and *con-test*. Haraway's (1991) cyborg is not simply 'multiple, without clear boundary, frayed, insubstantial', it also actively contests the unitary categories and hierarchical divisions of conventional form. Prigogine's (1989) mutual stability-instability becomes mutual contestation. (2) Taussig's (1992) Nervous System and its 'doubleness of social being' is also a site of contest between the norm and the ab-norm. Derrida's (1987) postal system contests the unfinished heterogeneity of *division* as 'a debased, lateralized, repressed, displaced theme' which exercises 'a permanent and obsessive pressure from the place where it remains held in check' (Derrida 1987: 270). (4) Cyborganization/information, which earlier we called 'self-organized criticality' on the 'edge of chaos' (2), can now be more clearly seen as *test/con-test*.

The test/con-test of Turing's simulation is repeated in Vattimo's (1992) contention that modern cinema is the technical reproduction of an increasingly inconstant and superficial reality. And, as we've noted, Vattimo cites the film *Blade Runner* as an example of contest between the representation of stable identity and the intertextual doubling of mimetic instability. At the level of representation, *Blade Runner* tells the story of a small group of android replicants in a Los Angeles of the twenty-first century, who, having illegally returned to Earth from Mars, are targeted for elimination by a hired bounty hunter. The androids represent a genetically advanced type, endowed with abilities and capacities equal, and even superior, to those of human beings. The critical problem for the bounty hunter is to distinguish the androids from the real humans before destroying them. In effect, the firm repeats the essential features of the Turing simulation. At every step, the decidability of what's human/natural and what's unhuman/artificial is in question. To help make (and thus *confirm*) these distinctions, the bounty hunter applies an empathy test, designed to elicit differences in empathic capacity between androids and humans in response to a series of set questions. Here, let's note that the empathy test literally *makes* the desired distinctions and does not simply record what is *already* there. In other words, it's a test that contests or attempts to force a decision in a situation that seems intrinsically undecidable. In contrast, the Turing test con-tests or attempts to force an 'indecision' in a situation that seems so obviously decidable.

The test/con-test of Turing and *Blade Runner* repeats Deleuze's (1989) discussion around Kant's famous ontological question, 'What are we?' The con-test in the film is between those who think they know the answer to this question (the humans like the bounty hunter who 'know' they're 'human') and those non-human, technological forces (symbolized in the androids) which deny such absolute divisions and thereby suggest that the question is fundamentally inappropriate. Deleuze himself replies to the question by denying that it's answerable in terms of the simple binary opposition: we're human, you're machines. He goes on to argue (here following Michel Foucault) for the thesis that 'Man is dead' and that the '*surhomme*' (the 'more-than-Man') has begun to makes its appearance with the impact of cybernetics and information technology by which 'the forces within man enter into a relation with forces from the outside, those of silicon which supersedes carbon, or genetic components which supersede the organism' (Deleuze, 1989: 131–2). This creates a cyborganizational field of forces and forms which Deleuze calls an 'unlimited finity' (we might also call it a field of unfinished heterogeneity) in which a 'finite number of components yields a practically unlimited diversity of combinations' (1989: 131). Clearly, Deleuze's 'more-than-Man' is Haraway's (1991) cyborg which, as we've seen, realizes itself through the 'plasticity of informational patterns' which 'make possible the combinational play of matter and thus the continuous disassembly and reassembly of new forms and patterns' (Cooper and Law, 1995: 268).

Deleuze's unlimited finity appears in *Blade Runner* in many guises. The inhabitants of its cityscape speak a hybrid language of English, Japanese, Spanish, German, and so on. The viewer is thus reminded that language itself is a variable combination of letters that in this case burst through the order imposed in them by word and sentence. *Blade Runner*'s poly-glot dramatizes our earlier question: can we read the words *and* see them as media *at the same time?* In other words, it's Deleuze's con-test of the audiovisual again. Unlimited finity appears also in the form of the genetically engineered androids which are products—like the humans from whom they're copied—of combinations of genetic components, the chains of the genetic code, which 'supersede the organism'. In *Blade Runner*, in Deleuze, in Haraway, our attention is constantly drawn to the cybernetic information out of which things are made, and the conflict between speaking and seeing which this engenders for the human agent.

These insights help us to see *Blade Runner* as an example of Deleuze's view that cinema is not just a window on the world, is not simply about conventional representation, is not *what* we see but that *with which, according to which*, we see. No longer an opening onto a transparent visual field, cinema/film is surface on which moving data are inscribed, on which information can be received, recorded, and transmitted onwards. And, borrowing from the art theorist Leo Steinberg's comments on the painter Robert Rauschenberg, Deleuze (1989) compares cinema/film to a surface that stands 'for the mind itself—dump, reservoir, switching centre, abundant with concrete references freely associated as in an internal monologue—the outward symbol of the mind as a running transformer of the external world, constantly ingesting incoming unprocessed data to be mapped in an overcharged field' (Steinberg, 1972: 88) In short, cinema as *kinema*, nervous system, nervousness.

# REFERENCES

Bateson, G. (1973) *Steps towards an Ecology of Mind*. London: Paladin.
Benjamin, W. (1970) *Illuminations*. London: Jonathan Cape.
Benjamin, W. (1979) 'Doctrine of the similar (1933)', *New German Critique*, 17: 65–9.
Brunette, P. and Willis, D. (1989) *Screen/Play: Derrida and Film Theory*. Princeton, NJ: Princeton University Press.
Caillois, R. (1984) 'Mimicry and legendary psychaesthenia', *October*, 13: 17–32.
Calvino, I. (1987) *The Literature Machine*. London: Picador.
Clynes, M. (1995) 'Cyborg II: sentic space travel', in C. H. Gray (ed.), *The Cyborg Handbook*. London: Routledge. pp. 35–42.
Clynes, N. and Kline, N. (1995) 'Cyborgs and space', in C. H. Gray (ed.), *The Cyborg Handbook*. London: Routledge. pp. 29–33.
Cooper, R. and Law, J. (1995) 'Organisation: distal and proximal views', *Research in the Sociology of Organisations*, 13: 237–74.
Deleuze, G. (1986) *Cinema 1: The Movement Image*. London: Athlone.
Deleuze, G. (1988) *Foucault*. Minneapolis, MN: University of Minnesota Press.
Deleuze, G. (1989) *Cinema 2: The Time Image*. London: Athlone.
Deleuze, G. and Guattari, F. (1983) *Anto-Oedipus: Capitalism and Schizophrenia*. Minneapolis, MN: University of Minnesota Press.
Deleuze, G. and Parnet, C. (1987) *Dialogues*. London: Athlone.

Derrida, J. (1987) *The Post Card: From Socrates to Freud and Beyond*. Chicago: Chicago University Press.

Donald, M. (1991) *Origins of the Modern World*. Cambridge: Cambridge University Press.

Eco, U. (1989) *The Open Work*. London: Hutchinson.

Goodwin, B. (1994) *How the Leopard Changed its Spots*. London: Weidenfeld and Nicholson.

Haraway, D. (1991) *Simians, Cyborgs and Women: The Re-invention of Nature*. London: Free Association Books.

Jardine, A. (1987) 'Of bodies and technologies', in H. Foster (ed.), *Discussions in Contemporary Culture*. Seattle: Bay Press. pp. 151–8.

Johnson, C. (1993) *System and Writing in the Philosophy of Jacques Derrida*. Cambridge: Cambridge University Press.

Moravec, H. (1988) *Mind Children: The Future of Robot and Human Intelligence*. Cambridge, MA: Harvard University Press.

Poster, M. (1990) *The Mode of Information: Poststructuralism and Social Context*. Cambridge: Polity Press.

Prigogine, I. (1989) 'The philosophy of instability', *Futures*, 21: 396–400.

Taussig, M. (1992) *The Nervous System*. New York: Routledge.

Taussig, M. (1993) *Mimesis and Alterity: A Particular History of the Senses*. New York: Routledge.

Taylor, M. (1995) 'Rhizomic folds of interstanding', *Tekhnema*, 2: 24–36.

Turing, A. (1950) 'Computing machinery and intelligence', *Mind*, 59: 433–60.

Vattimo, G. (1992) *The Transparent Society*. Cambridge: Polity Press.

Virilio, P. (1994) *The Vision Machine*. London: British Film Institute.

Wiener, N. (1954) *The Human Use of Human Beings: Cybernetics and Society*. New York: Houghton and Mifflin.

Wood, M. (1988) 'Signification and simulation: Barthes' response to Turing', *Paragraph*, 11: 211–26.

# 12 Primary and Secondary Thinking in Social Theory

## The Case of Mass Society

*Robert Cooper*

(*Journal of Classical Sociology*, 2003, 3/2: 145–172. Reproduced by permission of SAGE Publications Ltd., London, Los Angeles, New Delhi, Singapore and Washington DC, Copyright © SAGE publications.)

**Abstract** The development of social theory is introduced as a dialectic between primary and secondary thinking. Secondary thinking views the social and cultural world in determinate, positive, rational terms; primary thinking recognizes the indeterminate, negative and irrational as forever immanent in human action. Max Weber's work illustrates the dynamic interaction between the two forms of thinking, which are further developed with the ideas from religion, the philosophy of pragmatism and the psychoanalysis of artistic imagination. The primary-secondary dialectic is then applied to a reanalysis of early sociological studies of mass society, which is reinterpreted as *social mass*. The primary nature of mass is revealed as an ever-present absence, which, like Weber's idea of 'meaningless infinity', resists all secondary attempts to express it in clear, determinate, positive forms. The primary-secondary interaction is further illustrated through the technologies of the modern mass media and the 'consumption' of space and time implied by globalization.

**Keywords** absence, differentiation, infinity, mass media, presence, rationality, religion, social mass, undifferentiation, vagueness

The history of European social thought suggests that it has vacillated between two ways of thinking the social and cultural world. One way prefers to structure the human world as a set of observed data that can be fitted into determinate, rational formats of understanding. The other way sees the human world as subject to irrational, other-worldly forces that not only lie beyond rational comprehension but also actively interfere with our attempts to understand them. The actual practice of thinking is caught up in an eternal dialectic between these two approaches. In his study of the dynamics of this dialectic in European social thought in the period 1890–1930, the intellectual historian H. Stuart Hughes (1959) has shown how the nascent disciplines of the social science at that time were torn between their desire to attribute rational identities and autonomous boundaries to their varied subject matters and their recognition that these same subject matters were completely intermeshed and thus intrinsically resistant to the divisions of rational specialization. The problems of these early thinkers were partly due to their attempts to give form and content to areas of intellectual understanding for which there were few or no professional academic antecedents; they were beginners trying to establish directions for a conceptual future that had no past. A further problem was the recognition that the human consciousness of which they were self-appointed public exponents was bedevilled throughout by unknown and seemingly unknowable forces that appeared only as a receding horizon that would forever refuse conceptual capture.

A central question for thinkers of this period was how the human mind can arrive at knowledge of society. It was recognized that consciousness in any form was always shadowed by an unconsciousness, an indeterminate presence that distantly threatened all attempts at certainty. The problem of conscious knowing was magnified by the lack of systematic tradition in social thinking. This was a period of intellectual beginnings in which the various fields of the social sciences had yet to be laid out and their vocabularies invented. Whereas earlier thinkers such as Hegel and Goethe saw reality as essentially spiritual and hence beyond the immediate consciousness of sense perception, the new breed of social thinkers began by reducing what was previously vague and uncertain in human experience to discrete, finite problems that they considered amenable to rational and even scientific explanation. At the same time they were fascinated by the irrational: 'They were obsessed, almost intoxicated, with a rediscovery of the nonlogical, the uncivilized, the inexplicable' (Hughes, 1959: 35). They defined themselves as tamers of the irrational, believing themselves capable of reducing the wild, extravagant and obstreperous forces of the non-human to the manageable mental frameworks they considered to constitute the rational. 'Sorel, Pareto, Durkheim, Freud—all thought of themselves as engineers or technicians, men of science or medicine' who 'were concerned with the irrational only exorcize it. By probing into it, they sought ways to tame it, to canalize it for constructive human purposes' and to make it fit 'the new world of industrial logic and the machine' (Hughes, 1959: 35–6).

The technician pre-defines the world in terms of manageable problems that offer expedient solutions. When, like Freud and Durkheim, you move beyond the manageable world of immediate accessibility and limited horizon into the wide-open and ineffable spaces of the unconscious and the religious, your aspirations to intellectual control are placed at considerable risk. This was certainly Freud's experience throughout much of his professional career, which began with the modest, technical-rational methodologies of positivism, but which, over the long years of his working life, was forced to give way to the more speculative methodologies he borrowed from philosophy and literature. Freud faced an unconscious whose social expression resisted the simplified repression imposed by his technical method of representation on the oceanic feelings and the uncanny convolutions of a sublime world that seemed increasingly unapproachable. His imagination was constantly seduced by a vision that was much grander than that outlined by the technical-rational language he preferred to use: his 'creative imagination—the work of the unconscious itself'—refused to be tied down by a vocabulary that had originally been devised for quite different purposes. . . . The positivist vocabulary remained—but the positivist mentality had been largely sloughed off' (Hughes, 1959: 135). This, too, was Durkheim's problem, especially when he came, later in his career, to take the social nature of religion seriously. In his study of religion, Durkheim sensed the presence of an ineffable force that constituted the basis of society: '. . . Durkheim was led to define society as religious in origin. Religion *created* society . . .' (Hughes, 1959: 285). The precise nature of Durkheim's problem was in translating the ineffability and unutterability of religion into the clear, speakable language of positivism. He saw the solution to his problem to lie in the *practice* of religion rather than in its spiritual dimensions. Sociological concepts such as social solidarity and collective consciousness were to be understood as creations of religious practice, and practice itself was the pragmatic response of collective members to an originating power that was intrinsically vague and beyond technical-rational understanding (Hughes, 1959: 285). In the context of religion, social *action* was the way one translated the unknowable into the do-able. Despite recognizing the hyper-physical sources of action and practice, despite the misty appreciation of the spiritual underpinnings of society, Durkheim remained within the technical-rational space of positivism: 'His formulations were more static than dynamic; they were cast in terms of structure rather than of process' (Hughes, 1959: 286).

Another important explorer of the human spaces of society at this period was Max Weber, who was also caught up in the eternal dialectic between determinate, rational understanding and the irrational and other-worldly. Like Freud and Durkheim in the stages of their mature thinking, Weber's intellectual tensions increased with his gnawing realization that rationality, instead of clarifying and edifying our understanding of society, made it more problematic: 'The problematic character of rationality in the Western world came to torment him ever more profoundly', intensifying 'the unbearable antinomies that had been apparent in his earlier work' (Hughes, 1959: 329). And like Durkheim's pragmaticization of religion, Weber's intellectual method was based on the efficacity of practice: if a concept makes practical sense, use it. This was Weber's way of dealing with the intrinsically unknowable spaces of the irrational. Human culture is a complex of methods that give value and significance to a world that defies our comprehension: it is 'a finite segment of the meaningless infinity of the world process, a segment on which *human beings* confer meaning and significance' (Weber, 1949: 81). By infinity, Weber intended to convey the idea of an invisible presence that could not be made finite or given the finish of a definable, rational form.

At best, we could only fill the infinite and vague spaces of the world with practical fictions that conferred a *sense* of reality—but could not reveal the reality itself—through the construction of 'ethical and cultural values whose origin and ultimate meaning were veiled in mystery' and which were made possible solely through the 'pursuit of certain frankly arbitrary methods that *in practice* gave comprehensible results' (Hughes, 1959: 310). Among these methods were *Verstehen* and the *ideal type*. *Verstehen*, for Weber, was a cross between the intuitive sensing of something through feeling and the modification of this crude sensing by strict scientific argument: vague hunches were thus turned into explicit and hence acceptable logics. The ideal type was yet another example of Weber's modulating of the basic sensing of finite segments of the world. Any ideal type, such as the state, the church or capitalism, did not exist in reality for their empirical manifestations were too far complex for the human to grasp. The ideal type was an intellectual convenience to gloss the complex, dynamic and infinite nature of the social and cultural world. Weber's originality lay in recognizing that his intellectual techniques were merely local devices for imposing orders o perspective on this virtually prodigal world.

To say that the human world is a 'meaningless infinity' is to suggest that it is lacking in original meaning and hence that it does not simply and naturally offer itself to human comprehension. When Weber says that *significance* has to be attributed to or imposed on this original void, he literally means that the actual *practice of signification* is the *making of signs* that give value, direction and purpose to specific contexts. Left to itself, Weber's 'meaningless infinity' is inherently unreadable; it is that which has not yet been prepared for human understanding. Organized religions were among the first social institutions to make ready the inchoate beginnings of the world for our mental and spiritual consumption, especially with their promises of salvation in a future life, which created a profound sense of communal feeling and meaning by transmuting an indeterminate and potentially menacing non-presence into the benevolent presence of the holy. With the fall of religion as a communal force and the rise of mass society, a further variation of 'meaningless infinity' appeared: the 'inarticulate mass' of the *demos* or the new urban masses (Weber, 1948: 225). Bureaucrarization was the modern response to the mass's inarticulation, its lack of direction and purpose, its shadowy substance. Bureaucracy replaced the lost sense of religion-based community with 'rationality ordered "societal action"' (Weber, 1948: 228) that remade society as a collection of specialized spaces—legal, educational, economic, political, even religious—subject to the 'rules, means, ends, and matter-of-factness' of techno-rational administration (Weber, 1948: 244). Bureaucracy was thus not simply an administrative technology for the direction and control of the newly emerging masses; it translated their raw and obtuse nature into a formal system of significations and identities.

Common to both these cases—religion and bureaucracy—was the need to make articulate the congenital dumbness of the material world and hence to make it readable for human habitation. In the case of the emerging urban *demos*, Weber did not just mean that the mass lacked a language to express its identity and needs; equally importantly was the implication that the mass was implicitly indeterminate and hence was capable of assuming any number of different forms and identities. 'Democratization', in Weber's eves, was the assumption by the *demos* of the power to explore this implicit potential and its many political, economic and cultural possibilities, in direct contrast to the requirements of bureaucracy for a constrained and limited identity based on techno-rational ascription. 'Inarticulation' thus drew attention to a primitive, pre-human force that reappeared in the modern world as an unlocatable and unspeakable power that motivated the forces of both constraint and freedom. This dialectic was recognized by Weber in his discussions of the dominant role of science in the modern world and of 'objectivity' in the social sciences, where in both places he argued for the tempering of the rational by the visionary potential and creativity offered by the *demon*— Weber's term—that courses through all our social acts as an expression of something more than human (Weber, 1948: chap. V; 1949: chap. II). Despite his general favouring of the clear and rational in the study of social life, Weber here affirms his recognition of the role of the vague and uncertain as sources of creative understanding.

   Weber's analyses lead us to the essential insight that the new mass society requires us to think of *social and cultural mass* as a continuous dialectic between two complementary aspects of mass: primal, raw matter—what Weber called 'meaningless infinity'—and its conversion into secondary products—what, adapting Weber, we might call 'meaningful finities'—that can be packaged and readily circulated for general consumption by the urban masses. Sociology itself was in danger of becoming a secondary product as the universities assumed the role of dividing the world of knowledge into discrete specializations. In this sense, the universities became part of the universal production system that specially characterized the industrial age in its major function of reproducing primal, raw matter's 'infinity' as finite, 'bites' or 'finites' for the physical and mental consumption of the emerging mass society. In our own time, the concept of social and cultural mass is undergoing further transformation as it moves from conventional mass society, where secondary, finished products dominated and defined the nature of social life, to the society of globalized communication and bio-technologization, where primary, undifferentiated mass reappears as 'a principle of accelerating supplementarity' in which Weber's 'infinity' reasserts itself as 'the productive receding of consciousness' in the never-ending dialectic between the rational-conscious and irrational-unconscious (Bersani, 1986: 48, 47).

## PRIMARY AND SECONDARY THINKING

Early social thinkers such as Freud, Durkheim and Weber were *makers* of new systems of knowledge. In their different ways, they were aware of 'something' that lay beyond the ordinary conscious representations of everyday life and that even resisted all attempts to give it conscious form. In Weber's case, the practical answer to this problem was the invention of intellectual 'fictions' such as the ideal type that translated the vague and uncertain into manipulable and convenient vehicles for public understanding and rational communication. As beginners, these early thinkers were necessarily faced with problems of *definition*, of identifying and articulating the outlines of a vague 'something' and thus *making* it palatable and consumable for an educated audience. In the specific cases of Durkheim and Weber with their absorption in the social and cultural implications of religion, the task of *definition* was quite literally a task of *divination* or the making clear and explicit of that which is holy and hidden. Definition as divination is also an act of prevision or prediction. Freud's mapping of the unconscious may also be seen as a dramatic attempt of divination as prediction in the sense of literally *making up* a field of knowledge out of an inarticulate 'something'. In this context, *prediction* is also literally an act of *production*, which is why we can view the works of Freud, Durkheim and Weber as *products* or *predicts* that set out new areas of intellectual consumption in the public domain. All acts of production—intellectual and industrial—share the same basic character: they represent the translation of raw, crude or inarticulate matter into usable, consumable, readable, finished forms. More simply, they are undetermined beginnings that have to be made over into human ends. Weber's 'meaningless infinity' was the necessary beginning for the methodological rationality that led to his concepts of *Verstechn* and ideal type; in both concepts Weber kept in mind (though not always in his intellectual practice) their active origins in and dependence on their raw beginnings. Weber especially recognized the mutual composition of beginnings and ends in his intuition that the rational revealed the irrational just as much as the irrational sourced and motivated the rational.

Hughes's (1959) analysis of the various attempts by early modern European thinkers to do intellectual justice to the mutual conception of the rational-irrational concludes that they failed because they expressed their intuited sensings of the unconscious and the irrational in language that was too methodologically formal and thus placed undue emphasis on the rational. The problem seems to inhere in the nature of rational thinking itself, which finds it difficult to deal with 'open', raw material 'without rounding it off prematurely' and without submitting it to a 'secondary revision' that imparts 'to such material a greater precision and compactness than it actually possesses' (Ehrenzweig, 1967: 39). Rational thought 'rationalizes' itself through a 'law of closure' which 'will always tend to round off and simplify the images and concepts of conscious thought' (Ehrenzweig, 1967: 39). Rational thought is a form of *secondary thinking* that organizes the complex flow of raw, crude and inarticulate experience into readily perceivable and consumable 'finities'. Weber's project began with the profound recognition that the study of social and cultural life had somehow to include a sense of the raw and inarticulate as currently originating forces in modern social organization. In other words, Weber's form of secondary thinking explicitly recognized its own formative and immanent origins in the primal, raw matter of 'meaningless infinity'. The big intellectual challenge for the visionary social thinker was how to express the creative dialectic between these secondary and primary forms of thought.

Curiously, Durkheim (1933) unknowingly signalled a possible strategy for pursuing this challenge in his classic study of the division of labour as the basis of society. The division of labour is a production-prediction system that makes secondary, determinate structures out of primary, indeterminable matter; it stresses specialization and functional organization in which everyone has their place and every place has its function. Outside this specialized, determinate world there is art, which Durkheim called 'the domain of liberty', free of conventional necessities and constraints. Art, therefore, has no useful place in systems of purposeful organization constituted by the division of labour. Art reaches out to the vague and infinite spaces of the world and, like religion, hints at irrational and other-worldly forces. But for Durkheim the irrational other-world was completely marginal to the practical everyday world of the division of labour, whereas for Weber it was an immanent and ever-present source of all social and cultural action. If we accept Weber's approach, we are compelled to reject Durkheim's simplistic and absolute division between the practical world and the other-world of art, and instead take seriously the possibility that they are both part of the same eternal dialectic between rational constraint and irrational freedom. This is precisely what the art theorist Anton Ehrenzweig (1967) does in his ground-breaking study of the thinking that inspires art as a way of comprehending the complex social and cultural motions of our world. In Ehrenzweig's study, art becomes much more than a marginal appendage or luxuriant excess to the exigencies of everyday living; art emerges as a radically incisive method for revealing the complex mobilities intrinsic to human existence. In Ehrenzweig's mind, art is no longer a rarefied institutionalized category raised above and beyond the practical and taken-for-granted routines of the everyday but reappears as a way of rethinking the all-pervasive dialectic between the rational and irrational, the conscious and unconscious.

The problem first addressed by Ehrenzweig was precisely Freud's problem in his conscious attempts to characterize the nature of the unconscious mind. For Freud, the distinction between the conscious and the unconscious was expressed early in his thinking as the distinction between two kinds of mental process; the *primary* and the *secondary*. While secondary process was defined in terms of the precise logic of focused attention, clear judgement, structured reasoning and controlled action, primary process was an undifferentiated and chaotic stream of experience that resisted all attempts to translate it into secondary structures. Whereas primary process was completely undifferentiated so that its presence was only roughly sensed as vague and spectral intimations of a possible other-world, secondary process differentiated events and objects in space and time, giving them idealized forms. Primary process thus approximated Weber's idea of 'meaningless infinity', while secondary process rendered his version of the rational. But while Weber initially saw the two processes as interacting and ultimately inseparable, Freud kept them apart, seeing them as expressions of quite different types of human experience. The significance of Ehrenzweig's contribution to our understanding of the conscious-unconscious relationship is in his showing that Freud was too partitional in his thinking and that the primary-secondary dualism of the conscious-unconscious is a dynamic dialectic in which both terms actively create each other. In this respect, Ehrenzweig's study is a refinement of Weber's rough insight that the rational and irrational endow each other.

Idealized secondary thinking views the forms of the world in terms of precise, even rigid, outlines; it focuses attention on specific forms and figures while the rest of the mental field 'recedes and fuses into a vague background of indistinct texture' (Ehrenzweig, 1967: 11). It thus emphasizes bounded, separate and static structures as the expense of dynamic and creative movement. Ehrenzweig de-emphasizes the role of bounded, separate forms and figure in secondary thinking by exposing the origins of secondary forms in primary process. His more active, creative vision is 'anchored in the undifferentiated unconscious', where it becomes 'more plastic and real (though less clearly defined)' than the purely secondary thinking of the rational, conscious mind (1967: 12). When secondary thinking is reconnected with primary process, reality becomes much more plastic and vivid; instead of bounded, separate objects and events that command our attention at the expense of their vague and indistinct backgrounds, we become aware of a wider dynamic field in which objects lose their distinctly separate characterizations and move as 'intensely plastic objects without definition outline' in a field of 'blurred plasticity' (1967: 14–15). Where conventional secondary thinking, with its narrow focus on specific forms and events, perceives their undifferentiated background as empty and vague and hence 'cannot grasp its wider more comprehensive structure', Ehrenzweig's dynamic combination of primary-secondary process 'can accommodate a wide range of incompatible forms' (1967: 20, 19). The complex, dynamic vision of the artist 'far outstrips the powers of conscious attention, which, with its pinpoint focus, can attend to only one thing at a time', since it recognizes that 'there is not sharp boundary between the differentiation that motivates the 'surface vision' of normal secondary thinking: the differentiation of surface vision, like the rational thought of Durkheim and Weber, idealizes its subject matter through 'a law of closure' that 'makes it difficult, if not impossible, for rational thought to handle "open" material without rounding it off prematurely', in contrast to the dedifferentiation of primary-secondary counter-changes, in which the thinker is freed 'from having to make a choice' between binary distinctions such as figure and ground (1967: 32, 39). The dedifferentiation of primary-secondary thinking thus requires what Ehrenzweig (1967: 21–31) calls a 'scattered attention', as opposed to the precise, focused attention of secondary thinking. Dedifferentiation and scattered attention are conceptual strategies for the revealing of what Weber sensed as the undivided wholeness between social and cultural products and their origins in the raw and inarticulate. Instead of the social and cultural world seen simply as a collection of finite forms and objects, the human world becomes a 'fertile motif' which 'often has something incomplete and vague about its structure' (1967: 48). Instead of the finite and finished, scattered attention looks to the infinite and unfinished as the source of creative movement. The fertile and creatable are by definition incomplete, raw, vague and uncertain, just like Freud's unconscious and Weber's 'meaningless infinity'. Cultural and spiritual renewal have their beginnings in the vague and uncertain, and it is this insight that connects Ehrenzweig's analysis of the primary-secondary basis of creative art with Weber's belief in the irrational other-world as the source of all social and cultural action.

Whereas rational, secondary thinking seeks closure and completeness of knowledge and understanding, the sourcing of secondary thinking in primary process exposes knowledge as always incomplete and unfinished. Knowledge of the world now appears less as secondary commodity or possession and more as a vehicle for moving about and exploring social and cultural mindscapes. Mind as primary-secondary dialectic is permanently incomplete and supplements itself through 'a principle of accelerating supplementary' in which its incompleteness or infinity is expressed as 'the productive receding of consciousness' into the vague and uncertain of the primary process (Bersani, 1986: 48, 47). Consciousness thus appears as a moving force that advances on the unconscious, from which it gets its motive power. The secondary thinking of consciousness detects the vagueness and infinity of the unconscious primary process as 'something missing' and seeks to fill the gap by translating it into some kind of meaningful form, but since the gap always recedes, it denies consciousness its full presence in space and time while simultaneously creating consciousness and keeping it continually alive. It is this sense of vagueness and incompleteness as lack of full presence that the philosopher-psychologist William James (1890) addresses in his treatment of primary process as 'the stream of thought' or, as it was later called, 'the stream of consciousness'. Rational definition of the world assumes the full and complete even static, presence of its field of understanding. Weber's ideal type leans towards the illusion of full presence despite Weber's warning that it was simply a conceptual convenience that helped to fill in the communicational gaps that necessarily constitute all human understanding, including social analysis. Like words and concepts in general, the ideal type is shadowed by vagueness and infinity; its power derives not from any claim it might make for comprehensive precision but from its allusion to phenomena too complex and polymorphous for all but a preconceptual and prelinguistic sensing of what it might mean. The preconceptual and prelinguistic is the incomplete and infinite flow of James's 'stream of thought' from which conscious, secondary thinking captures its transient forms, of which the ideal type is but an example. The ideal type attributes substance and thingness to the intrinsic flux and flow of the 'stream of thought'; it foregrounds experience in terms of substantives while backgrounding its stream-like, transient character. Through such conceptual devices rational thought frames knowledge as a collection of complete and possible commodities rather than acts of supple and transitive knowing that enables us to modulate and move with the flow of experience and its kinetic possibilities. Creative movement rather than stabilizing fixity reasserts itself in James's explorations and revelations of 'the stream of thought' and the virtuality of its fluid vagueness and infinity.

Vagueness as an expression of primary thinking assumes a dominant feature in James's philosophy, where it becomes the source of creative *practice* as opposed to the precisions and certainties constructed by rational, secondary thinking. James embraces a 'philosophy that recommends "vagueness" as a counteraction to the dogmatizing of existent truths and as the necessary condition resistant to the blandishments both of conclusiveness and of common sense' (Poirier, 1992: 42–3). James's vagueness is clearly a version of Ehrenzweig's 'fertile motif' with its requirement of scattered attention as the source and strategy of creative movement. The creative movement provided by the fertility of vagueness begins with a general loosening or 'unsaying' of accepted certainties, whether in common sense or rational thought; to unsay the rigidities of certainty is to open up experience to creative 'mutations and superfluities of meaning' (Poirier, 1992: 38). To be 'superfluid' is to be supermobile, to move creatively among an inexhaustible reservoir of possibilities and to make vagueness into the 'extra-vagant' of 'extravagence' (Poirier, 1992: 44). At this point in James's thinking, the superfluous— which in the language of common sense is the inessential and unnecessary— becomes the necessary essence of human expression inasmuch as it is the origin and goal of all cultural production and 'becoming'. Superfluity is a return to the raw and inarticulate source of all social and cultural creation; without this return and renewal, action becomes inertia, language becomes mere communication and thinking turns into 'mere thought' (Poirier, 1992: 28). Social and cultural production as 'becoming' is pure action—the action, in the words of Ralph Waldo Emerson, of the 'preamble of thought, the transition through which it passes from the unconscious to the conscious' and which never reaches the completed, finite state of a thing or object; in its pure 'becoming' it never 'becomes' anything in particular and simply only 'exists in the action of becoming' (Poirier, 1992: 25, 28). Superfluity and 'extra-vagence' are expressions of 'accelerating supplementary' or *supplement* as 'supple mind', in which 'the productive receding of consciousness' is the action of pure becoming (Bersani, 1986: 48, 47).

'Extra-vagence' is the emergence of proliferating, transient forms out of the fertility of vagueness, forms that are 'extra' in the double sense of being extracted from an implicit, secret source as well as being redundant, being more than is required. Vagueness as an implicit, unarticulated, secret source is the primary process of the unconscious; its 'extra' forms are products of the secondary work of consciousness, which extracts and extricates the polymorphic possibilities from their primary, raw, unconscious source. The secondary products of consciousness thus appear as *surface* expressions of a deep and supple space that can never be wholly exposed—a space that might be compared to Weber's 'meaningless infinity'. The secondary surfaces are like Ehrenzweig's (1967) differentiated 'surface vision', which, while providing finite, thinkable locations for consciousness to rest on, are also 'extra-vagently' superfluous and superfluid due to their equivocal and obscure origins in the dynamic infinity of primary process. Like all surfaces, they provide the conditions for movement, and just as legs can only walk on stable, physical surfaces, so mental movement requires a stable surface on which to form and perform its ideas and images. Weber's ideal type can thus be seen as an example of 'surface vision' that defines a stable, visible surface for itself as a way of resisting the latent instabilities of 'meaningless infinity'. Surfaces constitute our points of physical and mental contact with reality— we 'live amid surfaces', says Emerson—but they are only temporary stopping places for the human body and its various perceptual organs such as the senses of vision and touch (Poirier, 1992: 64). Like Ehrenzweig's scattered attention, Emerson's 'true art of life' is the creative movement of the mind on the surfaces of ideas, images and texts in a way that rejects both the conception of rational knowledge as fixed commodity and the assumption that the unconscious is totally foreign to and therefore excluded from the actions of practical life (Poirier, 1992: 64). Human action, Emerson reminds us, is the 'preamble of thought, the transition through which it passes from the unconscious to the conscious'; action as 'the art of life' enables the mind to move 'in two places at one': in and on its conscious surfaces as well as recognizing that these surfaces have a secret underside in the primary process that sources them (Poirier, 1992: 25, 65). Surfaces thus become the secondary-primary expressions of what we may now perhaps call 'meaningful infinity'.

Surfaces transform all acts of knowing into transitional actions that reveal the social and cultural world as essentially mutable and mobile. The 'extra-vagence' of the superfluous implies a capacious, even infinite, vagueness in which to explore and move freely and creatively. Instead of knowledge of finite things, it is the search for the un-knowable beyond things, the desire for 'meaningful infinity' that places us on the vagrant border between secondary forms and primary process. Hence, it is not knowledge of solid things and structures that we seek but the surfaces of contact between the things and structures that mediate the social and the cultural. This is how the philosopher Jean-François Lyotard (1993) understands society: a 'social body' made up of limitless surfaces that offer immense possibilities or permutable contacts and virtual contexts. The surfaces of the 'social body' include the skin of the human body and its multifarious folds, the hands and fingertips, the skeleton and its moving parts, 'the whole network of veins and arteries', 'the tongue and all the pieces of the vocal apparatus', including the sounds they produce; they further include all those surfaces of the world external to the human body on and around which the human organs and senses move—'sheets to write on', words on pages, pavements to walk on, 'canvases to paint', rooms to move in and out of, landscapes on and in which the eyes can roam (Lyotard, 1993: 1, 2). Even language is interpreted as a surface or 'skin' of the human body that reaches out to make an 'extra-vagant' world of multiple and creative contacts and contexts in which we can be superfluid (Lyotard, 1993: 76–82). Society as a 'social body' of energetic and energizing surfaces is depicted as 'the great ephermeral skin' in which Ehrenzweig's (1967) undifferentiated, plastic unconscious merges with Weber's (1949: 81) 'finite segments' (or ephemeral surfaces) of meaning and significance to produce a superfluous and 'extra-vagant' space of pure becoming. In contrast, idealized rational knowledge, with its tendency to closure, has already reached its final destination and has already 'become' something finite. For Lyotard, the message of modern science and mathematics promotes knowing as a process of pure becoming; it rejects the old idea that we can possess knowledge as certainty and use it as a means of enhancing control and material domination. The borders of knowledge are never fixed; they cannot help but dissolve in the superfluity of pure becoming: 'They do not reduce the unknown to the known, they make everything one thought one knew unstable in proportion to what one used to know . . .' (1993: 253). Science becomes more like fiction, all the time rendering itself 'precarious, obliged by the very abundance of its discoveries to doubt its vocation to the true', and, forging 'new surfaces of inscription', it 'no longer believes in anything, space and time become infinitely suspect to it, the concepts it received as *a priori* become obsolete' (1993: 253). All this means 'the death of the knowing subject' in a world that subscribes to the rational illusion that' knowable is in principle supposed to be assignable to a subject who could *possess* it', and where the modern scientist moves on transient surfaces, no longer a knowing subject but simply 'as a small transitory region in a process of energetic metamorphosis' (1993: 253). For Lyotard, science becomes more like art, creatively *fictive* in that 'productive receding of consciousness' or superfluity he dramatically calls 'the operational delirium' (Bersani, 1986: 47; Lyotard, 1993: 253).

The dissolution of the 'knowing subject' who inhabits a world of fixed and certain forms is also the point of departure for the exploration of the theme of 'sacred sociology' by Georges Bataille and his colleagues at the College of Sociology. 'Sacred sociology' addressed the question of the irrational and other-worldly as the motivating force of the taken-for-granted, everyday world of conventional certainties. Inspired by Durkheim's interpretations of primitive forms of sociality, the College of Sociology viewed the sacred as the aboriginal source of human culture. The sacred was beyond rational understanding because it was *infinitely whole* and thus far exceeded the conception of the human world as a profane collection of discrete individuals and functional objects. The sacred was an extreme version of the vague with its infinite space of pure becoming that human beings exalted and glorified because it held up the possibility—however remote or illusory—of completing their ontological incompleteness. But for Bataille the sacred was not just vague and infinite; it was a disappearing reality; it might be approached but could never be attained. Through 'obstinately pursued through successful, deceptive, and cloudy depths', the sacred appears in Bataille's vision as the supreme expression of Bersani's (1986: 48) 'principle of accelerating supplementarity': 'the opposite of a *substance* that withstands the test of time, it is something the flees as soon as it is seen and cannot be grasped' (Bataille, 1985: 241). Christianity may have made the sacred *seem* physically present by expressing it through religious property, 'but the nature of the sacred . . . is perhaps the most ungraspable thing that has been produced between men: the sacred is only a privileged moment of communal unity, a moment of the convulsive communication of what is ordinarily stifled' (1985: 242). Bataille's 'privileged moment of communal unity' is that moment of ambiguity *between* the bounded, separate objects and events of secondary thinking in which Ehrenzweig's (1967) primary undifferentiation actively emerges as a ground that unites everything in a 'blurred plasticity' while at the same time refusing itself to clear perception and understanding. The sacred is the undivided wholeness of the raw and inarticulate; through unlocatable in secondary thinking, its definitive vagueness circulates as a primal call in all human communication. The essential infinitude of the sacred is like the vagueness that circulates throughout William James's 'stream of thought': it invites us to work on it, to transform it into 'extra-vagant' surfaces, to translate it into Weber's practices of signification, to recognize its inexhaustible potential for creative superfluity, and to inspire the human will to 'surrender . . . to the passion of giving the world an intoxicating meaning' (Bataille, 1985: 245). Bataille's approach to the sacred refuses the more practical and rational characterization of religion by Durkheim and Weber in suggesting that its energizing source lies in feeling and not in intellect; the sacred moves us through feeling, through the *motion* of 'extra-vagant' *emotion*, and not through the methodologies of explicit and precise definition we uncritically assume to be the ideal of disciplined theory. In this way Bataille's sense of religion coincides with James's (1890) rejection of 'full presence' as the ideal criterion of formal thinking and his consequent embracing of vagueness as the preconceptual and prelinguistic origin of secondary thinking in the primary process of 'the stream of thought'.

## MASS SOCIETY

Weber's analysis of the emergence of modern mass society was based on the increasing formalization of its institutions with the consequent loss of contact with its primal sources in religion. The institutional spread of techno-rational administration buried any former sense of religion as the origin of sacred inspiration. Weber's concern was to remind his audience that the spirit of the sacred was still with us despite its censoring by the rational. The *demon* as an infinite, super-rational power was still a seminal stimulus for human experience and even rational action. Religion was the route to that demonic and 'extra-vagant' motion and emotion that Bataille sensed as the passion that gave the world 'an intoxicating meaning'. The task of religion was to translate this holy and hidden potation into manageable and meaningful signs for use in everyday practice, and to maintain this transla-tion as a life-giving force. This, too, was Weber's dream in his diagnoses of the problems emerging in the new mass society, and especially the problem of *disenchantment* and loss of the sense of sacred community caused by the deepening intrusion of the 'rules, means, ends, and matter-of-factness' of the techno-rational mentality into the cultures of everyday life (Weber, 1948: 244). The big question for Weber was how to *re-enchant* mass-administered society with the creative urge of sacred powers. Implied in Weber's vision of the *demos*—though never made conceptually explicit—was the suggestion that social mass was implicitly infinite, indeterminate and therefore unlocat-able and unknowable. It could never be directly perceived; only indirectly sensed through its translation into specific signs, objects and practices that in their turn were mere fragments of a larger, unlocatable whole. Weber's ideal type exemplifies this partial, transient expression of the ineffable whole of 'meaningless infinity'. The significance of such conceptual devices as the ideal type was not that was intrinsically indefinable; they were simply signs of direction that led to no conceptual finality.

The significance of religion for Weber was that its signs and symbols directed us to the ineffable and indefinable whole of the holy or sacred. Reli-gion indicated the powerful presence of a force that, while pointing to the remote and vague, was nevertheless an immanently creative constituent of everyday practical life. Religion underlined the indispensability of the irra-tional to the rational. For these reasons, religion had to be included in the intellectual analysis and understanding of human society and its cultures, despite the indigenous resistance of the holy and sacred to rational formal-ization. The holy could only be sensed through *feeling*; it was a primitive presence we could only approach indirectly through the vague *motion* of 'extra-vagant' *emotion*. In this sense, the holy was a presence that was also an absence or infinity; it could not be made into the 'full presence' noted by William James as the definitive product of formal thought. The holy symbol *Om* is one way of expressing the felt presence of the holy; not so much a concept but more an unarticulated sound, it is 'simply a sort of growl or groan, sounding up from within as the quasi-reflex expression of profound emotion in circumstances of a numinous-magical nature' (Otto, 1926: 197). The practices and properties of organized religions carry this quasi-reflexive contact with the holy even further in their suggestion that the primal vagueness of the holy is the ultimate source of all human creation and re-creation. In the Christian and Buddhist Masses especially, a felt absence mystically conveys a demand to be made present. The Mass itself offers no clear meaning and at best only intimates and suggests. Mass music such as Bach's Mass in B minor intimates this archaic, primal absence in its 'faint, whispering, lingering sequence(s)', its 'held breath and hushed sound', its 'weird cadences . . . its pauses and syncopations', all of which hint at something beyond formal definition and rational explanation (Otto, 1926: 72). The Christian Mass makes a particular ontological point in its suggestion that the signs, symbols and messages of human communication derive from these vague sounds and their intermittent silences that point significantly to a world—if we can call it that—empty of recognizably meaningful shapes and sounds in a way that reminds us of Weber's 'meaningless infinity'. The Mass echoes James's insistence on vagueness as the source of creative practice and Ehrenzweig's undifferentiation of primary process as the source of secondary indeterminacy and infinitude that invokes its human audience to give it more specific meaning and form; it is a space in which the rich and varied signs and symbols of human life seem to degenerate and condense in what Ehrenzweig calls the 'blurred plasticity' of primary process. 'Mass' thus offers itself as a plastic genesis of multiple possibilities, the creative origin of multiple worlds, which in itself must remain inexpressible, and thus absent from conscious understanding. The Christian Mass recognizes this creative absence when it *tropes* or embellishes its text with a special phrase or sentence: to trope means to express the plasticity of 'mass' in a play of multiple twists and turns. The generic absence troped by the Mass now appears as a *missive* or religious *message* that reminds the congregation of its source in a *missing* or absent power. The very language of the Mass performs its essential message as a series of tonal and verbal tropings that illustrate the infinite and inexhaustible power of primal absence to move cultural production in superfluent directions.

The symbolism and practices of the Christian Mass can be seen as early and pre-theoretical attempts to answer Durkheim's and Weber's questions about the origins of social life in religion. How does religion contribute to a vital sense of *community* and the *communications* that keep that vital sense alive? Weber vaguely sensed the answer to this question to lie in the idea of 'meaningless infinity' and its emergence in the social mass as 'inarticulation'. The Christian Mass reveals 'meaningless infinity' and 'inarticulation' as that aboriginal absence that, despite its inexpressibility, human being feels compelled to make present in some way. The *missive* communicated by the Mass points not only to a radical absence, a profound unfoundedness, but also to a generative need of the human being to express this absence. At the same time the *missive* communicates its essential absence and unfoundness as an infinite source that can only be approached indirectly through the twists and turns of its tropings, which serve only to *hint* at their superfluent and superfluous origins. The religious Mass thus offers itself as *the* model of social mass in its suggestion that human community and communication—the themes that obsessed both Durkheim and Weber in their pursuit of the nature and origins of sociality—are *founded in unfoundedness* and *made present through absence*. Unfoundedness and absence are simply versions of Weber's 'meaningless infinity' and 'inarticulation', which, strangely, call out to us for contact and communication, however rudimentary. William James's argument for the significance of vagueness in human life is based precisely on the power of the vague to evoke elemental feelings of community among social agents. Communication creates community by admitting that our knowledge of the world stems from a radical ignorance of a primal absence; at best we sense this absence as a vague presence that can never be articulated. Communication serves to cover over this perturbing presence and the gaps of incompleteness and infinitude it creates. At this level we communicate largely through feelings—the *motions* of *emotions*—rather than the rational concepts, a point that James more specifically makes when he asserts that formal, rational thinking is aboriginally founded in 'the sentiment of rationality' (Poirier, 1992: 148). Hence

> . . . we are brought together not by a shared commitment to explicitly defined values; we are bought together instead in a shared confidence that . . . we do really not know what is there or cannot agree on what it is; and yet we . . . to the fact . . . that there is 'something' rather than nothing.
>
> (Poirier, 1992: 148)

It is this lack of the explicit as ontological vagueness that lies at the heart of the communication of community. Language itself rests on an inarticulate foundation of brute sound so that human speech seems forever ghosted or demonized (to echo Weber) by the inscrutability of 'meaningless infinity'. The sound behind the words cannot yield all the significances its infinitude might offer and so must remain, like the sense evoked by the religious Mass, largely obscure, absent, even mysterious. The implicit and covert source of communication and sociability originating in 'the idea of sound as a sign of barely enunciated presence' now emerges as 'the gel of human relationships, even as the gel is forever melting away' (Poirier, 1992: 140). A fundamental lack in human communication becomes the principal stimulus of communal feeling in which 'barriers to clarity' paradoxically becomes 'modes of communication, expressions of human bonding' (Poirier, 1992: 148). The intrinsic vagueness that underlies and even threatens any desired clarity of expression is what actually moves us 'to create trust and reassurance instead of human separation'. Community and communication depend directly on the human glossing of the spaces, gaps and instabilities that originate in vagueness.

Mass in its religious context reminds us that the communication of community is a dynamic dialectic between primary matter and its secondary elaboration. In the case of language, mass is that prelinguistic phase of brute sound which has yet to find more explicit expression in the language of meaningful concepts or 'full presence'. When Bataille calls the sacred 'a privileged moment of communal unity' that 'flees as soon as it is seen and cannot be grasped' (1985: 242, 241), he means that the *sacred* is also the *secret*, that primal power that forever withdraws at the approach of conscious thought. The sacred as secret not only withdraws when challenged by the demands of secondary thinking, it also 'is always receding, drawing or provoking us . . . into even greater volatilities, meanderings, or excesses of usage' (Poirier, 1992: 46). This is why we can call the religious Mass a permanent and inexhaustible source of sacred missives whose absence to conscious thought is nevertheless an indirect and lateral presence that *reminds* us—that is, regenerates and renews us—of its superfluous and superfluent powers of re-creation. Mass in this sense is therefore never a definable thing but an absent space of possibilities that pervades the human world as the necessary stimulus for social and cultural renewal; its superfluity means that it can never come to rest in a finite concept or finished product but is always in a process of 'becoming'; it reminds us of unformed matter with its vast pool of possibilities that await productive formation. Here we begin to see the connection with Weber's sensing of religion as the basis of community: for what is *common* to all is that commonwealth of possibilities or that unrealized space of 'becoming' noted by Weber in his discussion of the 'democratization' of the unarticulated powers of the *demos*. The *common* is that *capacity to become* in which we all necessarily find ourselves without necessarily finding it. The brute sound that underlies the meanings we attribute to spoken language is common begins to disappear with the development of the different local languages; the sound thus serves as the basic mass or matter from which we constantly mutate and modulate our verbal and aural communications. Just as the religious Mass tropes itself as a space of possibilities and 'becoming', so the social and cultural spaces of everyday life respond to the provocative withdrawals and teasings of raw mass with their superfluent tropings that constitute the ever-mobile messages through which we re-present this 'meaningless infinity' to ourselves.

In the context of social mass, communication and community now have to be understood not simply as the transmission of discrete, meaningful messages but as the continuous translation of the inarticulate into the articulate. The fundamental sense of community sought by Durkheim and Weber in primitive religions is to be found not in some hidden and profound meaning secreted in the depths of a spiritual world beyond our own but in that basic absence of meaning intrinsic to all human communication that moves us to *re-cover* or cover it over with an equally basic presence of meaning. At this level, we are not confronted with a world that is already there and which we merely represent to each other; instead of communication as a series of 'statements' about an external reality, communication is more radically 'the crossing of intervals' or gaps created by absence and vagueness (Bersani, 1986: 26). Less to do with the representation of sense, communication is motivated more by the combined need 'to avoid the traps of meaning in language' and the 'dissolution of sense' implied by absence ('ab-sence' or 'off-sense') and the vague (Bersani, 1986: 27). Whereas religion can be interpreted as a return to this primal sense of communication and community (as distinct from its institutionalized meaning as a spiritual authority), rationality presupposes communication as the representation of a prior logical sense and meaning in the world that can be clearly expressed. Weber of course saw rationality as the surface expression of a more implicit space he called 'meaningless infinity', as though rationality were a form of 'rationing' or sharing our of something that was 'extra-vagantly' irrational or 'un-rationable'. He sensed that the products of the intellect were also deeply and creatively rooted in the receding or 'dissolution of sense' implied by absence or 'meaningless infinity'. Among other things, this meant that academic products such as sociology had themselves to be seen as part of that more basic process of translation of the inarticulate into the articulate that motivate all social and cultural production. Weber's intuition also meant that the intellectual products were never complete or finished or final since they were simply transitory, surface expressions of a power that at best could only be intimated.

The religious interpretation of mass emphasizes its infinite or unfinished nature. To be infinite is to exist as a space of implicit possibilities that awaits some form of explicit and finite determination. Mass is this radical sense is an ontological statement that says that human and social being is a process of dynamic suspension between the possible and the yet-to-be. The vagueness and incompleteness of William James's (1890) 'stream of thought', with its lack of 'full presence', is another version of this sense of mass. Ehrenzweig's (1967) elaboration of Freud's distinction between primary and secondary mental processes, and especially their dynamic interplay, is a further troping of aboriginal mass. The intrinsic infinity and infinitude of mass thus opens itself to a range of interpretations to do with indefiniteness, plasticity, play, supple-mindedness, mortality and superfluency, as opposed to the clarity of precise definition, focus and fixity, bounded specificity and solidarity. Viewed in this way, mass tells us that all social and cultural products are simply different ways of attributing form to an absent and unrepresentable primal source. We are reminded here yet again of Weber's recognition that the intuitions of *Verstehen* and the ideal type are essentially pragmatic conveniences that can no more than hint at the 'meaningless infinity' from which they originate. Mass is that aboriginal vagueness and infinity on which we found ourselves through those partial and transient glossings and tropings that constitute the ceaseless production of social life as 'becoming'.

At this point we can begin to recognize in Weber's diagnosis that the correlative and complementary logic that binds together the rational and the irrational becomes a central problem in social analysis, and perhaps especially in studies that take *social mass* as their underlying theme. How do we begin to do intellectual justice to such a strangely complicated complicity between apparently contrary and antithetical compulsions? The sociology and social theory of mass society, while sometimes hinting at these underlying complications, never directly address them. This neglect of the problem that Weber considered central to the complicity between the rational and irrational in urban sociality returns us to the distinction *between* primary and secondary styles of thinking, which Weber also saw as central to the academic production of knowledge in the emerging mass society: sociology was in danger of forgetting the primal, sacred origins of society in its increasing dependence on the secondary structures of narratable and readable order and clarity. In contrast to Weber's sense of pervasive power in human affairs that could not be contained and tamed in rational, secondary thought, more recent studies of mass society unreflectively express their analyses as if it had a natural narrative and readable visibility that just as naturally offered itself to secondary thinking.

The sociology of mass society starts with the assumption that modern 'social mass' is a product of scale: vast numbers of people engaged in the large-scale production and consumption of goods and services. The sociality of mass society is organized around the continuous circulation of a common pool of goods and information that binds together a distributed population of individuals. In this way a generic sameness is created to constitute the social gel of the mass 'in which similarities between the attitudes and behaviour of individuals tend to be viewed as more important that differences' (Kornhauser, 1968: 58). Individuals are undifferentiated units in an aggregate of people now subjected to the 'ascendance of organization' through which 'mass organizations replace communal groups as the characteristic units of society' (Kornhauser, 1968: 59). Sameness as undifferentiated aggregation reappears in the characterizing of mass society as 'the most consensual' of societies in that 'there is more sense of affinity with one's fellows, more openness to understanding, and more reaching out of understanding among men, than in any earlier society' (Shils, 1962: 53). The undifferentiation of social mass represented in these examples is expressed as a particular property of large-scale organizations or of individuals; they reflect the rational attitude of secondary thinking that seeks to locate acts of thought in bounded, separate objects and events. They also reflect Weber's argument that the unreflective use of rational, finite concepts in social analysis can conceal the 'meaningless infinity' of human experience from which they derive as convenient and transient intellectual 'fictions'. In Ehrenzweig's (1967) analysis of undifferentiation as a component of creative thinking, we are reminded that the 'undifferentiated unconscious' is that primal space of plastic possibilities that have not yet been captured as finished, bounded and reliable forms. Undifferentiation in this sense as yet to be differentiated and thus cannot be seen as a ready-made, specific property of a ready-made, specific concept: it is still vague and incomplete. In contrast, the sociologist's view of mass society depends, perhaps too unreflectively, on a form of secondary thinking that has forgone its primal origins. Weber's return to the religious sources of sociality was an attempt to reverse this forgetting by reminding the sociologist that the rational is a secondary version of the irrational. The nature of the relationship between the primary and the secondary becomes a central issue in understanding the methods we use to construct and make sense of social and cultural experience. The primary and the secondary constitute that eternal dialectic between rational, determinate understanding and the irrational, other-worldly agencies noted by Hughes (1959) in his study of the dynamics of European social thought in its early modern period. The primary is undifferentiated in the fundamental sense of being unlocatable, like Weber's 'meaningless infinity'; it is everywhere and nowhere at the same time; it is an immanent absence that occupies that negative space so necessary for the production of positive presences. The secondary is what seeks to locate the primary in a general structure of thinkable objects and events, like the map of a country that places the traveller in an identifiable context of towns and highways; the secondary gives specific form and content to what was previously vague and absent. The primary is Bataille's (1985: 241) sacred that 'flees as soon as it is seen and cannot be grasped' and yet is always 'drawing or provoking us into every greater volatilities, meanderings or excesses of usage' (Poirier, 1992: 46). It is this point that sociological analyses of mass society hint at without in any way developing, due no doubt to their unreflective over-reliance on secondary thinking to represent social 'reality'.

Behind the secondary descriptions of mass society as the hyperactive circulation of products, services and information, and the enhanced social consensus this creates, there is also the recognition that mass society is a space of possibilities in which 'man's nature' also becomes a 'product' of the 'opening of human potentialities on a massive scale' along with the profusion of attendant consumables (Shils, 1962: 60). In drawing attention to society as a space of production possibilities rather than a space filled with ready-made, consumable products, this observation implicitly designates mass society as a society of 'becoming' whose defining character is the continuous and hyperactive conversation *between* the primary and the secondary. More significance that the finished, secondary products and services of 'mass organizations' and their appropriation of individuals as producers and consumers is the never-ending and mutually constituting dialogue between the primary and the secondary in which the secondary is continuously working to redeem itself from the provocative withdrawals of the primary in that 'productive receding of consciousness' noted by Bersani (1986: 47). Mass society in this sense returns us to the religious interpretation of Mass as vagueness, unfoundedness and absence; what is primary is not merely vague and absent but also without foundation; hence the secondary is that which seeks to found and find itself in a primal unfoundedness. Every act of finding oneself necessarily depends on a complementary act of losing oneself, just as every act of location or foundation is dialectically defined by unlocation or unfoundation. The secondary is thus not possible without the primary, nor is presence without absence.

Philosophical commentaries on mass society reflect this insight when they include the appropriation of extensive territorial space—what we now call globalization—as one of its more special features; secondary social mass now includes the whole planet in its inexorable programme to re-find and re-found itself among the provocative withdrawals of primary mass. Writing in the 1920s on the then emerging mass society, the philosopher José Ortega y Gasset noted the 'consumption' of space and time as one of its developing features: 'Each portion of the earth is no longer shut up in its own geometric position, but for many of the purposes of human life acts upon other portions of the planet'; this results in a 'global ubiquity' in which 'this nearness of the far-off, this presence of the absent, has extended in fabulous proportions the horizon of each individual existence' (1932: 41). A similar contraction occurs with time: prehistory and archaeology are delivered to our personal body spaces through the 'illustrated paper and the film' (1932: 42). The contraction of space and time in these contexts returns us to the original meaning of consumption as collapsing or breaking down: the new social masses absorb everything in a voracious programme of common 'levelling' (1932: 28) or undifferentiation that provokes its own renewal through the differentiation of re-production. Mass production and consumption thus *renew each other* in a 'productive receding of consciousness' and 'accelerating supplementarity' that alternates presence and absence, appearance and disappearance, so that we see mass society less as the proliferation of consumable finite products and more as a massive strategy of endless composition and decomposition in which 'becoming' is the energizing power of social mass rather than the possession of rational, secondary structures. The vagueness of absence and the 'extra-vagance' of 'becoming' are reflected through the world 'containing many more things', though it is not the things themselves that matter but their potential for composition, troping and play: each thing 'is something which we can desire, attempt, do, undo, meet with, enjoy or repel; all notions which imply vital activities' (1932: 42). The act of consumption in modern mass society 'consists primarily in living over the possibilities of buying as such' because 'our existence is at every instant and primarily at the consciousness of what is possible to us' (1932: 42). Wherever we look in mass society we see the technologies of 'extra-vagance' at work: modern science has 'extended the cosmic horizon' and thus increased the space of possibilities available to us at the margins of planetary space; sport, too, in its absorption in record-breaking, also seeks to question the very idea of limit as the circumscription of space and time (1932: 45). Like the natural world, modern mass society appears as an organ of spontaneous production and proliferation that sees itself less as a self-maintaining system and much more as an exploration and expression of that primary space of possibilities and inarticulation Weber called 'meaningless infinity'.

Mass society appears now as a society of massive movement in which movement has to be understood as the continuous *displacement of presence* and the grasping of absence. The displacement of presence weakens our sense of certainty and definitive meaning; presence itself is revealed as a convenient fiction for articulating 'something' that cannot be fully grasped and hence can only serve to intimate absence as a 'meaningless infinity' that forever refuses conceptual capture. In this picture of mass society the realization of finished objects and forms is immediately and forever deferred; the presence of things is forever postponed in the continuous action of 'becoming'. Limits exist to be erased; what animates the social mass is less the same of appropriation and possession and more the anticipation of going beyond present limits. This effectively means that modern mass society is centrally motivated by a spirit of composition, troping and play in a continuous displacement of fixed and focused meanings in favour of a dialectic of composition. The tentative drawing of boundaries and the evanescent tracing of forms in composition return us to that uncertain and aleatory stage of social and cultural production noted by William James (1890) in the virtual forms of 'the stream of thought' and by Anton Ehrenzweig (1967) in the 'blurred plasticity' and 'scattered attention' of primary-secondary thinking. Traditional sociological accounts of mass society miss its compositional nature when they interpret their 'undifferentiated mass' in terms of an 'aggregate of individuals'. Their sense of 'individual'—though never explicitly discussed—is of finite human subjects who live in large-scale collectivities and who relate to each other from within their separate pyscho-somatic boundaries. The more primitive sense of 'individual' whose 'un-dividual' boundary is *shared* with others, and is therefore also *undivided* from them, is lost; in this interpretation the individual person is an uncertain and aleatory part of a larger mobile mass, and is at best 'merely one instance of provisionally stabilized and bounded being' (Bersani and Dutoit, 1993: 8). In this latter sense, social mass is a dynamically inlocatable field of trans-actions that radically undermine the fiction of a self-contained human subject. Any 'I' is the transient and uncertain result of boundaries dynamically shared with 'you', 'he', 'she', 'it' and 'them'. This shared 'I' is therefore *common* and *communal* in the most radical sense of a boundary as that which *separates and joins at the same time*.

> The boundaries of being given to us by [these] pronouns are at once external and internal: they help us to locate where we stop and others begin, but at the same time the beginnings of others are inseparable from the consciousness of self . . . There is no moment of self-identification that is not also a self-multiplication or dispersal.
>
> (Bersani and Dutoit, 1993: 75)

Social mass in this sense is the struggle of individual forms—human subjects, events, institutions—to emerge out of the half-forms and blurred distinctions of primary thinking into secondary consciousness; equally, it is the struggle of individualized, secondary forms against losing themselves in the half-forms and blurred distinctions of primary mass.

Modern mass society is the gigantic enactment of this creative struggle between primary and secondary forces. Its systems of mass production are less concerned with the creation of finished, secondary objects for the consumer's convenience and much more strategically focused on the production of *parts*. Whole objects suggest completion, finiteness, while parts presume transition, transience. The automobile leaves the factory as a seemingly whole object but its apparent wholeness is a secondary aspect of the part-assembly strategy that distinguishes mass production in general. To underlines this point, we may note that the automobile leaves the factory still essentially incomplete—awaiting its human driver, who is simply another part in this moving, unfinished assemblage. The mass production of parts characterizes mass society as a space of 'becoming' in which objects have at best a provisional existence, serving the need for movement and the displacement of presence; 'parts, in the long run, are the carriers of "being", not wholes, which are no more than the provisional array of parts' (Fisher, 1991: 213). Parts carry, and what they carry is a fundamental sense of incompletion that compels us to reinterpret *wholes* as *holes* or the missing links of mass. In this sense the emphasis on parts reconstitutes our ways of seeing the world. Instead of clearly formed objects with clear meanings and purposes, the active movement of parts lateralizes the perception of focused, substantive forms to the intervals between them: 'the configuration of parts at any moment is an interval of objecthood that is permutable, reassociable' (Fisher, 1991: 213). The part thus exposes the action of mediation *within* intervals or gaps and so questions our conventional ways of seeing intervals as absolute divisions between objects; permutable and reassociable, parts enact that primitive process of communion and communication as 'the crossing of intervals' created by absence and vagueness (Bersani, 1986: 26). Parts move us towards 'the undifferentiated unconscious' of primary process where the world becomes 'more plastic and real (although less clearly defined)' than the finite objects and events of secondary thinking (Ehrenzweig, 1967: 12). The logic of parts-production returns us to our earlier understanding of primal mass as a plastic genesis of superfluent possibilities; like the letters of the alphabet, the 'central set of parts . . . to open to assembly into finite combinations—words', and words, in their turn, do not merely represent the world but, by crossing it's intervals and gaps, compose mobile and mutable jigsaw in which the parts of the human body mediate external objects so as to deny their separateness: the domestic cup has a *hand-le* and a *lip*, jars have *mouths*, bottles have *necks*, chairs have *arms and legs* (Fisher, 1991: 247, 244). Language and mass production condense in a common strategy of 'scattered attention' and 'blurred plasticity' in which generalized suggestion and allusion supplant the perception and representation of clear, specific, bounded forms.

In its general strategy of object dissipation, mass production 'creates a space of uncertain or doubtful forms, of forms neither present not absent' (Bersani, 1986: 105). This view of mass production dramatically opposes its conventional interpretation as the mass provider of useful and reliable goods and services. Instead of a rationally conceived human world purposefully constructed for conscious use and understanding, the mass production of parts opens up a space of self-multiplication and dispersion; instead of the immediacy of solid presence, we are presented with the continuous displacement of presence, where 'nonpresentness' becomes the major motive of 'human attention and expression' (Bersani, 1986: 26). 'Nonpresentness' reminds us of a neglected feature of the taken-for-granted world of everyday objects: the existence of each positive form depends upon a reciprocal absence or negative space. Mass parts-production capitalizes on this insight in scattering and shattering our conventional perception of a reliable object-world and substituting for it 'a space of uncertain or doubtful forms' that are 'neither present nor absent' (Bersani, 1986: 105). Foregrounding parts and the moving intervals between them at the expense of static objects shows the world to be not so much a rationally knowable structure but more a plastic space of infinite possibilities in and from which forms both merge and emerge in a continuous 'becoming'.

Freud's (1960) famous analysis of verbal slippage in everyday communication illustrates the continuous presence of the unconscious as a version of 'nonpresentness': 'This book isolated and made analysable things which had heretofore floated along unnoticed in the broad stream of perception' (Benjamin, 1970: 237). For Freud, mistakes in speech represented obtrusions by the primary process into the conventional and practical order of secondary thinking; while they only momentarily disturb surface understanding, their real significance for Freud lay in their suggestion of an unrecognizable primal space whose 'nonpresentness' motivates the routine, taken-for-granted presences of everyday life. The technology of the camera, especially the movie camera, revealed to the eye a similar primal space that Walker Benjamin called the *optical unconscious*, in which close-ups and slow motion disclose 'entirely new structural formations' beneath the conventional surfaces of our routinely stable world—formations that seem to glide and float like supernatural presences (Benjamin, 1970: 238). The camera's capacity to trope and twist the world of knowable and reliable forms was technology's way of revealing the undifferentiation and 'blurred plasticity' already explored as a definitive feature of primary process by artists as well as by Freud (Ehrenzweig, 1967). Like Freud's exploration of the unconscious, the camera dramatically unsettled our habituated expectation of a world of stable, predictable forms and meanings.

The modern mass media combine camera and text in ways that seem deliberately designed to remind us of the ever-presentness of absence and the unconscious. The modern media appear as hyperactive transmissions of that absence and unfoundedness we noted earlier as prelinguistic reminders of the religious Mass, whose *missions* are negative messages we feel compelled to make present. The daily newspaper not only makes absence physically present to its readers' minds and bodies by presenting messages of distant events in the manageable space of its newsprint, but it also illustrates a more radical version of absence in the crossed or mixed words and meanings of its *crossword*. The newspaper divides its reported events into a series of sections—international, national, financial, sport—whose contents it then narrates in referential language so that the reader uses this language as though it naturally refers to a world that is already 'out there' and already has meaning. But the crossword suggests that the words and the ideas used to make the everyday world present to us are themselves subject to continuous degeneration and recession in that they are harassed on all sides by the negative messages of primal mass or absence. Absence here does not mean presence somewhere else but 'ab-sense' or 'off-sense' as primary, undifferentiated mass, which, like Weber's 'meaningless infinity', is a pervasive absence or immanent negativity so necessary to the production of positive presences. The newspaper, subject to the dissolution of sense that radical absence represents, as to repeat its presentations of the world on a daily basis, otherwise our sense of both presence and absence would disappear and with it the sense of mass society's own presence. Absence in this sense is a form if negation that presence requires for its appearance: a positive presence, in other words, derives its identity from that which it is *not*. Presence has to reassert itself continuously against its displacement by absence. The mass media thus do not simply represent a series of external, objective events; rather, they repeatedly make present—that it, *re-present*—forms that would otherwise recede into an horizon of nothingness.

In this interpretation, the mass media become the *media of mass* in the proto-religious sense of mass as a space of infinite and implicit possibilities that awaits some form of finite and explicit determination. The newspaper is merely one element of a massive, global technology whose business is to translate this infinitude of mass into the 'meaningless finities' of readily readable media reports and commentary. As the same time the newspaper occupies an ambiguous position between reporting, on the one hand, events as meaningful and consistent presences and, on the other hand, events that displace any idea of a world of full forms and absolute presences. The development of new technologies in photo-journalism has not only contributed to this revelation of the world as a theatre of changing forms but has also revealed the newspaper as an active agent in the displacement of presence. In the 1920s the telephoto lens began to be used as a mobile means of capturing the institutionalized presences of public life in 'unguarded moments' of relaxed informality: public figures were photographed from a safe distance to expose such private, oblique behaviour as political button-holing or inebriation (Russell, 1971: 68). Later developments in phototechnology and mass motorization led to the paparazzi phenomenon, which even more dramatically revealed the potential of the new media technologies to displace the stability of conventional forms. The paparazzi, enabled by a combination of ever more mobile cameras and personal transport, transformed 'the photographic moment into a kind of provocation' in the Rome of the 1950s (Mormorio, 1999: 26). Instant photography revealed public figures in their unguarded moments and often disclosed the desultory and even wanton behaviour behind their formally presented images. The paparazzi showed the world of institutionalized and authoritative forms to be double-edged and devious. The tabloid newspaper had no fixed stance and sought to report any event that would *provoke* the interest of its readers. Commenting on Federico Fellini's film *La Dolce Vita*, whose main character is a paparazzo who haunts the social scene of urban Rome looking for and even provoking convention-shattering events to report, the novelist Alberto Moravia emphasizes the director's skill in parading the mutable, disintegrative and irrational aspects of modern urban existence: the film reflects an urban life that has no plot, no beginning or end, no logical, coherent development but merely 'infinite repetition' (cited in Mormorio, 1999: 34). Moravia's 'infinite repetition' is the repetition of the finite as that primal, raw and forever unfinished origin that sources all our attempts to re-cover— that is, to cover over again—the world as a rational arrangement of meaningful events. Fellini's paparazzo works like the crossword compiler: by presenting the immanent negativity or non-presentation behind the positive presences directly reported in the newspaper, they both reveal social mass to be a 'blurred plasticity' of ever-changing forms that also seem to emerge and recede simultaneously in a superfluid movement of infinite, unfinished matter.

The technologies of the media portray mass less as the scene of gross aggregates of finished forms and objects more as the mutable origin of the variable manifestations of a receding negative space. In this sense, social mass is the endless dialectic between an unlocatable primary ground and our secondary strategies to translate it into locatable and meaningful forms, however transient these may be. Social mass thus appears to us as always in excess of the local and locatable meanings we give it; it is *mass* in the literal sense of being *massive* or 'too much' for secondary consciousness to grasp. Although the primary is an unlocatable, negative ground that recedes from every attempt to approach it, it is also that which sources and invisibly contains the multiple secondary manifestations of social mass. The alien vagueness and generant plasticity of the primary acts as a necessary provoker of secondary elaborations in the same sense that Weber saw his 'meaningless infinity' as the casual incitement of his 'convenient fictions'. The globalization of information in the late-modern world exemplifies this elaboration of the secondary into the alluring foreign and vacant spaces of the primary.

Globalization itself is merely one step in the pursuit of the primary by the secondary; it is already being superseded by current corporate plans to domesticate outer space as vacation playgrounds. The globalized world and the appropriation of outer space are contemporary illustrations of the continuing human preoccupation with mass as that excess of meaning through which the primary ceaselessly provokes or calls out the secondary. Here we are reminded of Ortega y Gasset's claim that the 'consumption' of space and time was perhaps the chief emerging feature of early mass society, with its extension of 'the cosmic horizon' and its opening of the space of possibilities at the margins of planetary space (1932: 45). All this simply underlines the general significance of the primary-secondary dialectic for understanding modern mass society as a hyperactive production-consumption system that is based on the continuous requirement of the social mass to bring near what is far, to convert the foreign into the familiar, to make clearly visible and manipulable what is remote and vague.

# REFERENCES

Bataille, Georges (1985) *Visions of Excess: Selected Writings, 1927–1939*. Minneapolis: University of Minnesota Press.

Benjamin, Walter (1970) *The Freudian Body: Psychoanalysis and Art*. New York: Columbia University Press.

Bersani, Leo and Ulysse Dutoit (1993) *Arts of Impoverishment: Beckett, Rothko, Resnais*. Cambridge, MA: Harvard University Press.

Durkheim, Emile (1933) *The Division of Labor in Society*. New York: Macmillan.

Ehrenzweig, Anton (1967) *The Hidden Order of Art: A Study in the Psychology of Artistic Imagination*. London: Weidenfeld & Nicholson.

Fisher, Philip (1991) *Making and Effacing Art: Modern American Art in a Culture of Museums*. New York: Oxford University Press.

Freud, Sigmund (1960) *The Psychopathy of Everyday Life, The Complete Psychological Works of Sigmund Freud*, Vol. VI, ed. James Strachey and Anna Freud. London: Hogarth/Institute of Psycho-Analysis.

Hughes, H. Stuart (1959) *Consciousness and Society: The Reorientation of European Social Thought, 1890–1930*. London: MacGibbon & Kee.

James, William (1890) *The Principles of Psychology*. New York: Holt.

Kornhauser, Walter A. (1968) 'Mass Society', pp. 58–64 in David L. Sills (ed.) *International Encyclopaedia of the Social Sciences*, Vol. 10. New York: Macmillan/Free Press.

Lyotard, Jean-François (1993) *Libidinal Economy*. London: Athlone.

Mormorio, Diego (1991) *Tazio Secchiaroli: Greatest of the Paparazzi*. New York: Harry N. Abrams, Inc.

Ortega y Gasset, José (1932) *The Revolt of the Masses*. London: George Allen & Unwin.

Otto, Rudolf (1926) *The Idea of the Holy*. London: Humphrey Milford/Oxford University Press.

Poirier, Richard (1992) *Poetry and Pragmatism*. London: Faber & Faber.

Russell, John (1971) *Francis Bacon*. London: Thames & Hudson.

Shils, Edward (1962) 'The Theory of Mass Society', *Diogenes* 39: 45–66.

Weber, Max (1948) *From Max Weber: Essays in Sociology*. London: Routledge & Kegan Paul.

Weber, Max (1949) *The Methodology of the Social Sciences*. New York: Free Press.

# 13 Making Present
## Autopoiesis as Human Production

*Robert Cooper*

(*Organization*, 2006, 13/1: 59–81. Reproduced by permission of SAGE Publications Ltd., London, Los Angeles, New Delhi, Singapore and Washington DC, Copyright © SAGE publications.)

**Abstract:** *In Niklas Luhmann's social theory, autopoiesis is the repeated work of human self-construction through which social and cultural forms are maintained against a background of their continuous dissolution and disappearance. Autopoiesis in this sense is the production and reproduction of the human world through which the human body constitutes and reconstitutes itself by making the raw material of the world fit the requirements of the body and its organs. Human production thus makes the world present to the human body and its parts such as we see in the examples of the supermarket which brings together the products of the world in one space for our visual and manual convenience and the domestic television set which literally brings home to us to the distant happenings of the world. Human systems and institutions can thus be seen as means for making the world's materials fit the human mind and body and for ensuring their continuous presence as meaningful forms. But, significantly, the production of presence depends on absence, disappearance and decay. Absence has to be seen as a major force in human production; it is the missing presence that haunts all human work and which helps us to understand the development of such modern production methods as mass production and information technology.*
**Key words.** *Absence; autopoiesis, being; division; presence; production; relationally.*

Everything human begins with *division*. The act of human birth is the first and perhaps most dramatic example of division as creative beginning from which follows that endless stream of productive elaborations we call human culture. And culture makes vision out of division. Division cleaves or cuts out a distinguishable space and is thus an act of *fission, but* it is also an act of *fusion* with the indistinguishable ground from which it is cloven. As material marks, *vision, fission* and *fusion* suggest a degeneration into a common space where they begin to lose their specific forms and meanings.

This is one way of approaching Niklas Luhmann's interpretation of auto-poiesis, which we might define as the cultivation of humanized forms out of the humus of uncomposed matter. For Luhmann, the state of uncomposed matter is that necessary 'unmarked space' he posits as 'an inaccessible pre-condition' for all human cultivation and making.

Let's begin, as Luhmann does, with some basic insights from the work of George Spencer Brown. And let us return to the act of human birth as an example of division. Spencer Brown generalizes the act of human birth as ontological division in which human being emerges. Division at this the primal level is that original distinction of the human out of the homogeneity of uncomposed matter. The human as homogene cuts itself in two: a state that *sees* or distinguishes and a state that is *seen* or is distinguished. As homogene, the human is by definition *only partially* itself. Whatever it sees and distinguishes can only ever be a *part* of that original distinguishable mass from which it served itself and in which 'it will always partially elude itself' (Spencer Brown, 1969: 105). In this process of self-construction, the human sees parts of the world more specifically but what it sees is 'only a minor aspect of all being'; its specificity or 'particularity is the price we pay for its visibility' (Spencer Brown, 1969: 106). This is what Luhmann (2000, 91) calls 'the invisibilization that accompanies making something visible'.

All this means that human autopoiesis derives from the incompleteness intrinsic to its homogeneity: activated always by its particularity and par-tialness, the human system seeks its invisible remainder in the necessary 'unmarked space' external to itself. Luhmann expresses this as part of the functional work of the system which needs to get rid of its clutter of past and present impressions so as to open itself to new thoughts and experiences: '. . . the continuing dissolution of the system becomes a necessary cause of its autopoietic reproduction. . . . All structures of social systems have to be based on this fundamental fact of vanishing events, disappearing gestures or words that are dying away' (Luhmann, 1986: 180). But there is another side to the human system's functional need to reproduce itself: it has to return to 'the paradox of a beginning that presupposes itself' where *beginning* is a rough condition of incompleteness or *becoming* and where a 'determined form always promises something else with defining it. It dissolves the homo-geneity of the unmarked space—everything that is not form—into a space replete with suggestions . . .' (Luhmann, 2000: 30–1).

In this introductory sketch of autopoiesis, certain terms strike us: partial-ness, incompleteness, invisibility, dissolution, vanishing. The act of human birth as an act of primal division is here presented as an agonistic field where vision, fission, fusion have to do creative battle, thus reminding us of Spencer Brown's (1966: 105) brief note on *act* as originating in *agonistics*. Autopoiesis tells us that human life is a series of self-constituting acts of creative division, acts which tell us that human life is a continuous pro-cess of founding and finding, re-founding and re-finding, oneself in a world motivated by incompleteness, decay and disappearance. The act of birth is an act of projection into a world the human being does not know but which is already there, ready with its social and cultural scripts to inscribe the newborn into its ways of being, its ways of founding and re-founding itself. This is how the cybernetic thinkers Terry Winograd and Fernando Flores (1986) interpret Maturana's original thoughts on autopoiesis when they suggest that Heidegger's concept of human *throwness* or projected being helps throw significant light on the general nature of autopoiesis and its more specific application to the human-computer relationship. Thrownness is a form of rough beginning or becoming from which the practical knowledge of the human world is extracted: human practice originates in the vague, implicit and incomplete; practice and knowledge are expressions of the human body and its organs in their interactions with the tools and objects of the physical world; a human being is essentially *social* and *interactive* and never simply a property of individual agents. Human being in this sense is another way of saying autopoiesis in the human context where agents act out and express a set of forces much larger and more extensive than themselves, and which forever remain never fully realized. Heidegger calls this condition *Dasein*, the continuous process of human being forming and expressing itself through the supports and incipient possibilities of everyday existence; 'A person is not an individual subject or ego, but a manifestation of *Dasein*, within a space of possibilities, situated within a world and within a tradition' (Winograd and Flores, 1986: 33). Thrownness as active being-in-the-world also means that the *fission* and *fusion* of *division* make being always pro-*vision*-al—perhaps appropriate and adequate for a particular occasion but no more than that. The forms of being are no more than temporary stabilizations, provisional events with aleatory boundaries. They seem to suggest that the space opened up by division is an infinite and bottomless receptacle—the *void* or empty space of *divide*—in which being tries to find its place. Here again we meet the 'unmarked space' and the 'inaccessible precondition' that leads Luhmann to talk of 'the invisibilization that accompanies making something visible'. It's as if some absent power were sending messages to say it is here, always here, even though it can never be directly observed. The *void* of *divide* where *vision, fission* and *fusion* meet in a degenerative, common space now appears to us as a *missing presence* whose absence literally makes possible the multiple presences that constitute the being of everyday life. Presence is a form of thrownness, a sensing of something that comes before us, a *pre-sence* of a prior power of which we are projections. Spatial presence and the temporal present come together as expressions of the missing presence incipient to division.

## MAKING ABSENCE PRESENT

Basic to Luhmann's presentation of autopoiesis in the context of social and cultural systems is the co-dependence of the positive and the negative which cannot exist without each other: marked *and* unmarked, visible *and* invisible, appearance *and* disappearance—all are co-definitive and even degenerative in the same way as primal division. Yet Luhmann seems to say more than this: that the positive is a product of its negative context, that marked forms emerge out of unmarked spaces, that absence is the hidden ghost behind those transient guests we call the visible supports of being, and even perhaps that the *present* is a *gift* that is provisionally *given* to us by a power we can only vaguely divine. A long and honourable tradition lies behind much of what Luhmann offers us; we see echoes of his thought in earlier religious and cultural thinking, perhaps not surprisingly in view of the immanence of his basic concepts to the very texture of pragmatic being. Eastern thought and practice still preserves and expresses this autopoietic sense of everyday being in which forms emerge more as a mutable compositions rather than static structures. Again, it is a question of the vision of division.

Vision, as we've noted, comes in two interacting forms: *fission* and *fusion*. Fission exemplifies Luhmann's marked spaces, the specified and specific spaces we consciously look for in directing ourselves through the labyrinth of objects and events of everyday life. Fusion reminds us that marked spaces depend on a generic unmarked space, and that fission is an attempt to fissure (and thus, we might add, to *fixture*) the degenerate and devious tendencies of its unmarked origin, which seem always to call back the marked spaces to their place of birth in the humus of uncomposed matter. All forms obey this pattern as the following illustration of the flower tells us. We see the flower normally as a separate, self-contained entity, and this is because we place it in a static frame that distinguishes it from its wider, unmarked context. The frame is a marking device that invites the viewing subject to look only at its content and nothing else. When the frame is withdrawn, the marked content begins to merge or fuse with its unmarked background. It is this unmarked background that the Japanese philosopher Keiji Nishitani calls 'emptiness' or 'radical impermanence', and it is this unmarked background that we screen out in distinguishing the forms we try to fix. In the case of the flower:

> Its existence is only a *phase* of incremental transformations between seed and dust, in a continuous exfoliation or perturbation of matter . . . Moved on to the field of . . . radical impermanence, the entity comes apart. It cannot be said to occupy a *single* location, since its locus is always the universal field of transformations; it cannot achieve, separation from that field or acquire any kind of bounded outline.
>
> (Bryson, 1988: 97–8)

The flower is never a thing on its own right, never something singularly positive; it exists as a *trans-form* of a wider, dynamic field. This is also how we have to see the flower's seed as well as the dust in which it ends. Each of the flower's different states or forms is a product of a more inclusive, generic space which in itself never appears.

The example of the flower is reflected in the words of language which are never singularly meaningful. The definition of a word in the dictionary is presented to us through *other* words. And in conversation and reading, the meaning of a word is revealed only as we proceed through its general context: 'As one reads a sentence, one does not know what a word in mid-sentence means until one reaches the end of the sentence, and that sentence in turn changes as one moves to the next sentence, or paragraph, or page' (Bryson, 1988: 98). Meaning is thus far from stable and more like a temporary stopping pace which never arrives at a final destination. Meaning is never fully present and is more like an unsettled sense 'in a continuous motion of postponement' (Bryson, 1988: 99). Here, we have Nishitani's field of radical impermanence where creative absence keeps us always on the move. It is also the unmarked space that Luhmann views as 'an inaccessible precondition' for autopoiesis as well as the invisibilization necessary for making something visible; it is also a way of understanding Spencer Brown's original indistinguishable space from which the human self serves as a *part* or visible particular and in which 'it will always partially elude itself'.

Flower, word and human self are thus examples of the *throwness* that constitutes human being. Their presence is always a *pre-sense* of an imminent yet ungraspable absence, or that missing presence which lies within and behind every act of division or distinction, every act of form-making. Presence is the *pre-sense* of that originary absence or *off-sense* of Nishitani's field of radical impermanence; it is the vague sensing of an invisibilization that lies beyond—and yet within—all the visible, positive objects and forms that make up the visuality of our everyday being. Throwness as pre-sense hints at the missing presence of absence; it reminds the observer that every object or form is the product of a frame that *excludes* the surrounding context. This is also Luhmann's (2000) way of thinking the visible world: for him, the work of art in the gallery is made present to us through its exclusion of the rest of the world as an unmarked space. And yet it is this absent remainder that centrally constitutes the visible object, which needs to be seen as something *pre-sented* out of the multiple possibilities that make up the object's remainder—the other possible and uncountable perspectives on the object which the viewer's *partial* siting/sighting as to exclude (Bryson, 1988: 103). How can we begin to think of the presence of forms as being actively constituted by the excluded remainder of unmarked space, by' the surrounding envelope of invisibility' (Bryson, 1988: 103)? It is here that throwness comes in.

The act of birth throws the human body into an invisibility of unmarked space. The body then founds and finds itself through a primal act of division which engenders the self as a collection of organs—eyes, hands, brain, nerves, etc.—that actively work on the physical matter of the world. The body's organs interact with the surfaces of the world in a multiplicity of ways, from the simple impression of a footprint in the snow to the imprinting of words on the pulp of the forest now transformed into newsprint. Both footprint and newsprint mark themselves out of a wider, indefinite contexts or margins of invisibility which remind us of the surrounding field of radical impermanence from which all our forms come and to which they return. And with these examples we too return to the mutual relationship between *fission* and *fusion* in the dialectic of division where vision is always constituted *by that which it is not*. Again, we meet the essence of the thrownness of human being which expresses its incompleteness through the temporary framing of a space that continually threatens it. Among the more vivid expressions of thrownness as being that is constituted by its more comprehensive negative space are the flung-ink technologies of Oriental painting and calligraphy; both aesthetic practices expose the fixed form to the random possibilities of the surrounding unmarked negative space. As the ink is thrown, it exposes the fixed form to the vicissitudes that lie beyond its boundaries; the physical and mental gesture of throwing is revealed to be part of the space from which it tries to sever itself. 'The image is made to float on the forces which lie outside the frame; it is *thrown*, as one throws dice. What breaks *into* the image is the rest of the universe, everything outside of the frame' (Bryson, 1988: 103). The image is no longer rigidly held in place by its fixed frame. When the movement of the calligrapher's hand is slow and deliberate, the graphic tracings obey the framework of control already prescribed by the fixed form of the calligraphic characters. When the hand's movement is accelerated, 'the ink flies faster than the hand can control it, and to areas of the paper or silk beyond the sway of the character's prescribed structure. It breaks free from the subject who controls it, and from scriptural form' (Bryson, 1988: 103–4). The calligrapher connects with the pre-sense of an absence which he or she begins to recognize as the *missing remainder* of a partial vision. It is this missing remainder which re-minds us that there is no such thing as pure presence and that we are haunted by allusion and suggestion. For Nishitani, this is the infinite space of all origins, the space of beginnings and becomings, of the simultaneous emergence *and* mergence of forms, and where nothing is allowed to complete itself. It is the very spirit of autopoiesis as ongoing incipience and initiation.

The production of human culture is autopoietic in this special sense of never completing itself. Human being is the autopoiesis or the making over of the forever absent primary space of being. Primary being is absent in a special sense: it withdraws from every attempt to represent it; it 'contains something like a hostility to its own presentations . . .' (Gadamar, 1976: 226). What we make present or re-present in human culture simply echoes this more pervasive absence, and we ourselves as the autopoietic products of thrownness are mere reflections of this absence that seems to *call* us into being. This is the primal absence or unmarked space of division. We need to remind ourselves that division is not only an act of binary severing which enables us to distinguish (at least) two separate terms; it also makes a space *between* the separate terms and this common space is 'the invisibilization that accompanies making something visible' (Luhmann, 2000: 91). We normally see only the separate terms of the marked space but it is the marked space that we move across in our daily acts of being. The reading of a message is a series of crossings between words and between the letters that make up the individual words. It is the continuous crossings *between* the marked elements of being that move us rather than the meanings and representations we ascribe to the words of the message. The divided spaces keep us moving and not the individual terms which are simply temporary stopping places on a journey that has no final goal or destination.

Language is less a system for representing the world and for communicating our representations of it to each other and more a means of founding and finding ourselves among the primal absence that divisions reveal as constituting power of human being. We do not speak language; it is rather that language speaks us. This is precisely Nishitani's point when he says that we are moved to create by the radical impermanence and emptiness intrinsic to all forms of vision. The emptiness of primal absence calls to us as if to plead: help my *spaces speak*. *Spacing* and speaking thus each re-mind us of their mutual origin in the primal act of division; both say the same thing: to speak is to reveal space, to reveal space is to speak it. In the same way, emptiness and radical impermanence—despite their indefiniteness and resistance to form—somehow have to be expressed. Even the unmarked space has to be marked in some way by language. Again, we see the primal division at work; it not only generates a marked space but at the same time reveals a space that has yet to be marked. It is another version of the flung-ink technique of Oriental calligraphy in which the marked character recognizes its dependence on the missing remainder. The emptiness of the unmarked space thus appears as the missing presence absence in all our conscious markings. This di-vision—or double vision—of the marked-unmarked also appears in other contemporary fields of analysis. In psychoanalysis, the relation between the conscious mind—the structure of marked space—and the unconscious—made up of unmarked space—is viewed as an effect of primal division. The unconscious is not marginal to the conscious mind; they define each other just as absence defines presence and vice versa: 'just as the cry does not stand out against a background of silence, but on the contrary makes the silence emerge as silence' (Lacan, 1979: 26). And just as the empty space of silence activates the cry, so does the unconscious motivate the movings of the conscious mind, appearing as a *lack* that has yet to be completed. No longer a repository of incomprehensible, unwelcome or menacing spectra, the unconscious functions as a missing presence whose absence or lack continually provokes us to complete it. A similar perspective on space is offered by chaos theory where unmarked space appears as a series of intermittent gaps between the marked spaces of information. Every form or item of information is accompanied by its absence just as a cry is inhabited by its silence or a conscious thought by its unconscious remainder.

When, for example, we read an academic text, we expect a sense of readability and meaningful flow:

> Yet this unity or sense of flow or movement is at the same time made up of jumps over gaps, juxtapositions, leaps—unpredictable, irregular . . . so, continuous as the process of narration might seem, the closer we inspect monographs, paragraphs, sentences, the more aware we are of internal discontinuities . . . Certainty itself appears partial, information intermittent. An answer is another question, a connection, a gap, a similarity a difference, and vice versa.
>
> (Strathern, 1991: xxiii-iv).

As we have already noted, the reading of a message is a series of crossings *between* the marked elements of being, *between* the letters and the words that make up communication. In short, we seem to cross *out* as well as *cross over* the unmarked spaces that all messages carry within themselves. Chaos theory adds something else to the observation: namely, that the *betweens* of crossings return us to a primal condition of partialness and incompleteness in which the individually marked terms of question and answer, connection and gap, similarity and difference, seem to decompose and fuse into each other. *Between* becomes another way of saying *division* as the missing presence that inhabits all binary distinctions.

Presence is thus never the complete, full presence of an object or event. Presence is never the immediacy of the here-and-now. Presence is the presense of an absence or gap that invites us to re-cover it as thrownness or projection; it is sense in continuous movement, always supplementing itself in an onward movement of deferral and anticipation. It does not and it cannot appear as a finite, finished form since its thrownness and non-immediacy means that is it neither fully present nor fully absent but forever suspended *between* the two.


## PRODUCING PRESENCE

Let us remind ourselves of Luhmann's interpretation of autopoiesis as life continually reproducing itself from dissolution and loss. Events, words, gestures come and go in a continuous flux, and it is this coming and going which specifically characterizes autopoiesis as the infinite flow of life. For Luhmann, the unmarked space of Spencer Brown's primal act of distinction is where autopoiesis begins. In our analysis, we are suggesting that absences, gaps and intervals are also ways of saying unmarked space. These various forms of absence announce themselves through the presence of marked spaces such as the letters, words and sentences that constitute spoken and written language. All communication, we are suggesting, emanates from absence as missing presence.

Thrownness and projection represent human being as a continuous process of finding and re-finding ourselves against a background that significantly lacks foundation. Thrownness means that we are forever borne on waves of *provisionality* which not only suggest transience, but also the means or provisions for anticipating and searching for ourselves in the mobile supplementarity of human being. Presence is provisional in that is provides temporary locations through which being can structure its future. In this sense, presence is form of *prediction* but not in the conventional sense of knowing the future or predicting an event according to the technical logic of statistical probability; prediction is the actual *production* of presence, the making present of that unlocatable space of absence of lack that motivates all our everyday acts of being. But all this is an ever-receding presence whose provisionality makes it prospective instead of fully present in the here-and-now. It is more like a *pre-sensing* of possibilities, of vague and hazy forms that will always remain vague and hazy. The presence of human beings as perceptual pre-sense reveals the essential incompleteness of being human.

In the philosophy of pragmatism, human incompleteness is the source of human production. William James' version of pragmatism rests on a conception of human being adds a 'stream of thought'—much like Heidegger's thrownness and Nishitani's radical impermanence—where flux, fusion, vagueness and gaps seem to carry us along rather than precise definition and objective clarity. Like Luhmann, James gives priority to the unmarked spaces that lie between the conscious marks of human communication; these unmarked spaces generate a sense of creative vagueness in which we are never really sure what we are thinking and saying, only that we have to jump over the gaps and abysses that pervade and surround every turn of our being. James's pragmatism of being at this point is strikingly similar to Lacan's view of the unconscious as a lack that the conscious mind has yet to complete as well as to chaos theory's understandings of space as a series of intermittent gaps which we have to cross over and cross out in order to move through the thrownness of human being. Each of these approaches to the way the mind travels in space recognizes the crude presence of *something* that resists formalization and which we can only fleetingly and indirectly sense. The *soul* is a traditional name for this *something* that can never be located, defined and therefore known. Soul was an early religious way of saying unmarked space. Like Oriental painting and calligraphy, which also found and find themselves in an absent *something*, soul is that original 'creative impulse' which 'discovers in the very first stages of composition that it wants to reach out beyond any legible form, that it wants to seek the margins, to move beyond limits or fate' (Poirier, 1992: 24–5). Soul returns us to an initiatory acts of composition or, in the words of the early pragmatist philosopher Ralph Waldo Emerson, to the 'preamble of thought, the transition through which it passes from the unconscious to the conscious' (quoted in Poirier, 1992: 25). The vague *something* of the soul never comes to full presence; like Luhmann's 'paradox of a beginning that presupposes itself', it is a perpetual process of *becoming* and 'only promises to make its presence known' without ever fully doing so (Poirier, 1992: 24). As original incompleteness, soul is the infinite source of all human production—economic, aesthetic, literary, scientific, technical—which it activates by 'always receding, drawing or provoking us . . . into every greater volatilities, meanderings, or excesses of usage' (Poirier, 1992: 46).

Ordinary language is necessarily part of James's 'stream of thought' in which waves of vagueness carry us along in that 'great human repertoire of muttering and murmuring' which 'remains free floating of any fixed point' (Poirier, 1992: 154). Its intrinsic restlessness and mutability makes language more messy, more blurred than perhaps we'd like but by the same token it is more malleable and hence more productive of new horizons and the possibilities and opportunities they suggest and incite. Language is thus shadowed by an inveterate missing presence—the soul's *something*—that demands we *somehow* complete it, at least momentarily, in order to repeat and defer, and thus preserve, its power to create and motivate the production of human culture. If the worlds and meanings of language were precisely fixed and logically defined—that is, were always fully present—human being would experience no thrownness, no sense of becoming, no anticipation of possibilities, no freedom to re-create its world, merely the constraints of full and explicit presence. In James's pragmatism, the missing presence of language is to be found in its *sounds* and the rich fund of tonal modulations they make possible. Sounds constitute the basis of James's 'stream of thought' and the shaping of sound into a meaningful word is no more—yet no less—than a temporary hold on the 'reality' to which is refers. Sounds, for James, are a form of *pre-sence* or *pre-diction* inasmuch as they pre-exist the precise definitions and finite specificities we try to impose on them; they remind us yet again that human being exists in and gains its power from vague and hazy forms, from its essential incompleteness. Sounds are a way of filling in the gaps and absences that necessarily constitute human communication but because of their intrinsic vagueness they too create gaps and absences that have to be filled in. Sounds come before diction or clear articulation; they are the unmarked spaces of speech which are overlaid by the order and meaning of specific words. In other words, unarticulated sounds has to be divided onto discrete packages of meaning; like the cry and the silence, the sounds and meanings of language engender each other in acts of creative division. And this is precisely how James sees the function of sound in human communication: its absence of clarity, its 'barely enunciated presence', its obscurity and incipience, provide the basic incompleteness that originates human sociability (Poirier, 1992: 140).

'Losing oneself in a world of sound' is how Jean-François Lyotard (1989: 212–9) addresses the theme of absence as the creative source of being in his essay on 'scapeland'. Scapeland—otherwise scopeland, spaceland—is that combination of radical impermanence, emptiness, unconscious remainder, missing presence, unmarked space which comes before all narrative, all definition and all sense-making. Scapeland is Lyotard's way of saying the *pre-sence* of *pre-sence* and *pre-diction*. Scapelands are 'those border-lines where matter offers itself up in a raw state before being tamed', before being submitted to the rationalizing marks of human description, before being landscaped in a mental map (Lyotard, 1989: 217). Like James's char-acterization of the vagueness of sound, Lyotard's scapeland is that which is there before description and definition; it is that which appears 'as the erasure of a support' . . . an absence which stands as a sign of a horrifying presence in which 'mind fails and misses its aim', leaving only 'an excess of presence' (Lyotard, 1989: 216–7). Scapeland is the absence of direction and destination; signless and timeless, it dissolves and withdraws into an innocence of space. Despite worldwide human domestication and techno-logical encroachment, such spaces still exist and still call us to wonder at their unplacability in the wider scheme of human endeavour. The landscape of Nevada, for example, can appear to the sensitive observer as a scapeland lacking in all human signs:

> . . . in the open extensiveness of Nevada . . . it is not easy to gauge whether one is looking at (or waiting for) the past or the future. The landscape. . . . Is so often prehistoric and futuristic at the same time—or, at least, it quickly guides the innocent spirit or imagination into that kind of thinking.
>
> (Thomson, 1999: 75)

Lyotard's deserts are scapelands 'without any destiny', without human sig-nificance, and 'they are therefore disconcerting' non-places that cannot be fitted into the mental menus of human consumption (Lyotard, 1989: 213); deserts return to us that limbo Luhmann calls 'an inaccessible precondition' which precedes all human-centred perception and thought and which, as Lyotard argues, re-minds us of that always present state of 'wretchedness' or impoverishment out of which we cultivate ourselves and to which we finally return. Lyotard calls this 'understanding of wretchedness' a 'void state' of 'superplentitude' from which *poetry* (which we can also call *poiesis)* emerges as a suspended condition between the unmarked space of indeterminate matter and the marked spaces of humanized forms and meanings (Lyotard, 1989: 217). In the 'disconcerting' non-place of the Nevadan desert with its attitude of defiance to all that is human, the *poetry* of *poiesis* emerges in the aesthetic play culture of Las Vegas. At the very edge of urban civilisation, Las Vegas looks out onto a scapeland that lacks all human direction in space and time; it invites us to fill its human absence with directions, with signs and messages that blot out its missing presence by transforming it into a humanized location that provides ever ready answers to its residents' contin-uous calls for the animated conversation of poeticized excitement. Aestheti-cized signs and symbols dominate Las Vegas: 'The graphic sign in space has become the architecture of this language. The sign is more important than the architecture' (Venturi et al., 1977: 13). But these signs are not merely signs of functional direction, they signify much more than the casino, the hotel or the filling station. They play with space and time, and rather than simply copy tradition, they reach out for new possibilities: ancient civilisations such as Rome and Greece are recreated as a collection of 'honky-tonk improvisations' (Venturi et al., 1977: 53): signs taller and wider than buildings project their commercial messages in such strange shapes that seem like products of artists from outer space; the famous Las Vegas strip is a series of shifting configurations that keeps the human eye and body forever at work in selecting and interpreting their clashes and changing significations. Las Vegas *overfills* its desert space with 'an excess of presence' that suggests a 'void state' of 'superplentitude' (Lyotard, 1989: 216–7) which as well as directing its residents to specific, functional ends also points in the direction of an indeterminate, unmarked space which complements the undetermined, directionless space of the surrounding desert. Las Vegas appears as a collective act of thrownness in which its vibrant and stupendous signs, shapes and colours refuse to settle into a coherent whole, thus reminding us of the *becoming* of Oriental painting and calligraphy which breaks free from prescribed control to return us to the autopoiesis of ongoing incipience and initiation.

## HUMAN PRODUCTION

The more-than-signs and aesthetic technologies of Las Vegas are super-sensory experiences made by humans to animate and even eroticize themselves. Despite their apparent other-worldness, they are made to connect with the limbs and the sensory organs of the human bodies that inhabit them. It is this point that Luhmann (2000) makes when he says that perception through the senses is the human way of creating marked spaces out of unmarked, invisible matter. The psychologist James Gibson (1968) views sensory perception not merely as the perceiving or sensing of things but as part of a wider process of *reaching out* by the living organism. In the case of the human being, this reaching or branching out can be seen as the body's trunk—just like the trunk of a tree with its branches and leaves—divides into four limbs and each limb into five digits; the head too is like a limb with its further specialized divisions into organs of seeing, hearing, and tasting. The limbs reach out into the limbo of unknown or unmarked spaces such as Lyotard's non-places or missing presences which are then are appropriated by means of humanized markings. The signs and technologies of Las Vegas work out in a similar way; as extensions of their makers' organs, they reach out into a limbic space—that of the desert of possibilities and rough beginnings—they can only dimly and roughly sense like the incompleteness of James's 'stream of thought' where fusion and vagueness carry us along rather than the full presence of precise and complete definition.

Reaching out, I want to suggest, is a manifest part of human production. All human production is *pre-diction* as the making present of absence, gaps, vagueness and infinity. Reaching out is the recompositon and renewal of the *soul* as that original 'creative impulse' which 'discovers in the very first stages of composition that it wants to reach out beyond any legible form, that it wants to seek the margins, to move beyond limits or fate' (Poirier, 1992: 24–5). This sense of reaching out implies a search for incomplete forms, for elements and parts that have yet to be brought together into meaningful wholes. The designers of the signs and symbols of Las Vegas found their inspiration in a creative limbo of shapes and parts that had not yet found a final pattern of wholeness and their products appeared on the Strip as a volatile collection of relationships that still refused to settle into a coherent whole. The transience of momentary perceptions cuts across the conventional representation of finite objects to remind us of Spencer Brown's (1969) primal act in a division in which human being sees only *parts* of that original indistinguishable mass from which it severed itself. All perception starts and remains in this condition despite all our attempts to cover it over with meaningful structures that provide us with a reassuring sense of full presence. At this stage of perception, 'there are no objects, only parts, and . . . the configuration of parts at any moment of time is an interval of objecthood that is permutable, reassociation, and yet sensible as just-this-thing, in harmony and functional interrelation with itself throughout' (Fisher, 1991: 213). Human production in this context returns us to *acts of composition* as distinct from completed products. Incomplete parts suggest that *betweenness* of the unmarked space or 'the invisibilization that accompanies making something visible' (Luhmann, 2000: 91)— those intervals of objecthood that enable the continuous permutability and reassociation of the parts and elements that make up human being. Here again, we meet presence as a provisional—that is, not just temporary but also anticipative—searching and reaching out to the rough beginning where marked and unmarked spaces emerge. Human being is the thrownness of partial acts which, like James's 'stream of thought', carry us along in an infinite, continuous flow: '. . . parts, in the long run, are the carriers of "being", not wholes, which are no more than provisional arrays of parts' (Fisher, 1991: 213).

At this point we observe a fundamental community between Spencer Brown's idea of primary division and Heidegger's idea of *Dasein*, the being-there of human being. Both refer to a condition of rough beginning where distinctions or divisions are not yet complete, where they condense together in a state of primal degeneration. Spencer Brown's first distinction can be expressed in many different ways since it is a primitive source—just like Lyotard's scapeland—that has yet to find itself; here we have 'a place so primitive that active and passive, as well as a number of other more peripheral opposites, have long since condensed together, and almost any form of words will suggest more categories than there really are' (Spencer Brown,

1969: 84). The *part-ness* of the human actor reflects this aboriginal condition of condensation in which human autopoiesis is the complex work of incomplete *parts* trying to capture their lost homogeneity. Heidegger's treatment of the spatiality and temporality of *Dasein* also starts with the recognition that spatial and temporal distinctions are versions of a more primitive human condition of same-ness or condensation. And this is how Heidegger sees presence and absence—as the division of a more degenerative state of human being which he expresses as *a-partness* (Ent-fernung). Heidegger's *a-partness* is another way of saying that 'parts . . . are the carriers of "being", not wholes, which are no more than the provisional arrays of parts' (Fisher, 1991: 213). As the active constituent of human being, *a-partness* is not the simple physical distance between things but the making *near* of what is *far*. In other words, *a-partness* is the making of presence out of absence; it is also the recognition that the *missingness* of absence is also a *missing presence* in which absence is a *felt* and *implicit* presence that always haunts human being like the shadowing of the visible by the invisible that Luhmann notes. Presence and absence, near and far, are themselves constituted by that basic dynamic of human being we earlier called, following Spencer Brown's analysis of the severed self, *part-ness* or the *simultaneity* of being *both* separate *and* joined or *both* fissured *and* fused. Heidegger's being is thus an active *betweenness* of movement in perpetual suspension and which never comes to rest.

When applied to the human body, *part-ness* necessarily includes all the limbs and sensory organs that reach out to absence and farness. *Part-ness* is thus necessarily part of any act of *production* and *pre-diction* or reaching out by the limbs and sensory organs into spaces and times in which they seek to complete themselves but which their constitutive *part-ness* must refuse. When we think of production-prediction in terms of the movement of parts, we are forced to recognize it as continuous *genesis* rather than the completion of *results*. And it is in this sense that production-prediction complements Heidegger's notion of being as a life process that is never finished but is always *to be*. We note here yet again the similarity between Heidegger's philosophy of being and Spencer Brown's way of thinking the *partial* human actor. It is also the flung-ink technique of Oriental painting and calligraphy which draws attention to the physical act of throwing the paint and ink from the human limbs via the brush to the canvas and paper; the hand and eye of the artist, the paint, the ink, the brush and the paper, are made to appear as incomplete parts of something bigger than themselves. The being of the human body works through the principle of *part-ness* and what we conventionally call production is essentially the reaching out of our body parts for some sense of completion, however, brief and transient. But equally it is the call of the body's parts for the external world to fit into their organic requirements—for the hands to manipulate something that is handleable, for the eyes to be shown something visibly meaningful, for the ears to hear something audibly coherent.

'Every cultural and productive act includes an elaboration of the self outside of the boundaries of the body' (Fisher, 1991: 233). But the 'self' in this context is the physical body of limbs, nervous system and sensory organs whose various parts have to *participate* in the production of a world that is actively present *with* them. The production of presence thus becomes the making of objects that actively materialize not just body parts but *acts of participation* in the world. The spoon, for example, materializes the act of eating in that its handle inversely re-presents the clenched hand, while the bowl of the spoon re-presents the space of the mouth. The domestic chair re-presents the shape of the human body in repose as well as a promised reversal of the state of human tiredness; the tea cup re-presents the hand in its handle and the human lips in its lip (Fisher, 1991: 243–4). As materialized acts, spoon, chair and cup serve to make the human body present to itself, however provisional their use may be. All objects are thus materialized acts that remind us that we are always incomplete, always moving on in a context of missing presences that are nevertheless always co-present.

What we conventionally call *representation* or making images and thoughts that refer to external objects and events has now to be seen in the more radical context of human being as *re-present-ation* or the production of presence out of absence. Human culture is a complex of the multiple presences of the non-human world, including nature, that are made to fir the body's parts and to answer their continuous calls for completion. The dynamic, never-ending interaction between presence and absence is like a conversation marked by questions and answers. The early farmers made the grass of the fields say 'milk' which eventually appeared on our breakfast tables along with other refined natural products such as cereals. The trees of the forest were converted into pulp, pulp into paper, paper into books and newsprint that could be held in the hand and before the eye. The early developments of industrial society expanded through a series of 'humanized' questions that sought to convert nature's unhumanised potential into products that would respond to the body's calls—in this case, the developing social body of the new mass society—by making 'mountain ranges say "ore" and ore say "iron" and iron say "bridge"' (Fisher, 1991: 242). In all these examples, we observe production as *pre-edition* or the question-answer conversation between the body's limbs and sensory organs and their calls for some sense of completion by presence. Production as *pre-diction* is at the same time the materialization of acts and helps us to understand Spencer Brown's (1969: 105) brief reference to the human *act* as originating in an *ago-nistics* of creative division and struggle in appropriating unhuman absence to human presence.

Human production makes the world present to the human body and its parts: the motor vehicle enables us to reach out to the wider world through its engineered connections with the various bodily organs; the personal computer helps us reach out from the fixed location of our workspace to the multiple communicational spaces offered by globalized cyberspace;

the domestic television set entertains and informs us day and night with immediately visible spectacles of distant goings-on. In these examples, we again see at work Heidegger's insight that the near and the far, presence and absence, are co-present and mutually definitive; they dramatize the *part-ness* of human production where presence is activated by its mutual absence; they illustrate presence as the encapsulating of distant, far-flung, multiple and varied happenings into the convenience of what has been called *hand-made space* (Fisher, 1991: 195–232).

The working spaces of industrial, domestic and personal production are generally located on horizontal and vertical planes close to the hands and eyes of the human producer: the work bench, the office desk, the kitchen worktop, the computer and television screens—all these enable us to manipulate the complex, dynamic and even messy events of the world by dividing them into parts which we can (at least momentarily) fix and focus and thus control. 'Assembly lines, work-benches, counters for the preparation of food, sales counters for the display of commodities that can be picked up: the world of production and consumption locates itself here' (Fisher, 1991: 202). The world of presence appears to us as a kind of table-top where its parts can be readily assembled, reassembled and transformed under the gaze of the eye and through the manipulability of the hand. It is this space of human presence that reaches out to the scapelands of nature and re-presents them to us as table-top products of hand-made space such as we see in the supermarket and the department store. And these products are *pre-dicts* in the very basic sense that they provide *provisional* directions for the thrownness Heidegger noted as characterizing human being: production is an ontological feature of the human condition when understood as a form of *pre-dicting* or projecting human being into the absences of unknown spaces and times. Like Heidegger's analysis of *a-partness* (Ent-fernung) as the mutual creativity of the near and the far, like Lacan's example of the cry and the silence that generate each other, production as *pre-diction* makes present a sense of absence *and* makes absent a sense of presence—as though the human limbs and organs needed to remind themselves that their acts of participation were actively generated by an aboriginal state of *part-ness* and incompletion.

The development of modern industrial production has concentrated on the making of *parts* which we see at its most obvious in the logic of mass production. By definition, parts are incomplete; they have no final sense or meaning; at best, they serve to make up temporary whole objects. The motor vehicle exemplifies this basic sense of incompletion and continuous movement: it is essentially an assemblage of parts which is still incomplete when it leaves the factory for the saleroom where it awaits its next necessary part in the shape of its human driver. All mass-produced objects are partial in this radical sense. They are 'like jigsaw pieces whose outer surfaces have meaning only when it is seen that they are designed to snap into position against the body' (Fisher, 1991: 243). It is in this sense that mass products are intended to serve as parts in a general process of composition rather than as whole objects which enable us to complete a task or reach a goal. Their specific utilitarian purposes take second place to their ceaseless movement between presence and absence, between actuality and possibility. They highlight the human body less as a whole organic identity and more as a collection of limbs and sensory organs that can be assembled, disassembled and reassembled in countless different ways. They point to absent possibilities rather than present actualities. The logic of parts-production emphasizes the call of absence and the power of this call to motivate human being with a continuous questioning of what absence actually is and how it can be made present—as well as the perhaps stranger logic of *betweenness* that makes presence and absence re-create themselves repeatedly out of each other. Parts, therefore, point to something other than themselves, to incompletion and continuous becoming. The drama of the modern world lies in its seduction by motion and its transgression of limits; as a consequence, modern reality is pre-eminently provisional and unsettled. Production is geared to the creation of a composite world of parts rather than whole, finite objects; relationality rather than thinghood becomes the driving force behind modern systems of work and living. This in turn creates a sense of agitated mutability in which 'objects become restless and weak' and subservient to the new reality of 'the system as a whole and to the play of transformations and possibilities that it invites' (Fisher, 1991: 249).

## AUTOPOIESIS AND HUMAN PRODUCTION

Autopoiesis is generally defined as *self-organization* but Luhmann's interpretation, as we have noted, puts the emphasis on continuous self-creation out of dissolution and disappearance. For this reason, I prefer to think of autopoiesis as *self-origination* where *origin* is the primal act of division that *originates* all form. But the origin of primal division lies always in unmarked space and hence is like a receding horizon that continually withdraws when approached. At best, we can feel a rough sense of it but any attempt to present it fully and formally only loses. Spencer Brown (1969) approaches the primal origin as a degenerative and condensed space where all forms are mixed together in an unmappable limbo replete with untold formational possibilities. Our initial discussion of *division* introduced the same idea in suggesting that *vision*, *fission* and *fusion* came from a common source, despite their separate and differing meanings in everyday usage. The three terms suggest they share a common horizon which we cannot directly observe but only glimpse through the interaction of the separate terms. A similar message appears in the psychology of perception where we see in the famous example of Rubin's double profile two faces sharing the same outline yet at the same time repressing each other or in the equally well known wife/mother-in-law figure where a portrait of an attractive young woman shares the same outline with the portrait of her aging mother-in-law. In each of these cases, we are made aware by suggestion of a shared space we can never reach but which at the same time seems to originate the separate terms we can specifically identify. The shared, receding origin begins to look like Spencer Brown's unmarked space and Luhmann's invisibilization. It is where forms dissolve and disappear but also out of which they are resolved and made to reappear. The special nature of autopoiesis as continuous genesis lies in this unmarked, invisible source.

Effacement is one of the chief features of human autopoiesis production which seems always to hide itself and to deny itself full presence. The development of mass production systems is a major modern form of effacement inasmuch as its stress on parts and their movement makes reality less obviously thing-like and much more relational and hence more mutable. Effacement is what presence does to absence: it makes it withdraw into its own special space, a space that is a permanent reserve of the not-yet or what Levinas (1969: 256) calls the 'essentially hidden' which 'throws itself toward the light, without becoming signification. Not nothingness—but what is not yet'. Effacement intimates that shared horizon hidden in *vision, fission* and *fusion* which we can never directly see; a reverse which is reserved but never as itself, always as a *part* that echoes something other than itself. This, too, is the hiddenness of the modern mass-production system which, behind its superabundant panorama of expedient products, nurtures a secret, unknowable space that must always remain a-part and what-is-not-yet. Modern production systems in general, thought dependent on this space, prefer to keep it hidden and even to deny it. The mass media of newspapers and television make their products presentable in the packaged forms of narrativized accounts which report facts and even fictions as immediate presences rather than what-is-not-yet. Knowledge-production systems such as schools and universities do the same: they package their knowledge-products for consumption in discrete field such as psychology, sociology, art and literature; each of these fields also narrativizes its products for ease of consumption and use, and each divides the world into viewable parts which serve the necessarily practical purposes of maintaining the routine movement of institutionalized life.

Autopoiesis suggests that such institutionalized routines obtain their energy, purposes and meanings from a censored absence of invisibility or unmarked space. At the everyday level of simple presence, institutions serve to convert the invisibility of what-is-not-yet into the mapped spaces of signs, symbols and directions that give structure to the thrownness of human being. They also train us to read their signs and directions without questioning them; easy, effortless and unquestioning consumption of their presented forms is the ultimate purpose of our institutions. In contrast, autopoietic theory in the human context asks the primal question of how forms come to be and how they disappear; it views the human world as a complex of uncertain and aleatory forms, as provisional tracings rather than objectified, firmed-up structures. In Luhmann's interpretation of autopoiesis the world of recognizable and meaningful forms are seen as transitory abductions from the invisibility of unmarked space to which they eventually have to return. What sociology has traditionally called the *division of labour* can be understood as society's programme for translating the unmarked space of the what-is-not-yet into the practically meaningful objects and events that map social and cultural space and thus give direction and purpose to social being. Here, the concept of *division* can be viewed as a version of Spencer Brown's primal *distinction* which reveals unmarked space as well as being a source for all subsequent divisions. Sociology's division of labour now has to be understood as a systemic technology for dividing the missing absence of unmarked space into the myriad specific forms and specializations of modern society. Behind these myriad divisions lurks that unidentifiable something we are calling the invisibilization or unmarked space of autopoiesis.

We forget how insidious and pervasive the influence of institutionalized structures can be in our thinking and actions. We take for granted that the world is divided into so many different categories and that the nature of our work and purposes is to affirm these divisions as practical presences in daily life: the work of the sociologist affirms the practical presence of society as an institution; the psychologist affirms the special existence of something called mind and behaviour; the fiction writer affirms the distinction between life as fiction and life as fact; the economist affirms the significance of economics as an institutionalized presence in modern life; the school teacher affirms the important presence in society of something called education. Each of these specialist activities presents and represents a particular method for dividing the unmarked space of the world into specialist fields that make consumable mental products for delivery to our bodily limbs and sensory organs. An important requirement of these specialized areas of production is the existence of strong boundaries that also help to affirm and confirm the visibility of their products. The general emphasis is on the production of *results*, of completed, usable products, of objects, events and forms that have a certainty of presence so that they are beyond question.

Autopoiesis begins with a series of more radical questions: how do social and cultural forms come and go, what is presence before it is presented, what is the nature of the unexamined work of human being that makes us see it as already accomplished rather than as a continuous process of coming-to-be? Such questions are radical in the sense that they demand a wholly different way of thinking than that which supports the affirmative presencing of conventional representation. The disaffirmation of negation and absence has to be recognized as a necessarily significant power in the way we construct our perceptions and thoughts, for what mobilizes us is not the certainty of static and stable presence but the uncertainty of the provisional and mutable. A common example of such mobilizing is the increasing emphasis on *speed* in modern methods of production: fast food is *fast* because it produces an impression of instant reality in which presence is *secured* or made *fast*. Absence has to be seen as a productive force in all aspects of human being but we also have to remind ourselves that absence is not the non-presence of something we know but the missing presence of something we do not know. In this interpretation, absence appears as the dissolution of presence and presence itself as the censoring of absence through the construction and affirmation of mappable—hence fixed and locatable—spaces, however, provisional they may be.

It is perhaps only in art and literature that we find a tradition of critical questioning of the nature of being that corresponds with the radical questioning of social and cultural forms raised by autopoietic analysis. Maurice Blanchot's (1982) creative analysis of literature and its origination in a primal negative space of total absence provides significant insights into how it can be approached laterally, if not directly. Blanchot addresses the question of literature's *space*, the emptiness of the unmarked space which continually provokes us to fill it with parts, bits and pieces of presence that we call words, ideas, images. Yet, however busy we are in this work of filling, we can never fully approach the secret space of literature. The work of filling is essentially a work of effacement which as well as eclipsing literature's space also importantly preserves its creative vagueness and other-worldness. Like the Nevadan desert surrounding Las Vegas, like Lyotard's scapeland, Blanchot's space of literature is a space of latency that is signless, directionless and purposeless. Blanchot also calls it *le vide* or the void of *di-vide*, which yet again returns us to the initiatory power we noted in our introductory discussion of *division*. Institutionalized literature is ignorant of literature's space because it gives it practical form and meaning; it assumes the authority of cultured discourse which tells us of profound meanings of life as well as providing focussed and disciplined themes for the work of living. Institutionalized work in general is always purposeful and productive, focussed on specific goals and results, its products always geared to positive, effective action. The 'work' of literature, in contrast leads nowhere, it creates an absence of productive work, it places the writer in a space of latency where the recognizable forms of life dissolve into certain and uncertain and aleatory boundaries which become difficult, even impossible to read and understand: '. . . the profound labour of literature which seeks to affirm itself in its essence by ruining distinctions and limits' (Blanchot, 1982: 220). Yet the space of literature is only revealed by the very distinctions and limits it opposes and in this respect it works like the autopoiesis of unmarked-marked space where visible distinctions are always accompanied by an inbuilt tendency to dissolve and disappear. Art and literature, in Blanchot's view, are the only areas of human being which expresses this act of primal origination out of disappearance and absence; they refuse institutional categorization into poetry, prose, sculpture, painting, all the while intimating their genesis in 'the menacing proximity of a vague and vacant outside, a neutral existence, nil and limitless; (they) point into a sordid absence, a suffocating condensation where being ceaselessly perpetuates itself as nothingness' (Blanchot, 1982: 242–243). Art and literature above all remind us of the ontological significance of unmarked space as missing presence and of its continuous repetition in autopoiesis as self-origination.

We are left with the more general question of how Blanchot's view of art and literature as especially sensitive indicators of the creative role of negative space connects with the everyday expression of human being. In their study of Caravaggio's art, Leo Bersani and Ulysse Dutoit (1998) have shown how important the theme of *relationality* is to the understanding of Caravaggio's work and thinking. Relationality, they suggest, is a fundamental way of thinking human being as the living connections between things, and they go on to suggest that 'the ontology most congenial to an age of information is one that identifies being as relationality, as the principle of connectedness assumed by all technologies of transmission' (Bersani and Dutoit, 1998: 110). This insight returns us to our earlier discussion of *partial-ness* and the role of *parts* in the logic of modern industrial production where the *play of relations* becomes more important than the presence of complete, finite objects and structures. The space of relational play and freedom is a way of reaching out to Blanchot's radical interpretation of art and literature is a space of latent possibilities, of what-is-not-yet, and it is the implicit latency of this space that connects it with the idea of relationality. Relationality is much more than the principle of connectedness between parts for it embraces the more general idea of the *latent* as the missing presence of unmarked space. To *re-late* is to acknowledge the presence of the hidden, secret and unknown as the aboriginal source of all our connecting parts; other inflections of the *latent* include the dispersed, the unrestrained, the wild and petulant, all which remind us of Blanchot's space of literature which retreats from any attempt to tame and rationalize it.

When we take the cue from Bersani and Dutoit and apply this interpretation of relationality to modern information technologies we begin to see connections between information as a form of human production and autopoiesis. Information theory tells us that information results from selecting an item of knowledge from a range of alternative possibilities such as when we ask someone the time or wish to know what the weather will be tomorrow. But information theory deals with *unselected space* rather than the radical absence of unmarked space; it emphasizes knowledge as presence and gives priority to information as certainty. Information is when we are given the correct time as answer to our question; it is the answer that is sought rather than the question. In contrast, autopoiesis persuades us to see information as a provisional event that is permanently subject to the seductions of absence; it is never fully present and draws its significance from the radical impermanence of its missing presence. When we place information in the context of relationality we see it as an expression of primary being which reaches out *via the body* to a wider field of multiple possibilities and uncountable perspectives which the viewer's partial siting/sighting has to exclude (Bryson, 1988: 103). Information now appears as sourced by its wider *latent* space which it *re-lates* as a missing presence and always 'in a continuous motion of postponement' (Bryson, 1988: 99). The *latent* now appears as something that we are always *late* for and which we are obliged to try and catch up with. In this sense, information is no longer a simple commodity to be cast aside after use; it is a constituting feature of the thrownness of being and hence of autopoiesis itself. On this reading, relationality is much more than simple connectedness between parts; it makes us see parts as belonging to a more original space of the what-is-not-yet that Blanchot explored in the space of literature and which resists all attempts to appropriate it for worldly purposes. And yet its practical appropriation is what motivates much of modern production technology as we see in the logic of mass production with its programme for inflecting the world through the play of parts and the transformations this makes possible. Information technology is an even more developed step in this strategy of attempting to make present that which is ultimately unpresentable. Hypertext is an especially dramatic expression of the relationality of being through the medium of computer technology. Hypertext is a form of 'non-sequential writing' which collates text, sound, images, diagrams and maps and allows them to be variously combined on a computer screen (Landow, 1992: 4). It has the power to make available the vast resources of libraries, museums, art galleries and other information sources to a single computer user. Hypertext hints at something we can never directly grasp and which we can only approach laterally; it indicates the virtual as opposed to the full presence of its subject matter, a tentative outline that seems to mediate between ungraspable, mutable beginnings and a world of fixed and finite things. It re-lates the latency of hyperspace to the body's limbs and organs through the hand-made space of the computer and its worktop and as such reveals production as the pre-diction or presensing of that 'inaccessible precondition' of missing presence basic to all aspects of being. And it is in this sense that autopoiesis makes us see all forms of human production as the pre-diction of incompleteness and postponement with which absence vitalizes presence.

## REFERENCES

Bresani, L. and Dutoit, D. (1998) *Caravaggio's Secrets*. Cambridge, MA: MIT Press.

Blanchot, M. (1982) *The Space of Literature*. Lincoln, NE: University of Nebraska Press.

Bryson, N. (1988) "The Gaze in the Expanded Field', in Hal Foster (ed.) *Vision and Visuality*. Seattle, WA: Bay Press.

Fisher, P. (1991) *Making and Effacing Art: Modern American Art in a Culture of Museums*. New York, NY: Oxford University Press.

Gadamer, H.-G. (1976) *Philosophical Hermeneutics*, trans. and edited by David E. Linge. Berkeley, CA: University of California Press.

302   *Robert Cooper*

Gibson, J. J. (1968) *The Senses Considered as Perceptual Systems.* Boston, MA: Harvard University Press.

Lacan, J. (1979) *The Four Fundamental Concepts of Psycho-Analysis*, trans. Alan Sheridon and edited by Jacques Alain-Miller. Harmondsworth: Penguin.

Landow, G. P. (1992) *Hypertext: The Convergence of Contemporary Critical Theory and Technology.* Baltimore, MD: Johns Hopkins University Press.

Levinas, E. (1969) *Totality and Infinity: An Essay on Exteriority*, trans. Alphonso Lingis. Pittsburgh, PA: Duquesne University Press.

Luhmann, N. (1986) 'The Autopoiesis of Social Systems', in Felix Geyer and Johannes van der Zouwen (eds) *Sociocybernetic Paradoxes: Observation, Control and Evolution of Self-Steering Systems.* Berkeley, CA: Sage.

Luhmann, N. (2000) *Art as a Social System*, trans. Eva M. Knodt. Stanford, CA: Stanford University Press.

Lyotard, J.-F. (1989) 'Scapeland', in Andrew Benjamin (ed.) *The Lyotard Reader.* Oxford: Basil Blackwell.

Poirier, R. (1992) *Poetry and Pragmatism.* London: Faber & Faber.

Spencer Brown, G. (1969) *Laws of Form.* London: George Allen & Unwin.

Strathern, M. (1991) *Partial Connections.* Savage, MD: Rowman & Littlefield.

Thomson, D. (1999) *In Nevada: The Land, the People, God, and Chance.* London: Little, Brown.

Venturi, R., Scott Brown, D. and Izenour, S. (1977) *Learning from Las Vegas.* Boston, MA: MIT Press.

Winograd, T. and Flores, F. (1986) *Understanding Computers and Cognition: A New Foundation for Design.* Reading, MA: Addison Wesley.

# 14 The Generalized Social Body
## Distance and Technology

*Robert Cooper*

(*Organization*, 2010, 17/2: 242–256. Reproduced by permission of SAGE Publications Ltd., London, Los Angeles, New Delhi, Singapore and Washington DC, Copyright © SAGE publications.)

**Abstract.** *The social context of the human body is discussed as a generalized field of energy and action in which the body reflects and transmits itself as a living part of its wider field of social and cultural action. A definitive feature of the generalized social body is action at a distance. All human action finds its source in the making present and immediate of that which is distant and faraway. Distance is discussed as an immanent absence which keeps human action forever on the move. Distance moves the generalized social body as a field of continuous dispersal and dissemination. The human body is thus viewed as an incomplete part which is forever trying to complete itself in a generalized field that continually recedes from human appropriation. The generalized social body also means that the conventional boundaries between the individual and its context dissolve in a fluctuating field of continuous movement. The ancient meaning of technology is discussed as a means by which the human body translates the mute and anonymous (i.e., distant and remote) matter of the world into meaningful human forms and objects. Technology in this sense is disclosive rather than simply instrumental: it reveals the mute and mutable matter of the world as a distant source of infinite potential. Significantly, the human agent is an ongoing product of this process.*
**Key words.** *Distance; human agency; social body; technology; transmission.*

Distance is basic to an understanding of human agency and social organization. Human action originates in such distances as *here* and *there, now* and *then, you* and *me*. Distance is a force that both divides and unites. It compels us to think more critically about our conventional ways of viewing such essential social terms as individual and group, self and other, subject and object. The individual, for example, is usually seen as a self-contained, positive figure, a self that is distinguished from the multiplicity of other selves that make up society. In contrast, the idea of distance suggests that the so-called individual is permanently suspended in a double action between body and environment, between self and other, between part and whole. Distance stresses the transmission *between* terms as the moving force of life. Instead of a society of individuals, we begin to see society as a generalized social body motivated by the transmission *between* terms, that is, by action at a distance.

Transmission makes us see the human agent as a transmission station in a dynamic field of ceaseless action. Transmission is the continuous sending on of the signs and symbols that keep society going. Without such transmission the human world would dissolve and disappear. The human body is the sensory route for the translation and transmission of bodily forces into the everyday technologies that support and sustain social life. The body itself is an integral part of this ongoing field of action. Thus we can never summarize the body as a thing in itself: 'The human body is not a thing or substance, given, but a continuous creation . . . The human body is an energy system . . . which is never a complete structure (and) never static' (Brown, 1966: 155). Since the body is always part of its living world, it is always a *social* body through which it reflects and transmits itself as a living part of its wider field of social and cultural action. In this wider context, the self or individual person is always secondary to the translation and transmission of bodily forces and sensings. Translation and transmission distinguish the social body as a series of dynamic parts which are always on the move, forever parting and departing from themselves. More fundamentally, the generalized social body is the continuous flow of matter between the human body and its environment. The work of the social body is the continuous translation and transmission of raw matter into meaningful human focus.

Organizing in its most basic sense is the work of the generalized social body as the creative transformation of the unformed rawness of the earth's matter into the meaningful human forms and objects that constitute social organization. On the interpretation, organizing is a fundamental compositional action which comes before the finished form or object; the tools and products of organizing now have to be understood as vehicles for the continuous construction and movement of the social body rather than individually identifiable and bounded structures. In this context, technology becomes a general vehicle for the movement of undifferentiated matter in which the human agent and its technologies merge together to underline the intrinsic unitary wholeness of the social body. Social organization is thus a flow of undifferentiated wholeness before it is understood as a collection of interacting individuals and objects. In this sense, technology and human agency do not merely interact with each other; the primal matter from which they both emerge continuously reclaims them as its own. Technology may be conventionally viewed as the creation of new human possibilities but it also significantly reveals the basic matter of undifferentiated wholeness as a forever receding distance which can never be captured in a stable system of human knowledge and organization. In the context of the generalized social body, technology is the continuous work of the social body trying to catch up with itself as a forever unfolding field of infinite matter.

The supportive technologies of everyday life are also necessary parts of the translation and transmission of bodily forces and sensings. The technologies of domestic building and furniture, for example, free the human body from its physical limitations and thus enable it to travel beyond itself: medical technologies serve to free the body from the limitations of physical illness; modern technologies of communication such as the mobile telephone, the computer and the television also serve to remove the body from itself and transport it to another place. In these examples, transmission is the act of departing from the present to another and distant space. It is as if the general purpose of technology were to liberate the human body from itself in order to remake itself through the hidden possibilities of mute matter.

## THE SOCIAL BODY

Before the self, before the individual person, there is the body. The body is the abode or base of human agency, the ground or bed of human action, is the source and foundation of human movement and creation, which 'is in perpetual inner self-construction and self-destruction . . . in order to make (itself) new' (Brown, 1966: 155). As the source of human sentience and desire, the body translates and transmits the forces of life in a field of ongoing transient forms. The social body is thus the field of dynamic interactions between the sentient body and its environment. The body does not merely feel and transmit. It sources the social body as the producer of forms out of the base matter of unarticulated experience. The body is the source of human organization as the creator of social and cultural products out of pre-human, unarticulated space of possibilities. The body is thus the translator and transmitter of events as continuous movement as well as disclosing the world as a source of infinite, potential forms. The social body is thus not so much a bounded, specific thing or structure but a generalized field of human motion and creation in which specific forms lose their specificities and merge together in a flowing field of movement that withdraws from the specific identities of conventional thinking.

The social body is dispersed and disseminated through the bodies of its individual members as a field of active relationships. 'Reality does not consist of substances, solidly and stolidly each in its own place; but in events, activity; activity which crosses the boundary; action at a distance' (Brown, 1966: 155). The body does not end at its physical limits but finds itself only through its sentient extensions, the tongue and the mouth extend themselves through spoken language; the hands and eyes, through the written word. All the limbs reach out to a limbo of negative space which calls out to the sentient body for some form of expression and representation. The social body is the reaching out of the sentient body into the distances that translate it into a field of social action. It spreads itself in space and time as a field of *otherness* in which individuals forms and objects lose themselves to become each other so that there is no individualised *me* and *you*, no specific *here* and *there*, no separate *inside* and *outside*. The so-called individual is simply a 'postural image' that knows itself as a provisional and transient location in a field of relative positions or postures: 'In an individual's own postural image many postural images of others are melted together' (Schilder, 1935: 234). The individual finds itself only as a mobile part of a more comprehensive and unlocatable space in which it is intertwined with other mobile parts.

The body itself lives outside itself, forever seeking to complete its incompleteness. The social body is thus not a thing or substance but the continuous creation of events or happenings. It recreates itself as a response to the repeated movement of distance in space and time. Distance is the *double stance* or di-*stance* that characterizes human movement *between* things. All human action occurs as the movement *between* the forms and objects that support human life and which imply that human action is essentially the *transmission* of action over the gaps and intervals that constitute the distances of space and time.

The work of the body is essentially the bringing near of what is faraway, the making immediate of that which is distant in space and time. The body's limbs and organs reach out to the margins of experience in order to make the forms and objects of the world fit closely to the body's sentient demands. The double stance of distance is thus the sentient alternation between the immediate and the absent, between approach and withdrawal. Distance as an existential force is the movement of the body in its existential work of making the world visible and meaningful. All human production is motivated by the need and desire to make present what is absent and to make visible what is invisible. All human products are subject to the co-presence of presence and absence, visibility and invisibility. Language originates in this existential alternation of the double stance of distance. Through the spoken and written word, the body makes immediate and present that which is faraway and foreign. Language is a fundamental human act that gives forms and appearance to an existential absence that lies always beyond human knowing. The limbs of the body reach out to translate their limbo of negative space into the positive forms and objects of the knowable world.

Distance reminds us constantly of its negative presence, that space and time are ultimately ungraspable horizons that forever withdraw from our attempts to approach them. The social body expresses distance as permanent withdrawal in the example of the city. The city is a mutable field of perspectives which changes according to the distances in space and time from which it is experienced; the forms and objects that constitute the city's contents—its buildings, roads, traffic and human occupants—also vary according to the distances from which they are seen. The totality of the city's contents are further contained in the even more remote distance of pre-objective space and time which can never be directly known but only indirectly sensed through the ever-changing relationships between its multiple contents. In other words, the specific, knowable distances between the city's varied forms and objects are partial and transient expressions of a more comprehensive and indeterminable distance which lies always beyond human grasp.

The city as a field of multiple and transient distances exemplifies the active nature of the social body which can never be located in a specific structure but which exists as the movement of distances whose source is fundamentally unlocatable. The social body is this sense is human action that is permanently suspended between the double stance of presence and absence, approach and withdrawal. The social body is thus partly constituted by that which it can never reach but which provokes its human members to extend themselves in a permanent act of distension. Like the city, the social body is ultimately indeterminable and therefore unknowable. We may map the city by projecting our systems of human knowing and locating onto it but this does not mean that we have uncovered that indeterminable space from which the city and its contents emerge. Beyond the city, beyond its mappable structure of locatable things and places, there is the *atopical*, a placeless place that forever withdraws from all attempts to make it humanly comprehensible:

> There is a place that is everywhere and nowhere, a place you cannot get to from here . . . This strange locus is another name for the ground of things, the preoriginal ground of the ground, something other to any activity of mapping.
>
> (Miller, 1995: 7)

This placeless place is the limbo which the body's limbs reach out to in their perpetual work of making visible and present that which is always on the verge of withdrawing and disappearing.

Distance is thus the double movement of alternation or the double stance. In the distances of the social body there are no naturally explicit forms or infinite objects. All human action is the disclosing of that which refuses disclosure; everything is a transient event in the double movement of distance. Instead of complete, finished forms, distance tells us that the social body is a field of movement characterized by dispersal and dissemination in which the forms of things continually depart from each other. Edges and boundaries rather than bounded forms and images become the essence of the social body as a field of permanent movement. The limbs lose their specific forms in a limbo of dispersal and dissemination: the tongue becomes a tongue of language; the hand, a handle; the foot, a unit of measure. In this sense, the body is a base or common ground that sources the alternations and interactions of distance rather than a system of functional organs. The body as base or ground implies a limbo which has yet to be articulated and expressed in specific forms. The base as the negative ground of things is both mute and mutable and, like the pre-objective space of the city, remains forever indeterminable and unknowable as the ultimate source of distance. The base of the social body is thus the source of continuous movement and transmission, a process which inexorably carries us along in a continuous process of withdrawal, despite all our attempts to appropriate it as forms of human production.

The social body as a transmission station helps us to understand formal organizations as forms of social production. Production in this wider context of social organization reminds us that the making and transmission of social and cultural products is an intrinsic and definitive feature of the continuous movement of human life. Organizing as a fundamental function of the social body is the continuous making and moving of human forms in order to maintain human life as the continuous unfolding and disclosing of the infinite possibilities of distance.

## THE TRANSMISSION OF DISTANCE

Transmission expresses the social body as a field of dynamic parts which are always on the move, always parting and departing from themselves. It is the movement *between* things that constitutes the power of transmission rather than the things themselves. This means that transmission is fundamentally motivated by the distances *between* social terms and not by the terms themselves. Distance is a fundamental *otherness* that moves human life so that we as so-called individuals are always *other* and never simply ourselves.

Distance means that the social body is an interactive field of *parts* and *wholes*. Distance tells us that parts and wholes are interactive in the most basic sense of constituting each other. Individual and group, for example, are never separate structures but *integrally imply* each other (Wagner, 1991). The part reproduces the whole just as the whole reproduces the part. This way of thinking the social body means that social terms are neither individual nor group, neither singular nor plural, but are both at the same time and thus are indistinguishable from each other. Relationship between terms is what distinguishes the action of the social body rather than the terms themselves. Relationship implies that the terms *relate each other in an integral interaction*. This means that nothing is complete or self-contained but is the result of the continuous movement *between* things. The work of the scientist, for example, is as much a product of the methodology and technology he or she uses it is of his/her ideas and actions. In other words, distance means that all the terms and elements in a situation imply and constitute each other in a process of transmission. Part and whole are thus conflated just as the subject and object of an action are mixed together in an origin that in itself must remain *implicit* and thus refuse *explicit* expression. Technology and the human body represent this existential conflation in that their interaction expresses an origin which is always beyond their individual structures. Both *imply* something other than that which they make explicit.

The transmission of distance is thus the making present and immediate of that which is distant and faraway. The body's organs and senses reach out to make the distant and faraway immediately sensible, meaningful and manipulable. But the immediate and manipulable 'is only veiled distance the absolute foreign passing for the habitual, the unfamiliar which we take for the customary . . .' (Blanchot, 1982: 40). Hence the double stance of distance is a double and reversible process in which the immediate already includes the distant. The transmission of distance is thus the continuous making present of that which is absent and invisible. Human organization is essentially the continuous translation and transmission of distance into the ready-made immediacies of the world. Beyond the immediate and ready-made, distance occupies an impersonal space and time that remains indifferent to human meaning, 'an abyss in which all things are equal in their utter indifference to the human mind and will' (de Man, 1983: 72). Distance in this context is that which withdraws from all our attempts to make it immediately meaningful. The withdrawal of distance is the way the world hides itself from human appropriation and which 'confirms the existence of a fundamental distance at the heart of all human experience' (de Man, 1983: 76).

Distance now appears as the base of human experience, out of which the forms and objects of the social and cultural world emerge. The social body is base in the special and particular sense that it is mute and inarticulate but which significantly serves as the negative source for all the body's products. The base of the social body in itself is featureless and without positive identity, a limbo or placeless place, yet which serves as an invisible and infinite medium for all our attempts to give it form and location. The transmission of distance is the continuous translation of this anonymous, limbic base into the transient forms and objects that constitute the immediate presences of the human world. But distance itself can never be reached. It is existential force that resists completion as if to say that the social body can never be a finished product, a finite form, but a restless suspension of action at a distance.

## DISTANCE AND TECHNOLOGY

Technology in its modern sense has largely forgotten its ancient connections with the social body. Its roots (e.g., in the Greek *tek, tik, tex,* etc.) take it back to its origins in the primal act of making the forms of the world out of raw matter: production, generation, creation, bringing something into existence. Significantly, this archaic meaning of technology also included bodily sensings and feelings as well as the idea of making the hidden and mute material of the world articulate and hence comprehensible to human intelligence. Technology in its archaic sense was thus seen as the work of the bodily senses making sense out of a primal condition that lacked sense and meaning. Technology reflected the idea of the limbs reaching out into a limbo or placeless place in order to give it sentient structure. In contrast, modern thinking sees technology as an instrument to extend human knowledge and control. Through technology, the human agent sees itself as a major source of control and power in the world. But the ancient understanding of technology stressed its corporate or bodily nature. Body and technology were viewed as expressions of a primal, impersonal life-force of incomplete and transient events in which the human agent was not so much a self-directed source of power and control but rather the constant movement of bodily forces forever trying to reconstitute themselves out of dissipation and loss. Technology in this context was the continuous work of making and unmaking, constructing and deconstructing, the appearances of the human world.

The ancient conception of the body-technology relationship is implied in the cybernetic thinking of Norbert Wiener (1954). Wiener thinks of human existence primarily in terms of patterns of relationship whose task is to 'perpetuate themselves':

> Our tissues change as we live: the food we eat and the air we breathe becomes flesh of our flesh and bone of our bone, and the momentary elements of our flesh and bone pass out of our body every day with our excreta. We are but whirlpools in a river of ever-flowing water. We are not stuff that abides, but patterns that perpetuate themselves.
>
> (Wiener, 1954: 86)

In Weiner's cybernetics, the body loses its distinctive boundaries and merges with the material of its surroundings, so that the body and environment become parts of a more encompassing whole. In this view, human agents and their bodies do not simply inhabit their world. Significantly, it is *the world that inhabits them*. Here we find some sense of the ancient understanding of technology as the movement and transmission *between* the things and elements of the world rather than the specificities of the things themselves. Food, flesh and bone become transmitters of a generic energy or life-force whose source is always faraway and distant yet strangely always present. Distance transmits only itself and not the specific elements that contribute to the transmission process. In this respect, transmission is like the body's tongue which becomes the tongue of the language; it is not the tongue itself that speaks but the transmission process which translates the tongue into the movement of language. Likewise, the hand becomes a handle, and the foot becomes a unit of measurement. Transmission begins to look like a form of disembodiment in which the body's limbs not only reach out beyond themselves but also serve to express and transmit themselves as parts of a more comprehensive and distant whole that continually withdraws from all our efforts to identify and appropriate it.

We now have to understand technology as a transmission process that translates the faraway of distance into the immediate and present. We are no longer thinking of technology simply as an instrument of human control. Here we are re-interpreting technology in existential terms where it is less to do with the invention of tools for the facilitation of everyday living and is, more significantly, revealed as a human production system for the continuous construction and maintenance of the world of human forms. Technology in this revised sense *discloses* the world as an infinite source of inventable forms that stimulates the human mind in its work of disembodiment and distension. The social body has to be seen as an infinite base for the disclosure of events rather than their simple representation. The ancient interpretation of technology again reminds us of its essentially disclosive nature since the *tech-* refers to the mute zero ground of the human mind (Kaplan, 1999: 67) out of which the *logos* extracts events and forms for the mind to transmit itself. Technology makes present the mute and inarticulate base of the social body. The immediacies and presences of everyday life are thus always accompanied by the receding horizons of distance. Technology reveals the space and time of the world to be an infinite and invisible receptacle that is able to receive and accommodate the continuous stream of impressions imposed on it by the gestures of human agency. No longer simply a source of instrumental production, the world appears as the infinite ground of the immediacies and presences that constitute the fabric of everyday life. The infinite ground of distance is that which has not yet been made into an immediate, meaningful form or object; it is limbo or placeless place that is curiously always present as a receding horizon whose continuous withdrawal is the necessary background for the making of the immediate and present, just as tomorrow and yesterday are necessary for the making present of today.

Here we are reminded that the double stance of distance is a double and reversible process in which the immediate and present already includes the distant and absent. The immediate and present already imply that which is distant and absent; they necessarily imply something other than themselves just as the newspaper, for example, implies that the news it presents has its sources in distant actions and places that in themselves can never be immediately experienced but only re-presented. But distance as double and reversible stance implies more. It is a fundamental *otherness* which moves through human action as in infinite background of impersonal space and time which remains indifferent to all our attempts to give it specifiable form and meaning. Distance is the invisible and infinite space and time of the social body, its mute and inarticulate ground, out of which specific forms and meanings are created, if only to withdraw into the limbo from which they emerge. Distance appears as a missing wholeness or invisible container like that indeterminable space from which the city and its contents emerge as determinable space from which the city and its contents emerge as determinable distances or like language which makes a world or presences out of absence and withdrawal.

Distance itself can thus never be made immediate and explicit; it always *implies* itself as a missing presence as if to say it is always with us but always as an invisible background to the specific forms and structures that constitute our everyday reality. Distance implies its existence as a receding horizon of withdrawal which can never be made specific and explicit but simply implies itself. Such specificities as individual or self are extractions from the mute base of the social body which exists as an invisible reminder of the placeless origin that sources all human action and its products. Distance implies itself only through the presentable immediacy of the explicit. In this sense, distance is basic to the ancient understanding of technology as the making explicit of the implicit or the mute zero ground of the social body: technology is thus a fundamental act of human production which originates in the action itself and not in the finished product. Science, for example, originates in acts of questioning the implicit and unknown. The scientist is never just an objective observer of his/her subject matter but is always a participating part of the research process in which he/she actively exists as a scientist in the interior of the research activity and not outside it as an independent and objective observer. In this sense, the scientist is constituted by the research activity and is thus not simply a subject who independently acts on an object. Subject and object become *mutually* intertwined and hence imply the *muteness* of the social body's base or zero ground. The base is mute because it has not yet been developed into a system of meaningful specific forms; it is the placeless place of the zero ground that has not yet been made into a readable social map of individuals and objects. Hence, the base of things is like the raw matter of the world out of which things are articulated. The mute base of the social body means that nothing is distinguishable but is mutable, simultaneous, interactive and merged together. At this level, the scientist is distinguishable from their research technology/ methodology just as much as the technology/methodology is indistinguishable from the scientist.

Here we meet again Norbert Wiener's (1954: 86) interpretation of cybernetic process which stresses the movement of patterns across different domains of experience and in which specific forms give way to general acts of translation: food into flesh, flesh and bone into working bodies, bodies into machines. Wiener's cybernetics denies the fixed term, the specific location, the subject-object dichotomy. Wiener seems to imply that the specific forms and locations of conventional thought are secondary and transient expressions of an underlying mute and mutable base which refuses formal identification and representation. Cybernetic process thus suggests that 'the cybernetic nature of self and the world tends to be imperceptible to consciousness' because self and environment are not separate forms but are intimately and implicitly interlaced in the 'circularities of the self and the external world' (Bateson, 1973: 419, 420). In cybernetic terms, the self disappears in the imperceptible base of distance. The self loses itself in a space of dispersal and dissemination. No longer a bounded, individual self, the human agent has to be understood in terms of the signs, symbols and signals that connect it with its external world. The bounded, individual self dissolves in the constant *inter-action* between body and environment and in which 'individual human identity' is merely one instance of provisionally stabilised and bounded being' (Bersani and Dutoit, 1993: 8).

Cybernetic thinking radically questions the conventional way of viewing the human agent as the source of technological power. It relativizes the difference between the human self and its technologies so that we are left with the idea of the *cyborg*, 'a *hybrid* of machine and organism' in which the separate terms 'machine' and 'organism' dissolve to become each other (Haraway, 1991: 177). The hybrid is this never a locatable thing or term. It is always *between* things, always on its way somewhere. Instead of thinking the human subject as a bounded individual that simply uses technology to extend its power, the hybrid demands that we think it in terms of the double stance of distance where, for example, *you* and *me, here* and *there, today* and *tomorrow*, constitute each other. Distance is thus a form of hybrid thinking in which space and time are convoluted or folded processes just like the mathematician's Möbius strip where outside and inside are identical. The cyborg is also folded together in the sense that it is neither this not that but *both* this *and* that, neither here nor there but *both* here *and* there, at the same time. The distance of technology challenges us to think the world *inter-actively* and thus to recognize that the human subject is a transient and passing product of an existential base which is indeterminably distant.

## THE DISTANCE OF DISTANCE

Distance requires that we think of the social body as a fluctuating network of interactions *between* the individual elements that make up the social and cultural world. The self and its subjectivity give way to the continuous movement *between* the individualized contents of the social body. Instead of purposeful, human-centred, rational action, the dispersal and dissemination of movement becomes the main motivator of action in the social body. Distance is central to this way of thinking. Distance tells us that the human self is a temporary and transient part of a wider whole which is infinite and unreachable. The existential work of the human self is the making present and immediate of this absent horizon. Language, as we noted, finds its source in the work of translating the absent into the present or the bringing near to the physical body that which is faraway and foreign. Language thus expresses a basic feature of the social body: the permanently active suspension of human action between presence and absence, between the known and unknown. The conventional view of the bounded self stresses its capacity to appropriate the world and to make it knowable; the self understands itself as a subject in a world of appropriatable objects. The idea of distance as reversible, double stance tells us that the self does not simply inhabit the world but is also inhabited by it. The self is never simply itself but is always *other*. Otherness is the dispersal and dissemination of the self in a world where the conventional boundaries between self and object are broken down to become fluidly *inter-active* in a fluctuating network of movement that defies human control and domination. Cybernetic thinking says essentially the same when it views human action in terms of 'the circularities of the self and the external world' (Bateson, 1973: 420). The cyborg repeats this interpretation in its idea of the hybrid nature of the self and its technology. The subject is thus no longer a detached observer of the world but is inter-actively caught up in the fluid movements *between* the forms and objects of the world. The human subject finds itself in 'a "field", a comprehensive realm of interrelated energies, which are organised yet indefinitely subject to mutation and inflection' (Bowie, 1978: 144). The 'field' of human existence is a field of otherness in which the subject is dispersed and disseminated by the force of distance which constantly questions the idea of the authoritative, bounded self and begins to return us to the mute zero ground of the social body in which our 'namable . . . selves' revert to a field of 'shifting positions within an untraceable network of forms in communication' (Bersani and Dutoit, 1993: 208). The mute base of the social body thus reminds us that it is essentially mutable and this resists all attempts to place it in a locatable map of knowledge.

Technology is the means by which the human subject attempts to attribute some sense of place and locatability to the distant mutability of the social body. Technology makes present and immediate that which is mutely distant and intrinsically resistant to human knowledge. In this sense, the social body expresses itself as 'action as a distance' (Brown, 1966: 155). This means that it is not so much the human agent that expresses itself but the distances between the agent and its fluctuating field of relationships. Like the continuous movement that constitutes the city, the actions of the social body constitute a dynamic field of approach and withdrawal. Never a capturable structure, the *wholeness* of the social body implies itself through its absence and withdrawal. It calls on the human body to detach itself from its limbs and organs in order to correspond with the absences that motivate the body's presences. Language illustrates this detachment of the body from itself and its general dispersal and dissemination throughout the social body. Language in this sense becomes a technology of detachable signs, signals and symbols that *imply* the mute and tacit nature of the social base's body. Language suggests that it is essentially a means for the social body to explicate itself, and thus to locate and find itself, out of a material base that is not naturally explicable and which remains in itself forever beyond human comprehension.

Distance in this sense is always in excess of the forms and objects of the social body; never reachable, it is like the tomorrow which never comes. The *limbs* of the body express this unattainable excess in their reflection of the *limbo* of negative space. The practical spaces of everyday life are *cut-outs* from the mute and tacit nature of the social body. When we express and locate the mute base of the social body, we also translate its intrinsic mutability and resistance to location by excluding its intrinsic tendency to wander and lose itself in its continuous movement of otherness. This is the work of the cut-out which creates definable figures and forms out of the social body's inarticulate base. The cut-out literally cuts out the excess which threatens the practical work of defining everyday reality with the degeneration of specific meanings. But significantly, it is the neutral and anonymous character of the social body's mute base that sources human agency in all its social and cultural acts of production. The everyday work of social organization finds its origins in the translating of the pre-human base of the social body into the ready-made presences of everyday life. In this way, absence and withdrawal are always covertly present in human production. Distance reflects this dynamic alternation of absence and presence, of withdrawal and immediacy.

The everyday work of social organization stresses presence and immediacy. The forms and objects of the everyday world affirm and confirm the social body as an immediate, taken-for-granted presence. Such a world is seen as a collective of focused and visible figures against a background that remains invisible and mute. But distance stresses the co-implication and intertwining of the immediate and present with the distant and faraway. The immediacy and presence of social organization is the result of the continuous work of human production without which the human world would disappear. Again, the ancient meaning of *technology* as a way of transforming the mute, raw matter of the world into the clear, practical language of human action reminds us of the existential significance of distance. Distance thus reminds us that human action is always suspended *between* the specific forms and objects of daily existence and in this sense is never finished. It stresses the continuous movement of existence in which so-called finite, bounded forms or cut-outs are always subject to the dispersion of excess implied by the mute, negative ground out of which they are extracted and which keep them forever on the move. The mute, negative ground of distance is like a distant and silent call that can never be answered.

The literary theorist Paul de Man describes the mute, negative ground of distance as 'a fundamental distance at the heart of all human experience'. . . . 'an abyss in which all things are equal in their utter indifference to the human mind and will' (de Man, 1983: 76, 72). This is a state of existence that pre-exists the idea of the social person who defines him/herself in terms of the language of a conventional social and cultural map. De Man draws our attention to an *impersonal* space in which no one longer shares a consciousness or a destiny with a number of others, but that one is reduced to no longer being a person, to being no one, because one defines oneself in relation to being and not in relation to some particular entity (de Man, 1983: 69).

Here we meet again the zero ground of limbo in which the human agent loses it sense of identity and specificity to become *part* of the continuous movement and inter-action *between* things just as the scientist loses his/her identity in the inter-action with their research technology and methodology to become a moving part *interior* to the research process. For de Man, this anonymous distance that questions the existential nature of the human subject and its subjectivity occurs distinctively in the literary work and the act of reading it. The printed word of the literary work is simply a set of anonymous marks on the white background of a page. The anonymous marks of the printed word are thus the mute and mutable base of language out of which forms and meanings are created. At this level, both reader and author lose their particular subjectivities and 'move beyond their respective particularly toward a common ground that contains both of them' (de Man, 1983: 64). This common, anonymous ground of language returns us to the idea of the *atopical*, a placeless, distant place which 'is another name for the ground of things, the preoriginal ground of the ground, something other to any activity of mapping' (Miller, 1995:7).

In this common, anonymous space, the human agent loses itself in a pre-human field of dispersal and dissemination. The 'I', 'me' and 'you' of the conventional social world disappear as bounded, specific objects of knowledge. The scientist, like the author and reader, loses him/herself in a receding field of uncertainty and ambiguity which questions the very idea of a subject who can authoritatively *know* the world. Modern science exemplifies this work of uncertainty in the continuous questioning of its findings: modern mathematics and science 'do not reduce the unknown to the known, they make everything one thought one knew unstable in proportion to what one used to know . . .' (Lyotard, 1993: 253). The scientist is no longer a knowing subject but a 'small transitory region in a process of energetic metamorphosis' (Lyotard, 1993: 253). Less a discoverer of foundational knowledge, the scientist becomes part of a general process of transmission in which he/she is carried along by the unreachability of distance.

The absence and withdrawal of distance assumes a major force in the existential structuring of the social body and tells us that the presence and immediacy are always transient attempts to give meaning and location to the mute and mutable ground of the social body. Technology in its manifold modern forms dramatizes this general movement of the unfounding of presence and immediacy. In the computerized world of the modern multimedia, the 'private I' and the 'autonomous individual subject' have no natural place since they are dispersed in the disseminated mediations of the electronic media where agents, computers, binary digits, signs and spaces mediate each other in a limbic, mutable, hybrid space in which the boundary of an object is neither part of the object itself nor part of its context (Miller, 1992: 59). The computerized space of the modern world is essentially the perpetual and infinite movement of distance which constantly reminds us that we are never fully constituted individuals but are incomplete *parts* that *participate* in an existential field of 'uncertain visibility' in which 'the drawing of boundaries and the tracing of shapes are still somewhat aleatory' (Bersani and Dutoit, 1993: 218). It is in this sense that the generalized social body of human agency and social organization is essentially *action at a distance*.

## REFERENCES

Bateson, G. (1973) *Steps Towards an Ecology of Mind*. London: Paladin.
Bersani, L. and Dutoit, U. (1993) *Arts of Impoverishment: Beckett, Rothko, Resnais*. Cambridge, MA: Harvard University Press.
Blanchot, M. (1982) *The Space of Literature*. Lincoln, NE: University of Nebraska Press.
Bowie, M. (1978) *Mallarmé and the Art of Being Difficult*. Cambridge: Cambridge University Press.
Brown, N. O. (1966) *Love's Body*. New York, NY: Vintage Books.
De Man, P. (1983) *Blindness and Insight: Essays in the Rhetoric of Contemporary Criticism*. London: Routledge.
Haraway, D. (1991) *Simians, Cyborgs and Women: the Re-invention of Nature*. London: Free Association Books.
Kaplan, R. (1999) *The Nothing That Is: a Natural History of Zero*. London: Allen Lane/Penguin.
Lyotard, J.-F. (1993) *Libidinal Economy*. London: Athlone.
Miller, J. H. (1992) *Illustration*. London: Reaktion Books.
Miller, J. H. (1995) *Topographies*. Stanford, CA: Stanford University Press.
Schilder, P. (1935) *The Image and Appearance of the Human Body: Studies in the Constructive Energies of the Psyche*. London: Kegan Paul.
Wagner, R. (1991) 'The Fractal Person', in M. Godelier and M. Strathern (eds) *Big Men and Great Men: The Development of a Comparison in Melanesia*, pp. 159–73. Cambridge: Cambridge University Press.
Wiener, N. (1954) *The Human Use of Human Beings: Cybernetics and Society*. New York, NY: Houghton and Mifflin.

# 15 Main Features of My Approach

*Robert Cooper*

(Excerpt from 'Interview with Robert Cooper' Robert C. H. Chia and Jannis Kallinikos, in Chia, R. (ed) (1998) *Organized Worlds: Explorations in Technology and Organization with Robert Cooper.* London: Routledge, 159–63.)

*It's clear that you see organization as a general process that is immanent throughout society and social practice rather than as a specific instrumental system. In answering this final question, could you summarize this main features of your approach and suggest how it might be developed?*

I'll begin with a general—and perhaps obvious—point. The social world is essentially an infrangible fusion of events and relations in which there are no neat divisions or categories. It doesn't easily lend itself to conceptualization, yet is forever committed to an endless struggle to make sense of itself, to organize itself, within a matrix of confusion. We saw this happening in John Wilkin's and Thomas Sprat's attempt to develop a rational language for science in seventeenth-century England. In that example, we noted that order grew out of disorder, that order and disorder defined each other. Wherever we look, we see all around this dynamic and creative antagonism between order and disorder. This is what I mean by organization as a *generic* process in society. Generic organization is not a thing, it's not a self-contained structure. We can't point to it and say 'That's *it*.' It's more like a network of relations that keeps on moving. So that even when we try to make sense of it, when we order or organize it, we have to be careful not to reduce it to a state, to a static condition. Yet we seem almost naturally to think of organization not as a general process but in terms of self-contained units which we call *organizations*. Usually, these are understood as administrative-economic systems with specific goals and rational procedures for attaining their goals.

Organizations in this sense are viewed primarily in instrumental terms, that it, they're understood as the means for satisfying society's needs. The more basic order-disorder theme is lost—even suppressed—in this interpretation. This seems to be especially true of the academic field of organization studies which has constructed for itself a professionalized object called 'an organization'. In other words, organization studies may itself be seen as 'an organization' that continues to produce a definable and identifiable *product* called 'organization theory' which is built on the assumption that there are self-contained, self-identical objects that can be academically 'consumed'. Organization theory replicates itself through those objects— namely instrumental organizations—constitute its subject matter. In other words, organization theory has itself become an organizational product. (I've dealt with this question in more detail elsewhere; see Cooper, 1986.) This is an example of the specific knowledge of the professions that we discussed earlier . . . the knowledge of things in specific, self-contained spaces.

In contrast, generic organization requires that we relax the requirements for specific, locatable things that have specific, functional roles. Instead, it thinks of organization as loose and active *assemblages of organizings*—not static structures but dynamic acts that are always on the move. For example, conventional organization theory understands Scientific Management as a strategy of business management applied solely to factory production, whereas generic organization views is as part of a much wider control movement in the early twentieth century which was applied to housework and the design of the domestic kitchen as well as to factory organization (Lupton and Miller, 1992). Lyotard's (1991) analysis of photography as a techno-scientific product is another example of organization as immanent acts of organizing.

Photography is merely one of many ways by which industrial technoscience pervades social practice and in which the amateur photographer acts as its agent in that wider context that Lyotard calls 'the management of infinite research'. Lyotard's example of photography is also important here for another reason—it reveals the socio-cultural aspect of generic organization. Techno-scientific organization becomes part of the life-world of mass society. I argued earlier . . . that generic organization is also the regeneration of human culture. This is exactly the point that Lyotard makes when he says that techno-science transforms the infinite and indeterminate into per-*formable* knowledge. It's not simply a case of producing objects such as the camera for functional consumption. In other words, it's not a case of organizing for production. For Lyotard, it's more like the *production of organization* (Cooper and Burrell, 1988) in which the *product* serves as a device for *predicting* or organizing the indeterminate future or the *not yet*. Industrial techno-science and the amateur photographer both share the same problem: how to order the as yet unknown. *Pre-diction* and *pro-duction* thus becomes forms of generic organization that participate in social practice in different yet common ways. Organization as pre-diction *and* pro-duction suggests another significant feature of generic organization—that various social meanings cohere and condense into the one social act. Generic organization does not simply mean that acts of organizing are distributed throughout social networks. Perhaps more significantly, it means that the various ways of describing and understanding social organization are concentrate in the most simple, elemental acts. It's where different becomes the same and vice versa.

This is the point that emerges out of Mark Taylor's (1995) analysis of electronic media and compu-telecommunications technology and the ways in which they're forcing us to rethink the nature of our social and personal realities. The new media technologies—television, radio, film, video, telephones, faxes, computers, the net—are radically reorganizing the sensory and intellectual forms by which we 'engage with reality'. At the same time, they compel us to rethink the nature of social organization itself. We are no longer in a world that is external to us and which we simply represent. The electronic media now actually produce the images and signs which constitute the world: 'The structure of the real is indistinguishable from the structure of the medium. In more familiar terms, the medium is not only the message but there is nothing less than reality itself' (Taylor, 1995: 26–27). The medium is where everything condenses; where, for example, *production* and *pre-diction* become each other. It's another way of expressing the mutually defining relationship between original and copy. In the medium there is neither beginning nor end but *both* beginning *and* end, neither here nor there but *both* here *and* there, neither this nor that but *both* this *and* that—all condensed together in a *middle* that is also a *muddle*. This is version of Geertz's (1975: 10) 'thick' description in which 'complex conceptual structures (are) knotted into one another'. We see the same interlacing process in the mutual connection between *organ* and *organization* where human organs do not merely see or hear but actively contribute to the wider socio-cultural meaning of organization. Organ and organization mediate each other.

This is also Lyotard's point in his analysis of photography as both expression and product of techno-scientific organization: the human eye becomes an organ of organization through the camera. The co-implication of organ-organization is more vividly portrayed in Avital Ronell's (1989) account of the development of the telephone and the Bell Telephone Company (which later became the American Telephone and Telegraph Company). Telecommunication is essentially the mediation of organs. The eye, for example, mediates distances. The same applies to the ear and mouth. This repeats Heidegger's (1971) argument that the human body and its organs are *part of*—or *participators* in—a mutually reflecting field of possibilities. The mouth, for example, 'is not merely a kind of organ of the body understood as an organism—body and mouth are part of the earth's flow and growth in which we mortals flourish . . .' (p. 98). Mouth and body are both *organs* and *origins* which *organize* continuous mediation that 'brings together what it holds apart and holds apart what it brings together . . . without integrating or synthesizing' (Taylor, 1995: 34).

Telephony as the communication of sound over distances through the media of the mouth and the ear was a dream of pagan times and began to take on technical form in the work of the English scientist Robert Hooke in the seventeenth century. In the Victorian period, it marked the beginning of modern techno-scientific research in telecommunications with international attempts to translate the organs of hearing and speaking into organization of mass communication. The Bell system in the USA was one of the more successful attempts at this translation. In more recent developments of technoscientific organization, we find the same mediation between organs and organizations: 'Microelectronics mediate the translations of labor into robotics and word processing; sex into generic engineering and reproductive technologies; and mind into artificial intelligence and decision making procedures' (Haraway, 1991: 166). It thus is no longer possible, as Marilyn Strathern (1991: 36) tells us, 'to sustain a division between the natural and artificial, between matter and consciousness or between who makes and who is made in the relations between human and machine'. Nor, we should add, between organs and organizations. For what we have here is another way of expressing the nature of Taylor's (1995) medium as a middle that is also a muddle. It's also another version of Geertz's (1975) 'thick' description in which structures are *knotted into one another*.

These observations underline the organ—organization relationship as *mediation* rather than as a collection of self-identical actors and tools. They repeat the earlier interpretation of organization as *participation* . . . with its emphasis on mediating *parts* rather than separate entities: 'parts, in the long run, are the carriers of "being", not wholes, which are no more than provisional arrays of parts' (Fisher, 1991: 213). Lyotard's camera produces a *framed* picture *cut out* of the infinite process of medium and media. The photographer temporarily withdraws a form from a background of endless transformation, frames and immobilizes it in a snapshot. This is an example of Lyotard's thesis that techno-scientific organization can only realize itself via the production-prediction of the infinite or 'unfinished'. The function of production-prediction is to censor or excise the field of mobile transformations by framing it in a simple location such as the snapshot. At the same time the camera is still part of the wider field of endless transformations the term 'snapshot' itself suggests with its instantaneous capture of a slice of an object in time. And the camera is also an organ that mediates between the eye and its context in that contact-copy transformation that Taussig (1993) saw as defining mimetic Otherness . . . in which the camera de-objectifies the world through the problematic of the original-copy counter-change.

Here we have two interrelated aspects of the organ-organization relationship: one that fixes forms and figures by screening out their mobile and infinite backgrounds; and the other that refuses fixity of location through the continuous motion of in-one-anotherness and mediation that characterizes the Other. Drawing on the work of the Japanese philosopher Keiji Nishitani, Norman Bryson (1988) has discussed the organ-organization interaction in terms of *framing*. Objects and entities are made to stand out against a background of 'radical impermanence' or 'nihility':

> The concept of the entity can be preserved only by an optic that casts around each entity a perceptual frame that makes a cut from the (universal field of transformations) and immobilizes the cut within the static framework. But as soon as that frame is withdrawn, the object is found to exist as a part of a mobile continuum that cannot be cut anywhere.
>
> (Bryson, 1988: 97)

As Derrida (1987) has convincingly shown, the frame of an object or concept performs an ambiguous and ambivalent role, for it is neither *part of* the object or concept nor *apart from* it. Derrida's name for the frame is *parergon*—where *par* means both *part of* and *apart from*, and *ergon*, work. The frame as paragon is thus neither a presence nor an absence. It reminds us that eyes, mouths and ears as organs and ergons are never objects that are complete in themselves but only come alive when, in the company of cameras and telephones, they enter the transformational field of 'radical impermanence'. The organ-ergon organizes only in that transitional and immanent space which I earlier called the *binary act*. Organization without object. Participal. Without end.

## REFERENCES

Bachelard, G. (1937) *Le Nouvel Esprit Scientifique*. Paris: Alcan.
Bachelard, G. (1968) *The Philosophy of No: A Philosophy of the New Scientific Mind*. New York: Orion Press.
Bateson, G. (1972) *Steps to an Ecology of Mind: Collected Essays on Anthropology, Psychiatry, Evolution and Epistemology*. London: Routledge.
Beer, G. (1989) *Arguing with the Past*. London: Routledge.
Beer, G. (1992) *Forging the Missing Link: Interdisciplinary Stories*. Cambridge: Cambridge University Press.
Berger, P. and Luckman, T. (1967) *The Social Construction of Reality: A Treatise in the Sociology of Knowledge*. Harmondsworth: Penguin.
Bledstein, B. (1976) *The Culture of Professionalism*. New York: W.W. Norton.
Blanchot, M. (1982) *The Space of Literature*. Lincoln: University of Nebraska Press.
Bové, P. A. (ed) (1995) *Early Postmodernism: Foundational Essays*. Durham, NC: Duke University Press.
Bryson, N. (1988) 'The gaze in the expanded field', in H. Foster (ed.) *Vision and Visuality*. Seattle, WA: Bay Press.
Buckley, W. (1967) *Sociology and Modern Systems Theory*. Englewood Cliffs, NJ: Prentice Hall.
Butler, S. (1970) *Erewhon*. Harmondsworth: Penguin.
Calvino, I. (1987) *The Literature Machine*. London: Picador,
Cooper, R. (1976) 'The open field', *Human Relations* 29 (11): 999–1017.
Cooper, R. (1983) 'The other: a model of human structuring', in G. Morgan (ed) *Beyond Method: Strategies for Social Research*. London: Sage, 202–218.

Cooper, R. (1986) 'Organization/disorganization', *Social Science Information* 25(2): 299–335.

Cooper, R. (1987) 'Information, communication and organization: a post-structural revision', *Journal of Mind and Behaviour*, 8 (3): 395–416.

Cooper, R. (1989) 'The visibility of social systems', in M.C. Jackson, P. Keys, and S.A. Cropper (eds) *Operational Research and the Social Sciences*. New York: Plenum Press, 51–59. Reprinted in K. Hetherington and R. Munro (eds) (1997) *Ideas of Difference: Social spaces and the labour of division*. Oxford: Blackwell, 32–41.

Cooper, R. (1993) 'Technologies of representation', in P. Ahonen (ed.) *Tracing the Semiotic Boundaries of Politics*. Berlin: Mouton de Gruyter, 279–312.

Cooper, R. and Burrell, G. (1988) 'Modernism, postmodernism and organizational analysis: an introduction', *Organizational Studies* 9(1): 91–112.

Cooper, R. and Law, J. (1995) 'Organization: distal and proximal views', *Research in the Sociology of Organizations* 13: 237–274.

Deleuze, G. (1990) *The Logic of Sense*. New York: Columbia University Press.

Deleuze, G. and Guattari, F. (1983) *Anti-Oedipus: Capitalism and Schizophrenia*. Minneapolis: University of Minnesota Press.

Deleuze, G. and Parnet, C. (1987) *Dialogues*. London: Athlone Press.

Derrida, J. (1987) *The Post Card: From Socrates to Freud and Beyond*. Chicago, IL: Chicago University Press.

Derrida, J. (1978) *Writing and Difference*. London: Routledge & Kegan Paul.

Doob, P. R (1990) *The Idea of the Labyrinth from Classical Antiquity through the Middle Ages*. Ithaca, NY: Cornell University Press.

Dukheim, E. (1933) *The Division of Labour in Society*. Glencoe, IL: Free Press.

Eco, U. (1989) *The Open Work*. London: Hutchinson.

Ehrenzweig, A. (1967) *The Hidden Order of Art*. London: Weidenfeld and Nicolson.

Fisher, P. (1991) *Making and Effacing Art: Modern American Art in a Culture of Museums*. New York: Oxford University Press.

Foucault, M. (1970) *The Order of Things*, trans. A. Sheridan. London: Tavistock.

Foucault, M. (1973) *Madness and Civilisation: A History of Medical Perception*, trans. A. Sheridan Smith. New York: Vintage/Random House.

Foucault, M. (1975) *The Birth of the Clinic: An Archaeology of Medical Perception*, trans. A. Sheridan Smith. New York: Vintage/Random House.

Foucault, M. (1977) *Discipline and Punish: the birth of the prison*. London: Allen Lane.

Geertz, C. (1975) *The Interpretation of Cultures*. London: Hutchinson.

Gillespie, G. (1995) 'Scientific discourse and postmodernity: Francis Bacon and the empirical birth of "Revision"', in P.A Bové (ed.) *Early Postmodernism: Foundational Essays*. Durham, NC: Duke University Press.

Gleick, J. (1988) *Chaos: Making a New Science*. London: Heinemann.

Haraway, D. (1991) *Simians, Cyborgs and Women: The Re-invention of Nature*. London: Free Association Books.

Heidegger, M. (1971) *On the Way to Language*. New York: Harper and Row.

Herbst, P. G. (1976) *Alternatives to Hierarchies*. Leiden: Nijhoff.

James, W. (1890) *Principles of Psychology*. New York: Henry Holt.

Johnson, C. (1993) *System and Writing in the Philosophy of Jacques Derrida*. Cambridge: Cambridge University Press.

Kenner, H. (1987) *The Mechanic Muse*. New York: Oxford University Press.

Lupton, E. and J.A. Miller (1992) 'Hygiene, cuisine and the product world of early twentieth-century America', in J. Crary and S. Kwinter (eds) *Incorporations*. New York: Zone.

Lyotard, J.-F. (1991) *The Inhuman*. Cambridge: Polity Press.

March, J. (1988) *Decisions and Organizations*. Oxford: Blackwell.

Melberg, A. (1995) *Theories of Mimesis*. Cambridge: Cambridge University Press.

Mey, H. (1972) *Field-Theory: A Study of its Applications in the Social Sciences.* London: Routledge and Kegan Paul.

Morgan, G. (1983) *Beyond Method: Strategies for Social Research.* Newbury Park, CA: Sage.

Parker, M. and Cooper, R. (1998) 'Cyberorganization: cinema as nervous system', in J. Hassard and R. Holliday (eds) *Organization/Representation: Work and Organization in Popular Culture.* London: Sage.

Ronell, A. (1989) *The Telephone Book: Technology, Schixophrenia, Elective Speech.* Lincoln: University of Nebraska Press.

Rotman, B. (1994) 'Exuberant materiality—de-minding the store', *Configurations* 2: 257–274.

Royle, N. (1995) *After Derrida.* Manchester: Manchester University Press.

Schoenwald, R. L. (1973) 'Training urban man', in H. J. Dyos and M. Wolff (eds) *The Victorian City*, vol.2. London: Routledge and Kegan Paul.

Scott, N. A (1969) *Negative Capability: Studies in the New Literature and the Religious Situation.* New Haven, CT: Yale University Press.

Serres, M. (1982) *Hermes: Literature, Science, Philosophy.* Baltimore, MD: Johns Hopkins University Press.

Simon, H. (1979) *Models of Thought.* New Haven, CT: Yale University Press.

Strathern, M. (1991) *Partial Connections.* Savage, MD: Rowman & Littlefield.

Strathern, M. (1995) *The Relation: Issues in Complexity and Scale.* Cambridge: Prickly Pear Press.

Taussig, M. T. (1993) *Mimesis and Alterity: A Particular History of the Senses.* New York: Routledge.

Taylor, M. C. (1995) 'Rhizomic fields of interstanding', *Tekhnema* 2: 24–36.

Taylor, M. C. and Saarinen, E. (1994) *Imagologies: Media Philosophy.* London: Routledge.

Vattimo, G. (1992) *The Transparent Society.* Cambridge: Polity Press.

Weber, S. (1987) *Institution and Interpretation.* Minneapolis: Minnesota University Press.

Whitehead, A. N. (1925) *Science and the Modern World.* Cambridge: Cambridge University Press.

Wiener, N. (1954) *The Human Use of Human Beings: Cybernetics and Society.* New York: Doubleday.

Williams, R. (1983) *Keywords.* London: Flamingo.

# 16 Complete List of Robert Cooper's Work

This list doesn't include conference papers, translations or poetry. It might not be a complete list either, because the only CV we have (from about 1990) is oddly unreliable. Some of the items on it were incorrectly or vaguely dated or titled, others were missing altogether. This might be partly because of the passage of time and the failures of memory, but there are also hints of evasiveness, particularly concerning his earlier work.

Cooper, R. (1964) 'What makes a good work leader?' *New Society*, 20 August, 11–13.

Cooper, R. and R. Payne (1965) 'Age and absence: A longitudinal study in three firms' *Occupational Psychology* 39/1: 31–43.

Cooper, R. (1965) 'The psychology of organizations' *New Society*, 22 April, 14–17.

Cooper, R. (1966) 'Leader's task relevance and subordinate behaviour in industrial work groups' *Human Relations*, 19/1: 57–84.

Cooper R. and R. Payne (1967) 'Extraversion and some aspects of work behaviour' *Personnel Psychology* 20/1: 45–57. Reprinted in H. Eysenck (ed) (1971) *Readings in Extraversion-Introversion: Volume II*. London: Staples Press.

Cooper, R. (1968) 'The psychology of boredom' *Science Journal* 4/2: 38–42.

Cooper, R. (1969) 'Alienation from work' *New Society*, 30 January, 9–11.

Cooper, R. (1970) 'Task-oriented leadership and subordinate response' and 'A summing up', in B. M. Bass, R. Cooper and J. A. Haas (eds) *Managing for Accomplishment*. Lexington, MA: DC Heath and Co, 14–25 and 286–294.

Cooper, R. and M. Foster (1971) 'Sociotechnical systems' *American Psychologist*, 26/5: 467–474.

Cooper, R. (1972) 'Man, task and technology: Three variables in search of a future' *Human Relations* 25/2: 131–157.

Cooper, R. and R. Payne (1972) 'Personality orientations and performance in soccer teams' *British Journal of Social and Clinical Psychology* 11/1: 2–9.

Cooper, R. (1973) 'How jobs motivate' *Personnel Review*, 2/2: 4–12. Reprinted in M. Weir (ed) (1974) *Job Satisfaction*. London: Fontana.

Cooper, R. (1973) 'Task characteristics and intrinsic motivation' *Human Relations* 26/3: 387–413.

Cooper, R. (1973) A Review of: 'Job satisfaction: A study of computer specialists', by Enid Mumford. *Ergonomics* 16/5: 724.

Cooper, R. (1974) *Job Motivation and Job Design*. London: Institute of Personnel Management.

Cooper, R. (1976) 'Work and meta-work' *Personnel Review*, 5/4: 51–52.

Cooper, R. (1976) 'The Open Field' *Human Relations*, 29/11: 999–1017.

Gadalla, I. and R. Cooper (1978) 'Towards an epistemology of management' *Social Science Information* 17/3: 349–83.

Cooper, R. (1983) 'The other: A model of human structuring' in G. Morgan (ed.) *Beyond Method: Strategies for Social Research*. Newbury Park, CA: Sage, 202–218.

Cooper, R. (1983) 'Some remarks on theoretical individualism, alienation and work', *Human Relations* 36/8: 717–723.

Cooper, R. (1986) 'Organization/disorganization', *Social Science Information*, 25/2, 299–335. Reprinted in J. Hassard and D. Pym (eds) *The Theory and Philosophy of Organizations*. London: Routledge, 167–197.

Cooper, R. (1987) 'Information, communication and organization: a post-structural revision', *The Journal of Mind and Behaviour*, 8/3: 395–416.

Cooper, R. and G. Burrell (1988), 'Modernism, postmodernism and organizational analysis: an introduction', *Organization Studies* 9/1: 91–112.

Cooper, R. (1989) 'The visibility of social systems' in M. C. Jackson, P. Keys, and S. Cropper (eds), *Operational Research in the Social Sciences*, New York: Plenum, 51–59. Reprinted in K. Hetherington and R. Munro (eds), *Ideas of Difference: Social Spaces and the Labour of Division*, Sociological Review Monograph, Oxford: Blackwell, 32–41.

Cooper, R. (1989) 'Modernism, post modernism and organizational analysis 3: the Contribution of Jacques Derrida', *Organization Studies*, 10/4: 479–502.

Cooper, R. and S. Fox (1989) 'Two modes of organizing' in R. Mansfield (ed) *Frontiers of Management: Research and Practice*. London: Routledge, 247–261.

Cooper, R. (1990) 'Canetti's Sting'. *Scos Notework* 9(2/3): 45–53.

Cooper, R. and S. Fox (1990) 'The texture of organizing' *Journal of Management Studies*, 27/6: 575–582.

Malavé, J. and R. Cooper (1991) 'On the (organizational) context of (managerial) competence' *Management Research News*, 14/7/8/9: 49–56.

Cooper, R. (1992) 'Formal organization as representation: remote control, displacement and abbreviation', in M. Reed and M. Hughes (eds), *Rethinking Organization*, London: Sage, 254–272.

Fox, S., R. Cooper and L. T. Martinez (1992) 'Postmodern management and organization: the implications for learning 1' *International Studies of Management & Organization*, 22/2: 3–14.

Cooper, R., S. Fox and L. T. Martinez (1992) 'Postmodern management and organization: the implications for learning 2' *International Studies of Management & Organization*, 22/3: 3–10.

Cooper, R. (1992) 'Systems and organizations: proximal and distal thinking' *Systems Practice* 5/4: 373–377.

Cooper, R. (1993) 'Technologies of representation' in P. Ahonen (ed.), *Tracing the Semiotic Boundaries of Politics*, Berlin: Mouton de Gruyter, 279–312.

Cooper, R. and J. Law (1995) 'Organization: distal and proximal views', in S. B. Bachrach, P. Gagliardi, and B. Mundell (eds), *Research in the Sociology of Organizations: Studies of Organizations in the European Tradition*, 13, Greenwich, Conn.: JAI Press, 275–301.

Cooper, R. (1996) 'Foreword', in J. Kallinikos, *Technology and society: interdisciplinary studies in formal organization*. Munich: Accedo, vii-x.

Kallinikos, J. and R. Cooper (1996) 'Writing, rationality and organization: an introduction' *Scandinavian Journal of Management* 12/1: 1–6.

Cooper, R. (1997) 'Millennium notes for social theory' *Sociological Review* 45/4: 690–703.

Cooper, R. (1998) 'Assemblage notes' in R. Chia (ed) *Organized Worlds: Explorations in Technology and Organization with Robert Cooper*. London: Routledge, 100–119.

Cooper, R. (with R. Chia and J. Kallinikos) (1998) 'Interview with Robert Cooper' in R. Chia (ed.) *Organized Worlds: Explorations in Technology and Organization with Robert Cooper*. London: Routledge, 121–165.

Parker, M. and R. Cooper (1998) 'Cyborganization: cinema as nervous system' in *Organization—Representation: Work and Organization in Popular Culture* (Eds J. Hassard and R. Holliday) London: Sage, 201–228.

Cooper, R. (2001) 'A matter of culture' *Cultural Values* 5/2: 163–197.

Cooper, R. (2001) 'Interpreting mass: collection/dispersion' in N. Lee and R. Munro (eds.) *The Consumption of Mass*. Oxford: Blackwell, 16–43.

Cooper, R. (2001) 'Un-timely mediations: questing thought' *ephemera* 1/4: 321–347.

Cooper, R. (2003) 'Primary and secondary thinking in social theory', *Journal of Classical Sociology*, 3/2: 145–172.

Cooper, R. (2005) 'Peripheral vision: Relationality' *Organization Studies*, 26/11: 1689–1710.

Cooper, R. (2005) 'Foreword', in D. Seidl, *Organizational identity and self-transformation: an autopoietic perspective*. Aldershot: Ashgate, ix-xii.

Cooper, R. (2006) 'Making present: autopoiesis as human production', *Organization*, 13/1: 59–81.

Cooper, R. (2007) 'Organs of process: rethinking human organization' *Organization Studies*, 28/10: 1547–1573.

Cooper. R. (2010) 'Georg Simmel and the transmission of distance' *Journal of Classical Sociology* 10/1: 69–86.

Cooper, R. (2010) 'The generalized social body: distance and technology', *Organization*, 17/2: 242–256.

Cooper, R. (2014) 'Process and reality' in J. Helin, T. Hernes, D. Hjorth and R. Holt (eds) *The Oxford Handbook of Process Philosophy and Organization Studies*. Oxford: Oxford University Press, 585–604.

# Contributors

**Gibson Burrell**, whilst employed in the Department of Behaviour in Organisations at the University of Lancaster from the mid-1970s till the mid-1980s, worked with Bob Cooper on a project which developed into a series of articles in the journal *Organization Studies* on Modernism and Postmodernism. This led to a continuing relationship of joint seminar and conference presentations well into the early 1990s until their mutual excitement around this particular topic came to diminish. Separated thereafter by institution and theoretical direction, no further academic collaboration took place but the relationship continued in a different guise in many a social setting in which both bit their lip about confronting the weaknesses of the other. That perhaps is what friendship is. Today Gibson holds a Fractional Chair in Organization Theory at the University of Leicester.

**John Law** is Emeritus Professor of Sociology at the Open University and an Honorary Professor at the Centre for Science Studies in the Department of Sociology at Lancaster University. He was written widely in STS on non-coherent methods, and on actor-network and other material semiotic approaches to ordering, mostly working through cases studies and ethnographies of organisations, technologies, agriculture and human-animal relations. His publications include *After Method: Mess in Social Science Research*. His personal web page is at www.hetero geneities.net.

**Martin Parker** worked with Bob Cooper at Keele University in England from 1995 to 2003. He was young and excited then, and learnt a huge amount from Bob as well as a variety of other clever people at Keele and elsewhere. Failing to apply most of it, he moved to Leicester University, and then briefly to Warwick Business School, and then back to Leicester again. He likes writing about odd things at the moment, such as pirates, angels, space rockets, shipping containers, circuses and secret societies.

**Sverre Spoelstra** is an associate professor at the Department of Business Administration at Lund University, Sweden. His research interests include organizational philosophy, the relation between work and play, and excellence and relevance in management research. He is currently writing a book about the relation between organization and leadership.

# Index

Note: Italicized page numbers indicate a figure on the corresponding page.